MW01294564

HOLMAN
Old
Testament
Commentary

HOLMAN
Old Testament Commentary

Psalms 76-150

GENERAL EDITOR

Max Anders

AUTHOR

Steven J. Lawson

HOLMAN
REFERENCE

NASHVILLE, TENNESSEE

ISBN: 978-08054-9481-5

Dewey Decimal Classification: 223.2
Subject Heading: BIBLE. O.T. PSALMS 76–150

Psalms / Steven J. Lawson
p.   cm. — (Holman Old Testament commentary)
Includes bibliographical references. (p.).
ISBN
  1. Bible. Psalms Vol. 1—Commentaries.   I. Title.   II. Series.

—dc21

4 5 6 7 8 9 10 • 16 15 14 13 12

Samara Preacher's Institute
and
Samara Theological Seminary
Samara, Russia

May God give
the Russian church
a new generation
of biblical expositors
who "preach the Word."

"Forever, O LORD,
Your word is settled in heaven."
Psalm 119:89 (NKJV)

Psalms 76-150

Contents

Contents

Editorial Preface

Today's church hungers for Bible teaching, and Bible teachers hunger for resources to guide them in teaching God's Word. The Holman Old Testament Commentary provides the church with the food to feed the spiritually hungry in an easily digestible format. The result: new spiritual vitality that the church can readily use.

Bible teaching should result in new interest in the Scriptures, expanded Bible knowledge, discovery of specific scriptural principles, relevant applications, and exciting living. The unique format of the Holman Old Testament Commentary includes sections to achieve these results for every Old Testament book.

Opening quotations stimulate thinking and lead to an introductory illustration and discussion that draw individuals and study groups into the Word of God. Verse-by-verse commentary interprets the passage with the aim of equipping them to understand and live God's Word in a contemporary setting. A conclusion draws together the themes identified in the passage under discussion and suggests application for it. Bible teachers and pastors will find the teaching outline helpful as they develop lessons and sermons.

Some of the major psalms are given additional treatment. A "Life Application" section provides additional illustrative material. "Deeper Discoveries" gives the reader a closer look at some of the words, phrases, and background material that illuminate the passage. "Issues for Discussion" is a tool to enhance learning within the group. Finally, a closing prayer is suggested.

It is the editors' prayer that this new resource for local church Bible teaching will enrich the ministry of group, as well as individual, Bible study and that it will lead God's people truly to be people of the Book, living out what God calls us to be.

Acknowledgments

I want to express publicly my deepest appreciation for several people who have made invaluable contributions to this second volume of the Psalms. Without them, this commentary would not be what it is.

First, I want to thank Julie Riley, who personally typed this entire manuscript. She has done this tirelessly and cheerfully as an expression of her deep devotion to Jesus Christ. Without her faithful efforts, this book would not be in your hands. Her commitment to this work has been unwavering.

Second, I want to thank a small group of people who have proofread this manuscript with a careful eye. I especially want to thank Thad Key, Karl Allen, Ben Stubblefield, Laurie Gibson, Beth Lamey, and Justin Hughes.

Third, I want to thank Steve Bond, my editor at Broadman & Holman. He has provided seasoned editing and skilled oversight for this commentary.

Fourth, I want to thank Christ Fellowship Baptist Church in Mobile, Alabama. They have heard me preach the Psalms in an abandoned warehouse, in a senior center, in a gymnasium, and in our new church sanctuary. They have been a model congregation, both hungry for the Word and humble before the Lord. No pastor ever had a more godly and supportive flock than I have in them. Pick up their well-worn Bibles, which by now open automatically to the Psalms, and you will discover my sermon outlines and their notes written in the margins of the Psalms.

Finally, I must thank my wife, Anne, and my four children, Andrew, James, Grace Anne, and John, who have sat on the front pew of our church and heard me preach virtually every one of these psalms. Except for the time my twin boys were away at college, my family has not missed a week of my preaching the Psalms over the last four years. I started expositing the Psalms when my boys entered college; and although they have now graduated, I am still preaching weekly, verse by verse, through this great book. My own family's excitement for the preaching of the Psalms has greatly encouraged me in its ongoing series. I am a blessed man.

Most of all, I must thank the divine Author of the Psalms, God himself, who has granted me this extraordinary privilege to preach the Psalms and write this commentary. May the unrivaled glory of God as revealed in the Psalms be unveiled before your eyes as you read this book, resulting in much honor being given to him.

Soli deo gloria.
Steven J. Lawson

Holman Old Testament Commentary Contributors

Vol. 1 Genesis
ISBN 978-0-8054-9461-7
Kenneth O. Gangel and Stephen Bramer

Vol. 2 Exodus, Leviticus, Numbers
ISBN 978-0-8054-9462-4
Glen Martin

Vol. 3 Deuteronomy
ISBN 978-0-8054-9463-1
Doug McIntosh

Vol. 4 Joshua
ISBN 978-0-8054-9464-8
Kenneth O. Gangel

Vol. 5 Judges, Ruth
ISBN 978-0-8054-9465-5
W. Gary Phillips

Vol. 6 1 & 2 Samuel
ISBN 978-0-8054-9466-2
Stephen Andrews

Vol. 7 1 & 2 Kings
ISBN 978-0-8054-9467-9
Gary Inrig

Vol. 8 1 & 2 Chronicles
ISBN 978-0-8054-9468-6
Winfried Corduan

Vol. 9 Ezra, Nehemiah, Esther
ISBN 978-0-8054-9469-3
Knute Larson and Kathy Dahlen

Vol. 10 Job
ISBN 978-0-8054-9470-9
Stephen J. Lawson

Vol. 11 Psalms 1-72
ISBN 978-0-8054-9471-6
Steve J. Lawson

Vol. 12 Psalms 73-150
ISBN 978-0-8054-9481-5
Steve J. Lawson

Vol. 13 Proverbs
ISBN 978-0-8054-9472-3
Max Anders

Vol. 14 Ecclesiastes, Song of Songs
ISBN 978-0-8054-9482-2
David George Moore and Daniel L. Akin

Vol. 15 Isaiah
ISBN 978-0-8054-9473-0
Trent C. Butler

Vol. 16 Jeremiah, Lamentations
ISBN 978-0-8054-9474-7
Fred C. Wood and Ross McLaren

Vol. 17 Ezekiel
ISBN 978-0-8054-9475-4
Mark F. Rooker

Vol. 18 Daniel
ISBN 978-0-8054-9476-1
Kenneth O. Gangel

Vol. 19 Hosea, Joel, Amos, Obadiah, Jonah, Micah
ISBN 978-0-8054-9477-8
Trent C. Butler

Vol. 20 Nahum, Habakkuk, Zephaniah, Haggai, Zechariah, Malachi
ISBN 978-0-8054-9478-5
Stephen R. Miller

Holman New Testament
Commentary Contributors

Vol. 1 Matthew
ISBN 978-0-8054-0201-8
Stuart K. Weber

Vol. 2 Mark
ISBN 978-0-8054-0202-5
Rodney L. Cooper

Vol. 3 Luke
ISBN 978-0-8054-0203-2
Trent C. Butler

Vol. 4 John
ISBN 978-0-8054-0204-9
Kenneth O. Gangel

Vol. 5 Acts
ISBN 978-0-8054-0205-6
Kenneth O. Gangel

Vol. 6 Romans
ISBN 978-0-8054-0206-3
Kenneth Boa and William Kruidenier

Vol. 7 1 & 2 Corinthians
ISBN 978-0-8054-0207-0
Richard L. Pratt Jr.

Vol. 8 Galatians, Ephesians, Philippians, Colossians
ISBN 978-0-8054-0208-7
Max Anders

Vol. 9 1 & 2 Thessalonians, 1 & 2 Timothy, Titus, Philemon
ISBN 978-0-8054-0209-4
Knute Larson

Vol. 10 Hebrews, James
ISBN 978-0-8054-0211-7
Thomas D. Lea

Vol. 11 1 & 2 Peter, 1, 2, 3 John, Jude
ISBN 978-0-8054-0210-0
David Walls & Max Anders

Vol. 12 Revelation
ISBN 978-0-8054-0212-4
Kendell H. Easley

Holman Old Testament Commentary

Twenty volumes designed for Bible study and teaching to enrich the local church and God's people.

Series Editor	Max Anders
Managing Editor	Steve Bond
Project Editor	Dean Richardson
Product Development Manager	Ricky D. King
Marketing Manager	Stephanie Huffman
Executive Editor	David Shepherd
Page Composition	TF Designs, Greenbrier, TN

Introduction to

Psalms

For centuries, the Book of Psalms has played a leading role in shaping the spiritual life of the church. This sacred collection of inspired worship songs has proven to be a strong catalyst for ushering in mighty seasons of revival and awakening. Its place in church history is virtually unparalleled.

During the Reformation, the Psalms was the first book that Martin Luther, the famed German Reformer, taught at the University of Wittenberg. Awed by its theological depth and God-centered message, Luther went so far as to call the Psalms, "the Bible in miniature." When enduring the most difficult year of his life (1527), Luther wrote his most famous hymn, "A Mighty Fortress," based upon Psalm 46. After his death, there was discovered but one verse handwritten in the front of his well-worn Bible—Psalm 119:92. John Calvin, the luminous Swiss Reformer, wrote a substantive commentary on the Psalms and preached carefully through all of Psalm 119. Further, Calvin integrated the Psalms as the divinely inspired hymnbook for St. Peter's Cathedral in Geneva. The Huguenots, who fled the bloody persecution of France, sought refuge in Geneva, where they sang and studied the Psalms to the comfort of their assaulted souls.

During the Scottish and English Reformations, the Psalms proved to be a lifeline for brave believers in those tumultuous times. In Sir Thomas More's refusal to acknowledge the validity of the marriage between Henry VIII and Catherine of Aragon, he was committed to the Tower of London for over a year. Though imprisoned, he found in the Psalms the strength and solace he needed to remain true to God. Likewise, George Wishart, the early Scottish martyr, gathered his friends together the night before he was to be put to death and sang with them Psalm 51, thus fortifying his soul for impending martyrdom. What is more, it was to this same psalmodic cadence that John Rogers, the first martyr burned at the stake during the terrible reign of Bloody Mary, marched triumphantly to the stake in front of cheering thousands, courageously citing Psalm 51.

In the golden Puritan Age, the Psalms yet again left its indelible mark upon the godly believers in that movement. Thomas Manton, a noted Puritan, preached 190 sermons on Psalm 119, which were later published in three volumes requiring 1,677 pages. When Oliver Cromwell became Lord Protector of England, he addressed Parliament and expounded Psalms 46 and 85 in his inaugural speech. The vivid language of the Psalms helped guide the gifted pens of John Bunyan in writing his all-time literary classic *Pilgrim's Progress* and John Milton in *Paradise Lost*. During the years of Bunyan's imprisonment, he confessed that it was Psalm 68:18 that so often kept rolling into his mind and strengthening his soul.

In the Great Awakening, the Psalms fueled a passion for God on both sides of the Atlantic. Jonathan Edwards, America's greatest pastor and theologian, observed that at the zenith of the revival an outbreak of singing the Psalms caught fire throughout the churches of New England. John Wesley, the founder of Methodism, was converted to Christ after attending St. Paul's Cathedral, London, and hearing the choir sing, "If You, LORD, should mark iniquities, O LORD; who could stand? But there is forgiveness with You" (Ps. 130:3-4 NKJV). Wesley died with this truth from Psalm 46:11 in mind: "The best of all is, God is with us."

In the modern missions movement, the powerful impact of the Psalms was again deeply felt. When William Carey lay dying in India, he read the Psalms as he prepared himself for entrance into heaven. But God spared his life, and he lived another eleven years. When Carey did die, he insisted that the Psalms be read at his funeral, a testimony to its soul-sustaining power. Henry Martyn, another missionary to India, saturated himself with the Psalms—his *Journals* filled with Psalms notations. Martyn committed Psalm 119 to memory and regularly rehearsed its truths to his heart. When the time came for David Livingstone to leave England for Africa, he sat with his family one last time at the breakfast table—never to see them again—and read Psalms 121 and 135. His mother prayed these psalms for him every day until she died.

Amid England's Victorian era, Charles Haddon Spurgeon distinguished himself as arguably the greatest preacher who ever lived. Spurgeon wrote only one commentary during his towering ministry, a seven-volume work on the Psalms, *The Treasury of David*. Before preaching Psalm 51, Spurgeon confessed that he was so awed by it that he felt unworthy to expound its riches. He delayed its preaching several weeks until his heart could recover. When it did, he noted he must remove his sandals as he stood on holy ground.

Martyn Lloyd-Jones, pastor of Westminster Chapel, London, sat down for breakfast one Sunday morning before preaching. In that quiet moment, he read Psalm 42 and was so struck with its heart-searching truth that he turned over his napkin, outlined the psalm, and preached it that morning. In the weeks that followed, he continued to expound its truths. These sermons became his all-time best-selling book, *Spiritual Depression*.

God has used the Psalms to bless his servants over the centuries in immeasurable ways. This is only a small sampling of countless other examples that could be offered here. The power of the Psalms to capture and conquer human hearts is unsurpassed. These incidents from church history are intended to whet your appetite for the Psalms with the hope that you will delve more fully into this book.

The Psalms is a vast ocean of truth, but it is a challenge to stretch one's arms around it. Consequently, the Psalms often remains untaught and unpreached. To reverse such a trend, this brief commentary on the Psalms, limited as it is, is a humble attempt to make this great book more easily accessible to you. These pages survey each of the psalms in the second half of the Psalter and are intended to help you grasp their richness. I hope this book will encourage you to teach and preach the Psalms. My prayer is that David's treasury will become all the more treasured by you—for God's glory and your good.

Soli deo gloria.
Steven J. Lawson

Psalm 76
Holy Wrath

Psalm 76

I. INTRODUCTION

*I*n today's postmodern world, the truth of God's wrath has become ridiculed as an outdated caricature of deity, or worse, denied altogether as a medieval myth. Even many Christians today seem to apologize for divine vengeance as if it is a blemish in God's character, or some irrelevant doctrine of Christianity. But the truth is, the Bible clearly presents the wrath of God as a necessary attribute of his holiness. Any true knowledge of God must be grounded in a clear understanding of his sin-hating wrath. To withhold teaching on God's fury toward sin is, in reality, idolatry—it is worshipping a god of one's own making. The holiness of God requires that he be full of righteous anger and fiery vengeance against sin. God's holy displeasure against sinners and the just punishment he metes out to them are the central thrust of this psalm.

Specifically, Psalm 76 is a celebration of God's strong defense of his holy city, Jerusalem, against invading evil forces. The psalmist here declares that God made himself known in Jerusalem by executing judgment against his adversaries in defending his own people. Many Bible commentators believe that the historical background for this psalm was the destruction of Sennacherib's Assyrian army in 701 B.C. by the angel of the Lord, the preincarnate Christ, resulting in 185,000 slain soldiers (cp. 2 Kgs. 18–19; Isa. 36–37). If

---

so, this psalm, *a psalm of Asaph,* was either written or led by a descendant of the Asaph of David's time. Possibly, this inscription could be a reference to a choir guild bearing Asaph's name.

II. COMMENTARY

> **MAIN IDEA:** *The psalmist praises God for the glory of his wrath revealed against his enemies.*

A God's Wrath Is Revealing (76:1–3)

76:1–2. With a radiant display of his glory, God has made himself **known** by destroying Israel's enemies. **In Judah** God is known by his powerful acts in defending the holy city, Jerusalem. **His name** (i.e., the total fullness of his holy character) is shown to be **great in Israel** as a result of these severe judgments upon his enemies. **His tent** pictures the temple as the field tent of a conquering general. This massive edifice is **in Salem**, a shortened form of Jerusalem and the ancient name of Jerusalem (Gen. 14:18). **His dwelling place**, where his glory is most manifested, is **in Zion**, yet another name for Jerusalem.

76:3. God's royal city is where he has clearly revealed himself. **There he broke the flashing arrows** (i.e., flaming, missile-like weapons) launched by invaders' bows over the city's defensive walls. Likewise, God broke **the shields and the swords** of the enemies' soldiers. He destroyed all **the weapons of war** that were brought against Jerusalem. Through this display of divine judgment, God made himself known to Israel as a powerful dispenser of holy anger. Any understanding of God that minimizes or explains away his fierce wrath is a false representation of the true God.

B God's Wrath Is Resplendent (76:4–9)

76:4. Far from apologizing for God's wrath, the psalmist announces, **You are resplendent with light.** This display of divine wrath upon their enemies (cp. v. 3) revealed the light of God's holiness, illuminating himself to his people. In this, God is shown to be **more majestic than mountains rich with game.** Literally, this is "mountains of prey," picturing Israel's oppressors as towering, intimidating mountains who have invaded the land to attack his people. But instead, God has preyed upon them, devouring them in judgment as if he were hunting wild game.

76:5–6. Although these invading foreign **warriors** were **valiant men,** brave and stouthearted, they, nevertheless, were **plundered** by God as dead corpses. They were soundly defeated and destroyed, now sleeping their **last sleep** in eternal death. They were rendered lifeless, unable to **lift** their **hands.** God's **rebuke** was no mere idle threat. Even the **horse and chariot lie still.**

God's wrath had so obliterated the enemies' fighters that none were left to fight.

76:7–9. In response to this terrifying display of divine fury, the psalmist says to God, **you alone are to be feared.** Such sobering reverence is the only right response to this God of wrath. **Who can stand before you when you are angry?** The obvious answer is no one. No mere man, nor army, can withstand God when his anger is vented. **From heaven you pronounced judgment,** resulting in death-delivering devastation upon the earth. The people of **the land** saw it, **feared** God, and were made **quiet.** They were stunned and speechless by this awesome display. Shock came upon the entire earth as God **rose up to judge** his enemies. In so doing, he worked **to save all the afflicted of the land,** that is, to deliver his own people.

C God's Wrath Is Restraining (76:10)

76:10. Still addressing God, the psalmist exclaimed, **Surely your wrath against men brings you praise.** In the unleashing of divine fury upon their invading foes, the execution of this **wrath** led to **praise** from God's people. Where bold blasphemies were once heard from these invaders, now praise is heard from the saints. In addition, the **survivors** of God's wrath are **restrained** from going any further in their sins. The consciences of the wicked were forever aware of this great God of Israel who judges sin.

D God's Wrath Is Renewing (76:11–12)

76:11. All who name the name of God should carefully consider his wrath. They should renew their allegiance to him. In light of this terrifying display of divine vengeance, every believer should pledge his support to God in **vows** and keep them. This spiritual commitment will surely impact all who live in **the neighboring lands.** To these who hear about God's righteous anger, the psalmist says, Let them **bring gifts to the One to be feared,** namely, God. These offerings should be brought as an act of adoration and submission to him.

76:12. Both vows and gifts should be given to the God who **breaks the spirit of rulers.** His wrath will subdue even the mightiest of men, causing the Lord to be **feared by the kings of the earth.**

III. CONCLUSION

Matthew Henry, noted Bible commentator of yesteryear, wrote centuries ago, "As God's mercies are new every morning toward his people, so his anger is new every morning against the wicked." This pslam has borne strong testimony to this truth. It is clearly stated that God's wrath is presently active toward all those who oppose him. This sobering reality should cause those who are not Christians to come to him in repentance, knowing he is full of vengeance and judgment toward the wicked. In addition, all God's people should live in holy reverence and awe of him. All the saints should renew their commitment to obey and serve him, knowing that he hates sin. Though God's children will never experience the wrath reserved for his enemies, Scripture makes it clear that God does not turn a blind eye toward the sin of believers (Hebrews 12:5–11). May we give him the fear and respect due his name.

IV. TEACHING OUTLINE

A. God's Wrath Is Revealing (1-3)
  1. It Makes His Greatness Known (1-2)
     a. In Judah and Israel (1)
     b. In Salem and Zion (2)
  2. It Makes His Omnipotence Known (3)
     a. By breaking flashing arrows (3a)
     b. By breaking shields and swords (3b)
     c. By breaking all weapons of war (3c)
B. God's Wrath Is Resplendent (4-10)
  1. It Shines Forth In Majesty (4-6)
     a. Valiant men lie plundered (4-5)
     b. Horses and chariot lie still (6)
     c. All men are terrified (7)
  2. It Sounds Forth in Might (8-10)
     a. Wrath is decreed in heaven (8a)
     b. His wrath is felt on earth (8b)
     c. His wrath is served on enemies (9)
C. God's Wrath Is Restraining (10)
  1. It Brings Forth Praise (10a)
  2. It Holds Back Sin (10b)
D. God's Wrath Is Renewing (11-12)
  1. God's People Should Respond Rightly (11a)
     a. Make vows to God (11a)
     b. Keep vows to God (11a)
  2. God's Enemies Should Respond Rightly (11b-12)
     a. Bring gifts to God (11b)
     b. Bring reverence to God (12)

Psalm 77
Defeating Despair

"*T*he beginning of anxiety is the end of faith, and the beginning of true faith is the end of anxiety."

George Muller

Psalm 77

I. INTRODUCTION

In the crucible of life, believers may find themselves spiraling down into dark times of discouraging despair. These low valleys may even bring with them seasons of devastating depression. No one is exempt from such shadowy valleys, not even the strongest saint. In such sinking spells, the righteous must train and discipline themselves to refocus upon the victories God has already given to his people in the past. Times of great distress can be faith-building and soul-strengthening as saints reflect upon the mighty works of God in generations past. Such a backward look provides encouragement to the downtrodden heart drowning in despair. God has worked powerfully in earlier times and is fully capable of doing so again today.

Such a purposeful reflection was the personal experience of the psalmist in Psalm 77, *a psalm of Asaph*. It was written after a time of extreme personal crisis in which he found great relief in meditating upon the past triumphs of God. In this case, the earlier event upon which he reflected was the exodus, a momentous hour in which God worked powerfully to rescue his people from the tyranny of Pharaoh and the oppression of the Egyptians. Choosing to focus on this past divine triumph brought renewed encouragement to Asaph as he faced this new ordeal. This God-focused concentration greatly bolstered his faith. His troubling distress was soon transformed into triumphant rejoicing by remembering what God had done in the past.

II. COMMENTARY

MAIN IDEA: *Although Asaph despairs because he feels deserted by God, he finds encouragement in reflecting upon God's past mighty deeds.*

A Asaph's Depression (77:1–6)

77:1–2. Finding himself in a low, devastating place, the psalmist Asaph was emotionally depressed in a dark day of great trouble. In desperate need of divine help, he **cried out to God** all day and **night**. He earnestly **sought the Lord** because his soul was **in distress**. Throughout the night, he **stretched out untiring hands** to God, a posture of humble prayer and fervent faith. Yet, no matter how much he prayed, his **soul** was in such despair that it **refused to be comforted**. Although he looked to God to be the true comforter of his soul, his effort to find relief in prayer failed him.

77:3. In this distress and devastation, Asaph **remembered** to look to **God**. But he found no relief from this debilitating state. He only **groaned** within himself. Reflecting upon God's past mercies only further exacerbated his pain. He **mused** upon God's past goodness, but his **spirit grew faint** because such mercy was far from him in his present crisis.

77:4–6. Sleep evaded him, which he felt was God's doing. Unable to sleep, he was **too troubled to speak** rationally. He **thought about the former days** when God's blessings were clearly displayed toward him. He **remembered** the **songs** he once sang **in the night** that previously had comforted his heart. But looking back upon happier times only deepened his depression. His heart **mused** upon past glory days, and his **spirit inquired** of himself possible solutions to his present dilemmas. Tragically, his despondency was deepening, not lessening.

B Asaph's Desperation (77:7–9)

77:7. Overwhelmed and perplexed, Asaph asked God a series of rapid-fire rhetorical questions. These inquiries give voice to the very root of his dismay. Feeling abandoned and forgotten by God, he pondered, **Will the Lord reject forever?** The answer was no, but he certainly felt that way. **Will he never show his favor again?** He now doubted that God would ever bless him again. Such is the exaggerated reasoning of a discouraged soul.

77:8–9. How long would God withhold his **love**? The psalmist had convinced himself such love would never be shown to him again. He had persuaded himself, wrongly so, that God's **promise** had failed. **Has God forgotten to be merciful?** No, but the psalmist was starting to believe this. **Has he in anger withheld his compassion?** No, but God was seemingly restraining his tender love toward him. These questions are negative, reflecting his depressed state. However, voicing these questions would soon push him closer to God.

C Asaph's Determination (77:10–15)

77:10. Shifting his mind upon God's earlier triumphs in generations past, Asaph contemplated previous times when God protected and strengthened his people. This refocus is the turning point of this psalm. He began to draw hope from God's saving acts of the past: **To this I will appeal: the years of the right hand of the Most High.** Here is a reference back to earlier days (Gen. 14:22), seeing God's powerful rule as protector and provider of his covenant people.

77:11–12. Reflecting back on years gone by, the psalmist purposes, **I will remember your miracles of long ago.** The remembrance of God's past actions taken on behalf of his people bolstered his faith. **I will meditate on all your works,** that is, these past **deeds** and miracles of God. Asaph redirected his mind away from his present troubles to God's past **mighty deeds** and found renewed strength in the midst of his troubles.

77:13. With mounting confidence, Asaph acknowledged that the past miracles of God were **holy.** With a burst of boldness, he declared the greatness of God. **Your ways, O God, are holy,** meaning absolutely perfect and morally pure, without the slightest hint of error in his decisions and ways toward mankind. This led to a changed man. **What god is so great as our God?** The implied answer is none. God alone is transcendent, far above his creation, upright in all his ways.

77:14–15. You are the God who performs miracles, unleashing **your power among the peoples.** What God purposes to do, he accomplishes with unlimited power. **With your mighty arm you redeemed your people.** "Redeemed," a synonym for "delivered" or "rescued," means that God delivered his people in the past from the bondage of their oppressors. God did this for **the descendants of Jacob and Joseph,** indicating that he had long remained faithful to his people. Thus, the psalmist can expect God to do the same in his own life. What God had done in the past, he is able to do once again in the present (vv. 11,14–15).

D Asaph's Declaration (77:16–20)

77:16. In particular, Asaph described one divine act from Israel's past in which God displayed his power—the exodus (Exod. 14). Here is a vivid description of divine power, parting the Red Sea, expressed in highly poetical language. **The waters,** referring to the Red Sea, **saw you, O God** and **writhed** and **convulsed,** knowing they were to be parted. The entire earth trembled.

77:17–19. In this miraculous intervention, God displayed his might in **the clouds**, which poured down rain, **the skies**, which thundered, and the lightning, pictured as **arrows**, which **flashed back and forth**. **The whirlwind** is the cloud that stood between God's people and Pharaoh's armies and divided the sea. **Thunder** was heard coming from this powerful cloud, as well as **lightning**. The very ground of **the earth** beneath them **trembled and quaked** at this unleashed power. God's **path led through the sea**, which parted before the Israelites. His **footprints were not seen**, meaning that his presence was not visible to them. Nevertheless, it was apparent that this was the hand of Almighty God at work.

77:20. Through this dramatic, supernatural deliverance, God **led** his **people** like a shepherd would lead his flock, tenderly yet powerfully, protecting them like sheep. He led them through the Red Sea, through the Desert of Sinai, and ultimately, into the promised land. It was through **Moses and Aaron**, his chosen leaders, that God faithfully led them forward to safety and security.

III. CONCLUSION

What strong encouragement there is here for discouraged believers in this passage. All saints should reflect upon the past triumphs of God throughout redemptive history. Written in the pages of Scripture and recorded in the annals of church history, the mighty exploits of God are designed to tell the story of God's working in the affairs of men. Each episode should infuse powerful hope into hearts. The God who has worked so mightily in the past stands ready to help his people in the present. By looking back, we find strength for today, as well as for the future. May all the saints find comfort in this present hour by focusing upon what great exploits the sovereign Lord has done in generations past.

IV. TEACHING OUTLINE

A. Asaph's Depression (1-6)
   1. I Cried Out to God (1)
      a. To help me (1a)
      b. To hear me (1b)
   2. I Sought God (2)
      a. In the day of trouble (2a)
      b. In the night of tribulation (2b)
   3. I Remembered God (3)
      a. My soul groaned (3a)
      b. My mind mused (3b)
      c. My spirit feinted (3c)

4. I Recalled My Former Days (4-6)
   a. My eyes wearied (4a)
   b. My mouth stammered (4b)
   c. My mind reflected (5)
   d. My heart mused (6)

B. Asaph's Desparation (7-9)
   1. Will the Lord Forsake Me? (7)
   2. Will the Lord Fail Me? (8)
   3. Will the Lord Forget Me? (9)

C. Asaph's Determination (10-15)
   1. I Will Refocus on God's Deeds (10)
   2. I Will Remember God's Deeds (11)
   3. I Will Reflect on God's Deeds (12)
   4. I Will Rejoice in God's Deeds (13-15)
      a. God's ways are perfect (13)
      b. God's wonders are powerful (14)
      c. God's works are protective (15)

D. Asaph's Declaration (16-20)
   1. God's Power Was Displayed at the Red Sea (16-18)
      a. The waters withered (16)
      b. The clouds poured (17a)
      c. The skies thundered (17b)
      d. The lightning flashed (17c)
      e. The thunder sounded (18a)
      f. The earth quaked (18b)
   2. God's Path Was Decreed Through the Red Sea (19)
      a. His path was invincible (19a,b)
      b. His presence was invisible (19c)
   3. God's People Were Delivered from the Red Sea (20)
      a. He led them like a flock (20a)
      b. He led them by his servants (20b)

Psalm 78
Remember to Remember

"To test the present you must appeal to history."

Winston Churchill

Psalm 78

I. INTRODUCTION

The year was 1897, and England found herself at the height of her colonial power. It was then that the vast British Empire turned its attention to the jubilee celebration of Queen Victoria. Around the globe, the rulers of the British-held colonies returned to London for a long summer of self-congratulation. In this golden hour of Britain's zenith, Rudyard Kipling, England's best known poet, was asked to write a piece for this historic occasion. Taking this opportunity to sound a much-needed warning, he wrote a powerful poem entitled "Recessional 1897." It began:

> God of our Fathers, known of old,
> Lord of our far-flung battle line,
> Beneath whose awful hand we hold
> Dominion over palm and pine—
> Lord God of hosts, be with us yet,
> Lest we forget—lest we forget.

In this brilliant work, Kipling called upon England to look to her storied past not with pride but with humility and dependence upon God. He challenged Britain to trust in God, not in herself, lest she repeat the now-forgotten mistakes of her past. This daring reminder that all earthly success comes from God alone, and that God must not be forgotten, was believed to be the reason Kipling was passed over as the nation's poet laureate. A proud people did not want to think like that, especially during the Queen's jubilee celebration. But Kipling was right, even though his message was not received. If

England was to be prosperous in the future, he believed, she must not forget the lessons of the past. Most especially, she must not forget that her many successes were not self-originating but were from God.

Along this line, Psalm 78 recounts the past history of Israel in order to draw practical lessons for the present. This psalm recalls how God's people wrongly responded to him in the past. These truths are designed to show how God's people in a new generation must not repeat the same failures of other generations. This psalm is the longest historical psalm in the Psalter, the other historical ones being Psalms 105–107; 114; and 135–136. It is a didactic song divided into six stanzas, each unit offering a unique perspective on Israel's past failures.

The first stanza (vv. 1–8) serves as a preamble to the history that is to be surveyed in each stanza. Each successive stanza introduces a failure of Israel's past, one that should be avoided at all costs in the present. Yet through it all, the psalmist notes that God remained faithful to his people and preserved them in spite of their rebellion and unfaithfulness. Such is the long-suffering grace of God.

II. COMMENTARY

> **MAIN IDEA:** *Asaph surveys the long-repeated rebellion of Israel in the face of God's goodness, encouraging believers not to repeat this same sin.*

A The Importance of Israel's Past (78:1–8)

> **SUPPORTING IDEA:** *Asaph calls upon God's people to learn many lessons from their past failures.*

78:1–3. Focusing on Israel's past, the psalmist begins with a passionate appeal to be heard by others. **O my people, hear my teaching** and **the words of my mouth.** Asaph must be heard! **I will open my mouth in parables** (*mashal*, a comparison), a form of illustrative teaching that places one incident or story alongside something else so that a comparison of the two may be made. In this case, the past history of Israel is set before the present generation so that they might not repeat the mistakes of the past. **I will utter hidden things . . . from of old.** Speaking of forgotten truths from Israel's past, the psalmist looked beyond the actual events of history to discern their true, spiritual significance. He will now provide appropriate commentary on what God has been doing throughout Israel's past (see Matt. 13:35).

78:4–7. These lessons from redemptive history must be told to **the next generation** so that the mistakes of the past will not be repeated. These divine acts involved God's **power,** intervening miraculously into Israel's affairs, provoking **wonders** in everyone. In giving **the law,** God **commanded** his people **to teach their children,** who **in turn would tell their children** (Deut. 6:6–7). Each generation should entrust God's Word to the next generation, urge them to **put their trust in God,** and **keep his commands.**

78:8. This present generation should **not be like their forefathers,** who were **stubborn and rebellious, not loyal** and **not faithful to him.** Israel's history has been one long, unbroken record of unfaithfulness to God in spite of his abundant grace and undeserved loving-kindness to them. They must choose to respond differently toward God than past generations, who proved to be faithless.

Ⓑ The Insurrection of Israel's Past (78:9–16)

SUPPORTING IDEA: *Ephraim, a symbol of national apostasy, rebelled against God.*

78:9–12. The psalmist addressed **the men of Ephraim,** one of the twelve tribes of Israel, whose failures represented the sins of the entire nation. **Though armed with bows,** ready for war, they, nevertheless, **turned back on the day of battle.** This is a reference to Israel's history of retreating from trusting and obeying God. Consequently, they were continually defeated by their enemies because of their disobedience. **They did not keep God's covenant** because they repeatedly **forgot what he had done.** If they had remembered God's faithfulness to them, they would have been motivated to be faithful to him. But they forgot God's past mighty interventions and, thus, fell into disobedience again and again. **He did miracles** before their eyes in **Egypt** and **Zoan,** the latter being the Egyptian city of Tanis northeast of the Nile Delta. Yet Israel, God's chosen people, still refused to keep his word.

78:13–16. The Lord faithfully led them through the Red Sea, in spite of their unfaithfulness. **He divided the sea and led them through** it, making **the water stand firm like a wall** (Exod. 15:8; Josh. 3:13,16). This describes God's dramatic deliverance of Israel at the Red Sea, escaping Pharaoh's army. Further, God led them through the wilderness **with the cloud** and **light from the fire;** and when Israel was thirsty, he **split the rocks in the desert and gave them water.** Even in the face of their disobedience, God remained good to them, bestowing his undeserved blessings.

Ⓒ The Ingratitude of Israel's Past (78:17–31)

SUPPORTING IDEA: *Israel often rebelled against God, doubting his ability to provide and not trusting him, but he gave them water and manna, repeatedly demonstrating his faithfulness.*

78:17–20. But in the face of this divine goodness, Israel **continued to sin against him,** being ungrateful and disobedient. The more gracious God was, the more they rebelled. They were **rebelling** even when God provided them food in the wilderness. They were **demanding the food they craved**, all the while doubting God's ability to provide in the desert. When **water** came gushing from **the rock** that Moses struck, they were skeptical that God could **supply meat**.

78:21–26. How did God respond to their disobedience, unbelief, and ingratitude? **He was very angry** and **his wrath rose**, sending **fire** (Num. 11:1–3). He did this because **they did not believe in** him. Yet, in spite of his holy displeasure, he still fed them. God **opened the doors of the heavens**, and **he rained down manna** for his unthankful people to eat, **all the food they could eat** (Exod. 16:14–31). How graciously and patiently he dealt with them.

78:27–31. Then, God fed them **meat** from **flying birds**, or quail (Exod. 16:13), which he made fall **inside their camp** next to **their tents**. God fed them plentifully, yet they still remained disobedient; and **God's anger rose against them**. Amazingly, although they repeatedly provoked him, God still provided for them.

Ⓓ The Insincerity of Israel's Past (78:32–39)

> **SUPPORTING IDEA:** *Israel repeatedly offered shallow repentance toward God, yet he still forgave and favored them.*

78:32–37. Even in the face of such divine goodness, the people **kept on sinning** and **did not believe**. Consequently, **God slew them**, and only then did they **seek him**. Sadly enough, God had to deal with them severely before they remembered he was their **Rock** and **Redeemer**. When they finally turned to him, **they would flatter him** with **lying** words of insincerity, failing to be **loyal to him**. Though they supposedly repented, it was insincere and meaningless, a counterfeit turning back to God. They suffered the self-deception of a false sorrow for their sin. Theirs was a bogus belief, a pseudo repentance that caused them to return to their unfaithfulness when tested.

78:38–39. Nevertheless, in spite of their unfaithfulness, God **was merciful** to them, forgiving **their iniquities**, and he **did not destroy them**. He repeatedly **restrained** the full expression of **his anger**, remembering that they were weak and lived fleeting lives like **a passing breeze**.

Ⓔ The Insubordination of Israel's Past (78:40–55)

> **SUPPORTING IDEA:** *Israel often rebelled against God, tempting him and forgetting him; yet he still brought them out of Egypt into the promised land.*

78:40–43. Shifting back to the time of the exodus, the psalmist recalled the same theme: Israel's rebellion and God's redemption. **How often they rebelled against him in the desert**, Asaph lamented. **Again and again**, Israel vexed the Holy One by forgetting **his power** that had been clearly displayed on the day of the exodus. In their deliverance from Egypt, **he redeemed them** from Pharaoh, **the oppressor**. They grieved God in spite of his display of **miraculous signs in Egypt** by their repeated rebellions demonstrated by their disobedience.

78:44–51. Even when God sent plagues upon Egypt (Exod. 7–12), Israel did not repent of her rebellion against God. These plagues included **rivers** of **blood**, **swarms of flies**, **frogs**, **grasshopper**, **locust**, **hail**, and **lightning**. In all this, God **unleashed** his **anger** against Egypt, even striking dead **all the first-born**. God did all this to deliver his people, yet they remained hard-hearted much like the Egyptians.

78:52–53. God unleashed the ten plagues brought upon Pharaoh and **brought his people out** of Egypt **through the desert**. Though Israel was hard-hearted like the Egyptians, God delivered Israel while destroying the Egyptians. Faithfully, God **guided them safely** through the Red Sea, which **engulfed their enemies** (Exod. 14).

78:54–55. In spite of Israel's forty years of disobedience in the wilderness, God remained faithful to them. He led them like a flock to the **border of his holy land** and gave each tribe its allotted inheritance. He led them into the promised land and **drove out nations before them**. All this God did to bless them. In spite of their prolonged rebellion, God still fought for them, defeating their enemies and favoring them in the land.

F The Idolatry of Israel's Past (78:56–72)

SUPPORTING IDEA: *Israel continually turned away from God, but he remained faithful, fighting for them and favoring them.*

78:56–58. Despite their new location, Israel continued their relentless rebellion against God. Once in the promised land, they did not change. They still **put God to the test** by being disobedient against him. Just **like their fathers**, Israel was **disloyal and faithless**, setting up **high places** for Baal worship. All this **angered** God and **aroused his jealousy** as Israel once again worshipped false **idols**.

78:59–64. In righteous indignation, God **rejected Israel completely** and had **the tabernacle of Shiloh** plundered. Since the days of Joshua, Shiloh had been the center of Israel's worship (Josh. 18:1,8; 21:1–2; Judg. 18:31; 1 Sam. 1:3). But the capital city was **abandoned** by God, and **the ark** was captured by **the enemy** (1 Sam. 4:4–11). He gave Israel **to the sword** and many **people** were killed at that time, including the **priests** Hophni and Phinehas.

78:65–72. But then **the Lord awoke**, as if his momentary inactivity gave the appearance that he had been asleep. Aroused and stirred to action, he **beat back his enemies**. Then God **rejected the tents of Joseph and Ephraim**, representing the ten northern tribes, in order to choose **the tribe of Judah** for the location of **his sanctuary**. Likewise, God **chose David**, who had earlier tended his father's sheep, **to be the shepherd of his people Jacob** and **Israel**. Once again, this was God's blessing upon his people, though much undeserved. As their king, David ruled over them **with integrity of heart** and **skillful hands**.

> **MAIN IDEA REVIEW:** *Asaph surveys the long-repeated rebellion of Israel in the face of God's goodness, encouraging believers not to repeat this same sin.*

III. CONCLUSION

George Santayana observed, "Those who cannot learn from history are doomed to repeat it." History, it is argued, is an insightful teacher of the present and a trusted guide into the future. But history, if it is to be viewed profitably, must have a realistic view of the past. A naive perception of "the good ole days" will be no help for the present. The past has always been marred by sin, just as the present is; and profitable lessons may be learned from the past only when it is recognized for what it is—a past marred by sin. Much can be learned from the failures of the past, sometimes even more than from its successes. This is the valuable role of Psalm 78, and much of it can be applied to the lives of believers today.

Two dominant themes have reoccurred throughout the centuries of God's people and must never be forgotten—their failures and God's faithfulness. Over the many years, believers have repeatedly disobeyed the Lord and turned to go their own way. In spite of this reoccurring distrust, God has remained longsuffering and patient, providing undeserved blessings for his wayward people. This amazing patience of God's grace, enduring with his people in spite of their sin, underscores the marvelous mercy of God. He rewards his people, not according to their sins but according to his lovingkindness. This psalm reminds us that the Lord remains graciously faithful to bless his people, even when they are unfaithful to him.

IV. LIFE APPLICATION

As believers look to God's past dealing with his people, they should be encouraged to note several timeless truths.

1. *God's Word never changes.* In spite of the disobedience of believers, God's Word remains the same—unchanging, immutable, forever true. Cultures change over the centuries. Values change. Morality changes. But not God's Word. It is the one constant that endures from generation to generation. What

was wrong yesterday remains wrong today. You can always look to the unchanging standard of Scripture and know what God expects.

2. *God's ways never change.* In the face of human rebellion, God remains gracious and long-suffering, slow to anger, quick to forgive. He is always faithful to bring back a wayward people to himself when they humble themselves and repent. Believers should be as quick to repent as God is to forgive.

V. PRAYER

God, according to your infinite grace, forgive us our many sins committed against you. As you have so faithfully shown grace in the past, show grace in this present hour. We thank you that where our sin has abounded, so your grace has more than abounded. In Jesus' name. Amen.

VI. DEEPER DISCOVERIES

A. Covenant (78:10,37)

This is the first usage of the word *covenant* (*berit*) in the Psalms. A *berit* was a binding pact or agreement between two parties whether between individuals (Gen. 21:27) or nations (Josh. 9:6,15). God often used this word in describing his relationship with Israel, his chosen people. Yet unlike a covenant between people involving a mutual agreement, the covenant between God and his people was a unilateral covenant, or an agreement based upon the faithfulness of God alone. This covenant was initiated and instituted by God alone to protect and preserve his chosen ones. The one-sided nature of this covenant is clearly evident in the statement, "I will . . . be your God, and you will be my people" (Lev. 26:12; Exod. 19:5).

B. Shame (78:66)

The word *shame* (*herpa*) is a noun that occurs seventy times in the Old Testament. It means "to disgrace, scorn, shame, contempt, or rebuke." In some instances *herpa* carries the idea of an accusation or blame that is cast upon someone (Isa. 25:8; Jer. 31:19; Ezek. 36:30). In addition, *herpa* is used of a person or persons who are despised (Gen. 30:23; Neh. 2:17; Isa. 4:1; Joel 2:17,19; Dan. 9:16). It is used to describe the taunting of one's enemies (Judg. 8:15; Ps. 119:42) and of the defamation of a person's character in order to discredit him (Neh. 6:13).

VII. TEACHING OUTLINE

A. The Importance of Israel's Past (1-8)
  1. I Will Teach You (1-3)
    a. Truths in parables (1-2a)
    b. Things hidden from old (2-3)
  2. You Will Teach Others (4-8)
    a. The wonders of God (4)
    b. The word of God (5-8)
B. The Insurrection of Israel's Past (9-16)
  1. They Rebelled Against God (9-11)
    a. They forsook his word (9)
    b. They forgot his works (10-11)
  2. God Rescued Them(12-16)
    a. God did wonderful things (12)
    b. God divided the sea (13)
    c. God directed them through the sea (14)
    d. God divided the rock (15-16)
C. The Ingratitude of Israel's Past(17-31)
  1. They Defied God (17-19)
    a. They sinned against him (17)
    b. They tested him (18)
    c. They spoke against him (19)
  2. God Delivered Them (20a)
    a. He struck the rock (20a)
    b. He served them water (20b)
  3. They Disbelieved God (20b)
    a. They doubted he would give them bread (20b)
    b. They doubted he would give them meat (20b)
  4. God Disciplined Them (21)
    a. He was wrathful toward them (21a)
    b. He was angry with them (21b)
  5. They Denied God (22)
    a. They did not believe him (22a)
    b. They did not trust him (22b)
  6. God Delighted Them (23-31)
    a. God commanded the clouds (23)
    b. God rained down manna (24)
    c. God fed them abundantly (25-29)
    d. God disciplined them (30-31)

D. The Insincerity of Israel's Past (32-39)
    1. They Rejected God (32-37)
        a. They sinned against God (32-33)
        b. They sought God (34)
        c. They remembered God (35)
        d. They lied to God (36)
        e. They left God (37)
    2. God Remained Faithful (38-39)
        a. He forgave them (38)
        b. He remembered them (39)
E. The Insubordination of Israel's Past (40-55)
    1. They Rebelled Against God (40-42)
        a. They turned from God (40)
        b. They tempted God (41)
        c. They forgot God (42)
    2. God Rescued Them (43-55)
        a. He performed signs (43)
        b. He sent plagues (44-51)
        c. He led them (52-53)
        d. He directed them into the land (54)
        e. He drove out the nations (55a)
        f. He divided up the land (55b)
F. The Idolatry of Israel's Past (56-72)
    1. They Rebelled Against God (56-58)
        a. They tested him (56)
        b. They turned back from him (57)
        c. They provoked him (58)
    2. God Disciplined Them (59-61)
        a. He abhorred them (59)
        b. He abandoned them (60-64)
    3. God Favored Them (65-72)
        a. He fought for them (65-66)
        b. He chose Judah (67-68)
        c. He constructed the temple (69)
        d. He chose David (70-72)

Psalm 79
For Your Glory

I. INTRODUCTION

All that God does, he does primarily to pursue and promote his own glory. This is the highest end and chief ambition that stir the passion of God's own heart, namely, the magnification of his own most holy name. Here is the supreme good for which God acts, the promotion of his own honor. If this is the loftiest pursuit of God, then so it must be for man. All people must live for what is greater than themselves if they are to be elevated to experience life as God purposes. Men either live for the greatness of God, or they merely exist. This is the highest goal and most honorable aim of man, the passionate pursuit of the glory of God.

In this psalm, the glory of God grips the heart of Asaph as he approaches the Almighty with a humble request. He petitions the Lord to act for the display of his own supremacy. The historical setting behind this psalm is the occasion of a devastating national defeat for ancient Israel. Most probably, the background was the aftershock of the dreaded invasion of the Babylonian ruler, Nebuchadnezzar, who invaded the promised land in 588 B.C. and destroyed the temple. This foreign attack that led to Israel's Babylonian captivity was caused by Israel's own sin of disobedience committed over many years. Having suffered for their own iniquities, Asaph called upon God to atone for their sins and avenge their own blood by turning his wrath upon their enemies. In so doing, Asaph appealed to God by the grandest motivation of all. He asked God to act for the sake of his own glory. He prayed that God would guard the greatness of his own name in the world.

II. COMMENTARY

MAIN IDEA: *Asaph laments that Jerusalem has been devastated and cries out to God to act for the sake of his own glory.*

A A Prayer of Lamentation (79:1–4)

79:1. Bemoaning the complete devastation of the holy city **Jerusalem**, the psalmist laments its defeat at the hands of a fierce foreign oppressor. **The nations**, a reference to this advancing army, **have invaded your inheritance**, Israel's homeland, the place God uniquely possessed. In so doing, they have **defiled your holy temple** in Jerusalem, the city where God's glory has been most prominently displayed through the ages. The walls and buildings of the city, which was witness to the glory of God, were **reduced . . . to rubble** under this rampage.

79:2–3. In this foreign invasion, many of God's people were killed and their **dead bodies** fed **to the birds**, picturing a devastating defeat without any burial. Their **flesh** had been eaten by the wild **beasts**, and their **blood** poured out **like water**. This loss of human life was enormous. The savages ruthlessly killed everyone in their way as they pillaged the city.

79:4. As a result, Israel suffered embarrassing **reproach** in the eyes of their surrounding **neighbors**, the adjoining nations in the region. God's people were objects of **scorn and derision** to all who saw them. This national disaster was cause for great lamenting for the psalmist and the people.

B A Prayer for Restoration (79:5–8)

79:5. In response, the psalmist pled with God to relent and restore Israel to her former strength and stature. This would require that God, first, release her from her former sins. **How long** must they endure this painful chastening for their iniquities? Rightly so, God has been **angry** with them. The **jealousy** of a holy God has burned **like fire** against them. Yet Asaph wondered how much longer this would continue?

79:6–7. Asaph petitioned God, **pour out your wrath** upon these pagan **nations** just as they have poured out the blood of your people. They had **devoured** and **destroyed** Israel, the **homeland** of **Jacob**. This was a fervent request for divine vengeance to defeat and crush Israel's enemies.

79:8. Israel had already suffered much because of the **sins of the fathers** of past generations. So the psalmist prayed that God would not continue to hold these previous sins of Israel's ancestors against them any longer. In

desperate need, he pled that God's **mercy** would **come quickly** before it was too late and all of God's chosen people were completely annihilated.

C A Prayer for Glorification (79:9–11)

79:9. Appealing to God's highest motive, the psalmist asked God to answer these requests for restoration based upon the **glory** of his own **name**. **Help us** and **deliver us** from the oppression of these invading nations. **Forgive our sins**, he pled, asking for divine forgiveness for the treacherous failings of Israel. The foundation of this request was the glory of God's name, that is, that his greatness should be proclaimed. If God were to deliver Israel and reverse his judgment, God's mercy would vividly display God's glory.

79:10. Burdened for the honor of God's name, the psalmist prayed, **Why should the nations say, "Where is their God?"** If God should not forgive them and restore them soon, this would defame God's name and honor. The psalmist pled, **make known among the nations that you avenge the outpoured blood of your servants**. That is, reveal yourself to be a God of wrath who visits his enemies.

79:11. Asaph interceded for the survivors of Jerusalem's destruction, for those fellow Jews held captive in Babylonian exile as **prisoners . . . condemned to die: May the groans of the prisoners come before you**. He besought God that he would hear their prayers for relief and release them from their oppressors. **By the strength of your arm**, he asked, **preserve** them from death.

D A Prayer of Imprecation (79:12)

79:12. Repeating his earlier request for divine vengeance (vv. 6,10), the psalmist expressed the same request again. **Pay back into the laps of our neighbors seven times the reproach they have hurled at you, O Lord**. Their assault upon God's people in Jerusalem had, in reality, been an attack upon God himself, who is inseperably identified with his people (cp. Acts 9:4–5). **Seven times** is a figurative way of conveying fullest measure. He requested complete and swift retribution from the Lord.

E A Prayer of Adoration (79:13)

79:13. Upon God's destruction of Israel's enemies, his people will **praise** him **forever**, thus, bringing glory to God, the glory Asaph promised if the Lord would grant his request. This **praise** will be so fervent that it will pass **from generation to generation**, enduring **forever**.

III. CONCLUSION

A similar supreme passion for God's glory should saturate the heart and focus the prayers of every believer. There must be a seeking first of the kingdom of God by every child of God before there should be the pursuit of earthly things (Matt. 6:33). In whatsoever the believer does, every activity must be for God's own glory (1 Cor. 10:31). This is God's own chief pursuit (Rom. 11:36). So should it be with believers. The greatest appeal to God in prayer should always be the advancement of his name and the spread of his fame among the unbelieving nations (Ps. 67:4).

IV. TEACHING OUTLINE

A. A Prayer of Lamentation (1-4)
1. The Situation Is Desolate (1
   a. The nation is devastated (1a)
   b. The temple is defiled (1b)
   c. The holy city is destroyed (1c)
2. The Saints Are Dead (2-3)
   a. Dead bodies feed the birds (2a)
   b. Dead flesh feeds the beasts (2b)
   c. Spilt blood runs in Jerusalem (3a)
   d. Dead corpses are unburied (3b)
3. The Survivors Are Dispised (4)
   a. We are objects of reproach (4a)
   b. We are objects of scorn (4b)

B. A Prayer for Restoration (5-8)
1. God, Restrain Your Anger Toward Us (5)
   a. How long will you be angry? (5a)
   b. How long will you be jealous? (5b)
2. God, Release Your Wrath Toward Them (6-7)
   a. For they defy you (6)
   b. For they devour us (7a)
   c. For they destroy us (7b)
3. God, Renew Your Mercy Toward Us (8)
   a. Pardon our former sins (8a)
   b. Pity our present suffering (8b)

C. A Prayer for Glorification (9-11)
1. Magnify Your Own Name (9)
   a. Deliver us for your glorious name (9a)
   b. Pardon us for your name's sake (9b)

    D. A Prayer of Imprecation (12)
        1. Pay Back to Our Neighbors (12a)
        2. Pay Back for Reproaching You (12b)
    E. A Prayer of Adoration (13)
        1. We Will Give Thanks Forever (13a)
        2. We Will Give Praise Fervently (13b)
            a. From this generation (13b)
            b. To the next generation (13b)

Psalm 80
The Great Awakening

| Q u o t e |

"*W*hen God is about to do a great work,

He pours out a spirit of supplication."

J o n a t h a n   E d w a r d s

Psalm 80

I. INTRODUCTION

In the early days of colonial America, intense seasons of heaven-sent revival often came to the churches. In the 1730s and 1740s, spiritual awakenings swept through many congregations with great power and effect. Many gifted preachers were raised up by God to bring people to the awareness of their need for repentance. Before these movements of God's Spirit caught fire, the American colonies were at a low ebb, both spiritually and morally. But God raised up many faithful ministers to help restore the church. Chief among them was Jonathan Edwards, the great theologian and preacher of Northampton, Massachusetts, whose biblical preaching impacted the land.

Edwards spent days in prayer for the spiritual vitality of the churches. His pulpit was mighty because the Spirit's power upon his ministry was dominant. For him, the connection between the Spirit's power and strong preaching, clearly, was vitally linked by prayer. Edwards also encouraged his young people to form small groups for serious prayer. Adults soon joined these seasons of intercession as well. Prayer, literally, paved the way for the First Awakening which followed. As the Word was preached, hearts were pierced, sin was exposed, and souls were saved. A spark was lit that ignited a fire of revival that soon spread quickly throughout the Connecticut River Valley. Over the next six months, Edwards saw nearly three hundred people converted in Northampton, a town of only twelve hundred people. But where was this awakening ignited? The fires of revival were begun in prayer, first by

Edwards, then by the youth, later by the adults. Prayer *is* the forerunner of revival.

This is the theme of Psalm 80, a prayer for Israel's restoration after she had been ravaged by a foreign oppressor. But more than a cry for national restoration, this psalm is a plea for spiritual revival that God would awaken himself and come to renew them. Most probably, the historical occasion was the Assyrian captivity of the ten tribes of the Northern Kingdom in 722 B.C. (2 Kgs. 17:6). Psalm 80 then was written from Jerusalem where the Asaph singers lived, as the title indicates. It reveals the shock that this foreign invasion and resulting defeat had upon God's people in the Southern Kingdom who found themselves exposed to Assyria and a similar attack. They cried out to God as their one true Shepherd to protect them (vv. 1–7) and as their vinedresser to nurture them (vv. 8–19). It is *a psalm* to be sung *to the tune of "The Lilies of the Covenant"* (cp. Ps. 45) and is *of Asaph,* meaning the singers were descendants of Asaph who served in the temple.

II. COMMENTARY

> **MAIN IDEA:** *Asaph pleads with God to restore his people who, like a vine ravaged by boars, have suffered excruciating defeat by foreign enemies.*

A Asaph's Plea (80:1–3)

> **SUPPORTING IDEA:** *Asaph asks God to save and restore his people.*

80:1. Asking God to send a spiritual revival, Asaph expressed an urgent plea, **Hear us, O Shepherd of Israel, you who lead Joseph like a flock** (cp. 74:1; 77:20; 78:52,71–72; 79:13). Pictured as a Shepherd to his people (cp. 23:1; 28:9), God is always guarding and guiding them in the presence of much danger. **You who sit enthroned between the cherubim** is a reference to the ark of the covenant, a symbol of God's presence (Exod. 25:18). God is pictured as sitting **enthroned** above the gold-covered cherubim (Ps. 99:1; 1 Kgs. 6:23–28). **Shine forth,** Asaph pleaded, a request that God's glory be seen again in their midst as in days of old (Exod. 24:16–17; 40:34–35). All revival puts God's glory on display.

80:2. Do so, he asked, for the good of **Ephraim,** located in the Northern Kingdom, and **Benjamin,** where Jerusalem was in the Southern Kingdom, and **Manasseh,** partly across the Jordan River. These three names are intended to represent the entire nation of Israel. **Awaken your might,** he requested. That is, no longer be inactive and seemingly indifferent toward us. **Come and save us** from the destruction which they have suffered by the Assyrians.

80:3. More than a cry for mere national resurgence, the psalmist prayed for spiritual revival. **Restore us, O God; make your face shine upon us, that we may be saved** (cp. vv. 7,14–15,19). This repeated refrain is a fervent prayer for Israel's restoration after suffering a major, devastating defeat by the Assyrians. They will be **saved**, or rescued from defeat, only if God will **shine** his grace and power upon them (cp. Num. 6:25; Pss. 4:6; 13:1). This was more than a cry for national prosperity, but a request for spiritual revival (cp. Ps. 80:18).

ⓑ Asaph's Pain (80:4–7)

SUPPORTING IDEA: *Asaph laments over the Lord's severe punishment of his people.*

80:4–6. With a heavy heart, Asaph lamented, **How long will your anger smolder against the prayers of your people?** When will God turn his fierce discipline away? In the midst of their painful ordeal, it was as if God, their Shepherd, had **fed them with the bread of tears** and they had been made to **drink tears by the bowlful.** This pictures their uncontrollable weeping in the midst of this painful tribulation. So great was this defeat and humiliation that they had become, worse, **a source of contention** to the enemies who **mock us.** This ridicule and taunting was their greatest pain.

80:7. So Asaph repeated the reoccurring refrain, **Restore us, O God Almighty** (cp. vv. 3,19). The identification of God as **Almighty** was intended to emphasize his all-sufficient power. He was able to overrule their enemies and **restore** them to safety and prosperity in their land if they would turn to him.

ⓒ Asaph's Perplexity (80:8–15)

SUPPORTING IDEA: *Asaph recognizes that Israel, once God's fruitful vine, is being punished for its present fruitlessness and begs for divine favor.*

80:8–9a. Speaking of Israel as a **vine,** Asaph stated that God brought her **out of Egypt.** That is, he had earlier transplanted the nation out of Egyptian soil into the promised land. In so doing, God prepared the land in that he **drove out the nations.** He removed the pagan peoples who inhabited Judea. As a farmer would prepare the land for sowing or planting, God **cleared the ground for** Israel to dwell successfully in it.

80:9b–11. The transplanting of Israel into their land was so successful that the nation, like a flourishing vine, **took root and filled the land.** The people grew so prolifically that **the mountains were covered with its shade.** Even the **mighty cedars,** the tallest trees of the area, were covered **with its branches.** This symbolizes the extraordinary prosperity of the nation, so phenomenal that Israel, this vine, **sent out its boughs** to the Mediterranean Sea, **its shoots as far as the** Euphrates **River.** Israel fully occupied her promised land.

80:12–13. But devastation came. The Lord had **broken down its walls**, removing his divine protection. These walls have been removed by God himself, allowing all nations **who pass by** to pick its prosperity. The surrounding enemies are represented as devouring **boars from the forest** who **ravage** Israel and **feed** on them.

80:14–15. The reoccurring refrain (vv. 3,7,19) is once more stated, this time in slightly different terms, but it conveys the same message. **Return to us, O God Almighty** in order to restore us, Asaph pleaded. **Look down from heaven and see** our desperate need. **Watch over this vine** in order to protect us. Shifting metaphors, this vine is **the son you have raised up for yourself**, picturing God's tender compassion for this vine as a **son** (Exod. 4:22; Hos. 11:1). However, the Hebrew word for "son" may also be rendered "branch" (Gen. 49:22).

D Asaph's Petition (80:16–19)

> **SUPPORTING IDEA:** *Asaph concludes with a prayer for the restoration of God's people.*

80:16. Before stating his petition, Asaph summarized what he had been saying to God. He lamented, **Your vine is cut down, it is burned with fire; at your rebuke your people perish**. He realized that all of their troubles had come from the chastening hand of God.

80:17–18a. Now the petition was expressed by Asaph. **Let your hand rest on the man at your right hand, the son of man**. This imagery may allude to Benjamin, the name meaning "son of the right hand." Or it could signify the entire nation of Israel, pictured earlier as a son (v. 15). Either way, Asaph was saying, **Then we will not turn away from you**. If God would bless his people again, their hearts surely would be more faithful to him. From a prophetic prospective, "son of man" may refer to the Davidic dynasty on a larger scale and point, ultimately, to the Messiah, the Lord Jesus Christ. It should be noted that Christ most often referred to himself by this title, the son of man.

80:18b–19. Asaph concluded this section as he had each previous unit with the same closing refrain: **Revive us, and we will call on your name**. This is a much repeated prayer for a renewed devotion to God, a restored loyalty to God, and a rekindled passion for God. God himself must so work in their hearts. **Restore us, O LORD God Almighty**, he asked, to a place of blessing. **Make your face shine upon us** as a king would look favorably upon his subjects, granting this request. Then, **we may be saved** from the defeat of our enemies.

> **MAIN IDEA REVIEW:** *Asaph pleads with God to restore his people who, like a vine ravaged by boars, have suffered excruciating defeat by foreign enemies.*

III. CONCLUSION

Ultimately, God answered this prayer, but only after a period of severe chastening and suffering by those in the Southern Kingdom in the Babylonian captivity. Over many years, God's people had removed themselves from his blessings through their apostasy and rightly experienced his disciplinary love. But in God's perfect timing, God did revive his people and restore his work under the ministries of Ezra, Nehemiah, and the postexilic prophets. Even so, God will restore his people today who call out to him, all in his proper time.

IV. LIFE APPLICATION

In his work *The Reformation in England,* historian J. H. Merte d'Augbigue concludes that "the only true reformation is that which emanates from the Word of God." So it is with every revival that inevitably leads to reformation. It will be through the ministry of God's Word that true revival will come—or it will not come at all. What must we do today to see great revival come?

Preach the Word. Revival is spread through the preaching of God's Word. A biblical pulpit is the fuel for the fire of revival. In the eighteenth century, Bible preachers such as George Whitefield, John Wesley, Daniel Rowland, and Howell Harris were used mightily by God in seeing great multitudes converted. Preaching fed the flame of this revival. Pray that God will raise up biblical expositors in this hour who preach the full counsel of God.

Submit to the Word. In a time of revival, there is a new humility before God's Word. The authority of Scripture reigns in the hearts of God's people again. There is a new submission in believers who place themselves under the Bible, desiring to do whatever it requires. Pride is dethroned, and biblical authority once again rules the day. There is a coming *back* to the Bible, which is a coming *under* the Bible.

Obey the Word. Revival always brings a new allegiance to keep the Word. It is not to be measured by fanatical emotions running high but by a new obedience to the commands of Scripture. Repentance from disobedience comes. A return to embracing the requirements of Scripture comes back in full bloom. The Word preached becomes the Word practiced.

V. PRAYER

God, restore and revive your church in this hour. We confess our sin of lukewarmness and compromise with the world. We repent and return to you. Restore your work in the midst of this decadent hour. Rend the heavens and come down. In Jesus' name. Amen.

VI. DEEPER DISCOVERIES

A. Almighty (80:4,7,14,19)

The word *Almighty* (*sebaot*) refers to a large number of hosts such as human armies (Exod. 7:4; Ps. 44:9), the celestial bodies (i.e., the sun, moon, and stars) (Gen. 2:1; Deut. 4:19; Isa. 40:26), or heavenly creatures such as angels (Josh. 5:14; 1 Kgs. 22:19; Ps. 148:2). The title, the Lord Almighty, or the Lord of hosts, conveyed the idea of the sovereignty of God over all powers in the universe. It also referred to God as the God of armies, both the heavenly army (Deut. 33:2; Josh. 5:14; Ps. 68:17) and the armies of Israel (1 Sam. 17:45). It occurs 486 times in the Old Testament as a special name for God that speaks of his sovereign rule over the entire created order. The Lord is the mightiest Warrior and the omnipotent King. While having military connotations, *sebaot* denotes more than military meanings to encompass the forces of the realms, both heavenly and earthly (cp. 1 Sam. 17:45). Thus the divine name, Lord Almighty, or the Lord of hosts, denotes the God who sovereignly reigns above all, showing himself to be ready to intervene on behalf of his people (Pss. 80:19; 84:1; Isa. 28:5–6; Amos 4:13; 5:8–9; 9:5–6).

B. Son of Man (80:17)

The title "son of man" (Heb. *ben 'adam*) was deliberately chosen by the psalmist to underscore man's frailty, mortality, and weakness. *Ben* is used almost five thousand times in the Hebrew Bible, and it refers to the human male offspring. Sometimes *ben* is used as an idiom for children, descendants, remote descendants, and sons. "Man" (*adam*) is used more than five hundred times throughout the Hebrew Bible to speak of mankind, but it is also used of individuals.

"Son of man" is a poetic term that emphasizes man's frailty (Num. 23:19; Job 25:6; 35:8). It was used at times as a proper title. Ezekiel referred to himself ninety-three times with the phrase "son of man." It denoted the finitude of the prophet against the infinite God. This title was often used in reference to the coming Messiah (Dan. 7:13, in Aramaic). Jesus used it to refer to himself in all four Gospels.

VII. TEACHING OUTLINE

A. Asaph's Plea (1-3)

    1. Hear Us, Shepherd of Israel (1a)

    2. Shine on Us, Sovereign over All (1b-2a)

        a. Enthroned between the cherubim (1b)

        b. Enthroned over Israel (2a)

3. Save Us (2b)
   a. Awaken your power (2b)
   b. Come to your people (2b)
   c. Deliver your people (2b)
REFRAIN: Restore Us, God! (3)
B. Asaph's Pain (4-7)
   1. You Discipline Us in Anger (4)
      a. How long will you burn with anger? (4a)
      b. How long will you refuse our prayers (4b)
   2. You Inflict Us with Tears (5)
      a. You make them eat tears (5a)
      b. You make them drink tears (5b)
   3. You Expose Us to Shame (6)
      a. You make our neighbors contend with us (6a)
      b. You make our enemies mock us (6b)
REFRAIN: Restore Us, God! (7)
C. Asaph's Perplexity (8-15)
   1. You Planted a Vine (8)
      a. You uprooted it from Egypt (8a)
      b. You uprooted the nations (8b)
   2. You Prepared the Ground (9a)
   3. You Prospered the Vine (9b-11)
      a. It filled the land (9b)
      b. It covered the mountains (10)
      c. It extended to the sea (11a)
      d. It stretched to the river (11b)
   4. You Plummeted the Walls (12)
      a. Why did you break down the walls? (12a)
      b. Why did you expose its fruit? (12b)
   5. You Permit Its Ravaging (13)
      a. Boars destroy it (13a)
      b. Creatures devour it (13b)
REFRAIN: Return to Us, God! (14-15)
D. Asaph's Petition (16-19)
   1. Examine Your Vine (16)
      a. It is cut down by foes (16a)
      b. It is burned with fire (16b)
   2. Extend Your Hand (17-18a)
      a. May you bless the son of man (17)
      b. May the sons of God not turn away (18a)
REFRAIN: Restore Us, God! (18b-19)

Psalm 81

Radical Repentance

"*We* are all responsible to God for repentance."

J .   C .   R y l e

Psalm 81

I. INTRODUCTION

Throughout one's Christian life, every believer must be brought back, again and again, to the place of repentance. Brokenness over sin and turning away from sin are to be an ongoing lifestyle, not an occasional event. No matter how long a person has walked with the Lord, a habitual practice of sin-confessing, sin-forsaking repentance must be an ongoing reality. No Christian grows spiritually beyond his need to acknowledge and abandon sin with a broken heart and godly sorrow. Not only does Christianity begin with repentance, it continues and progresses with the very same steps of repentance. Is it any wonder that God is always calling his people to repent?

This is the central thrust of Psalm 81, a song that was an annual sermon delivered at the Feast of Booths. In this message, Israel was repeatedly called to repent of sin and return to paths of obedience. After the opening call to worship (vv. 1–5), God speaks in first person, reminding Israel of her past disobedience and discipline from God (vv. 6–12). If Israel would now listen to God and walk in his ways, he would defeat her enemies and give them the best he has to offer (vv. 13–16). But God's people must first repent. This is the clear message of this psalm, an ongoing reminder to their hearts. The superscription states that this was a psalm *of Asaph* (see Ps. 73), *according to the gittith,* a guitar-like harp associated with Gath in Philistia.

II. COMMENTARY

MAIN IDEA: *Asaph calls God's people to rejoice in God who has blessed them, to remember their past deliverance by the Lord, and to repent lest they forfeit his blessings.*

A A Call to Rejoice (81:1–5)

81:1–2. This psalm starts by calling Israel to worship God in a holy feast, most likely the Feast of Tabernacles. Asaph urged the people, **Sing for joy to God our strength**. **Shout aloud** and celebrate the **God of Jacob**. "Jacob," a reference to the entire nation of Israel, should celebrate because God is their "strength." Calling out to the instrumentalists, he said, **Begin the music, strike the tambourine**, an instrument used on joyful occasions (Ps. 68:25; Jer. 31:4). In addition, **play the melodious harp**, a long, narrow-necked instrument resembling a guitar, and **lyre**. This was a designated time for God's people to worship God joyfully.

81:3. **Sound the ram's horn**, a trumpet-like instrument that was used to summon God's people together to praise him. The occasion was **the New Moon**, or **the day of our Feast**, probably the Feast of Tabernacles. This occasion was a seven-day annual festival celebrated every fall, beginning on the fifteenth day of the seventh month, to: (1) call the people to remember God's providential care of them during their wilderness journey (Lev. 23:43), (2) express thanksgiving for God's provision in the fall harvest (Lev. 23:39–40; Deut. 16:13–15), and (3) mark the end of the year's religious festivals.

81:4–5. **This is a decree for Israel**, meaning this festival was required by God in his law, **an ordinance** recorded in Scripture. God **established it as a statute for Joseph**, meaning for all the descendants of this patriarch, or the entire nation Israel. The basis for this New Moon festival was **when he went out against Egypt**, namely, when Israel was delivered out of Egypt. At this time, they **heard a language** they **did not understand**, the Egyptian language. This "going out" was the entire exodus experience.

B A Call to Remember (81:6–12)

81:6–7. God himself called the people to remember his dealings with them in the past. Referring to their time of Egyptian bondage, God says, **I removed the burden from their shoulders**, picturing when God released **their hands** from forced labor. It was in this context that God reminded them, **you called and I rescued you**. On many occasions during this exodus, God delivered his people. One such rescue involved a **thundercloud**, a reference to God's presence on Mount Sinai at the giving of the law (Exod. 19:16–25; 20:18–21). Another occasion was **at the waters of Meribah** when Israel tempted God, yet he remained faithful to them (Exod. 17:1–7; Num. 20:1–13; Pss. 95:8; 106:32).

81:8–10. God continues as the speaker, saying, **Hear, O my people, and I will warn you.** He declared sternly, **You shall have no foreign god among you** from the surrounding nations. This was the fundamental requirement of the first of the Ten Commandments (Exod. 20:3). God requires exclusive loyalty from his people. They are never to **bow down to an alien god.** Identifying himself as **the LORD your God, who brought you up out of Egypt,** he lovingly urged his people to look completely to him. By remembering how God had delivered them in the past, they would be encouraged to trust him in the present. **Open wide your mouth and I will fill it,** God pledged, just as he had provided for them earlier in their wilderness wanderings.

81:11–12. But in stark contrast to the gracious works of God, Israel was stubborn and would not listen to him. God reminded them of this insubordination, saying, **But my people would not listen to me.** Israel resisted him and **would not submit** to him, choosing instead to follow their own ways. They were an obstinate people. Because of their unbelief, God **gave them over to their stubborn hearts to follow their own devices.** They had abandoned God, and he, in turn, abandoned them, giving them over to their sins. Such abandonment by God is the most fearful of judgments (Rom. 1:24–31; Isa. 6:9–10).

C A Call to Repent (81:13–16)

81:13–15. In light of such past terrifying dealings with God, Israel must be concerned to repent in the present, lest God abandon them again. But the hearts of the people remained unchanged. **If my people would but listen to me,** God says, and **follow my ways, how quickly would I subdue their enemies.** In the Mosaic Law, God had already promised Israel that he would defeat **their enemies** if they would obey him (Num. 33:52–56; Deut. 6:16–19; 7:16–24). If they would repent, **those who hate the LORD** (i.e., Israel's enemies) **would cringe before him** because God would utterly defeat them. So complete would be **their punishment** that it would **last forever.**

81:16. As for Israel, if they would repent and obey God, he promised, they **would be fed with the finest of wheat**—a reference to the full blessings of the promised land—and be satisfied **with honey from the rock.** This pictures his sweet and abundant provision (Deut. 32:13). The goodness of God should lead them to repentance.

III. CONCLUSION

It is entirely possible to go through the motions of worship, yet at the same time stand in dire need of repentance. This all too often characterizes many religious people today who remain inwardly carnal. Quoting the prophet Isaiah, Jesus said of the religious leaders in his day, "These people honor me with their lips, but their hearts are far from me" (Matt. 15:8; cp. Isa. 15:8). Even so, believers must guard their hearts against worshipping God externally while their hearts remain set on sin. Is our worship like this? Let us heed the warning of this psalm and be those who come as repenters whenever we gather to worship our God.

IV. TEACHING OUTLINE

A. A Call to Rejoice (1-5)
  1. How Israel Should Worship God (1-3a)
    a. Sing for joy (1)
    b. Strike the timbrel (2a)
    c. Strum the lyre (2b)
    d. Share the harp (2b)
    e. Sound the ram's horn (3a)
  2. When Israel Should Worship (3)
    a. At the new moon (3a)
    b. On the day of feast (3b)
  3. Why Israel Should Worship (4-5)
    a. It is a decree for Israel (4a)
    b. It is an ordinance of God (4b)
    c. It is a statute for Joseph (5)
B. A Call to Remember (6-12)
  1. Remember How God Rescued Them (6-7)
    a. He relieved their bondage (6)
    b. He answered their cries (7)
  2. Remember What God Required of Them (8-9)
    a. He must be heard (8)
    b. He must be honored (9)
  3. Remember How God Replinished Them (10)
    a. He delivered them out of Egypt(10a)
    b. He filled them with food (10b)
  4. Remember How God Reproved Them (11-12)
C. A Call to Repent (13-16)
  1. God's People Should Hear His Word (13a)
  2. God's People Should Heed His Ways (13b)
  3. God's People Would Have His Victory (14-16)
    a. God would defeat their adversaries (14-15)
    b. God would delight their appetites (16)

Psalm 82

Inescapable Judgment

"Those who will not observe the judgments of God's mouth shall not escape the judgments of His hand."

M a t t h e w   H e n r y

Psalm 82

I. INTRODUCTION

Deep within the heart of every believer, there exists an intense longing for the day when God will finally render perfect justice on the earth. In that last day, the Lord will make right every wrong that has been suffered by believers. In that final hour, God will punish the wicked who prosper in this perverse world. Presently, many unjust judges pervert the scales of justice, allowing the righteous to suffer. As a result, many saints cannot defend themselves, suffering many judicial abuses from corrupt men. Evil is all too often rewarded. The innocent are consistently reproached. God's people long for divine justice one day to come to the earth. *That* day is surely coming. And when it does, the unjust judges of the earth will be judged by God *himself*.

Psalm 82 addresses these present inequities, envisioning a future judgment scene in which God is holding court, presiding over the evil judges of this age, dispensing true justice. As the supreme Judge of all the earth, God is seen as calling into account all corrupt rulers who were responsible for defrauding the weak, the fatherless, the poor, and the oppressed. This wisdom psalm declares that all earthly powers are subject to God, who is sovereign over all. Here is a plea for divine justice to be rendered by God himself toward all who withhold justice from the earth.

II. COMMENTARY

MAIN IDEA: *The psalmist pronounces divine judgment upon Israel's unjust judges, reassuring them that God will judge them.*

A The Assembly Before God (82:1)

82:1. The psalmist envisioned a scene yet to take place in which **God presides** over **the great assembly**, ready to judge the earth. In that day, there will be no judge but the Lord. The author saw the **gods**, meaning either (1) human rulers and judges of the earth, (2) demon spirits, (3) pagan deities, or (4) foreign rulers. The reference is probably to the first, human rulers, who are seen standing before **God**, subject to his **judgment**. These judges are described in corrupt terms (vv. 2–4) as gods, sarcastically speaking, as if to express belittling contempt for their evil ways. The biting irony is that these human judges were seen standing in this final judgment before the one, true Judge of heaven and earth, God himself, anticipating his final verdict.

B The Accusations by God (82:2–7)

82:2. God himself is the speaker, examining these corrupt human judges: **How long will you defend the unjust**? The phrase "how long" (cp. Pss. 13:1–2; 74:10) introduces the charge that they **defend the unjust** rather than sentencing them. They **show partiality to the wicked**, perverting the justice which they were installed to execute. They have done this at length.

82:3–4. It is the duty of judges and rulers to protect those who are powerless to **defend** themselves (Isa. 11:4; Jer. 22:3,16). But that obigation is forsaken here. So God said to them, **Defend the cause of the weak and fatherless** from the injustices they face. In other words, they should protect the innocent from the injustices of evil men who drag them into court. **Maintain the rights of the poor and oppressed** from those who take advantage of them, God demanded. **Rescue the weak and needy** from being exploited by **the wicked**.

82:5. But these self-serving judges **know nothing** of divine equity, impartial fairness, or true justice. **They walk about in darkness**, a picture of ignorance, iniquity, and folly. **All the foundations** of the present social order **are shaken** because of their corrupt courtrooms. The entire world order was reeling under their injustice.

82:6–7. It was God himself who said they were **gods**, or judges (cp. v. 1), and **sons of the Most High**, meaning these human rulers served by God's sovereign appointment and were directly accountable to him. **But you will die like mere men**. In spite of their high position, these exalted men were soon to be brought low by death, just **like every other ruler**, and then they would give strict account to God. God put them into positions of power, and God will remove them.

C The Appeal to God (82:8)

82:8. The speaker shifts from God to the psalmist. He pleaded, **Rise up, O God, judge the earth**. With this petition, he asked that God would come quickly to preside in judgment over the whole world. **Judge** these earthly rulers, he pled, and do what they failed to do. That is, defend the weak who are oppressed by these ruthless judges. This coming judgment by God was certain, **for all the nations are your inheritance**. God possessed them, and thus, they are his to judge.

III. CONCLUSION

In this psalm, the final prayer of the psalmist, "Rise up, O God, judge the earth" (v. 8), is, ultimately, a petition for the second coming of Israel's Messiah, Jesus Christ. Perfect justice will not be completely served until the Judge himself returns. Not until the final day will perfect justice be served upon the earth. Only then will evil men be stopped, and every wrong will be made right. Believers should pray this prayer today, asking God to judge the earth. This fulfillment will occur in its fullest and final form when heaven's Judge, the Lord Jesus Christ, comes back to inherit the earth. In that day, God's kingdom will come and his will will be done on earth as it is in heaven. Even so, come, Lord Jesus!

IV. TEACHING OUTLINE

   A. The Assembly Before God (1)
      1. God Presides in the Assembly (1a)
      2. God Prevails over the Rulers (1b)
   B. The Accusations by God (2-5)
      1. God Interrogates the Rulers (2)
         a. They defend the unjust (2a)
         b. They favor the wicked (2b)
      2. God Instructs the Rulers (3-4)
         a. Defend the weak and fatherless (3a)
         b. Defend the poor and oppressed (3b)
         c. Deliver the weak and needy (4)
      3. God Indicts the Rulers (5-7)
         a. They are ignorant of justice (5a)
         b. They are instigators of chaps (5b)
         c. They are inferior to God (6)
         d. They are impuned to death (7)

C. The Appeal to God (8)
    1. Rise Up (8a)
    2. Render Justice (8a,b)

Psalm 83

Divine Intervention

Psalm 83

I. INTRODUCTION

When believers have found themselves in their darkest hours, they have often prayed that God would directly intervene and remove them out of their ordeal. With no hope except in God, they have petitioned him, longing for heaven dramatically to intrude and deliver them. In so doing, they have pleaded with God to vindicate their unjust suffering and protect them from their encroaching adversaries. Their firm conviction is this: God *does* over-rule the threats of evil men and act powerfully in order to protect them, his people. Salvation belongs to the Lord. Only God can rescue his people out of their painful trials. So it is to God that they must pray for deliverance.

Psalm 83 is such a prayer, a national lament in which the psalmist prays for the Lord's intervention against Israel's enemies. The psalmist prays for God to crush his enemies in a day when many nations had joined together to destroy Israel. It was a desperate hour, yet it became the occasion for the psalmist to plead with God for protection by frustrating the international conspiracy against his people. It was a foreboding day in which it seemed that the entire world stood against them. But God is greater than all. It is to God they will look. This is *a psalm of Asaph,* the last of the psalms attributed to Asaph (Pss. 50; 73–83).

II. COMMENTARY

> **MAIN IDEA:** Asaph pleads for God's help against Israel's enemies, requesting divine deliverance and vindication.

A A Plea for God's Intervention (83:1)

83:1. Abruptly, the psalmist pleaded, **O God, do not keep silent.** God's quiet inactivity gave the appearance that he was not concerned. **Be not quiet, O God, be not still.** He pleaded with God to intervene in this troublesome situation in which Israel found itself. This was an urgent cry that God should speak and rout their enemies, causing them to tremble. The psalmist's desperate plea was that God would take action immediately against their adversaries.

B A Plea for God's Inspection (83:2–8)

83:2. Asaph asked that God would take notice of their adversaries. **See how your enemies are astir.** In this, he invited God to behold how these foes were preparing to attack them. Quite the opposite of God's apparent silence and stillness, Israel's foes were very active in their plotting evil against them. He lamented to God, **how your foes rear their heads,** rising up in overt hostility and arrogant defiance (Judg. 8:28). He viewed these foes as **your enemies,** that is, God's foes. This enmity is, ultimately, against God himself.

83:3–4. Asaph reminded God, **With cunning they conspire against your people.** They had forged a multination alliance to attack Israel. They **plot** harm **against those you cherish,** a tender description of God's own people, the object of his love. **Come . . . let us destroy them as a nation.** They joined together to defeat and obliterate Israel from the earth. Their malicious intent was **that the name of Israel be remembered no more.** These vicious enemies sought their complete defeat and utter destruction.

83:5. Restating the evil intent of their unified opposition, the psalmist reminded God, **They form an alliance against you,** that is, against the Lord. This was not merely against God's people but an attack upon God himself. Their alliance against him expressed the solidarity of their evil aggression.

83:6–8. The psalmist identified this hostile coalition of nations which defiantly opposed God and his people, Israel. This ten-nation confederation was: (1) **Edom,** descendants of Esau, (2) **the Ishmaelites,** descendants of Ishmael, (3) **Moab,** descendants of Lot, (4) **Hagrites,** living east of the Jordan River, (5) **Gebal,** a Phoenican city, (6) **Ammon,** also descendants of Lot, (7) **Amalek,** descendants of Esau, (8) **Philistia,** (9) **Tyre,** and (10) **Assyria,** Israel's dreaded enemy to the north. This league of nations formed a powerful alliance to oppose Israel.

◆ A Plea for God's Imprecation (83:9–18)

83:9–12. Having identified Israel's enemies, Asaph petitioned God to defeat them as he had done in the days of the judges. **Do to them as you did to Midian**, he prayed—a reference to Gideon's great victory over the Midianites (Judg. 7:19–25). Likewise, **do to them** as you did to **Sisera and Jabin**, a recalling of Barak's defeat of the Canaanite coalition (Judg. 4–5) which occurred at **Endor** near Taanach (Judg. 5:19). Asaph pointed back to Gideon's victory over the Midianites (Ps. 83:9a) in which their leaders, **Oreb and Zeeb** and **Zebah and Zalmunna**, were soundly defeated. These foreign **nobles** and **princes** had said, **Let us take possession of the pasturelands of God**. But it was to no avail. God intervened and defeated them, just as the psalmist prayed would happen again. Thus, he was asking that God defeat their present foes (vv. 6–8) just as he had done in the past (vv. 9–12).

83:13–15. Asaph used several powerful metaphors to describe the desired destruction of their enemies. **Make them like tumbleweed**, easily swept away in divine judgment. Also, he prayed, cause them to be **like chaff before the wind**, picturing fleeing armies blown away in battle. Furthermore, Asaph prayed, **as fire consumes the forest**, so destroy these enemies. And he petitioned, may God overthrow their evil plotting as with a **tempest** or a **storm**, confusing and confounding them.

83:16. Asaph asked that God would **cover their faces with shame** in humiliating defeat. He requested this not for personal gain, or for national prominence, but for purely selfless, spiritual reasons, namely, **that men will seek your name, O LORD**. Even in stating this request for vengeance, a door of grace was opened to these hostile nations to **seek** the Lord.

83:17–18. If they did not repent, Asaph concluded, **May they ever be ashamed and dismayed** in suffering a devastating defeat by the Lord. **May they perish in disgrace**, meeting an ignominious death. **Let them know that you, whose name is the LORD—that you alone are the Most High over all the earth.** Again, the desire was that these foreign nations would come to acknowledge the Lord as the "Most High," meaning the absolutely sovereign ruler over all.

III. CONCLUSION

What confidence believers should have that God intervenes in the affairs of men. He reroutes the course of human history. God hears the prayers of his people and sees the troubles they face, both on the individual and national levels. God hears, and God acts, even in the most difficult situations. So let Christians everywhere take courage and have confidence to call out to him who is the Most High over all the earth. May all believers petition God, as did the psalmist, to be silent or still no longer.

IV. TEACHING OUTLINE

A. A Plea for God's Intervention (1)
   1. God, Be Not Silent (1a)
   2. God, Be Not Still (1b)
B. A Plea for God's Inspection (2-8)
   1. See How Great Their Corruption Is (2-4)
      a. They rear their heads (2)
      b. They plot their plans (3-4)
      c. They raise their voices (4)
   2. See How Great Their Confederation Is (5-8)
      a. Edom and Ishmaelites (5-6a)
      b. Moab and Hagrites (6b)
      c. Gebal, Ammon, and Amalek (7a)
      d. Philistia and Tyre (7b)
      e. Assyria and Lot's descendents (8)
C. A Plea for God's Imprecation (9-18)
   1. Defeat Them (9-12)
      a. As when Gideon defeated Midian (9a, 10-12)
      b. As when Barak defeated Canaan (9b)
   2. Destroy Them (13-16)
      a. Bear them away like tumbleweeds (13a)
      b. Blow them away like chaff (13b)
      c. Burn them up like wood (14)
      d. Blow them away like a storm (15)
   3. Disgrace Them (16-18)
      a. Cover them with shame (16)
      b. Confound them with dismay (17)
      c. Cause them to know (18)

Psalm 84

A Holy House

Psalm 84

I. INTRODUCTION

As an elderly lady was being conducted through a great cathedral in Europe, the guide carefully pointed out the stunning beauty of its design. He called special attention to its exquisite statues and wonderful paintings. Being spiritually minded, the old lady was unimpressed with the external trappings of the building. At the conclusion of the tour, she asked the guide, "How many souls have been saved here this year?" "My dear lady," said the embarrassed guide, "this is a *cathedral*, not a chapel."

Unfortunately, many large and impressive church buildings are just that—little more than ornate cathedrals built to impress people rather than truth-filled chapels where God is glorified. Bricks and mortar should never be the chief focus of any church. Whether their facility is large or small, impressive or plain, the primary concern should always be the genuineness of the worship inside. Wherever believers gather to worship, it should be a place where the Word of God is proclaimed, the name of God is magnified, and the will of God is pursued. What matters most to God is the pursuit of his glory, not the promotion of the facility itself. In this sense, every church is to be a chapel, not a cathedral, a place where God's glory is put on display.

This is the main focus of Psalm 84, a prayer of earnest longing for the house of God, but most of all, for God himself. Not unlike other psalms in which the psalmist concerns himself with a deep passion to be in God's house (Pss. 27; 42; 43), the author expressed a consuming desire to be in the house of worship. He possessed a genuine zeal to worship God in the temple. In Old Testament times, great importance was placed upon Israel's temple built in Jerusalem where, admittedly, a unique manifestation of God's glory resided. Nevertheless, when the psalmist spoke of his love for the temple, he was actually thinking of God, whose greatness filled the temple. This psalm pronounced blessing upon the person who trusted God, and ultimately, that is all that truly matters.

According to the superscription, this is *a psalm* written by the *Sons of Korah,* referring to the Levitical choir comprised of the descendants of Korah. They had been appointed by David to serve in the temple as gatekeepers and musicians. Thus, this psalm was written either by or for Korah's descendants. As one of eleven psalms ascribed to the "Sons of Korah," it is the first of four such psalms that occur in Book Three (Pss. 84–85; 87–88). It is to be sung *according to the gittith,* most probably a guitar-like harp associated with Gath in Philistia.

II. COMMENTARY

MAIN IDEA: *The psalmist expresses his excitement for the temple where the Lord's presence is greatly enjoyed.*

A A Passion for God's House (84:1–4)

SUPPORTING IDEA: *The psalmist declares that his supreme passion for being in the temple is to worship the Lord.*

84:1–2. The psalmist burst forth with praise for the divine **dwelling place** of the LORD **Almighty**, a reference to the holy temple in Jerusalem that had been built by Solomon (1 Kgs. 6). Describing the worship center as **lovely** (i.e., "loved" or "beloved"), this place was special to Old Testament saints because it allowed them to come, uniquely, into the presence of God (Pss. 27; 42:1–2; 61:4; 63:1–2). Thus, the psalmist's soul **yearns** passionately to come into the temple. He **even faints** to enter **the courts** of the temple. His entire inner being (i.e., his **heart** and **flesh**) **cry out** for God. More than merely desiring the building, he earnestly sought the holy presence of God himself. To yearn for the temple, in reality, was to yearn for God.

84:3. Expressing this intense passion for God's house, the psalmist pointed to the birds that flew into the temple, building their nests there, and thus, were able to live in the courts of God. **Even the sparrow has found a home** in God's house **and the swallow a nest for herself, where she may have her young**. The psalmist envied these birds that built their nests in the temple courtyard near the **altar**. They enjoyed a close proximity to where his own heart was. This altar probably refers to where the burnt offerings were placed (Exod. 27:1–8). Or it could refer to the smaller altar where the incense was placed before the Holy of Holies (Exod. 30:1–10). Thus, the psalmist envied this privilege the birds had of being close to the LORD Almighty, his King and God. The first part of this expanded divine name emphasizes God's sovereign power, the latter, the closeness of the relationship between the psalmist and God.

84:4. If the birds who live in God's **house** are to be admired, how much more are those believers who **dwell** there. They are **blessed**, especially favored and abundantly happy in God. A special manifestation of God in the temple had descended in the form of the Shekinah glory, and God's people uniquely experienced the presence of God there. No wonder the psalmist longed to be in the temple and be declared blessed with all who dwell there.

B A Pilgrimage to God's House (84:5–7)

> **SUPPORTING IDEA:** *All who travel to the temple are blessed even as they anticipate worshipping God there.*

84:5. The psalmist declared the blessing of all who travel to Jerusalem to be in God's house. **Blessed are those whose strength is in you.** Those who find their **strength** in God are truly **blessed.** Their faith in God transforms their own human weaknesses into a God-given strength. The genuineness of their faith is seen in their **pilgrimage** to the temple, pursuing the glory and knowledge of God.

84:6. On their way to the temple, they pass through the **Valley of Baca**, an enigmatic name which is either (1) an unknown place or (2) a figurative place, representing a state of the soul. Probably, the latter is intended here. The Valley of Baca means "balsam trees," which are those trees which grow in arid places. Literally, the word *Baca* means "weeping" or "the place of weeping." These expectant pilgrims started out in a place of sorrow, spiritually speaking, until they **make it a place of springs.** In this process, their broken, barren souls are transformed into blessed hearts. **The autumn rains also cover it with pools,** picturing the replenishment and refreshment of their hearts by God. The person who trusts and worships God may have his burdens transformed into blessings, even on his way to Zion, as he anticipates worshipping God there.

84:7. Whatever the burdens of their hearts or the obstacles faced in the journey, **they go from strength to strength,** greatly energized in their souls, **till each appears before God in Zion.** Not only does worshipping God in **Zion** strengthen hearts, but so does the anticipation of doing so, as they meditate upon his greatness throughout the long journey.

C A Prayer in God's House (84:8–9)

SUPPORTING IDEA: *Once at the temple, prayer is offered for the king, God's anointed.*

84:8–9a. Upon arrival in the house of God, the journey to Zion was complete. Once in the temple, the psalmist lifted up his soul to heaven: **Hear my prayer, O LORD God Almighty**. He turned to the **God of Jacob** and offered his prayer on behalf of their king, identified as **our shield**. As Israel's monarch, he was the protector of the people, leading the armies of Israel in the day of battle.

84:9b. The psalmist interceded for the king: **Look with favor on your anointed one**. Israel's ruler was God's anointed one because he was energized to serve by the Spirit's power. The psalmist prayed that God, heaven's King, would **favor** their earthly king with wisdom, power, and courage. The psalmist prayed this so that he might return in peace to his ministry in the temple.

D A Prizing of God's House (84:10–12)

SUPPORTING IDEA: *One day in the temple is better than a thousand elsewhere.*

84:10. The psalmist concluded by affirming the privilege of being in God's house and not anywhere else on earth. **Better is one day in your courts than a thousand elsewhere**. Just one day in God's house, he reasoned, is superior to many days anywhere else. He stated, **I would rather be a doorkeeper in the house of my God**, referring to his regular, humble service in the temple, **than dwell in the tents of the wicked**. Better to be a lowly servant in the temple than to be an exalted sovereign on a throne surrounded by the wicked.

84:11. Explaining why it is better to be in God's house, the psalmist concluded by stating, **For the LORD God is a sun** who shines down favorably on his people. With beaming grace, God empowered them and brightened their days. God is an impenetrable **shield** who protects his people from their foes whenever attacked. As a result, **no good thing does he withhold from those whose walk is blameless**. God is an infinite source of good for his people.

84:12. The psalmist repeated with his third **blessed** of the psalm (vv. 4–5,12) promised to God's people. He declared, **O LORD Almighty, blessed is the man who trusts in you**.

MAIN IDEA REVIEW: *The psalmist expresses his excitement for the temple where the Lord's presence is greatly enjoyed.*

III. CONCLUSION

No church building should be an end in itself. Never should it become the chief focus of our attention. Rather, a church facility should merely play a supportive role as a place where, above all, God is praised by true worshippers. But such is not always the case. All too often, the building itself overshadows the intended purpose of the bricks and mortar. One such example is a well-known cathedral whose planning and building has spanned two centuries. It is reported to be the sixth largest church building in the world and has been built at a cost of many millions of dollars. It includes a bell tower over three hundred feet tall. Over two hundred ornate stained-glass windows decorate the building. Gargoyles line the structure overhead. Some of the figurines on the rainspouts reportedly resemble world leaders, whether they be Christian or not. This famous church hosts over one hundred thousand visitors each year just to view its stained-glass windows and vast collections of religious art. But is this the purpose of a church?

What makes a church? Not the building itself. Surely it is the glory of God made known to worshippers there. The greatness of a church is not measured by how many visitors come to admire the building, but how many worshippers come to admire God. A church building should never overshadow the spiritual activity within. Let all believers choose a church, not by the grandness of the building but by the greatness of God being made known there. The preaching of the Word and the all-consuming worship of God inside the building mark its true greatness.

IV. LIFE APPLICATION

In choosing a house of worship to attend, the following questions must always be asked:

1. *Is God's Word being proclaimed there?* A true house of worship is a place where the truth of Scripture is rightly taught to all who enter its doors. It must be a place where the Bible occupies the central place in the worship service, as well as with each supporting ministry.

2. *Is God's worship being pursued there?* A true house of worship is a place where God himself is exalted, magnified, and adored. It is a place where people worship God in spirit and in truth. It is a place where a high view of God is championed and a sense of his presence is conveyed.

3. *Is God's will being practiced there?* A true house of worship is a place where God's Word is not only heard but also applied and obeyed. It is a place where the Scripture is put into practice in the lives of the people.

4. *Is God's work being performed there?* A true house of worship is a place where God's work is being carried out. It is a place where God is served and

people are ministered to in God's name. It is a place where believers are not inactive spectators but are active servants, doing God's work.

V. PRAYER

God, may we long to come together with your people to worship you in spirit and truth. May we not forsake our assembling together as is the habit of some. Keep our hearts singular in the pursuit of magnifying your greatness. In Jesus' name. Amen.

VI. DEEPER DISCOVERIES

A. God (84:3,7–11)

The word *God* (*elohiym*) is used throughout the Hebrew Bible as a general name for the true God. Although it is sometimes used to refer to pagan gods or deities (Gen. 35:2,4; Exod. 12:12; 18:11; 23:24; Judg. 17:5; Ruth 1:15; 1 Sam 7:3; 17:43; 2 Sam. 7:23; 1 Kgs. 11:2; 2 Chr. 2:5; Ps. 86:8), angels (Ps. 8:5), men (Ps. 82:6), and judges (Exod. 21:6), it is used primarily to refer to the one true God who created all things out of nothing. In fact, *elohiym* is often used for God in the early chapters of Genesis. The meaning of *elohiym* is debatable, but it seems to refer to the transcendence of God. The plural form indicates plentitude of power and majesty and also makes allowance for a plurality of persons in the one God. This would certainly allow for the trinity of the Godhead which is more fully developed in the rest of the Old and New Testaments. This plurality is clearly identifiable in selected passages (cp. Gen. 1:26; 3:22; Isa. 6:8).

B. Blessed (84:4,5,12)

The word *blessed* (*'ashrei*) means an overflowing joy and full contentment in God, a satisfaction and happiness in the Lord. This noun occurs forty-four times in the Old Testament, twenty-five of which are found in the Psalms. The word *happy* is a good synonym, although it must be understood that this word conveys far more than mere feelings of settled peace and contentment. Also, this word is in the plural, which intensifies its meaning, expressing God's multifaceted, redemptive favor upon the person who fears the Lord and pursues his will. An alternate translation in Psalm 1:1 would be, "Oh the blessednesses." This blessedness is not deserved, but it is a gift of God, not dependent upon one's circumstances but upon the vitality of one's relationship with God.

C. Anointed One (84:9)

The anointed one (*mashiah*) refers to any anointed king who is seated on the throne of David. Occurring about forty times in the Old Testament, it was used in reference to the office of the high priest (Lev. 4:3), kings (1 Sam. 24:6; Isa. 45:1), patriarchs (Ps. 105:15), and prophets (1 Kgs. 19:16). To be the Lord's anointed meant this person had a special relationship with God, being chosen, consecrated, and commissioned by him for a special function or task. Referring to David in a near sense, nowhere is this demonstrated more clearly than when David stood before Samuel, and the Lord said to Samuel, "Rise and anoint him; he is the one" (1 Sam. 16:12). It is from *mashiah* that the English word *messiah* is derived. But, ultimately, the title finds its fulfillment in the New Testament. In fact, "Christ" is the Greek equivalent of the Hebrew term *Messiah,* both meaning "the Anointed One." The psalmist's reference to the Anointed One goes beyond King David to the coming of the Lord Jesus who is the Christ. The early church rightly understood this psalm to be fulfilled by the Lord Jesus Christ (Acts 2:32; Heb. 1:5; 5:5).

D. Good (84:11)

The word *good* (*tob*) is a broad Hebrew adjective that describes something or someone who is excellent, favorable, pleasant, lovely, or sound. It is used in a wide variety of ways to describe the abstract. Here as in other passages (cp. Gen. 2:18; Num. 11:18; Deut. 6:24; 15:16; 2 Sam. 16:12; Neh. 2:18; 13:31), good denotes one's overall well-being.

VII. TEACHING OUTLINE

A. A Passion for God's House (1-4)
  1. I Extoll the Beauties of the Temple (1-2)
     a. It is God's dwelling place (1)
     b. It is God's own court (2)
  2. I Envy the Birds in the Temple (3)
     a. The sparrow has a home there (3a)
     b. The swallow has a nest there (3b)
  3. I Exclaim the Believers in the Temple(4)
     a. They are blessed in you (4a)
     b. They are boasting in you (4b)
B. A Pilgrimage to God's House (5-7)
  1. God's People Set Out on the Journey (5)
     a. They are satisfied in God (5a)
     b. They are strengthed by God (5b)
     c. They are set upon God (5c)

2. God's People Advance to the Valley of Baca (6)
    a. They make it to a place of springs (6a)
    b. They cover it with autumn rains (6b)
3. God's People Arrive at Mount Zion (7)
    a. They grow in strength (7a)
    b. They appear before God (7b)
C. A Prayer in God's House (8-9)
    1. Listen to My Prayer (8)
        a. Hear me, Lord God Almighty (8a)
        b. Hear me, God of Jacob (8b)
    2. Look upon Our King (9)
        a. Favor him as our shield (9a)
        b. Favor him as your anointed (9b)
D. A Prizing of God's House (10-12)
    1. God's House Is Better Than Anywhere Else (10)
        a. Any day here is better (10a)
        b. Any duty here is better (10b)
    2. God's Holiness Is Better Than Anything Else (11)
        a. He is a sun (11a)
        b. He is a shield (11a)
        c. He is a source (11b)
        d. He is a sustainer (12)

Psalm 85

Revive Us Again!

Quote

> "*W*hen God has something very great for His church, it
>
> is His will that there should precede it the extraordinary
>
> prayers of His people."

J o n a t h a n   E d w a r d s

Psalm 85

I. INTRODUCTION

On July 8, 1734, Jonathan Edwards stepped into the pulpit to preach his now famous sermon, "Sinners in the Hands of an Angry God." Edwards had actually preached from the same text several times previously, as recently as one month earlier to his own congregation in Northampton, Massachusetts. But while the guest preacher in Enfield, Connecticut, he preached this sermon yet again; and the people in that New England church were deeply affected. Eleazer Wheelock, one of the leading preachers in the Great Awakening, said the people were "bowed down with an awful conviction of the sin and danger." One man under deep conviction sprang up and cried, "Mr. Edwards, have mercy!" Others caught hold of the backs of the pews lest they should slip into the pit of hell. Many thought that the day of judgment had suddenly dawned on them. Still others were alarmed that God, while blessing others, should in anger pass them by.

Revival had come to New England, restoring God's work among his people in colonial America, empowering them to do his will. What is revival? Literally, the word itself means a restoring back to fullness of life that which has become stagnant or dormant. It is a rekindling of spiritual life in individual believers and churches which have fallen into sluggish times. True revival always returns God's people to a fresh and vivid emphasis on the holiness and righteousness of God, his judgment on sin, true repentance, and the overflowing effect of personal conversions to Christ. This sudden awareness of the overwhelming presence of God is the hallmark of any revival. It is a supernatural work of God in which he visits his people, restoring spiritual life to their hearts, as well as ushering salvation into many souls. Such a revival is always a sovereign work of God, in response to the prayers of his people, and it leaves a lasting mark on his work forever.

This is the central theme of Psalm 85, a prayer offered in difficult days for the reviving of God's people in days of spiritual apathy. Although the historical setting of this psalm cannot be firmly established, it is believed to be the time soon after ancient Israel returned to her land in Palestine after her seventy-year captivity in Babylon. In 538 B.C. under the leadership of Zerubbabel, the first Jews returned to Jerusalem. Then in 458 B.C., a group under Ezra returned. At first, the people rejoiced at being able to return to their homeland. But when the rebuilding project came to a standstill, the holy city fell into difficult times.

If this is the actual setting for this psalm, then it is a prayer that God would revive their work and restore the city to its former glory. Accordingly, the answer to this prayer came in 445 B.C. with the arrival of Nehemiah, who did, in fact, restore God's work in a time of spiritual revival. Here is a psalm intended to inspire God's people with the prospects of a bright tomorrow whenever his work comes to a standstill. It is yet another psalm of the *Sons of Korah* (Pss. 42; 44–49; 84–85; 87–88).

II. COMMENTARY

> **MAIN IDEA:** Remembering God's favor in the past, the psalmist calls for God to restore and revive his people.

A Looking to the Past (85:1–3)

> **SUPPORTING IDEA:** The psalmist recalls God's past blessings to his people.

85:1. Looking back to the past, the psalmist reflected upon God's mercies displayed in previous years. Such a remembering of God's mighty working in the past breeds confidence in the present. Pointing to yesteryear, the psalmist reflected, **You showed favor to your land, O LORD.** This favor is probably a reference to Israel's return to their promised land after their seventy-year exile in Babylon. In their return to Judea, he testified, **You restored the fortunes of Jacob** (Jer. 29:14), a reference to the entire nation of Israel.

85:2. The psalmist wrote, **You forgave the iniquity of your people,** sins for which they had suffered greatly. By his mercy, God **covered all their sins,** graciously making an atonement for their sins. Their restoration was not only a physical relocating to their land but a spiritual one, involving their relationship with God that had been greatly affected.

85:3. You set aside all your wrath, his righteous anger being appeased. By being propitiated, God **turned** from his **fierce anger**, a remarkable display of divine mercy and grace toward his disobedient people.

B Longing for the Present (85:4–7)

SUPPORTING IDEA: *The psalmist asks God to stay his anger and grant salvation, bringing about their revival and restoration.*

85:4. Having reviewed God's past mercies (vv. 1–3), the psalmist urged that this same divine mercy be granted to their present troubles (vv. 4–7). **Restore us again, O God our Savior** is a humble request that God's favor be once more extended in this present hour. Having restored them in the land in the past, the psalmist asked God to do it once more. The phrase **put away your displeasure toward us** indicated that their present crisis was because of their own sin.

85:5. The psalmist lamented, **Will you be angry with us forever?** This introduces three rhetorical questions, the expected answer being negative. Surely God will not be **angry** indefinitely, he reasoned. **Will you prolong your anger through all generations?** Surely God will turn back or relieve his anger soon.

85:6. Will you not revive us again, that your people may rejoice in you? This was a plea for the spiritual awakening of God's people, a petition that God would restore their hearts with renewed devotion toward him. If God would **revive** them, they would rejoice again. But, conversely, there can be no true rejoicing without spiritual revival.

85:7. The psalmist concluded this stanza with one final request: **Show us your unfailing love** (*hesed,* covenant commitment), **O LORD.** He asked that God make known his loyal, unfailing love in faithful devotion to them, even in spite of themselves, based upon his permanent covenant commitment to his people. **Grant us your salvation** out of our present problems and spiritual apathy, he asked.

C Living on the Promises (85:8–13)

SUPPORTING IDEA: *God promises peace and salvation to those who fear him.*

85:8. The psalmist probably recorded the words of a priest or Levite here. Possibly, they are those of the psalmist himself. **I will listen to what God the LORD will say.** The speaker expected to hear a direct revelation from the Lord. **God promises peace to his people**, a peace that, initially, is a general benediction (Num. 6:22–26) and, ultimately, finds fulfillment in the future coming of the Messiah's kingdom (Luke 2:14). This peace (*shalom*) signified a wholeness or fullness of life, or abundant life as it is intended to be. **But let them not return to folly**, which is living independent of God, a sin which would only provoke God's displeasure again.

85:9. **Surely his salvation is near**, close to delivering his people out of their ordeal. Such salvation is reserved for **those who fear him**, reverencing his name. Such a God-sent revival would cause **his glory** to **dwell in our land**. The deepest longing of the psalmist's heart is the manifestation of God's awesome presence. The restoration of his people would make known his supreme greatness and majesty to all.

85:10. When God inaugurates this new day, many divine attributes will be revealed. **Love and faithfulness meet together**. His unconditional, steadfast, loyal love (*hesed*) will work together with his faithfulness, his unfailing commitment to the truth of his Word. Also, **righteousness and peace** (*shalom*) **kiss each other**, a poetic way of describing their working together in perfect harmony. All four of these spiritual qualities are expressions of God's abundant favor toward his people.

85:11. Reiterating the second of these divine attributes, the psalmist stated, **Faithfulness springs forth from the earth**. The effect of his faithfulness was like new produce coming from the fields to bless them with a bountiful harvest. **And righteousness looks down from heaven**. The third divine attribute was pictured as if being extended **down** directly from God. Thus, from both heaven and earth, God's blessing surrounds his people.

85:12. These four characteristics of God's kingdom, expressed in verses 10–11, were pictured as coming in largest measure. In the promised **land**, they will enjoy an extreme, God-given prosperity, symbolized by a fruitful **harvest**. **The LORD will indeed give what is good**, namely, love, faithfulness, righteousness, and peace (vv. 11–12).

85:13. **Righteousness**, emphasized twice in the previous verses (vv. 10–11), **goes before him**, as if leading the way in this restoration and revival of God's people. This divine attribute will be featured in the future establishment of Messiah's kingdom (Isa. 11). Like a forerunner before him, **righteousness** is seen preparing **the way for his steps**. Wherever God's presence is manifested in the restoration of his people, righteousness will be clearly seen in the lives of God's people.

MAIN IDEA REVIEW: *Remembering God's favor in the past, the psalmist calls for God to restore and revive his people.*

III. CONCLUSION

Oliver Cromwell, the Lord Protector of England from 1653 to 1658, reigned during the stormy times following the English Civil War. Possessed of an iron will and military genius, Cromwell inspired more love and respect from his followers, if not more fear and hatred from his critics. He led the armed forces of Parliament to victory over Charles I and served as the leader of England until his death in 1658.

On September 16, 1656, the day before the second meeting of the second Parliament of the Protectorate, Cromwell was reading Psalm 85. As he meditated on this psalm, he was greatly inspired regarding the future of England. What this psalm promised he desired for his beloved nation. Cromwell desperately longed for England to be marked by righteousness and peace, a place where God's abundant blessings were clearly seen. When Parliament convened, Cromwell addressed the members, expounding these very verses as an expression of his vision for the great island of England. He desired that by their faithfulness to God, righteousness might reign in England and with it a happier and more harmonious age of peace might come to the land.

What Oliver Cromwell longed for England—a day when righteousness and peace would meet and kiss—so believers today should pray for as well. They should intercede and petition God for such a time of revival in their lives, ministries, and churches. Spiritual awakening is the need of every believer in every generation. This present hour is no different. Only God can send such a time of spiritual restoration and renewal to his people. That is why we must pray, as did the psalmist, that God in his grace will revive us again. May God's people pray this psalm afresh in these days and ask God to stir the hearts of his people again.

IV. LIFE APPLICATION

Historically speaking, revivals have always been marked by the same spiritual characteristics, and it would do believers well to reacquaint themselves with these benchmarks. Whether it be during the days of Ezra and Nehemiah in Old Testament times or the Reformation, Puritan age, and Great Awakening in church history, revivals have always demonstrated the same qualities. They are as follows:

1. *A proclamation of Scripture.* Any period of revival has always been preceded by a dramatic return to the Word of God. Certainly, this was true in the revival at the Watergate under Ezra and Nehemiah (Neh. 8:8). The centrality of the Scripture in any revival is undisputed. "Preserve my life according to your word" (Ps. 119:37). And this clearly was the dynamic of the early church in Jerusalem which exploded on the scene as "they devoted them-

selves to the apostles' teaching" (Acts 2:42). The same was true in the days of Martin Luther, Jonathan Edwards, and George Whitefield. There was a return to the divine revelation of Scripture being read, studied, taught, and preached.

2. *An intercession with God.* A genuine spiritual awakening is further marked as a time in which God's people humble themselves and seek the Lord in unceasing prayer. It is a new season of petitioning God, seeking his face, and asking him to revive his people and restore his work. While all revivals are sent by the sovereign initiative of God, nevertheless, prayer is always the forerunner of his people. It was this way in the early church as they regularly met together to pray (Acts 1:13–14; 2:42; 3:1).

3. *A confession of sin.* True revival ushers in a deep conviction of personal sin, a confessing of sin, and a turning away from sin. This means that sin made known must go. Iniquities are revealed by the Word, and hearts are broken with deep contrition. Sin is put away. This is precisely what happened in Ezra's day as the people confessed their sin to God, while openly grieving that they had departed from God's standard (Neh. 9:1–37). In fact, they put on sackcloth, threw dust on their heads (v. 1), and acknowledged their sin (v. 3), bringing it out into the open before God (v. 37).

4. *A devotion to holiness.* Old paths of obedience, previously forsaken, are once more pursued. The Word is not only taught and heard anew, but it is also received and kept. Suddenly, there is an overwhelming desire to apply the Scripture to one's own life, putting it into practice with a new resolve. Revival always brings about this effect. It is a time of renewed commitment to return to the Scripture in order to obey it.

V. PRAYER

Father, we ask that you would send another great awakening to your people and that it would begin with each one of us individually. As you have worked in the past, in previous generations, we ask that you would work again. Restore us in the fullness of your favor. Cause your glory to be put on display before our eyes in ways that are unmistakable. Give your Word success in our own hearts. In Jesus' name. Amen.

VI. DEEPER DISCOVERIES

A. Iniquity (85:2)

The term *iniquity* is translated from the Hebrew word *awon*, meaning "corrupt, twisted, bent, perverse, or crooked." While the first word for sin (*transgression*) describes sin in view of our relationship to God, and the second word deals with our relationship to God's Word, this word focuses upon a person's relationship to himself. All sin is a self-defilement, a self-corrupting, a twisting of one's own character, and a bending of one's integrity. To the degree that a person sins, he becomes a twisted creature within his own soul. When David sinned, he became unclean and dirty. Psalm 51:2 says, "Wash away all my iniquity and cleanse me." Psalm 51:10 pleads, "Create in me a pure heart."

B. Forgave (85:2)

The Hebrew word for "forgave" (*nasa*) means "to raise," "to lift up," "to bear," "to carry," "to take away," "to lift up the head" (i.e., "to take a census") (Exod. 20:12), "to lift up one's face" (i.e., "to look someone straight in the eyes") (2 Sam. 2:22), "to lift up one's hand" (i.e., "taking an oath") (1 Sam. 20:21), "to lift up one's voice" (i.e., "to wail or lament") (Gen. 21:16), "to lift up one's soul" (i.e., "to be entirely dependent") (Deut. 24:15). But here, it is not man who lifts up and removes his sin but God. God rolls man's sin off him when he confesses it.

C. Salvation (85:7,9)

The term *salvation* (*yesha*) refers to deliverance, rescue, victory, help, or liberty. In its first usages, *yesha* referred to physical deliverance from one's enemies (Num. 10:9; Exod. 2:17; 3:12; 14:30; Judg. 8:22; Pss. 18:3; 44:7; Jer. 1:8,19), but later it came to connote a redemptive meaning (Pss. 51:14; 67:2; 68:19; 79:9; Isa. 45:17,22; 49:6; 52:10; Ezek. 37:23).

D. Truth or Faithfulness (85:10)

The word *truth* (*emet*) is a derivative of *aman* which denotes the idea of certainty, dependability, firmness, or sureness and is often translated as truth or faithfulness. This word (*emet*) is used 127 times in the Old Testament, often to speak of the divine attribute of truthfulness (cp. Gen. 24:27; Exod. 34:6; Pss. 25:5; 31:5; 71:22; Jer. 4:2; 42:5). It is also applied to the words and commandments of God because he possesses truth (cp. 1 Kgs. 17:24; 2 Chr. 18:15; Pss. 26:3; 30:9; 43:3; 69:13; 86:11; 91:4; 108:4; 117:2; 119:142,151; 138:2). Likewise, it is a characteristic of those who know God (Exod. 18:21; Neh. 7:2; Ps. 15:2; Zech. 8:16). Here, the word *truth* or *faithfulness* means moral integrity and reliable living or that which conforms to the standard of God's truth in his word.

E. Righteousness (85:10–11,13)

The term *righteousness* (*sedeq*) means in the figurative sense to do right and is used to speak of someone or something that is honest, just, equitable, and moral. *Sedeq* is used to denote judges who judged impartially (cp. Lev. 19:15; Deut. 16:18; Pss. 9:4,8; 72:2; 89:14; 96:13; 98:9; 119:7,62,75).

Between individuals it refers to ethical and moral conduct in relationships. Here it refers to God's righteousness, a righteousness of justice which he will bring to Israel.

VII. TEACHING OUTLINE

A. Looking to the Past (1-3)
  1. You Have Shown Us Favor (1)
    a. Revealing your mercy (1a)
    b. Restoring our fortunes (1b)
  2. You Have Shown Us Forgiveness (2-3)
    a. Covering all our sins (2)
    b. Turning from your anger (3)
B. Longing for the Present (4-7)
  1. Restore Us Again, God (4-5)
    a. Put away your displeasure (4)
    b. Put away your anger (5)
  2. Revive Us Again, God (6-7)
    a. Show us your love (6)
    b. Give us your deliverance (7)
C. Living on the Promises (8-13)
  1. God Promises to Manifest His Glory (8-9)
    a. Providing peace to his people (8)
    b. Revealing salvation to his people (9)
  2. God Prepares to Magnify His Goodness (10-13)
    a. Love and faithfulness meet (10a)
    b. Righteousness and peace kiss (10b)
    c. Faithfulness and righteousness proceed (11a)
    d. Righteousness looks down (11b)
    e. Goodness grows forth (12)
    f. Righteousness leads out (13)

Psalm 86

Have Mercy!

"*The* best of men need mercy and appeal to mercy, yea to nothing else but mercy."

Charles Haddon Spurgeon

Psalm 86

I. INTRODUCTION

Precious is the tender mercy of God toward his people, undeserving though they be of such divine care. To be sure, the Lord is not a stoic sovereign or a robotic ruler, empty of emotions and compassion. Rather, God is filled with affectionate pity and deep longings toward his saints. He feels for them with a heart full of warmest sympathy. What is mercy? It is the fond compassion and tender expression of God's love toward his creatures who find themselves in a desperate plight. Mercy is the deep heart feeling of benevolence that God has for his own, especially in their troubles. Flowing from his all-compassionate heart, mercy is God's infinite kindness and unending favor toward his people whose lives have been ruined by sin or stressed by trials.

This attribute of God, his tender mercy, is the underlying focus of this psalm. It is *a prayer of David,* the only such psalm by David in Book III. In this lament song, David finds himself in the day of trouble (v. 7), attacked by a band of ruthless men (v. 14) who are avowed enemies (v. 17) and who seek to take his life (v. 13). In this ordeal David calls out to God to save him, appealing to God's tender mercy, goodness, and compassion (vv. 3,5,13,15).

II. COMMENTARY

MAIN IDEA: *David prays for God's guidance and strength when attacked by his seemingly unrelenting enemies.*

A David's Appeal (86:1–4)

86:1. Feeling mounting pressure upon him, David burst forth, **Hear, O LORD, and answer me.** He pleaded with God to incline his ear to his urgent plea. Rather than approaching God as if God owed him something, David humbly confessed he was **poor and needy** (cp. Ps. 35:10)—needing mercy.

86:2. Guard my life and **save your servant,** he requested, from evil men who sought to do him much harm. The basis of his appeal was, he was **devoted** (*hasid,* "faithful") to God. He was not claiming sinlessness but a position of total commitment to God, as one **who trusts in** the Lord, looking to him with the eye of faith and thus demonstrating that he is righteous.

86:3–4. Pouring out his heart to God, David yearned, **Have mercy on me, O Lord.** So desperate was his state that he called upon God **all day long,** never ceasing. **Bring joy to your servant** in the midst of this ordeal, something that only God can do. **To you, O Lord, I lift up my soul** in humble prayer, David implored the Lord.

B David's Assurance (86:5–7)

86:5. Although surrounded by proud enemies who were attacking him (vv. 14,17), David, nevertheless, remained confident in the Lord regarding several unchanging truths about the divine character. **You are forgiving and good, O Lord, abounding in love to all who call to you.** In spite of the sin in David's life, he knew that God would forgive him and work for his good. God's very nature is to pardon his servants. David knew God overflowed in boundless love toward him. This was his assurance, a confidence rooted in the unchanging character of God.

86:6–7. Repeating the opening verse, David once more pleaded for a hearing: **Hear my prayer, O LORD.** Confident of God's love toward him (v. 5), he poured out his soul to the Lord. **In the day of my trouble** (i.e., this present trial) **I will call to you, for you will answer me.** With unwavering trust, David believed that God would hear him and come to his rescue. In the furnace of affliction, David's faith remained strong and steadfast not in himself or his circumstances, but in God.

C David's Adoration (86:8–10)

86:8. The fact that God loved him, heard him, and would deliver him (vv. 5–7) caused his heart to burst forth in praise for God (vv. 8–10). **Among the gods there is none like you, O Lord.** David understood that the Lord is God, the only true God among the false gods of the polytheistic nations surrounding Israel. **No deeds can compare with yours.** How could they? God alone works with unlimited power and unrivaled authority.

86:9. All the nations you have made, even these peoples who threaten the psalmist as the enemies of Israel. In due time, they **will come and worship before you, O Lord.** Whether in this lifetime or in the final judgment, **they will bring glory to your name.** One day even his enemies will praise God, even if it was in their damnation.

86:10. For you are great in every way **and do marvelous deeds,** a fact that elicited utter amazement from David. **You alone are God,** and there is none other, not in heaven, on earth, or under the earth.

D David's Affirmation (86:11–13)

86:11. David's prayer and praise were not confined to a merely theoretical realm. He desperately wanted to live what he believed. So he asked God, **Teach me your way, O LORD, and I will walk in your truth.** He desired to pursue the path of God's will relentlessly, but the Lord must illumine the way. **Give me an undivided heart, that I may fear your name.** David realized that his own heart was prone to wander and was in continual need of divine intervention and influence in order to rightly reverence the Lord (Phil. 2:13).

86:12. God's sovereignty over David's spiritual life (v. 11) caused him to rejoice humbly. **I will praise you, O Lord my God, with all my heart; I will glorify your name forever.** Expressed as a vow of thanksgiving, this praise was not to be a one-time, isolated occurrence but an ongoing lifestyle of worship as he devotedly sought to glorify the Lord.

86:13. Such praise flowed out of David's experience of the steadfast **love** of God. **For great is your love toward me,** he declared, a love that has **delivered me from the depths of the grave.** David anticipated a positive answer to his prayer, convinced that God would rescue him from this life-threatening situation.

E David's Adversaries (86:14–15)

86:14. Though confident of God's deliverance (vv. 7,13), David continued to plead his case before the heavenly throne. In so doing, he affirmed two realities to the Lord. The first was, **The arrogant are attacking me, O God; a band of ruthless men seeks my life.** David reminded God of the desperate and possibly life-ending situation in which he found himself, facing enemies who sought his life and had no **regard** for God. In other words, David's foes were God's foes.

86:15. The second truth was, **But you, O Lord, are a compassionate and gracious God**, unlike his malicious enemies. Amid his many dangers, David rested in the tender care of God, whose heart was drawn toward his plight. He knew God to be **slow to anger, abounding in love and faithfulness**. This strong affirmation echoed David's earlier praise (v. 5). He had every reason to trust in God and God's steadfast character.

F David's Address (86:16–17)

86:16. This psalm concluded as it began (vv. 1–4), with David making an urgent appeal to God. **Turn to me and have mercy on me**, he pleaded, just as the opening verses of this psalm expressed. **Grant your strength to your servant**, David asked, no doubt aware of his own weakness. In so doing, he requested, **save the son of your maidservant**. This was a veiled, humble reference to himself as one born of lowly stature.

86:17. Anticipating the Lord's answer, David concluded, **Give me a sign of your goodness**. David's deliverance by God would be a strong witness to others that God is worthy to be trusted and can deliver his people from their most desperate and precarious circumstances.

III. CONCLUSION

John Calvin, the famed Reformer, once wrote, "The only haven of safety is in the mercy of God, as manifested in Christ, in whom every part of our salvation is complete." If we are to be saved, we all need divine mercy, not justice. This is true whether the salvation be God's eternal deliverance from his wrath in hell or his temporal deliverance from the wrath of men on the earth. Salvation is always by the undeserved mercy of God, never by his inflexible justice. If the Lord ever gave us what we deserved, we would suffer eternal punishment in much affliction. So it is not justice that we need, but mercy. It is the tender compassion of God toward those in great danger and stress who need his saving, sustaining grace. So it is mercy that we must request of the Lord. And it is mercy that will activate God's unlimited power to work for our good.

IV. TEACHING OUTLINE

A. David's Appeal (1-4)
   1. Grant My Prayer (1)
     a. For I am poor (1a)
     b. For I am needy (1b)
   2. Guard My Life (2)
     a. For I am devoted to you

        b. For I am trusting in you

    3. Gladden My Soul (3-4)

        a. For I call out to you (3)

        b. For I reach up to you (4)

B. David's Assurance (5-7)

    1. God Is Abounding to Me (5)

        a. Ready to forgive (5a)

        b. Rich in love (5b)

    2. God Will Answer Me (6-7)

        a. Able to hear (6)

        b. Alert to answer (7)

C. David's Adoration (8-10)

    1. You Are Unlike Other Gods (8)

        a. Unique in your person (8a)

        b. Unique in your works (8b)

    2. You Alone Are Sovereign (9)

        a. All nations are made by you (9a)

        b. All nations will worship you (9b)

    3. You Alone Are God (10)

        a. Great in your person (10a)

        b. Great in your deeds (10b)

D. David's Affirmation (11-13)

    1. I Will Walk in Your Way (11)

        a. So I may follow your truth (11a)

        b. So I may fear your name (11b)

    2. I Will Worship Your Name (12-13)

        a. For great is your love toward me (13a)

        b. For great is your deliverance of me (13b)

E. David's Adversaries (14-15)

    1. The Arrogant Persecute Me (14)

        a. Men who are ruthless (14a)

        b. Men without regard (14b)

    2. The Almighty Protects Me (15)

        a. He is compassionate and gracious (15a)

        b. He is patient and loving (15b)

F. David's Address (16-17)

    1. Grant Me Your Strength (16)

        a. Sustain me (16a)

        b. Strengthen me (16b)

        c. Save me (16b)

    2. Give Me a Sign (17)

        a. That the ungodly may be ashamed (17a)

        b. Because the Lord has helped me (17b)

Psalm 87

The Celebrated City

| Q u o t e |

"*Glorious things of thee are spoken,*

Zion, City of our God."

J o h n   N e w t o n

Psalm 87

I. INTRODUCTION

John Newton, the former slave trader turned gospel preacher and hymn writer, wrote many great songs, among them "Amazing Grace." But certainly one of his most beloved works is "Glorious Things of Thee Are Spoken, Zion, City of Our God." The first line of this grand hymn comes from the third verse of Psalm 87, a statement of praise for Zion. One of the stanzas of this masterpiece that is often omitted ends with the lines, "Fading is the world-lings pleasure, all his boasted pomp and show; solid joys and lasting treasure, none but Zion's children know." Newton had tasted the passing pleasures of this world, and they left a bitter taste in his mouth. He preferred the joys of Zion, and so should everyone.

Psalm 87 is a glorious celebration of Zion, Jerusalem, "the city of God," as the special object of his love and the royal city of his kingdom. As the holy city, it represents all that is holy and good in the working of God among his people. Further, it looks ahead prophetically to the ingathering of the nations into Jerusalem as the reigning religious city of the world in the coming messianic kingdom. Israel will remain the chosen nation of God as the nations of the world will come to Zion to worship God. As the title indicates, this psalm was written by the *Sons of Korah*, the Levitical choir made up of the descendants of Korah.

II. COMMENTARY

MAIN IDEA: *The psalmist celebrates Zion as the holy city of God.*

A The Glorious City of Zion (87:1–3)

87:1. Declaring God to be the builder of Jerusalem, the psalmist declared, **He has set his foundation on the holy mountain.** The Lord himself has laid the very foundation of Zion. This God-founded city is located in the hill country of Judea, set upon the holy mountain, Mount Zion. Being holy, it is immovable, set apart unto God's special purposes. "Mountain" is in the plural, underscoring its stability and transcendent majesty.

87:2. Consequently, **the LORD loves the gates of Zion** as his most cherished city. He chose Zion to be his dwelling place, the city where his glory would be specially displayed. The city "gates" refers to the activity of the people there, those coming into the city to worship God and departing to serve him. Thus, he **loves** this place **more than** the other **dwellings of Jacob.** This city is the God-chosen place to be his center of worship on earth. **Jacob** is a synonym for the entire nation of Israel (Gen. 32:28).

87:3. In response to these truths, **Glorious things are said of you.** The people spoke highly of the holy city because it was the **city of God,** the place where God uniquely met his chosen people in intimate, awesome worship.

B The Gathered Crowd to Zion (87:4–6)

87:4. God is now the speaker, saying, **I will record Rahab and Babylon among those who acknowledge me.** "Rahab" symbolized Egypt (Ps. 89:10; Isa. 30:7; 51:9), the great power to the southwest. The psalmist also named **Philistia,** a closer power located to the west, and **Tyre,** a powerful city-state to the north, along with **Cush,** a reference to Ethiopia, a far distant nation to the south. All these foreign powers will say, **This one was born in Zion.** In a future day of blessing, all the nations of the world will come to Jerusalem to worship God and while there will bear children. The emphasis is upon the global scope of the praise to be offered to God. There was a near fulfillment of this prophecy on the day of Pentecost when worshippers came to Jerusalem from all around the known world (Acts 2:9–11). Ultimately, it looks ahead to the millennial kingdom where Gentiles and Jews alike will worship together the Lord of Israel in the holy city (Rom. 11).

87:5–6. It will be said of Zion, **This one and that one were born in her.** Many Gentile worshippers will come to Jerusalem and be **born** there. Various people, **this one and that one,** will be born there as their parents come to worship God. In the process, **the Most High himself will establish her,** making her glorious as the epicenter of worship. **The LORD will write in the**

register of the peoples: "**This one was born in Zion.**" Jerusalem is so loved by God (v. 2) because glorious praise will be given to him there (v. 3). To be born in Jerusalem, therefore, will be considered a special honor (Zech. 8:20–23).

C The Glad Celebration in Zion (87:7)

87:7. **As they make music**, these worshippers who come to Jerusalem **will sing** to the Lord. They will declare to Zion, **All my fountains are in you**. That is, all their spiritual blessings will flow from Jerusalem where God is worshipped and will manifest his glory. "Fountains," or springs, pictures the source of divine blessings from God. The Lord is enjoyed with great pleasure by those who seek him at Jerusalem.

III. CONCLUSION

To this present hour, Jerusalem remains the apple of God's eye, the city in which he has promised to display his glory uniquely. It was in the holy city, Jerusalem, that Jesus died for sins, becoming a curse under the law for sinners. It was in Jerusalem that Jesus rose from the dead, triumphant over the grave. It was from the Mount of Olives at Jerusalem that Jesus ascended back to heaven. It was to Jerusalem that Jesus sent the Holy Spirit. It was in Jerusalem that Christ built the first church. It will be to Jerusalem that Jesus shall return at the end of this age. And it will be in Jerusalem that Christ will rule and reign over the earth for one thousand years. How special Jerusalem is to God. So should it be to all who love him as well.

IV. TEACHING OUTLINE

    A. The Glorious City of Zion (1-3)
        1. God Laid Its Foundations (1)
        2. God Loves Its Gates (2)
        3. God Lives in Its Worship (3)
    B. The Gathered Crowd to Zion (4-6)
        1. The People Will Praise Zion (4a,b)
           a. Rahad and Babylon (4a)
           b. Philistia, Tyre, and Cush (4b)
        2. The People Will Populate Zion (4c-6)
           a. People will be born there (4c-5a)
           b. God will establish the city (5b)
           c. God will record their names (6)
    C. The Glad Celebration in Zion (7)
        1. Worshippers Will Make Music (7a)
        2. Worshippers Will Be Refreshed (7b)

Psalm 88
Dark Despair

"A man is not known by his effervescence but by the amount of real suffering he can stand."

C. T. Studd

Psalm 88

I. INTRODUCTION

No believer is exempt from the trials of life. As long as one is in this world, suffering is a required course in the school of faith, never an elective to be passed or dropped. Rather than being spared pain, the saints are supported by God through their adversities, sustained triumphantly. No one should be surprised to read in these verses that the psalmist is undergoing the dark night of the soul. Such difficulty is common to life. However, in other psalms, the psalmist moves through his tribulation to be restored to a state of bolstered hope. That is not the case in this psalm. Here the psalmist remains in despair, unable to shake his deep discouragement. Deliverance by the Lord had not yet happened. Neither had spiritual encouragement. Darkness shrouded the psalmist without and within, and he could not shake it.

This psalm has the unique distinction of being called the saddest psalm of the entire Psalter. This song of lament is a desperate cry out of the depths of one's being, the painful prayer of one who has been ill or injured since the days of his youth (v. 15). Throughout his lifetime, he has suffered ill health followed by unanswered prayers. He has known one disappointment after another. Because the Psalms speak to all troublesome times of life, this particular psalm is appropriately included for those who suffer with no end in sight. The superscription is a double title, the first being *A song. A psalm of the Sons of Korah. For the director of music. According to mahalath leannoth.* This refers to "a dance of affliction" and describes the despair of this psalm.

The second title is *a maskil* (a contemplation) *of Heman the Ezrahite,* a musician from the family of the Kohathites (1 Kgs. 4:31; 1 Chr. 15:16–19).

II. COMMENTARY

MAIN IDEA: *The psalmist expresses his deepest lamentation as he faces darkness, despair, and even death.*

A The Crisis He Faced (88:1–9)

88:1–2. With a sudden burst of desperation, the psalmist exclaimed, **O LORD, the God who saves.** He understood that the only deliverance out of his present troubles must come from God. Such was the desperate, bleak outlook of his situation. This was the only ray of hope in the entire psalm. **Day and night I cry out before you,** without ceasing. But feeling as if he were not being heard in heaven, he pleaded, **May my prayer come before you; turn your ear to my cry.** He had been praying, but there was no answer. His unanswered petitions left the impression that God was not listening and had turned a deaf ear to his pleas.

88:3–5. Living on the threshold of death, he lamented, **my life draws near the grave.** This **trouble** cannot be identified, but it was undoubtedly life-threatening. Reinforcing the seriousness of this peril, the psalmist stated, **I am counted among those who go down to the pit,** a reference to the grave. He did not have the **strength** to go any further. As if he already had one foot in the **grave**, he was resigned to this hopeless fact: **I am set apart with the dead.** From his perspective, death will cut him off from God's **care** to be remembered by him **no more.** The psalmist felt utterly forsaken and forgotten by the Lord.

88:6–7. The psalmist believed that God was the one who had brought this trial. **You have put me in the lowest pit,** emphasis upon *you* (i.e., God). Illustrating his point, the psalmist made another graphic reference to death and the grave as the **lowest pit** and **darkest depths.** Assuming this trouble to be divine discipline and punitive judgment, he stated, **Your wrath lies heavily upon me** (cp. v. 16). His trouble-filled circumstances had **overwhelmed** him like large **waves,** leaving him drowning in deepest despair.

88:8–9. With mounting discouragement, the psalmist lamented, **You have taken from me my closest friends.** He suffered alone, without support from friends, now made to be **repulsive to them** (cp. v. 16). Thus, they hid from him. **Confined** by his surrounding troubles, he **cannot escape** to find relief. With unending tears, his swollen eyes were **dim with grief.** He called to the Lord, but there seemed to be no answer.

B The Case He Presented (88:10–12)

88:10. The psalmist made his appeal to God, reasoning with him in the form of a series of questions. Addressing God, he attempted to persuade, **Do you show your wonders to the dead?** That is, "How can you show your saving acts toward me if you wait until I am dead?" **Do those who are dead rise up and praise you?** He knew he could not praise God on earth from the silence of the grave.

88:11. The appeal continued. **Is your love declared in the grave?** He knew that he could not proclaim God's love to others once he was dead. So he pleaded with God to preserve his life. Or, **your faithfulness in Destruction?** Neither could he declare God's steadfastness to earthly men if he died. The psalmist's death would prevent others from seeing God's faithfulness.

88:12. Are your wonders known in the place of darkness? The answer was no. **Or your righteous deeds in the land of oblivion?** Again, no. The psalmist reasoned with God to deliver him from darkness and oblivion, two results of death, that he might praise and serve God.

C The Confusion He Felt (88:13–18)

88:13–14. With no relief in sight, the psalmist voiced, **But I cry to you for help, O LORD.** Yet no answer came. **In the morning my prayer comes before you.** But still, there was no response from God. With deep confusion, he expressed, **Why, O LORD, do you reject me and hide your face from me?** The more he prayed, the more he seemed to be refused by God. The silence from heaven was deafening and discouraging.

88:15. This rejection had been the psalmist's lifelong experience, or so he felt at the moment of writing. **From my youth I have been afflicted and close to death.** His present suffering was a long-standing pattern of trouble, all from God: **I have suffered your terrors and am in despair.** What he now suffered was familiar pain.

88:16–17. Like a wave crashing upon his helpless soul, he testified, **Your wrath has swept over me.** This left him drowning in despair. **Your terrors have destroyed me.** He was done! Without any relief, **all day long they surround me like a flood; they have completely engulfed me.** He was totally submerged in sorrow, unable to surface for the life-sustaining air of hope.

88:18. Sinking further, the psalm again claimed that the Lord had turned his friends against him: **You have taken my companions and loved ones from me.** This isolation was because he was repulsive in their sight (v. 8), perhaps involving a quarantine because of a life-threatening illness. He could only conclude, **the darkness is my closest friend.** This darkness alluded to his despair, depression, and seeming nearness to death. Such was the hopelessness he felt. He was engulfed in the darkness of despair, fearing that he would never see the light of hope.

III. CONCLUSION

No believer is immune from times of major discouragement. In spite of many high times on the mountaintop, there are also low seasons in the valley. This is true of every Christian's life. Accordingly, this lament song reveals just how discouraged a true believer may become. In the midst of adversity God's people often have to persevere with unshakable faith in God. This psalm, admittedly somber, has a reality to it that makes it relevant to every life. It is in such difficult times that the believer must turn to the Lord for strength. What an encouragement it is to know that his grace is always sufficient.

IV. TEACHING OUTLINE

A. The Crisis He Faced (1-9)
   1. I Have Cried to God (1-2)
      a. By day and night (1)
      b. Before God in heaven (2)
   2. I Am Crushed by God (3-7)
      a. My life is near death (3)
      b. My life is weak (4)
      c. My life is forgotten (5)
      d. My life is darkened (6)
      e. My life is afflicted (7)
   3. I Am Constrained by God (8-9)
      a. My friends are removed (8a)
      b. My goings are restricted (8b)
      c. My eyes are wasted (9a)
      d. My prayers are wasted (9b)
B. The Case He Presented (10-12)
   1. Will You Deliver the Dead? (10a)
   2. Will the Dead Praise You? (10b-11)
      a. Is your love declared in death? (11a)
      b. Is your faithfulness declared in death? (11b)
   3. Will You Be Made Known in Death? (12)
      a. Are your wonders declared in death? (12a)
      b. Are your works declared in death? (12b)
C. The Confusion He Felt (13-18)
   1. I Have Agonized to God (13-14)
      a. Why do you reject me? (14a)
      b. Why do you hide from me? (14b)
   2. I Am Afflicted by God (15-18)
      a. I have long been afflicted (15a)

    b. I have been suffering deeply (15b)
    c. I have been destroyed painfully (16)
    d. I have been engulfed completely (17)
    e. I have been isolated entirely (18)

Psalm 89

Forever Faithful

"*H*ow blessed to lift our eyes above this scene of

ruin, and behold One who is faithful in all things,

at all times."

A . W . Pink

I. INTRODUCTION

In contrast to the unfaithfulness of man, God shows himself to be forever faithful to his people, especially in keeping his promises. How soul strengthening it is to behold One who keeps his word at all times. God always stands committed to do what he says he will do. He never forgets his word, never forfeits his promises, never violates his covenant. Never does he pledge something and then fail to bring it to pass. Never does he speak and fail to fulfill it. Even when we are faithless, he remains faithful. God is a faithful God.

The faithfulness of God is the chief focus of this royal psalm. It is an agonizing prayer offered for the nation Israel, pleading that God would honor the Davidic covenant (2 Sam. 7:8–16). It is a prayer that God would remain faithful to the promises he made to David. This psalm is attributed to *Ethan the Ezrahite*, a Levite (1 Chr. 15:17–18) and wise person (1 Kgs. 4:31) who interceded with God on behalf of his people at a time when they faced the defeat of their anointed king who stood in the promised line of David. Thus, the psalmist beseeched God to remember his covenant which he had made with David and deliver them from their affliction.

II. COMMENTARY

MAIN IDEA: *The psalmist rejoices in God's faithfulness to his covenant with David and his descendants.*

A The Praise for God's Faithfulness (89:1–2)

89:1a. With an initial burst celebrating God's love and faithfulness, the psalmist declared, **I will sing of the LORD's great love forever.** He rejoiced in God's perfect, unconditional love for his own people, a special focus of this psalm (vv. 1–2,14,24,28,33,49). Likewise, *forever* is a critical word in this psalm, used eight times (vv. 1–2,4,28–29,36–37,46). God's love is without end.

89:1b–2. The psalmist continued, **With my mouth I will make your faithfulness known through all generations.** Divine faithfulness was yet another unique focus of this psalm, used seven times (vv. 1–2,5,8,14,33,49). By his faithfulness, God remained unconditionally committed to do for his people what he had promised to do. For this reason, he declared God's love and faithfulness **forever.**

B The Promise of God's Faithfulness (89:3–4)

89:3–4. The psalmist examined one specific aspect of God's faithfulness, a subject that will occupy the entirety of this psalm, God's covenant with David. God said, **I have made a covenant with my chosen one.** This **covenant** referred to the Davidic covenant (2 Sam. 7:8–16) that God made with **David**, a covenant that will extend to his descendants and establish the royal **line.** Thus, the rightful heir to the **throne** would always be a descendant of David. Ultimately, this royal recipient would be the Messiah (Luke 1:31–33).

C The Perfections of God's Faithfulness (89:5–18)

89:5–8. Focusing on this divine attribute, faithfulness, it is a quality that uniquely distinguishes God from all other beings and powers. **The heavens praise your wonders, O LORD, your faithfulness too.** This worship of God comes from **the holy ones,** or the angelic beings, depicted here as the **heavenly beings.** They are declaring God's unique holiness, **for who in the skies can compare with the LORD?** The answer to this question was no one. In their midst above, **God is greatly feared** because his faithfulness surrounds him.

89:9–14. Day by day, the Lord remains unwaveringly faithful to rule over and sustain all creation. **You rule over the surging sea** and all that it contains. God **founded the world and all that is in it,** including **the north and the south,** a reference to **Tabor and Hermon,** the two tallest mountains that surrounded Israel. All this, God **created** and controlled by his **right hand.** Likewise, the psalmist cited other attributes of God that work for the good of his people, causing them to praise him. **Righteousness and justice are the foundation of your throne**, meaning God can do only that which is right, just, equitable, and fair. **Love and faithfulness**, both already mentioned, **go before you**, meaning they proceed from God's **throne** to work his will. Everything God does emanates from the foundation of his throne as he rules as the only sovereign.

89:15–18. It is because God possesses these many perfections that his people are **blessed**. They are greatly favored, happy, and satisfied who have learned to **acclaim** him in worship and **walk in the light** of holiness. **They rejoice** and **exult** in God's **righteousness** because he is their **glory and strength**. **Our shield**, a metaphor for the king as their defender (Ps. 84:9), **belongs to the** LORD.

D The Pledge of God's Faithfulness (89:19–37)

89:19–25. The psalmist here returned to a subject he introduced earlier, namely, God's covenant with David (vv. 3–4). God **spoke** in a revelation to both Samuel (1 Sam. 16:1–12) and Nathan (2 Sam. 7:4–16) in which he made known that he had chosen **David**, a **young man** and **warrior**, to be king. He was divinely **anointed**, sustained, and strengthened, enabled to withstand **his foes**. God decreed that David's rule would reach from the Mediterranean Sea to the **rivers**.

89:26–29. The writer described the special father-son type relationship that will exist before **God** and David. As if he were God's **firstborn** son, this anointed king will have the highest position and holy privileges in the earthly kingdom, making him the **most exalted** of all **kings**. God promised to keep his **covenant** with David **forever**, as well as **his line** (dynasty) and **throne**, as long as the **heavens endure** (2 Sam. 7:12–13,16).

89:30–37. Although the Davidic covenant was unconditional and eternal, disobedience would lead to suffering. **If his sons forsake my law**, then God promised, **I will punish their sin with the rod**. Disobedience would bring divine discipline. In spite of his divine covenant with David's descendants, the Lord said, **I will not take my love from him**, nor **violate my covenant**. God has **sworn** this by his **holiness** that the terms of the covenant with David will stand **forever**. This is because God is faithful to keep his word even if David's descendants are unfaithful.

E The Perplexity with God's Faithfulness (89:38–45)

89:38–39. With this pledge in mind, the psalmist lamented that their king had been afflicted and defeated. How can God's apparent rejection of Israel be reconciled with his Davidic covenant? In what is probably a description of the Babylonian captivity, the psalmist asked, **But you have rejected, you have spurned, you have been very angry with your anointed one**. God had rejected David's descendants with painful consequences. In a state of perplexity, Ethan wrote, **You have renounced** (literally, "disdained") **the covenant with your servant**. How could God seemingly break the covenant which he said was forever? This was the psalmist's dilemma.

89:40–45. Pointing to the demise of the holy city, he said, **You have broken through all his walls**, referring to the city walls of Jerusalem. Its protection was gone, and the city was rendered defenseless, subject to being **plundered** and being made the object of **scorn**. As an unwalled city, it seemed as if God had **exalted the right hand of his foes**, giving their enemies the opportunity to defeat and destroy them. The outward appearance was that God had **not supported** his own people **in battle** against the invading Babylonians as he had promised he would do. Instead, it seemed that God had **put an end** to Jerusalem's **splendor**, a total contradiction to his pledge in the Davidic covenant. Likewise, concerning the king, God had **cast his throne to the ground**, ending his reign, and **cut short the days of his youth**, abruptly ending his life. In all this, God had **covered him with a mantle of shame**, ending his glory. In light of God's promises, no wonder the psalmist was bewildered and distraught.

F The Prayer for God's Faithfulness (89:46–52)

89:46. In this final stanza, Ethan petitioned the Lord, **How long, O LORD? Will you hide yourself forever?** Because God had allowed Jerusalem to be destroyed and the Davidic dynasty disrupted, it seemed as though God was hiding himself. Thus, **how long will your wrath burn like fire?** There appeared to be no end in sight to the divine discipline being inflicted upon them.

89:47–48. So the psalmist prayed, **Remember how fleeting is my life**. God must act now, he desired, before he died and failed to live to see the restoration of his people. **What man can live and not see death?** Certainly not the psalmist, nor this entire generation. Death was imminent. They would not **live to see** the faithfulness of God if the Lord did not act soon.

89:49–51. The psalmist's only hope was to appeal to God's **former great love**. Where is the love which God in his **faithfulness** swore to **David**? This appeal asked that God keep his covenant with David. He pleaded with the Lord to come to their aid in order to avoid being **mocked** by **the taunts of all the nations**. These pagan peoples would use the opportunity to divide the covenant-breaking God of Israel.

89:52. This psalm concluded, **Praise be to the LORD forever! Amen and Amen**. This verse was probably added by the final editors who compiled Psalms 73–89 into Book III. In summary of all God's glory revealed in these seventeen psalms, the compilers offered fervent praise. With this declaration of praise, Book III comes to a conclusion.

III. CONCLUSION

The unchanging faithfulness of God, forever reliable and firm, is a glorious treasure to believers. Even when God's people have been unfaithful to him, he remains faithful to them. People are prone to break their word. They are apt to go back on their promises. They are subject to altering their commitments. But not God. The Lord remains forever faithful to do what he purposes and pledges he will do. Herein is true comfort for all the saints. God will never deny us, never disappoint us, never desert us. All his promises are yes and amen. All of his plans are immutable and eternal. Great is his faithfulness because of the power he wields to keep his word. May all God's people anchor themselves to him alone who is perfectly faithful in all things, at all times. The divine promises may be late in their fulfillment, but, be assured, they will surely come to pass in the lives of believers. Such is God's faithfulness.

IV. TEACHING OUTLINE

A. The Praise for God's Faithfulness (1-2)
  1. I Will Sing of His Faithful Love (1)
  2. I Will Speak of His Faithful Love (2)
B. The Promise of God's Faithfulness (3-4)
  1. He Has Established a Covenant with David (3)
  2. He Has Established a Line Through David (4a)
  3. He Has Established a Throne for David (4b)
C. The Perfections of God's Faithfulness (5-13)
  1. His Faithfulness Is Declared in Heaven (5-8)
    a. God is praised for his faithfulness (5)
    b. God is feared for his faithfulness (6-7)
    c. God is surrounded by his faithfulness (8)
  2. His Faithfulness Is Demonstrated on Earth (9-13)
    a. God rules over the surging sea (9)
    b. God rules over the sea monsters (10)
    c. God rules over the surrounding earth (11-12)
    d. God rules with the strongest power (13)
  3. His Faithfulness Is Delighted in by Believers (15-18)
    a. It works with his other attributes (14)
    b. It goes before his throne (14b)
    c. It causes his people to rejoice (15-16)
    d. It gives his people protection (17-18)
D. The Pledge of God's Faithfulness (19-37)
  1. It Was Revealed to the Davidic King (19-29)
    a. God selected David to be king (19-20)

        b. God strengthened David as king (21)

        c. God protected David as king (22-24)

        d. God exalted David as king (25-27)

        e. God blessed David as king (28-29)

     2. It Is Reenforced with Divine Discipline (30-32)

        a. If his people disobey God's word (30-31)

        b. Then God will punish their sin (32)

     3. It Remains with Divine Love (33-37)

        a. God will not banish his love (33a)

        b. God will not betray his faithfulness (33b)

        c. God will not breach his covenant (34a)

        d. God will not break his word (34b)

        e. God will not batter David's line (35-37)

E.   The Perplexity with God's Faithfulness (38-45)

     1. God Has Rejected the King (38)

     2. God Has Renounced the Covenant (39)

     3. God Has Ruined the City (40-41)

        a. He has destroyed the walls (40)

        b. He has plundered the wealth (41)

     4. God Has Rewarded Their Foes (42)

        a. He has exalted them (42a)

        b. He has exulted them (42b)

     5. God Has Refused the King (43-45)

        a. He has disregarded the king (43)

        b. He has defeated the king (44)

        c. He has dishonored the king (45)

F.   The Prayer for God's Faithfulness (46-52)

     1. The Psalmist Reasons with God (46-49)

        a. How long will you be angry? (46)

        b. How can man escape death? (48)

        c. Where is your former love? (49)

     2. The Psalmist Reminds God (50-51)

        a. Remember my mockings (50a,51)

        b. Remember my tauntings (50b,51a)

Doxology: PRAISE THE LORD (52)

Psalm 90
Eternal Perspective

"O God, stamp eternity on my eyeballs!"

Jonathan Edwards

I. INTRODUCTION

A famous cathedral in Europe is known for its three arched doorways that lead from the vestibule into the sanctuary. Over the right entrance, these words are carved into the marbled archway: "All that *pleases* is but for a moment." Over the left entrance, leading worshippers into the sanctuary, are chiseled these words: "All that *troubles* is but for a moment." Visibly etched over the main archway, leading down the center aisle, is this inscription: "All that is *important* is eternal." The message is clear for all who enter the sanctuary. All that is temporal is ultimately trivial. What is truly important in the present is that which will be important ten thousand years from today.

This engraved message, chiseled over the center aisle, is the central theme of Psalm 90. In life, we often become concerned with what is passing away, that which troubles or pleases only momentarily. Unfortunately, we are then most prone to lose sight of what is eternal. This psalm is transcendent, towering over time and eternity, written to remind us that what matters most in life is not the temporal but the eternal, not the physical but the spiritual, not the visible but the invisible. In other words, all that truly matters is eternal.

The inscription above this psalm reveals it to be written by Moses—the only psalm written by the aged prophet. Thus, it is the oldest of all the psalms, written over fourteen hundred years before the coming of Christ. This psalm is also quite possibly the oldest piece of all Scripture, depending upon whether Moses wrote this before the Pentateuch, and contingent upon who wrote Job and when. Most probably, it was written during Israel's wilderness wanderings.

What should have been a relatively short sojourn of a few months for Moses and Israel, traveling from Egypt to the promised land, turned into a forty-year ordeal. The people of God went in endless circles in the wilderness, going absolutely nowhere, dying off before they could reach their destination across the Jordan River. They were living in ignominious defeat, disappointment, death, and despair. In the midst of these difficult circumstances, Moses lifted up his heart to heaven in order to anchor his soul to God. He looked to God afresh that he might reestablish his eternal perspective. Here is living with an eternal perspective.

II. COMMENTARY

MAIN IDEA: *Moses asks that the people be taught to number their days in light of God's eternality, sovereignty, and mercy.*

A God's Eternality (90:1–2)

SUPPORTING IDEA: *Moses acknowledges that from eternity past to eternity future God is God.*

90:1. Addressing God directly, Moses declared, **You have been our dwelling place**. For forty years in the wilderness, God's people had no place to call home. Wandering like nomads in the desert, they had been without any earthly dwelling place of their own. They never unpacked to settle down but were like a tumbleweed driven by the wind, never tied down to one place. In the midst of this vagabond existence, Moses acknowledged that his soul rested in God, who was his true dwelling place. **Generations** come and go, but God is the one constant in the midst of uncertainty.

90:2. Before the creation of the world, God alone existed. Before the foundation of the world, before there was anything or anyone else, there was God. There has never been a time when God was not. This God, who is without beginning, shall be God throughout all eternity future, never ceasing to be God. In a world that is constantly changing, God is the eternal constant. **From everlasting to everlasting**, God remains the one true God.

B God's Sovereignty (90:3–6)

SUPPORTING IDEA: *Moses states that God controls man's days, turning him back to dust.*

90:3. In stark contrast to God, man is nothing but dust. At the end of man's days, God, who created man out of dust (Gen. 2:7), is the one who returns him **back to dust**. God formed man out of the earth and breathed into him the breath of life. God is sovereignly governing the length of man's life, the number of his days being preordained and divinely determined.

90:4. From the perspective of God's infinite eternality, a **thousand years** of human history is a mere twenty-four-hour **day**, quickly passing away. A thousand years for man is like a short three-hour **watch in the night**. This is how temporal mortal man's days are. Man is transitory, but God is eternal.

90:5a. Men's lives are swept away by God in **death**, as if being ushered along by powerful floodwaters. Alive for only a fleeting moment, man soon closes his eyes in the **sleep of death**. This sobering end is appointed not by man but by God.

90:5b–6. In the desert conditions, the early **morning** dews caused small twigs of **grass** to grow. But when the noon sun blazed, it withered and perished. So it is with man, who always lives under the constant sentence of death.

Ⓒ God's Severity (90:7–12)

> **SUPPORTING IDEA:** *Moses confesses that the sin of the people has provoked God's anger, shortening their lives.*

90:7. In the Sinai wilderness, Israel's sin provoked God's divine **anger**, leading to their death. God's people were **consumed** and **terrified** in the face of this divine severity. Their unbelief and idolatry grieved God and aroused his anger, causing an entire generation to die in the wilderness without entering the promised land.

90:8. Moses explains that God has set **our iniquities** before him. God sees all their unbelief, murmuring, disobedience, and rebellion (Heb. 4:13). **Secret sins**, hidden on earth, are fully exposed in the blinding **light** of God's holy **presence**. Nothing is hidden from the Lord.

90:9. All man's **days pass away** under divine **wrath**. Human life is short-lived because it is spent under God's judgment upon man's sin. This consuming wrath sentences men to live under the sure end of divine judgment.

90:10. Even the most God-fearing of men have only a limited time to live on earth. For some, an average life span is **seventy years**. For others, it is **eighty** years due to **strength**. The best that man has to show for his life is **trouble** (i.e., hard work), **sorrow**, or disappointment, and then, death.

90:11. Who takes to heart the full intensity of God's holy anger against sin? The truth is, no one gives God the **fear** that is rightly due him. No one understands God's fierce wrath nor responds in fitting reverence due the Lord.

90:12. In response, Moses petitioned God, **Teach us to number our days**. That is, man must be taught by God to number his days here on earth because they are few. He must weigh them and value them. Because God has numbered man's days, so all men must do the same. Once each person numbers his days, only then will he be able to present to God a **heart of wisdom**. Man must be careful not to waste his life in temporal frivolities but to invest it for eternity.

ⅅ God's Mercy (90:13–17)

> **SUPPORTING IDEA:** *Moses requests that God restore and establish his people by his mercy.*

90:13. This psalm concludes with a prayer for God's **compassion. Relent, O LORD!** or, literally, return to us with divine grace before you return us to the dust. **How long,** O Lord? The people have gone for a long time under God's discipline without his blessing. How much longer must they endure this chastening?

90:14. Interceding for Israel, Moses requested, let a new day of grace dawn **in the morning.** Let the long night of divine anger cease. Let the rest of **our days** be different. Let them be filled with **joy** and gladness.

90:15. Moses knew the people were suffering under God's severe discipline that had **afflicted** them. All this **trouble** was God's chastisement upon them, a painful correction caused by turning their backs on God. Bring as much gladness, he prayed, as they had known sadness.

90:16. Restore your **deeds** in and through our lives, Moses interceded. Cause us to stop going in endless circles in the wilderness, he prayed, but lead us into the promised land and the fullness of your blessing. This is a prayer that God would put his glorious **splendor** on display once again.

90:17. This request concludes that God would bestow his undeserved **favor** upon his people rather than consume them with his wrath. Further, Moses asked that the Lord would establish the **work of our hands,** making them effective and enduring.

> **MAIN IDEA REVIEW:** *Moses asks that the people be taught to number their days in light of God's eternality, sovereignty, and mercy.*

III. CONCLUSION

Perspective is critically important in the Christian life. One's vantage point determines how one sees, how one lives, and for what one lives. This underscores how important it is that every believer should maintain an eternal perspective. We are allotted by God only so much time. Therefore we must live strategically in light of eternity. Maybe you feel that you are going in aimless circles, like Israel in the wilderness. Perhaps you are living with disappointment and despair. Maybe you are being squeezed into the tyranny of the urgent with all its pressing deadlines but have lost sight of eternity. This psalm is intended to bring the eternal perspective back into focus in your life. It is designed to redirect you to live for the kingdom of heaven, not for the kingdoms of this world. It calls us to live every day for the approval of God, not for the applause of men. It directs us to be laying up for ourselves treasure in heaven, not riches on the earth. Wisely investing one's life requires living in light of eternity. It necessitates living with an eternal outlook on all of life.

IV. LIFE APPLICATION

An old adage says, "Aim at nothing, and you will hit it every time." So it is with life. A misdirected life is a wasted life. In order to hit the target of God's will, one must live for what is truly important and will stand the test of time. One must choose to live for what will be vastly important ten thousand years from today. One must live for God and his eternal kingdom today. Only a life lived for God will be a truly satisfied life. Living for the world, independent of God, yields an empty and hollow existence. A round world will never fit into a triangular heart that was made for God and God alone.

This psalm is a passionate plea, calling us to live every day with an eternal perspective. Every person has only so much divinely allotted time during his stay on earth, an amount of time sovereignly determined by God. The message is clear: Redeem the time. Use time wisely. Invest it carefully. There are only two things going out of this world, the Word of God and the souls of men. One must pour his or her life wisely into these eternal realities.

V. PRAYER

God, cause us to invest our lives wisely in that which matters most in eternity. Prevent us from squandering our days and wasting our lives in trivialities. Allow us to see our present opportunities and responsibilities in light of eternity. Help us to live our lives to the fullest while we can. In Jesus' name. Amen.

VI. DEEPER DISCOVERIES

A. Lord (90:1)

The word Lord (*adonay*) means "master or lord." *Adonay* is most likely a modified, plural form of *adon,* with a first common singular pronominal suffix. In this form, *adonay* signifies majesty or intensification and is always used of God. Found throughout the Hebrew Bible, in the Pentateuch it is used as a reverent way of addressing God (Exod. 4:10,13; Josh. 7:8). *Adonay* is prominent in the prophets and is used fifty-five times in the Psalms. Its use in certain passages, "Lord of all the earth" (Josh. 3:13; Ps. 97:5; Mic. 4:13), "Lord of lords" (Deut. 10:17), "the Sovereign LORD, the God of Israel" (Exod. 34:23), and the contexts of other passages alludes to the meaning of *adonay* as being the sovereign Lord who has ultimate authority, power, and rule. Interestingly, it is used of the Messiah in Psalm 110:1.

B. World (90:2)

The term *world* (*tebel*) is used three different ways in the Old Testament: (1) It refers to the physical mass of the earth (Ps. 89:11; 1 Sam. 2:8; 2 Sam. 22:16); (2) it refers to the people of the earth (Pss. 9:8; 24:1; 33:8; 96:13; 98:9; Isa. 13:11; 18:3; 24:4; 26:9,18; Lam. 4:12); and (3) it is used to refer to the habitable part of the land (Job 37:12; Ps. 90:2; Prov. 8:31; Isa. 14:17; Nah. 1:5).

C. Power (90:11)

The word *power* (*oz*) is used throughout the Psalms to describe the attribute of God's omnipotence (Pss. 62:11; 63:2). It is used to speak of God's mighty voice that rules over all (Ps. 68:33) and his powerful arm that overcomes all opposition (Ps. 89:10). This strength was clearly demonstrated by God in the exodus when he overcame all opposition and obstacles in order to lead Israel out of Egypt, through the wilderness, and into the promised land (Exod. 15:13). This word is used to convey the security, stability, and safety to be found in God (Ps. 30:7), who is a "strong" tower (Ps. 61:3) and a "mighty" rock (Ps. 62:7). The strength of God is to be ascribed to him by his people as they worship him (Pss. 29:1; 96:7).

VII. TEACHING OUTLINE

A. God's Eternality (1-2)
1. God Is Our Dwelling Place (1)
2. God Is the Only God (2)
   a. Before the mountains were born (2a)
   b. Before the earth was created (2b)
   c. Throughout eternity past (2c)
   d. Throughout eternity future (2c)
B. God's Sovereignty (3-6)
1. God Sentences Man to Death (3a)
   a. He turns man to dust (3)
   b. He transcends man within time (4)
2. God Subjects Man to Death (5-6)
   a. He sweeps away man like sleep (5a)
   b. He cuts down man like grass (5b-6)
C. God's Severity (7-12)
1. God Judges Man's Sin (7)
   a. We are consumed by God's anger (7a)
   b. We are confounded by God's fury (7b)
2. God Exposes Man's Sin (8)
   a. God has set our sin before him (8a)

    b. God has set our sin in the light (8b)

  3. God Shortens Man's Life (9-10)

    a. Life is lived under wrath (9a)

    b. Life is finished with moaning (9b)

    c. Life is shortened by God (10a)

    d. Life is filled with trouble (10b)

  4. God Exceeds Man's Understanding 911)

    a. God's anger is inscrutable (11a)

    b. God's wrath is infinite (11b)

PROPER RESPONSE (12):

    1. Teach Us to Number Our Days (12a)

    2. Give Us a Heart of Wisdom (12b)

D. God's Mercy (13-17)

  1. Grace Us (13)

    a. Change your mind (13a)

    b. Show your compassion (13b)

  2. Satisfy Us (14-15)

    a. Bring in a new day (14a)

    b. Bring in a new gladness (14b-15)

  3. Enlighten Us (16)

    a. Show us your deeds (16a)

    b. Show us your splendor (16b)

  4. Establish Us (17)

    a. May your favor rest upon us (17a)

    b. May your favor remain with us (17b,c)

Psalm 91

Sovereign Security

"*A* sovereign Protector I have,

Unseen, yet forever at hand,

Unchangeably faithful to save,

Almighty to rule and command."

Augustus M. Toplady

I. INTRODUCTION

The Golden Gate Bridge, located at the entrance of San Francisco Bay, is one of the largest and most spectacular suspension bridges in the world, spanning 8,981 feet through midair. When this world-famous bridge was being constructed, several workmen lost their lives, falling from precariously high positions, two hundred feet above the waters. Consequently, the work was constantly behind schedule. That is, until someone hit upon the idea of building a safety net directly under the construction area. Then, with such security in place, any workman who fell would not tumble to his death but would be caught by the net.

So a giant safety net was made of stout, sturdy cord and swung under the construction work—the first time in the history of major construction that such a net was used. The cost for the net was one hundred thousand dollars, a staggering figure in those postdepression years. But the effect was both immediate and noticeable. The work suddenly proceeded at a much faster rate because the workmen knew that if they did slip, the net would catch them and their lives would be spared.

This was the same effect that God's sovereignty had upon the psalmist, as recorded in Psalm 91. But his security was not beneath him; it was above him. God himself was his security, the one who would protect him from the harm that surrounded him. He would rest under the shadow of the Almighty as God, the Most High, would be his refuge and fortress. Under this security—an incomparably *sovereign* security—the psalmist could move forward in his life with great confidence and efficiency. This psalm vividly describes God's continuously sovereign protection of his people from their many threatening dangers and alarming terrors. In reading these verses, believers are encouraged to trust God, knowing that nothing can harm a child of God unless the Lord himself permits it. Further, there are many references in this psalm to the future kingdom of the coming Messiah. Thus, it should also be seen as prophetic as well, awaiting final fulfillment at the end of the age.

The historical background of this psalm of trust is uncertain. It may well be that of Israel's army proceeding into battle. The author is anonymous, perhaps the one who was leading the troops of Israel into conflict. Regardless of the setting, the message is clear. The basis of security for the believer is found in God's character (vv. 1–2), care (vv. 3–8), protection (vv. 9–13), and love (vv. 14–16). This is a psalm to be read when facing times of great danger and being confronted with the powers of evil.

II. COMMENTARY

MAIN IDEA: *The psalmist affirms the absolute security of all who put their trust in God.*

Faith in a Powerful God (91:1–2)

SUPPORTING IDEA: *The psalmist trusts God to be his shelter and protective care.*

91:1. In the face of mounting dangers, the psalmist declared his personal trust in God. He did so with a sharp focus on the divine character, using three names for God: Most High (*El Elyon*), emphasizing God's strength and sovereignty; Almighty (*El Shaddai*), picturing God as the active, self-existent One; and God (*Elohim*), the strong one, mighty leader, supreme deity. The believer **who dwells in the shelter of the Most High** can expect to find God's strong, sure protection. He dwells close to God, under the shelter of divine care. This shelter is later pictured as the overarching wings and invincible armor of God (v. 4). The psalmist **will rest** with much calm and peace in the **shadow of the Almighty**, depicting God's overseeing guardianship of every believer's life. This will be accomplished by the Most High, the divine name emphasizing

God's overruling sovereignty, and the Almighty, the all-powerful, invincible God.

91:2. With unwavering resolve, the psalmist professed, **He is my refuge and my fortress**. Here is dynamic faith, a reliance upon God's invincible might to be his refuge (*mahceh*, a place to flee for protection) and fortress (*metsudah*, a castle, stronghold). He added, **my God, in whom I trust** (*batach*, to attach), firmly fixing himself to God in the midst of his threatening circumstances. This is what true faith is, a committing of oneself to God with full reliance on his ability to provide and protect.

Ⓑ Favor from a Protecting God (91:3–13)

> **SUPPORTING IDEA:** *The psalmist describes the protection he is sure he will receive from God.*

91:3. Anticipating a positive future, the psalmist described the protection he will receive from God as he lives in the Lord's presence: **Surely he will save you from the fowler's snare**. This image pictures danger as a hunter who stalks him as prey. But the Lord will deliver **from the deadly pestilence**, another metaphor for the harm he faces, a harm that is like a life-taking plague.

91:4. Like an eagle protecting its young, God **will cover** believers **with his feathers** and **wings** (Ps. 17:8; Deut. 32:11). In yet another shifting of metaphors, the psalmist represented God's **faithfulness** in guarding him from all harm like a **shield** and **rampart**, depicting God as protecting a warrior in the day of battle.

91:5–6. Such safeguarding brings a settled peace. The psalmist will not fear the **terror of night** when he would be most vulnerable to an enemy's surprise attack. Nor will he dread the **arrow that flies by day** aimed for his destruction and death. Neither will he fear the **pestilence that stalks in the darkness**, the attacks begun even in the night. Nor will he be terrified of the **plague**, picturing everything that threatens him. The reason he **will not fear** is because God is his sure protection.

91:7–8. So overwhelming is God's intervention, **A thousand may fall at your side** in battle, even **ten thousand** who would seek to harm you. But, in sharp contrast, **it will not come near you**. God is far greater than any human, and thus, any harm that could come near to man. In the presence of such danger, **you will only observe with your eyes** this onslaught, not as a victim, but as an untouched victor.

91:9–10. With mounting confidence, the psalmist repeated his opening declaration of faith to **make the Most High your dwelling** (v. 1) and **the LORD** his **refuge**. In this unassailable position of total reliance, **then no harm will befall you** from the hands of your enemies. And **no disaster will**

come near your tent because the Lord's shield of protection will act as a hedge of protection.

91:11–12. In part, this sovereign guardianship will be carried out by his angels whom the Lord will command and commission to guard you in all your ways. Satan quoted these verses to Christ in his temptation and shrewdly omitted this last phrase, "in all your ways" (Matt. 4:6; Luke 4:10–11). This divine protection extends only to the place of trusting and obeying God. The angels will lift you up in their hands, so that you will not strike your foot against a stone (Ps. 34:7).

91:13. Standing in this elevated place of safety, you will tread upon the lion and the cobra, not literally, but figuratively. You will trample the great lion and the serpent. These threatening beasts pictured his foes and the many dangers brought upon him by his enemies.

Ⓒ Fellowship with a Personal God (91:14–16)

SUPPORTING IDEA: *God declares that he will deliver the person who honors him.*

91:14. A sudden shift in speaker now moves from the psalmist to God himself. Note the reciprocal nature of the mutual fellowship that exists between the Lord and the one who loves him. Because he loves me . . . I will rescue him. True faith involves a deep, mutual love between God and his servant. The believer who loves God will, in turn, be delivered by God. I will protect him, means, literally, "I will raise him up to a high, secure place." This rescue results because he acknowledges my name. Those whose allegiance is to the Lord will find that his protective allegiance is theirs.

91:15. God continues as the speaker, saying that the person who loves and acknowledges him (v. 14) will call upon me, and I will answer. Such is the binding covenant relationship that exists between the Lord and his people. God will answer the prayer of the believer who is in deep trouble and be with him in his adversity. I will deliver him, God promised, out of his trouble, and then, honor him with divine reward and favor, especially when suffering for his name's sake.

91:16. God concluded, with long life will I satisfy him. That is, the Lord will deliver a person who trusts him out of life-threatening adversity (vv. 7–8,13), giving him long life. In so doing, God will satisfy him with fullness of life. God will add years to his life and life to his years. The believer will live a long and full life, within the boundaries of God's eternal decree, because the Lord will show him my salvation.

MAIN IDEA REVIEW: *The psalmist affirms the absolute security of all who put their trust in God.*

III. CONCLUSION

In a sermon, Juan Carlos Ortiz spoke of a conversation with a trapeze artist. The performer admitted the net underneath was there to keep the trapeze artists from breaking their necks. Then he added, "The net also keeps us from falling. Imagine there is no net. We would be so nervous that we would be more likely to miss and fall. If there was not a net, we would not dare to do some of the things we do. But because there is a net, we dare to make two turns, and once I made three turns—thanks to the net!" Ortiz then made this observation: "We have security in God. When we are sure in His arms, we dare to attempt big things for God. We dare to be holy. We dare to be obedient. We dare, because we know the eternal arms of God will hold us if we fall."

This is the bold confidence inspired by the sovereign security which God provides for all believers. Knowing of this divine protection, especially in the face of mounting dangers, God's people have courage to move forward with great faith. This psalm points the believer to the source of true security—God himself. The person who trusts completely in God, not in self or in this world, will experience God's divine protection in all of life.

IV. LIFE APPLICATION

In the many circumstances of life, we must learn to put our trust in God. The Lord is our security, our only sure shield and shelter from all harm. We may always have confidence that his protection is greater than any danger that threatens us. No matter how great the adversity we may face, God is bigger than the adversity and remains in full control. He is always over all. Thus, we must trust him completely.

Trust God's protection. Nothing can come into our lives unless it comes through God's hands first. He can keep out any danger he chooses. Whatever he allows into our lives is there by divine appointment to work for our good.

Trust God's power. As we abide under God's protection, we are enabled by divine grace to bear up under the greatest trial. In our weakness God's strength is made perfect. He gives a greater grace that enables us to press on in the midst of the storm.

Trust God's peace. Peace is more than the absence of trouble. It is the presence of a supernatural calm in the midst of our trouble in which God steadies and satisfies our hearts with himself. When all others are distant, we have a divine peace that surpasses all comprehension.

V. PRAYER

God, how our troubles so often rise up around us and cause us great fear. We confess how weak and fragile we are before them. Draw our focus away from these trials and place our attention on you. Enable our hearts to rest fully in you. Enlarge our understanding of your greatness. Expand our confidence in you. Make us mighty in you. Then we will not be afraid. We thank you for your sovereign security in all things. We declare your awesome power that always protects us. In Jesus' name. Amen.

VI. DEEPER DISCOVERIES

A. Refuge (91:2,9)

This word (Heb. *mahseh*) refers to a strong, secure structure that provides shelter from the elements (Job. 24:8; Isa. 4:6). In the figurative sense, as it is used here, *mahseh* refers to a shelter from one's enemies who seek to harm and destroy, even kill. The psalmist understood that God was a refuge for his people (Pss. 14:6; 46:1; 61:3; 62:8; 71:7). This word was used to emphasize God's watch care over his people.

B. Save (91:3)

The word *save* (Heb. *nasal*) means to be snatched away, rescued, drawn out of, saved, pulled away, or to escape. The word was used countless times by David when he petitioned God to rescue him from his enemies who sought to take his life. In other psalms, the word is used in a salvific sense to speak of a deliverance from one's transgressions (Ps. 39:8) and the grave (Ps. 86:13). Asaph wrote, "Help us, O God our Savior, for the glory of your name; deliver (*nasal*) us and forgive our sins for your name's sake" (Ps. 79:9). The word was also used in requesting God for the power to resist sin (Ps. 120:2). Considering the numerous appearances of *nasal* in the Psalms, the theme of deliverance is one of the dominant themes of the Psalms.

C. Harm (91:10)

This word (Heb. *ra*) is an adjective meaning "that which is bad, evil, wicked, or corrupt." It is used of evil words (Prov. 15:26), evil thoughts (Gen. 6:5; 8:21), and evil actions (Prov. 2:14; Exod. 5:22–23; Deut. 17:5; Neh. 13:17; 2 Kgs. 3:2).

VII. TEACHING OUTLINE

A. Faith in a Powerful God (1-2)
   1. He Lives in the Lord's Presence (1)
      a. I dwell in God's shelter (1a)
      b. I Rest in God's shadow (1b)
   2. He Trusts in the Lord's Protection (2)
      a. He is my refuge
      b. He is my fortress
      c. He is my God
B. Favor from a Protecting God (3-13)
   1. God Will Save You (3)
      a. From the fowler's snare (3a)
      b. From the deadly pestilence (3b)
   2. God Will Shield You (4a, b)
      a. With his feathers (4a)
      b. Under his wings (4b)
   3. God Will Safeguard You (4c)
      a. Like a shield (4c)
      b. Like a rampart (4c)
   4. God Will Shelter You (5-6)
      a. Not to fear the terror (5a)
      b. Not to fear the arrow (5b)
      c. Not to fear the pestilence (6a)
      d. Not to fear the plague (6b)
   5. God Will Sustain You (7-10)
      a. You will escape disaster (7)
      b. You will only observe disaster (8)
      c. You will escape the harm (9-10)
   6. God Will Secure You (11-12)
      a. His angels will protect you (11)
      b. His angels will lift you up (12)
   7. God Will Strengthen You (13)
      a. To tread upon the lion (13a)
      b. To tread upon the cobra (13a)
      c. To trample the great lion (13b)
      d. To trample the serpent (13b)
C. Fellowship with a Personal God (14-16)
   1. He Enjoys a Loving Relationship with God (14)
      a. He loves God (14a)
      b. God will rescue him (14b)

       c. God will protect him (14c)
       d. He acknowledges God (14d)
  2. He Enjoys a Living Relationship with God (15-16)
       a. He calls upon God (15a)
       b. God will answer him (15b)
       c. God will be with him (15c)
       d. God will deliver him (15d)
       e. God will honor him (15d)
       f. God will satisfy him (16a)
       g. God will save him (16b)

Psalm 92

Exuberant Praise

"*Be not afraid of saying too much in the praises of God; all the danger is of saying too little.*"

M a t t h e w   H e n r y

Psalm 92

I. INTRODUCTION

For all Christians, Sunday is the Lord's day, a special day to gather together with other like-minded believers to worship God and honor Christ. While the Old Testament saints met for public worship on the Sabbath, the last day of the week (Exod. 20:8–11; Lev. 23:3), Christians in New Testament times assembled to offer public praise to God on the first day of the week (Acts 20:7; 1 Cor. 16:2). In addition to this designated time to render their weekly praise, believers should worship God every day. Worship is a lifestyle, a continual experience of magnifying the glory of God. This adoration should be carried out through a Christian's actions, thoughts, and words. Wherever we are, that place should be transformed into a palace for praise. Whatever we are doing, that activity should be a platform for worship. Ceaseless praise, all day every day, should be a living reality to every believer.

Nevertheless, the public gathering of God's people is always a special privilege and should be maximized to the fullest. But *how* should the Lord's day be observed? *How* should praise be brought to him? And *why?*

Psalm 92 gives helpful instruction in worshipping God in the public gathering of his people. The superscription on this psalm, *for the Sabbath day,* was originally intended to direct worshippers in their Sabbath worship of God. In the postexilic community, this psalm came to be sung in the temple on the Sabbath at the time of the morning sacrifice. It is an exuberant, joyful celebration of the person and work of God over the earth. All the particulars of praising God detailed here are equally applicable for New Testament worshippers today. Here is the rightness of (vv. 1–3), reason for (vv. 4–11), and results of (vv. 12–15) praising God. The guiding principle of this psalm is to be observed by all believers today.

II. COMMENTARY

MAIN IDEA: *The psalmist praises God in the Lord's house for his righteous rule over all.*

A The Rightness of Praise (92:1–3)

92:1. The central theme of this psalm is found in the very first verse. The psalmist exuded, **It is good to praise the LORD**. That is, worshipping God is fitting, the most reasonable thing to do. It is a glorious thing, precious and delightful, **to make music** to God's **name, O Most High** (cp. Ps. 7:17) as he is exalted above all others. He is to be worshipped because of the surpassing greatness of who he is and what he has done.

92:2–3. It is fitting **to proclaim** divine **love** and **faithfulness**, two theological truths about God prominently mentioned in the Psalms (cp. Pss. 85:7; 89:5). His **love** (*hesed*) refers to God's steadfast, loyal love, which is unconditionally directed toward his own people. Likewise, his faithfulness, which causes him to remain devoted to his believers, is cause for greatest praise, both **in the morning** and **at night**, or all day long.

B The Reasons for Praise (92:4–11)

92:4–5. In verses 4–6, the psalmist gives the reason praising God is so essential. He continues, **For you make me glad by your deeds**, referring to God's saving acts in delivering his people from their enemies (cp. vv. 10–11). **I sing for joy at the works of your hands**, pointing to what God has done in history. **How great are your works**, awesome and majestic, and **how profound**, meaning they are deep or incomprehensible, not immediately discernible to the average observer.

92:6–7. The senseless man, meaning one who is dull or stupid, a brute beast (Ps. 73:22), **does not know** how deep and profound are God's ways. Thus, he cannot praise him whom he does not understand. These who cannot see the great works of God are **the wicked**, and they **spring up like grass** and temporarily **flourish**, only to be, eventually, **forever destroyed**.

92:8–9. But, by dramatic contrast, **you, O LORD, are exalted forever**, ensuring the destruction of his enemies. **For surely your enemies**, the psalmist declared, **will perish** and **be scattered**. They cannot succeed long-term against God, who will see to it that they meet their deserved end.

92:10–11. You have exalted my horn is a picturesque way of saying that the psalmist triumphed in the face of much opposition. An animal **horn** represents strength, and **fine oils** that God has **poured upon** him picture much joy in the midst of labor. Thus, in face of this great difficulty, much divine enablement and heart celebration are given to the psalmist. He has every reason to praise God because he has witnessed **the defeat of my adversaries**.

C The Results of Praise (92:12–15)

92:12–13. This psalm concludes with an affirmation of the abundant blessing that rests upon the righteous who praise God. **The righteous will flourish like a palm tree**, bearing fruit in every season and circumstance of life. **They will grow like a cedar of Lebanon**, the largest trees of the Near East, a symbol of majestic size and strength. In contrast to the wicked who sprout up and wither like grass (v. 7), the righteous are **planted in the house of the LORD** and thus perennially **flourish**. Such vitality, stability, fruitfulness, and strength result from worshipping God.

92:14–15. They will still bear fruit in old age, never losing their spiritual vitality. **They will stay fresh and green**, full of godly virtues, all because they are rooted and grounded in God, continually worshipping him in both good times and bad times. They do not cease proclaiming, **The LORD is upright**, always doing what is blameless and right. God is **my Rock**, perfectly stable, **and there is no wickedness in him**, since he is absolutely holy.

III. CONCLUSION

It is important for Christians to gather faithfully on the Lord's day to give glory to God. This is a repeated emphasis of Scripture, even in this psalm. The New Testament says, "Let us not give up meeting together, as some are in the habit of doing, but let us encourage one another—and all the more as you see the Day approaching" (Heb. 10:25). Believers must make it a regular practice to come to God's house on God's day with God's people to hear God's Word and sing God's praises. Such a spiritual discipline is necessary for the vibrant faith of any believer. This psalm echoes this truth and becomes a strong exhortation to join with all the saints in worshipping him. May this song direct all hearts to praise God with enlightened minds and hearts.

IV. TEACHING OUTLINE

A. The Rightness of Praise (1-3)

    1. It Is Good to Praise the Lord (1)

        a. To make music to his name (1a)

        b. To make music to the most high (1b)

2. It Is Good to Proclaim to the Lord (2)
   a. His love in the morning (2a)
   b. His faithfulness at night (2b)
3. It Is Good to Play to the Lord (3)
   a. With the lyre (3a)
   b. With the harp (3b)

B. The Reasons for Praise (4-11)
1. Praise God for His Exploits (4-5)
   a. His deeds make me glad (4)
   b. His deeds are great (5a)
   c. His deeds are profound (5b)
   d. His deeds are inscrutible (6-7)
2. Praise God for His Exaltation (8-9)
   a. His exaltation is forever (8)
   b. His enemies are defeated (9)
3. Praise God for His Enablement (10-11)
   a. His horn is exalted (10a)
   b. His head is anointed (10b)
   c. His adversaries are defeated (11)

C. The Results of Praise (12-15)
1. The Righteous Are Spiritually Productive (12)
   a. Like a palm tree (12a)
   b. Like a Lebanon cedar (12b)
2. The Righteous Are Securely Planted (13)
   a. In the house of the Lord (13a)
   b. In the courts of our God (13b)
3. The Righteous Are Steadfastly Prolific (14)
   a. Bearing fruit in old age (14a)
   b. Staying fresh in old age (14b)
4. The Righteous Are Strongly Passionate (15)
   a. The Lord is upright (15a)
   b. The Lord is my rock (15b)
   c. The Lord is holy (15c)

Psalm 93

The Lord Reigns!

| Quote |

"*D*ivine sovereignty simply means that God is God."

A . W . Pink

Psalm 93

I. INTRODUCTION

The foundational truth of all Christian theology is that bedrock doctrine of all doctrines, the sovereignty of God. Here is the immovable mountain that towers above all theology, the Mount Everest of all truth. The absolute reign of God represents his undisputed right to govern all that he has created. God's reign is the continual, unhindered free exercise of his supreme authority over all. This must be the first article of doctrinal creed, the chief cornerstone of all divine truth. Every other doctrinal teaching must be brought into alignment with this God-exalting truth and rest squarely upon it. The sovereignty of God means, quite simply, that God *is* God, not merely in name but in full reality. That is, God always does *as* he pleases, *when* he pleases, *where* he pleases, *how* he pleases, *with whom* he pleases. Herein is the truth of divine sovereignty, his unrivaled right to rule over all the works of his hands.

Psalm 93 is an enthronement psalm, one which celebrates God's sovereign kingship over all the earth. The eternal, universal kingdom of the Lord is its unmistakable, central focus. This worship song is the first of a short series of theocratic psalms extending through Psalm 100. The phrase "The LORD reigns" is repeated in these psalms and punctuates this overarching message of divine sovereignty (Pss. 93:1; 96:10; 97:1; 99:1). To be sure, God reigns over every realm of his universe, whether it be over nature, nations, history, salvation, or the eternal destinies of men. Here is declared the undisputed, unrivaled sovereignty of God over heaven and earth.

II. COMMENTARY

MAIN IDEA: *The psalmist rejoices that God reigns triumphantly over all, even despite the sinful rebellion of human beings.*

A The Sovereign Reign of God (93:1–2)

93:1a–b. The psalmist begins this song with a declaration of the ultimate truth about God, the first reality to be established in worship. **The LORD reigns.** God is enthroned in the heavens, constantly exerting his will and exercising rule over everything. He is **robed in majesty**, describing the regal garments worn by a victorious king after a decisive conflict. God is so depicted here with regal grandeur, dignity, and stateliness. He is clothed with the apparel that attends the supremacy of a king's reign. Further, he is **armed with strength**, or the might appropriate to a victorious warrior king, a strength that overshadows all earthly kingships.

93:1c. Because God is Sovereign, **the world is firmly established**. Not only the physical planet, but the moral, social, and spiritual laws of this world order have been ordained by God himself. The Lord has put everything in its proper place, and it is fixed. His providential reign over the earth **cannot be moved** by men or nations. In spite of the threats of earthly powers, the eternal counsel of the Lord cannot be altered by the plans of mere man.

93:2. Further, **your throne was established long ago; you are from all eternity**. Uncreated and without beginning, God has eternally existed. He has supremely reigned from before time began, when he first decreed his eternal purpose for all that comes to pass (Eph. 1:4–5,11; 2:10). God has been the sovereign ruler since before the foundation of the world. His throne was long ago established, never to be overturned, usurped, or overrun.

B The Sinful Rebellion of the World (93:3–4)

93:3. In opposition to God's sovereignty is this rebellious world, ruined by man's fall into sin. **The seas have lifted up their voice; the seas have lifted up their pounding waves**. This roaring thunder from these chaotic waters is a poetic representation of the moral disorder present in the world, especially among the Gentile nations (cp. Isa. 17:12; Jer. 6:23; 50:42). Like the relentless pounding of the waves against the beach, the seas symbolize all that comes against and opposes the Lord's kingdom (Ps. 2:1–3). All the destructive powers of sin and Satan are embodied in this sea that threatens God's established order in and on the earth. Man's sinful rebellion is set against the sovereign Lord.

93:4. In spite of the sinful revolt of men, the strong resistance of God is far greater. **Mightier than the thunder of the great waters, mightier than the breakers of the sea—the LORD on high is mighty**. This is a clear assertion of

God's sovereignty over history and every human development that seeks to oppose his heavenly government. The truth is, God is mightier than all, and he freely exercises his unrivaled authority over all without any hindrance (Pss. 103:19; 115:3). Man proposes, but God disposes.

C The Sure Revelation of God (93:5)

93:5. This final stanza now declares two more characteristics of God's kingly rule. First, his kingdom is a kingdom of fixed law. The psalmist emphatically states, **Your statutes stand firm**. The Lord's commands are spoken and sure, never to be rescinded. His statutes are all life-giving directives for his people, forever the same, completely trustworthy (Ps. 19:7). Likewise, God is unchanging in his **holiness**, a transcendence and purity that **adorns your house for endless day**. God is eternal, absolutely holy, unchangeably perfect in his person and all his ways.

III. CONCLUSION

The Lord reigns supremely over all the earth. Let all God's people rejoice. All the sinful resistance of men cannot thwart his eternal purposes. All their rising up against God, like the rising waters of the sea, cannot succeed against him, who alone reigns on high. Therefore, all believers should confidently trust in the Lord, who causes all things to work together for their good. God is the sovereign King over everything. His universal reign has been established from all eternity past and will never come to an end. Let all believers have grand and lofty thoughts of the Lord, who alone is worthy of praise. Let God's people give him the glory due his name. *God* reigns. Not Satan, not man, not other gods. Not world rulers, not foreign powers, not circumstances, not random fate, but God. The Lord *reigns!*

IV. TEACHING OUTLINE

A. The Sovereign Reign of God (1-2)
   1. The Lord Is Enthroned (1)
      a. He is attired with majesty (1a)
      b. He is armed with might (1b)
   2. The World Is Established (2)
      a. It is fixed by God (2a)
      b. It cannot be moved (2b)
B. The Sinful Rebellion Against God (3-4)
   1. The Seas Have Lifted Up (3a)
      a. Their voice against God (3a)
      b. Their waves against God (3b)

  2. The Sovereign Is Over All (4)
   a. Mightier than the thunder (4a)
   b. Mightier than the breakers (4b)
 C. The Sure Revelation of God (5)
  1. His Statutes Stand Firm (5a)
  2. His Holiness Stands Out (5b)
   a. Adorning his house (5b)
   b. Enduring forever (5b)

Psalm 94
Unjust Suffering

"*T*hose who will not deliver themselves into the hand of God's mercy cannot be delivered out of the hand of His justice."

M a t t h e w   H e n r y

Psalm 94

I. INTRODUCTION

Believers often find themselves oppressed by the wicked, but when they do, they should leave vengeance with God. Rather than seeking their own retribution, the saints should patiently wait upon God, who pledges to judge all evil. Even when they are reeling under personal attack, God's people should never retaliate in like manner. Rather, they must live in peace with all men, leaving room for the wrath of God. Better to suffer unjustly and wait for God to make right a wrong than to take matters into one's own hands with fleshly retaliation. The attribute of divine wrath should bring both patience and peace to God's people, knowing that one day God will settle all accounts.

Psalm 94 is the inspired record of the psalmist's urgent cry to God, calling upon him to avenge the wrongs suffered at the hands of the ungodly. This psalm is a royal song, an appeal to God as "Judge of the earth" (v. 2) who "avenges" (v. 1) the attacks brought against the defenseless (v. 21) by the ungodly (vv. 3–7,16,20). How practical this psalm is. Surely the righteous often find themselves suffering attack in this world by evil people (Matt. 5:10–12; John 15:18–20; 16:33; 2 Tim. 3:12). This psalm is a model cry for help for all who are oppressed by ungodly leaders (v. 20) who abuse their power by dominating the innocent (v. 3). There is no superscription attached to this psalm, being anonymous as to the author and historical setting.

II. COMMENTARY

MAIN IDEA: *The psalmist appeals to God to judge the wrongs suffered at the hands of wicked rulers.*

A The Psalmist's Appeal (94:1–3)

94:1–2. This first stanza is an urgent appeal to **God** to **rise up** as the **Judge of the earth** and **pay back to the proud what they deserve**. Although the specific details are unknown, the wicked are revealed here as persecuting God's people. Thus, the psalmist pleads with God to **shine forth** in judgment to deal with their oppressors. Vengeance, or just retribution, belongs to **God** alone to inflict upon all violators of his holy law.

94:3. How long will God be, seemingly, slow to act, and thus, allow **the wicked** to **be jubilant**? This is a fervent plea for God to act immediately in judgment.

B The Psalmist's Accusation (94:4–7)

94:4. This second stanza voices the psalmist's indictment of the wicked. Here is a graphic picture of total depravity, involving the mouths, hands, thoughts, and wills of sinners. Their perverted mouths **pour out arrogant words** and **are full of boasting**. The perverse character of the unrighteous is revealed by their words.

94:5–6. Their hateful hands **crush** God's **people** and **slay** the defenseless, specifically, **the widow**, **the alien**, and **the fatherless**. Those who cannot stand for themselves are most vulnerable. Under such onslaught, God's people are vulnerable and defenseless.

94:7. Insanely, the sin-mangled minds of the wicked conclude, **The LORD does not see**. They foolishly think that God does not know what they are doing. This is the self-deceived condition of the godless. In their sinfulness, they are unable to see God and thus assume that he is ignorant of their actions.

C The Psalmist's Admonition (94:8–11)

94:8–9. The psalmist now utters a sober warning to these **senseless ones**, calling them to repent and forsake their wickedness. With simple but compelling logic, the psalmist reasons, **Does he who implanted the ear not hear?** The presumed answer is yes, he hears. God who made the human ear can surely himself hear the arrogant words of the wicked (v. 4). Again, he asks, **Does he who implanted the eye not see?** Of course, God can see their wicked ways. The one who created the human eye can himself see. How absurd to think otherwise.

94:10-11. Does he who disciplines nations not punish? Obviously, God avenges all wrongs, this in spite of what the wicked claim and think (v. 7). The truth is **the LORD knows the thoughts of man** and will act accordingly.

D The Psalmist's Assurance (94:12-15)

94:12. Shifting focus, the psalmist concentrates upon the favor bestowed by God on the righteous. **Blessed** ("happy, favored"; cp. Ps. 1:1) **is the man you discipline** as loving punishment for sin. That is, the evils God's people endure are, in actuality, designed by God for their spiritual good. A loving, all-wise God is always correcting and training his people, using even their adversity for eternal good.

94:13-15. Though the process is painful, God will **grant him relief from days of trouble**, namely, a relief from the adversity brought on by sin. Even while in the fire of tribulation, the Lord will never utterly **reject his people**. In all discipline, God's perfect **judgment** will be according to his **righteousness**, bringing about a positive result, causing **the upright in heart** to **follow** the truth of the law. For God's people, his discipline is always for their good.

E The Psalmist's Affirmation (94:16-19)

94:16. A personal testimony is now in order regarding the blessedness God offers when his people call out in the midst of their adversity. The psalmist asks, **Who will rise up for me against the wicked?** The implied answer is no person can deliver him.

94:17-19. Unless the LORD had given me help, the psalmist would have died. God himself rescued him out of his near-death experience. When he was about to be overwhelmed with **anxiety**, the Lord **supported** him with his steadfast, permanent **love** and **brought joy** to his **soul**. All this God did for him, even in troubling times, and he gladly declares it.

F The Psalmist's Alliance (94:20-23)

94:20. The psalmist now returns to the place he began this psalm, declaring God to be the Judge of all the earth. He renounces every **corrupt throne**, a reference to any position of authority occupied by a corrupt ruler who uses his power unjustly, especially in oppressing those who cannot defend themselves. The psalmist asks, **Can a corrupt throne be allied with you?** The anticipated answer is negative. A holy God cannot approve human corruption.

94:21-22. Although these wicked rulers **band together against the righteous**, seeking to take their lives, they, to be sure, are not in alliance with God, nor God with them. Instead, the psalmist declares his own unwavering alliance with God. The Lord has become his **fortress** (*misgob*) and **rock**. God alone provides him perfect protection.

94:23. Vengeance belongs to the Lord who will **repay** the wicked **for their sins** and utterly **destroy them** in the final judgment.

III. CONCLUSION

In the midst of unjust suffering at the hands of evil people, believers must always choose the right response. The proper reaction is recorded here. Here is the God-honoring way to endure persecution. When attacked by the wicked, believers should call upon the Lord, who alone vindicates the injuries brought against them. God is holy and righteous. He will avenge all wrongs inflicted upon his people. So let the godly seek the Lord in the hour of their most painful affliction. Let them patiently wait for God to arise and act in judgment against their enemies. Vengeance belongs to the Lord, not man. God will surely repay the wicked for their sins against the defenseless innocent. As God's people live in a world that is increasingly hostile toward Christ, this psalm will become increasingly relevant and precious.

IV. TEACHING OUTLINE

A. The Psalmist's Appeal (1-3)
   1. O God, Shine Forth (1)
   2. O Judge, Pay Back (2)
   3. O Lord, How Long? (3)
B. The Psalmist's Accusation (4-7)
   1. Their Words Are Prideful (4)
      a. They pour out arrogance (4a)
      b. They are full of boasting (4b)
   2. Their Works Are Perverted (5-6)
      a. They crush the believers (5)
      b. They stay the defenseless (6)
   3. Their Words Are Pompous (7)
      a. God does not see (7a)
      b. God does not care (7b)
C. The Psalmist's Admonition (8-11)
   1. Take Heed, Senseless Ones (8a)
   2. Become Wise, Foolish Ones (8b-11)
      a. Does not God hear? (9a)
      b. Does not God see? (9b)
      c. Does not God punish? (10a)
      d. Does not God know? (10b)
      e. God knows man's thoughts (11)

D. The Psalmist's Assurance (12-15)
  1. God's People Are Blessed (12-14)
     a. They are corrected by God (12)
     b. They are comforted by God (13)
     c. They are connected to God (14)
  2. God's People Are Rewarded (15)
     a. They will be judged in righteousness (15a)
     b. They will follow righteousness (15b)
E. The Psalmist's Affirmation (16-19)
  1. He Requested God's Help (16)
     a. Will God rise up for me? (16a)
     b. Will God stand for me? (16b)
  2. He Received God's Help (17-19)
     a. God delivered me from death (17)
     b. God supported me with love (18)
     c. God consoled me with joy (19)
F. The Psalmist's Alliance (20-23)
  1. God Promotes Holiness (20-21)
     a. A corrupt throne is not allied with God (20)
     b. A corrupt throng is allied against the godly (21)
  2. God Protects Believers (22)
     a. He is my Fortress (22a)
     b. He is my Rock (22b)
  3. God Punishes Unbelievers (23)
     a. He will repay them (23a)
     b. He will ruin them (23b)

Psalm 95

Worthy of Worship

Psalm 95

I. INTRODUCTION

Whenever a monarch of the British Empire ascends to the throne of England, the royal coronation is traditionally held at historic Westminster Abbey, London. This dramatic service has been the venue for every British ascension since 1066. On this solemn occasion, the sovereign-to-be proceeds to Westminster Abbey to the playing of "I Was Glad," accompanied by the acclamations of the Westminster Scholars, representing the shouts of approval of the people. The sovereign, seated in the coronation chair, is anointed with oil, followed by the crowning with St. Edward's crown. This is the most solemn moment of this august occasion.

The sovereign then rises from the coronation chair and moves to the throne, the first time the crowned king or queen is visible to the gathered dignitaries. This is when the monarch takes possession of the British Empire. The sovereign, now crowned and visible, is ready to receive the homage of the people. The archbishop speaks to the congregation three separate times, "I present to you [the sovereign's name]. Will you do her/him homage?" The people, seeing their sovereign now robed, crowned, and enthroned, respond three times with shouts of acclamation, "We will."

This is what the psalmist is doing in Psalm 95, but in a far greater way. The author is setting before the people of God their crowned Sovereign, the sole ruler of heaven and earth, God Almighty. In essence, he asks, "Will you give him the worship due his name?" The psalmist is eliciting the reader's "I will" to the invitation to worship their great and awesome God. Herein is the heart of worship. It is acknowledging the "worthship" of the true Sovereign, God himself. It is declaring his greatness and bowing before his throne. True worship is approaching God, lowering one's self in his presence, and adoring him, as a subject would kneel before his king and kiss his extended hand. God alone is worthy of such worship.

Psalm 95 is a passionate call to the people of God to praise the Lord, who is sovereign above all supposed gods, who are but lowly idols of gold, silver, wood, and stone. This worship psalm extends a fervent call to worship God, who is their Creator and Shepherd. Dramatically, it concludes with a warning to the people to avoid the unbelief of their forefathers. Such apostasy provokes the living God.

II. COMMENTARY

MAIN IDEA: *The psalmist calls God's people to worship the Lord by singing praises and bowing before him.*

A The What of Worship (95:1–2)

SUPPORTING IDEA: *The psalmist calls for God's people to sing and shout to the Lord.*

95:1. With dramatic beginning, the psalmist invites all God's people, **Come, let us sing for joy to the LORD**. The entire congregation is called to **sing for joy** to God, who alone is worthy to be praised. How celebrative and exuberant the saints should be in worshipping the Lord. Inviting all believers, he says, **let us shout aloud to the Rock of our salvation**, a metaphor referring to the rock from which the water in the wilderness flowed (Exod. 17:1–7; Num. 20:1–13). Ultimately, the rock is God himself, the people's steadfast sufficiency and security.

95:2. They should **come before him with thanksgiving** and express humble gratitude for his abundant provision, while magnifying his name **with music and song**. Singing expresses God's truth in a way that stirs the soul of the worshipper. True religion is not stoic, leaving worshippers emotionally flat, but it ignites the affections of the heart, especially with joy.

B The Why of Worship (95:3–5)

SUPPORTING IDEA: *Believers should worship God, who is the great King over all.*

95:3. God's people have every reason to worship him. The psalmist describes the first of those compelling reasons: **For the LORD is the great God**, meaning that he alone is God and is awesome. He is **the great King**

above all gods, ruling and reigning over all dumb idols, over all the mythical, imaginary gods of pagan religion. The psalmist exhorts the reader to worship the Lord because he is the one, true God.

95:4–5. Second, God should be worshipped because he holds all creation **in his hand**, both **the depths of the earth** and **the mountain peaks** and everything in between. God the Creator of everything also is the sustainer of all. The creation must show proper homage by worshipping the Creator. God is their maker, and both the **sea** and **dry land** belong to him. All that exists is his possession. So worship God, the Creator and sustainer of all.

The Way to Worship (95:6–7b)

SUPPORTING IDEA: *Believers should humble themselves before God in worship.*

95:6. This great God should be worshipped in the appropriate manner. **Bow down** (*shaha*) means to prostrate oneself, especially before a superior. Most specifically, "bow down" refers to an attitude of the heart, not necessarily a prostrated position. This word describes the total self-humiliation, submission, and adoration to be rendered by those who approach God.

95:7a–b. God's people should worship him **for he is our God**, indicating their personal intimate relationship with him. The Lord is their gracious Shepherd (Ps. 23:1), and thus, the psalmist says, **we are the people of his pasture, the flock under his care**. He is God, mighty, enthroned, ruling, yet tenderly caring for his own. God's people are like sheep—dumb, defenseless, and wayward. Thus, all worshippers should lower themselves before God, who gently leads and feeds his own people.

The When of Worship (95:7c–11)

SUPPORTING IDEA: *The psalmist calls for God to be worshipped now—today!*

95:7c–8a. With evangelistic zeal, the psalmist pressed his appeal: **Today, if you hear his voice, do not harden your hearts**. God was clearly speaking through his Word. The only question was: Were his people listening? Would they heed his voice in repentance and faith, or harden their hearts in unbelief? Hear (*shama*) means "to listen with strictest attention with a view to obedience." The first step of worship is to respond with submissive faith. There can be no true worship of God apart from a humble, obedient relationship with him.

95:8b–9. The psalmist gave a negative example from Israel's past for those who gathered to worship that day. Do not refuse God, he warned, **as you did at Meribah, as you did that day at Massah in the desert**. This notorious incident (Exod. 17:1–7) involved Israel's revolt against Moses, who brought God's message and led them into God's will. When the people rebelled against Moses, they, in reality, were rebelling against God himself. This disobedience **tested** God and **tried** him, provoking his patience, inviting his judgment and, more importantly, endangering their souls.

95:10–11. This wilderness episode of rebelling against God marked the people's lives for the next **forty years.** For the next four decades, God **was angry with that generation** because they went **astray** from his Word. Thus, they **have not known** by personal experience God's **ways.** Consequently, God said, **I declared on oath in my anger, "They shall never enter my rest."** This means that they were never to enter into the promised land of Canaan. Neither would they enjoy the fullness of God's favor and blessing. The message was clear. Israel must respond immediately with obedience whenever they hear his voice or forfeit divine blessings.

MAIN IDEA REVIEW: *The psalmist calls God's people to worship the Lord by singing praises and bowing before him.*

III. CONCLUSION

A man was touring an art gallery, observing the beautiful masterpieces on display. As he approached one painting in particular, he recognized it as a rendering of the crucifixion of Christ. He stopped and stared at its majestic brushstrokes and stunning depiction of Christ's death. As he was observing the painting, a tour guide approached him, motioning for him to lower himself. "If you want to truly appreciate the beauty of this painting, you must assume a lower position. The artist intended it to be viewed from a lower posture." So the man bent down.

"Lower," the guide responded, motioning with his flashlight. The man followed this instruction and bent over lower at the waist. "No, no," the persistent guide responded. "Lower still." Finally, the man was bowed down, kneeling on the carpet, looking up at the canvas painting. Only now from such a lowly posture could he behold and appreciate the true beauty of the masterpiece.

This is the only proper posture for worshipping God as well. All who would approach God must bow down before him. All worshippers must lower themselves in the Lord's presence. Those who would rightly approach God must look up from a humble posture if they are to behold the transcendent glory of God. Only in kneeling before him can we worship him as we should.

IV. LIFE APPLICATION

To be sure, there are a right way and a wrong way to worship God. Careful thought must be given to what distinguishes each of the two. It is dangerous, even life-threatening (Acts 5:1–11; 1 Cor. 11:29), to worship the Lord in a way that is offensive to him. How should God be worshipped? John 4:24 teaches that we must worship the Lord "in spirit and in truth." What does this mean?

1. *Worship in spirit.* Jesus meant that we must worship God with the proper heart attitude. The emphasis is not upon external religious rituals but upon the internal realities of a person's soul. The place of worship is irrelevant as it relates to the outward trappings such as the building's architecture and the worshipper's attire. What truly matters is the heart. So prepare your heart to worship. Humble yourself. Yield yourself to him.

2. *Worship in truth.* All true worship must be consistent with the written Scripture. Truth matters greatly in God-exalting worship. Theology produces doxology. The Word inspires worship. Worship is the proper response of the soul of man to the revelation of God through his written Word. Thus, all believers study the Scripture. They must sit under the Word and understand sound doctrine, rightly dividing the Word of truth. Only the truth from God leads to proper worship of God.

V. PRAYER

God, we believe that you have made us for yourself, to worship you and give you glory. We humbly bow before you. You are our Sovereign, and we gladly acknowledge your right to rule our lives. We bow before you this day and ascribe to you the greatness that belongs to you alone. In Jesus' name. Amen.

VI. DEEPER DISCOVERIES

A. Bow Down (95:6)

The phrase "bow down" (Heb. *shaha*) means "to prostrate oneself," especially before a superior (Gen. 18:2; 19:1; 43:26,28; 1 Sam. 24:8; 2 Sam. 9:8; 15:5), although rarely it is before an equal (Gen. 23:7; 1 Kgs. 2:19). The word occurs over 170 times in the Hebrew Bible, most often of prayer (Gen. 22:5; 1 Sam. 1:3). It is used most often of worshipping God (Exod. 11:8; 24:1; 33:10; Deut. 26:10; 1 Sam. 15:30; Isa. 27:13), but sometimes it describes idol worship (Deut. 8:19; 11:16; 30:17; Josh. 23:7; Judg. 2:19; 2 Chr. 7:19; 25:14). In ancient times, a person would fall down before someone who possessed a higher status. People would bow before a king to express complete submission to his rule. Following the example of the ancient people of faith, true Christian worship must express more than love for God; it must also express submission to his will.

B. Anger (95:10)

The Hebrew word for *anger* (*'aph*) (2 Kgs. 13:3; 17:11; 21:6,15; 22:17; 23:26; 24:20) signifies either "nose," "nostril," or "anger" (Gen. 2:7; Prov. 15:1). This term often occurs with words describing burning. Throughout the Old Testament, figures of speech such as "a burning nose" typically depict anger as the fierce breathing of a person through his nose (Exod. 32:10–12). Most of the Old Testament references using this word describe God's anger (Deut. 4:24–25; Ps. 103:8). The righteous anger of God is reserved for those who break his covenant (Deut. 13:17; 29:25–27; Josh. 23:16; Judg. 2:20; Ps. 78:38).

C. Rest (95:11)

The word *rest* (Heb. *shaqat*) (Josh. 1:13; 21:44; 22:4; 23:1) means "to be at peace." Rest implies freedom from anxiety and conflict. God promised the Israelites rest in the promised land (Exod. 33:14; Deut. 3:1–20; 12:9–10). In the Book of Joshua, the idea of rest is related specifically to the conflicts and hostilities Israel had with its neighbors. God promised his people a peaceful place to settle. Obtaining this rest depended on Israel's complete obedience to God's command to drive out the Canaanites (Josh. 11:23; 14:15). The New Testament writers also speak of the concept of rest. Christians are told that heaven will bring them rest from death, pain, sin, and all other earthly struggles (Heb. 4:1; Rev. 21:4).

VII. TEACHING OUTLINE

A.   The What of Worship (1-5)
  1. Sing Joyfully to Him (1a)
  2. Shout Loudly to Him (1b)
  3. Show Gratitude to Him (2a)
  4. Shout Joyfully to Him (2b)
B.   The Why of Worship (3-5)
  1. The Lord Is the Great God (3a)
  2. The Lord Is Above All Gods (3b)
  3. The Lord Is Above All Creation (4-5)
C.   The Way to Worship (6-7a)
  1. Come, Worship the Lord (6)
    a. Bow humbly before him (6a)
    b. Kneel lowly before him (6b)

    2. Consider Why Worship the Lord (7a,b)
       a. The Lord is our God (7a)
       b. The Lord is our Shepherd (7b)
D. The When of Worship (7c-11)
    1. Hear God's Voice Today (7c)
    2. Heed God's Voice Today (8-11)
       a. Not as when Israel resisted him (8)
       b. Not as when Israel tested him (9)
       c. Not as when Israel strayed from him (10-11)

Psalm 96

All Peoples, All Praise

"*B*efore Jehovah's awesome throne

Ye nations, bow with sacred joy;

Know that the Lord is God alone;

He can create; and He can destroy."

Isaac Watts

Psalm 96

I. INTRODUCTION

That God is absolutely sovereign over the nations is a truth that demands a reverential response from all people. How could any heart consider God's supreme authority and remain apathetic? Such silence is sinful, completely incongruent with the majesty of God. The unrivaled, worldwide rule of God demands the praise of all people everywhere. If the Lord were a mere regional deity, possessing only a limited dominion, then he should be adored only by the few who live under his localized government. But there is no restriction to his global dominion. The Lord is King over all the nations of the earth. Thus, he must be worshipped by every person. It is too small a thing, the pslamist argues, that he should be praised only by the remnant of Israel. Such would be far too small a congregation to declare God's true greatness. Because his sovereignty is extended over all nations, his praise must come from all peoples.

This call to all nations, imploring them to praise the Lord, is the central focus of Psalm 96. It is another enthronement psalm in which the reign of God is declared (v. 10) among "the nations" (vv. 3,5,7,10) and among "all peoples" (v. 3). Clearly, this is a psalm with a global perspective, calling for all to "worship" (v. 9) and "praise" (v. 2) the Lord, giving him "the glory due his name" (v. 8). Implied in this psalm is that God's people should go into the world and declare the sovereignty of the Lord to all nations. This is the only way that all peoples may come to worship God. Here is the highest purpose behind all evangelism. It is, ultimately, to add worshippers to the great choir of those who praise our sovereign God.

II. COMMENTARY

> **MAIN IDEA:** *The psalmist invites all the nations to praise the Lord as the one, true God.*

A The Invitation to Worship (96:1–3)

96:1–2. Issuing a worldwide summons, the psalmist invites **all the earth** to **sing to the** LORD. All creation is enjoined to **praise his name** by lifting to him **a new song**. This new song is contrasted with the old songs offered to pagan gods and dumb idols. These songs of **praise** should be offered to the one, true God for **his salvation**, a deliverance from sin and its consequences that can come only from the Lord. Likewise, **a new song** is offered for his new saving acts performed for his people. Such singing to God should occur **day after day**.

96:3. If all the earth is to praise the Lord, then God's people must, first, **declare his glory among the nations**. This calls for a bold, global evangelistic thrust by all believers. To **declare his glory** is to proclaim the greatness of God's **marvelous deeds**, who he is, and what he has done. This salvation is to be announced **among all peoples**.

B The Inspiration for Worship (96:4–6)

96:4–5. This second stanza expresses *why* all peoples should praise the Lord. Worship should be rendered because God is great and glorious (v. 6). God is **most worthy of praise** and **to be feared above all gods** because he alone is **great**. He is great in his attributes, great in his creative acts as when he **made the heavens** out of nothing, and great in his saving acts (v. 2). By comparison, all other so-called gods are nothing but dumb **idols**. The Lord is the one, true, living God, and thus worthy of praise.

96:6. Two pairs of divine attributes are personified as guardians of his throne. God's attributes of **splendor and majesty are before him**, radiating from his awesome holiness in heaven. **Strength and glory are in his sanctuary**, surrounding his royal enthronement. Such sovereign splendor should elicit the praise of all the people of the earth.

C The Instruction for Worship (96:7–9)

96:7–8. This third stanza describes *how* the Lord is to be praised and worshipped. First, worshippers are to **ascribe to the** LORD . . . **glory and strength**. They should declare that God alone possesses true glory and strength. All **nations**, without exception, should **ascribe to the** LORD **the**

glory due his name. This call prohibits the giving of praise to false idols, affirming a strict monotheism. The Lord is an intensely jealous God and will not share his glory with another. So **bring an offering** to God and **come into his courts**, the psalmist declared. True worship is purely theocentric and gives glory to God alone, not dumb idols.

96:9. Worship the LORD in the splendor of his holiness. Give him praise because of the unsurpassed greatness of **his holiness**. Describing God as holy represents all his divine perfections that set him apart from all creation. He, uniquely, is transcendent above and beyond his creation. When approaching such blazing holiness, people should **tremble before him** in reverential awe. Worshipping God is never a casual experience but soul-gripping, even traumatic.

D The Impact of Worship (96:10–13)

96:10. This final stanza is a passionate call to God's people to announce to all nations that **the LORD reigns**. All believers should declare that God rules over all the affairs of men. In spite of any chaotic appearances to the contrary, in spite of the turmoil and threats of the nations, **the world is firmly established**. All events and developments are under the overruling government of God. Although evil temporarily escapes unpunished, God **will judge the peoples with equity**. This final judgment of all mankind should be declared to the nations (Acts 17:31), bringing about their repentance unto eternal life. Such a proclamation will surely yield new worshippers of God.

96:11–12. The psalmist anticipates the day when all creation will respond enthusiastically to this proclamation: "the LORD reigns" (v. 10). **Let the heavens rejoice, let the earth be glad**. He calls on all nature to rejoice, including the **sea** and the **fields** and the **trees**. All peoples should rejoice in the sovereignty of God over human history.

96:13. This celebration of God's universal reign (vv. 11–12) looks ahead to the final consummation of human history, when Christ returns to the earth and **will judge the world in righteousness**. The Lord will come in the person of his Son, Jesus Christ, and **judge the earth** and **the peoples in his truth**. In that final day, perfect righteousness will be executed, the wicked will be punished, the righteous will be rewarded, and the Lord's reign will be established in all the earth. This is the confident hope of all who worship God in this present hour.

III. CONCLUSION

Let this message—"the Lord reigns"—be declared far and wide to all nations and peoples. God is enthroned in the heavens and reigns over all the earth. There is only one Sovereign, God himself. May this God-exalting truth be proclaimed to all the earth. God alone is seated on high, and his government rules over all. This theme of his universal reign should promote a missionary zeal throughout the earth. There is no conflict between divine sovereignty and worldwide missions. The former fuels the latter. Both Scripture and church history substantiate this fact. This psalm demands that all believers participate in global evangelism in one way or another, whether by going, praying, supporting, or training. It is encumbent upon the church to take this message of God's supremacy into all the earth and say to them, "The Lord reigns!" Let God's people say to the world, "Come bow down before God in repentance and faith in his Son!"

IV. TEACHING OUTLINE

A. The Invitation to Worship (1-3)
   1. Sing to God (1-2)
      a. What: a new song (1a)
      b. Who: all the earth (1b)
      c. How: praise his name (2a)
      d. When: day after day (2b)
   2. Speak of His Glory (3)
      a. Where: among all nations (3a)
      b. What: his marvelous deeds (3b)

B. The Inspiration for Worship (4-6)
   1. The Lord Is Great (4-5)
      a. He is above all gods (4-5a)
      b. He is above all creation (5b)
   2. The Lord Is Glorious (6)
      a. Splendor and majesty are his (6a)
      b. Stength and glory are his (6b)

C. The Instruction for Worship (7-9)
   1. Give Glory to God (7-8a)
   2. Give Offerings to God (8b)
   3. Give Worship to God (9a)
   4. Tremble Before God (9b)

D. The Impact of Worship (10-13)
   1. Declare God's Sovereignty (10)
      a. The Lord reigns over the earth (10a, b)
      b. The Lord judges the peoples (10c)
   2. Delight in God's Supremacy (11-12)
      a. Let the heavens rejoice (11a)
      b. Let the earth resound (11a-12)
   3. Declare God's Settlements (13)
      a. The Lord is coming (13a)
      b. The Lord is Judge (13b,c,d)

Psalm 97
A God-Centered Worldview

Psalm 97

I. INTRODUCTION

The vantage point from which one views all of life is often referred to as a worldview. Such an all-inclusive perspective is the lens through which one sees world history, society, culture, education, philosophy, art, music, and the like. One's worldview is the paradigm through which a person sizes up life and tries to understand it as one cohesive unit of thought. A worldview answers the basic philosophical questions such as: *Who* am I? *Why* am I here? *Where* did I come from? *Where* am I going? *What* is reality? *What* is the state of the world in which I live?

There is no shortage of worldviews from which to answer these questions. Be it biblical theism, dualism, humanism, fatalism, deism, synergism, secularism, relativism, pragmatism, positivism, or hedonism, many worldviews are possible. But the reality is, there is one—and only one—true and adequate worldview. Only the belief system that God actively, moment by moment, rules over all things for his own glory and for the good of his people will suffice. This is the comprehensive worldview presented in the Bible and, specifically, in the Psalms.

Psalm 97 is a worship song that succinctly declares a God-centered worldview. It provides an all-inclusive vision of the world through the lens of God's holy attributes and divine character. This psalm is yet another enthronement psalm (Pss. 93–100), which declares the absolute sovereignty of God over all creation. Having a correct worldview begins with having a proper view of God himself. Nothing on the earth will make any sense until one has first beheld God in his supreme glory, high and lifted up in heaven. This psalm provides great help in giving a theocentric vision of all things.

II. COMMENTARY

MAIN IDEA: *The psalmist rejoices in God's righteous reign over all the earth.*

A God Is Sovereign (97:1)

97:1. The psalmist begins with the familiar refrain, **The LORD reigns**. This declaration means that God is absolutely sovereign over all human history. It states that God does only and always as he pleases, continually exercising his all-inclusive authority. **Let the earth be glad** is the only rightful response appropriate to this grand truth of divine sovereignty. The **earth** represents the large land masses of the globe. The **distant shores** represent the smallest land areas of the earth.

B God Is Severe (97:2–6)

97:2. **Clouds and thick darkness** represent a violent storm of divine wrath soon to break upon the earth in the last days. Having been introduced to the throne of God (i.e., "the LORD reigns") (v. 1), **the foundation of his throne** is now revealed. Here is an angry thunderstorm with violent flashes of lightning on earth, unleashed and directed from God's throne. Here is a destructive storm brewing in heaven around God's throne, ready to break on the earth and inflict terrifying fury. **Righteousness and justice** refer to God's strict judgment of sinners when he will preside over their lives, examining the evidence, rendering his verdict, and executing his sentence.

97:3. **Fire** represents the divine wrath and fury that **goes before** God. It is the unquenchable fire of his wrath, full of the flames of his vengeance, to be unleashed on a Christ-rejecting world. Literally, **his foes** will be burned up like a dry log, consumed by his fury. This divine wrath will in the last day burn up all who reject the Lord Jesus Christ.

97:4–5. **His lightning lights up the world; the earth sees and trembles.** The entire world population will be thrown into convulsions in the day of judgment. The entire earth will experience a monumental meltdown in cataclysmic fashion **before the LORD**.

97:6. In response to this divine wrath, the redeemed in the **heavens** will lift up their voices and **proclaim his righteousness**. The redeemed will magnify the triumph of these righteous divine judgments on the earth. In the end, Christ himself will come in blazing **glory**. When he bursts on the scene, every eye will **see** him for who he is.

God Is Solitary (97:7–9)

97:7. In this final hour of human history, the irreversible judgment of God will be executed. All false religions will be exposed for what they are—nothing but man-made lies, satanic-inspired shams, and soul-damning deceptions. All sham, satanic religions are an offense to the one, true God. Such practice will end in their **shame**. Metaphorically, all these false **gods** are called on to bow their knee to the one, true God and **worship him**. Moreover, those who follow these gods must repent.

97:8. Zion, Jerusalem, and the **villages of Judah** (Israel) rejoice because of the Lord's **judgments**. God's judgments in the last days will reveal that he alone is the solitary God. There is none other than God.

97:9. The psalmist declares that God alone is God. He only is **Most High** (Gen. 14:19) and is elevated over all, **exalted far above** all other so-called **gods**.

God Is Savior (97:10–12)

97:10. God's people are called to **hate** all **evil**, not coddle it. Believers must reject all sin, never compromise with it. To the extent that a person loves the Lord, he will hate evil. Loving God increases hating evil. Whenever a person compromises with evil, it is only because he or she has become lukewarm toward God. God **guards the lives of his faithful ones**, his true believers. God **delivers** believers **from the hand of the wicked**, not always from death but always from final harm inflicted by unbelievers.

97:11. Light pours out on **the righteous**, a reference to the true knowledge of God. Such outshining revelation illumines the souls of the righteous, who grow in their personal relationship with God. Light also means that they grow in their understanding of the truth in God's Word and in personal holiness. The result of this divine light is **joy**. The knowledge of God and the pursuit of holiness produce joy.

97:12. The psalmist concludes by calling on all believers to **rejoice in the** Lord. Rightly should they exult in God himself and in his kingdom. All true joy is in the Lord. The fact that "the Lord reigns" (v. 1) makes the heart glad. Knowing that God is causing all things to work together for our good and for his glory (Rom. 8:28) is cause for deepest gladness.

III. CONCLUSION

God is absolutely sovereign over all the works of his hands. This is the firm foundation of all Christian truth. The supremacy of God over all creation is the center of gravity of all Christian doctrine. This core biblical teaching is the sun around which all the lesser planets of subordinate truth circulate. Either God is sovereign over all, or he is not sovereign at all. There can be no partial sovereignty—only that which is absolute. The sovereignty of God is the continental divide of all theology. One drop of man-centered thought runs down the other side of the mountain into creeks, streams, and rivers, ultimately to pour into an ocean of man-centered worship, living, and ministry. Yet, conversely, one drop of theocentric truth that is rooted in this statement—"the LORD reigns"—flows down the opposite side of the mountain. Such biblical truth empties into an ocean of God-centered worship, living, and ministry. May God's people always put God in his rightful place in their minds, hearts, and lives. The Lord alone is the One who rules over all.

IV. TEACHING OUTLINE

A. God Is Sovereign (1)
  1. The Lord Reigns (1a)
  2. The Earth Rejoices (1a,b)
B. God Is Severe (2-6)
  1. The Lord Judges (2-4a)
    a. Clouds and darkness surround him (2a)
    b. Righteousness and justice uphold him (2b)
    c. Fire goes before him (3)
    d. Lightning lights up the world (4a)
  2. The Earth Trembles (4b)
    a. The world shakes (4b)
    b. The mountains melt (5)
  3. The Heavens Proclaim (6)
    a. The heavens shout his righteousness (6a)
    b. The people see his glory (6b)
C. God Is Solitary (7-9)
  1. Idolators Are Shamed (7a,b)
  2. Idols Are Taunted (7c)
  3. Israel Hears and Rejoices (8-9)
    a. God's executions are over all (8-9a)
    b. God's exaltation is over all (9b)
D. God is Savior (10-12)
  1. God Guards the Faithful (10a,b)
    a. Those who love him (10a)
    b. Those who live for him (10b)
  2. God Delivers the Faithful (10c)
  3. God Enlightens the Upright (11)
  4. God Gladdens the Righteous (12)

Psalm 98

Highest Praise

> "*T*he first foundation of righteousness
>
> undoubtedly is the worship of God."

John Calvin

Psalm 98

I. INTRODUCTION

When God saves a sinner, it is always a glorious triumph of his sovereign grace. This is the greatest of all miracles—the salvation of a human soul. In this divine act of mercy, God plants a new song of praise within the newly converted heart. In the divine act of regeneration, the redeemed become genuine worshippers of the one, true, living God. Here is the highest purpose of our salvation. It is that more voices join in the magnification of the glory of God. God saves those ruined by sin so that, ultimately, heaven and earth will be filled with true worshippers who magnify his grace.

But worship is far more than merely singing to the Lord one day a week. In its fullest reality, worship involves an ongoing lifestyle, one that encompasses every moment of every day, living for the glory of God in all that one does. A person's entire life is to be one continuous worship service, always bringing glory to God in all that he or she does. In the midst of life's daily routine, there is to be a song of praise that *must* be sung. God seeks perpetual praise and worship from his people. Everyone has been created for this high and holy purpose of giving glory to God.

Psalm 98 is a royal psalm written to celebrate the righteous reign of God. Psalms 93–100 are a cluster of royal psalms that celebrate the lofty enthronement of God over all the earth. Psalm 98 has three stanzas of three verses each, a total of nine verses. There are three unfolding aspects of God for which the psalmist praises God: as Savior (vv. 1–3); as Sovereign (vv. 4–6);

and as Judge (vv. 7–9). Let all people give praise to God for these three awesome truths.

II. COMMENTARY

> **MAIN IDEA:** *The psalmist calls all creation to worship the Lord as Savior, Sovereign, and Judge.*

A Sing to Our Saving God (98:1–3)

98:1. This first stanza is a call to **sing** with exuberance and celebration a **new song** to God. This means to offer fresh praise because of some new act of his grace. The reason for this call is clear: **He has done** wonderful **things**. This refers to his saving acts on behalf of his people, divinely intervening with both eternal and temporal salvation. No sinner is beyond God's saving power. No situation is beyond his rescuing power. With **his right hand and his holy arm**, he has **worked salvation**. God's hand and arm symbolize his great strength and power in his saving work. Because he is holy, there is no other way for unholy man to find acceptance with him except through his salvation.

98:2. God is a saving God whose very nature is to save. Therefore, he has made **his salvation known**, even to the nations, a salvation that reveals **his righteousness**. In regard to temporal salvation from earthly trials, he is righteous, rewarding the godly and punishing the ungodly. Regarding eternal salvation, he provided the righteousness that the ungodly sinner needs to be reconciled to God through his Son, Jesus Christ.

98:3. He has remembered his loyal, steadfast, and unalterable **love and his faithfulness to the house of Israel**. God's commitment to save his chosen people is unchanging and eternal. **All the ends of the earth** have seen God's **salvation**. He is the Savior not only of those in Israel who believe but of all peoples around the world who trust him. Far from every person being saved, rather, this teaches that God's salvation reaches out to all peoples. The wicked will perish (Ps. 1:6). God is worthy of praise because he is a powerful, holy, righteous, loving, faithful Savior forever.

B Sing to Our Sovereign Lord (98:4–6)

98:4–6a. The psalmist addressed **all** people on **the earth** and called every creature to **shout for joy to the LORD**. There is only one true God, and all the earth must worship him. They must forsake their pagan gods and dumb idols. Here is the highest purpose of evangelism—that there would be increased numbers of worshippers of the Lord. Pardon is secondary; praise is primary. Specifically, God should be praised with music. The psalmist called for loud, lively music to be given with the **harp and the sound of singing**, as well as with **trumpets** and the **ram's horn**. Such **jubilant song** should be given in the praise of God's name.

98:6b. Shout . . . before the LORD, the King is a summons to worship issued to all peoples of the earth. Give glory to God. There is no god like heaven's King.

C Sing to Our Severe Judge (98:7–9)

98:7–8. This last stanza calls all creation to make music to praise God, the righteous Judge. **Let the sea resound, and everything in it**. The ocean and all marine life within it were created for God's glory. The dry land **and all who live in it** are beckoned to praise. The **rivers** are to **clap their hands** unto the Lord as they carry his praise across the continents, rejoicing and celebrating in God. **The mountains** that tower over the land are to **sing together for joy**. Let every feature of the earth clap and sing for joy **before the LORD**.

98:9. God will come to **judge the earth** with **righteousness** and **equity**. God will have the last word in every matter and deal with every offense. God will decisively judge wickedness and reward all righteousness. This looks ahead prophetically to the future coming of God's Son, the Lord Jesus Christ, the One to whom he has committed all judgment (Acts 17:31). The call to praise God is, in reality, the call to praise his Son (Ps. 2:7,12). May Jesus Christ be praised!

III. CONCLUSION

Throughout the ages, God has eternally existed, perfectly fulfilled within his triune majesty, without sense of emptiness or loneliness, as if needing to be gratified by others. But in his lovingkindness, God the Father created the earth and all that is in it so the Father might express his love for his Son. The Father chose a people so there would be a people to praise the Son. God created all people for this purpose (Phil. 2:9–11). He expanded salvation far beyond Israel so that his redeemed community might include those among the nations who believe. God is the glorious Savior who redeems sinners by providing for them his own righteousness in his Son, Jesus Christ. He is the sovereign Lord who providentially rules over all the earth in his Son, Jesus Christ. He is the severe Judge of all peoples, having appointed his Son, the Lord Jesus Christ, to judge each person righteously. May every heart declare the excellencies of God's Son, Jesus Christ, to the honor of God the Father.

IV. TEACHING OUTLINE

A. Sing to Our Saving God (1-3)
  1. How He Is to Be Praised (1a)
    a. With singing (1a)
    b. With a new song (1b)

     2. Why He Is to Be Praised (1b-3)

        a. He has done wondrous things (1a)

        b. He has performed salvation (1b)

        c. He has revealed salvation (2)

        d. He has remembered love (3a)

        e. He has retained faithfulness (3b)

B. Sing to Our Sovereign Lord (4-6)

     1. How He Is to Be Praised (4-6b)

        a. With shouts of joy (4a)

        b. With jubilant song (4b)

        c. With the harp (5)

        d. With trumpets (6a)

     2. Why He Is to Be Praised (6b)

        a. He is Lord (6b)

        b. He is King (6b)

C. Sing to Our Severe Judge (7-9)

     1. How He Is to Be Praised (7-9a)

        a. Let the sea resound (7a)

        b. Let the world resound (7b)

        c. Let the rivers clap (8a)

        d. Let the mountains sing (8b-9a)

     2. Why He Is to Be Praised (9b,c,d)

        a. He came to judge the earth (9b)

        b. He will judge in righteousness (9c)

        c. He will judge in equity (9d)

Psalm 99

Absolute Sovereignty

"*A*bsolute sovereignty is what I love to ascribe to God. God's sovereignty has ever appeared to me, a great part of His glory. It has often been my delight to approach God, and adore Him as a sovereign God."

Jonathan Edwards

Psalm 99

I. INTRODUCTION

The most basic, underlying truth of all biblical theology is the fact of the sovereignty of God. Unwavering in carrying out his eternal purposes, unhindered by man's decisions to the contrary, God reigns supremely in absolute authority, the unrivaled ruler over heaven and earth. The entire universe is under his ominpotent rule. This truth prompted A. W. Pink to write, "Divine sovereignty means that God is God in fact, as well as in name, that he is on the Throne of the universe, directing all things, working all things after the counsel of his own will." That is, God always does as he pleases. God *alone* is sovereign and no other.

Absolute sovereignty is the message of Psalm 99, a worship song that trumpets the now familiar refrain, "The LORD reigns" (Pss. 93:1; 96:10; 97:1; 99:1). This psalm is an enthronement psalm (Pss. 93–100), one designed to affirm God's rule over the earth. It is a potent hymn, celebrating the Lord as the great and awesome King in Zion, who rules over all. It extols God for delivering his people while judging the nations. There are four stanzas of three Hebrew lines each, different in the English, giving this psalm perfect symmetry. A repeating refrain, "He is holy" (vv. 3,5,9), punctuates this song with a regal feel.

II. COMMENTARY

MAIN IDEA: *The psalmist declares the sovereignty of God over all the earth.*

A The Declaration of God's Sovereignty (99:1–3)

99:1. This psalm begins exuberantly with the proclamation of the absolute, unconditional sovereignty of God: **The LORD reigns**. No matter how much this world is beset with turmoil, this fact remains: God is enthroned. In response, all the people are called upon to **tremble**—to be deeply moved and disturbed, even thrown into commotion. All people should be moved with fear, with reverential awe, toward such a Sovereign. Presiding over history, God **sits enthroned** and actively reigns. The **cherubim**, a special order of angels, dwell in the immediate presence of God, guarding his enthronement. This fact should cause **the earth to shake**, sending reverberations through human hearts.

99:2. The LORD is **great**, towering over everything, possessing absolute dominion in the heavenly **Zion**. He is exceedingly great in authority, power, and sovereignty. His sovereignty is not restricted to Israel. He is not just a regional God with limited jurisdiction but is **exalted over all** the kingdoms and empires of men. All peoples are under his control.

99:3. In response, let all the nations and peoples **praise your great and awesome name**. As King, God must be given the honor due his name. **He is holy**, set apart from his creation, separated, transcendent, high and lifted up, above and beyond his creation, utterly distinct and different from it.

B The Description of God's Sovereignty (99:4–5)

99:4. **The King**, a lofty, regal designation for God, **is mighty**, able to do all that he pleases. Moreover, he **loves justice**. He delights in using his sovereignty with perfect equity and fairness. His power is never misused but is always exercised properly. God's **equity** means his righteousness, or his right set of rewards and punishments. God always does what is **just** and **right**.

99:5. The psalmist calls upon everyone to **exalt the LORD our God**. As God is exalted, this calls upon all to recognize his high exaltation by lifting high his name in praise. **Worship at his footstool**, the psalmist declared. In ancient times, the king's **footstool** was immediately before his throne as a low piece of furniture on which he rested his feet. It represented a lowly position before him, or one being prostrate before him, assuming deep humility and profound reverence. That God is **holy** is the strongest reason for lowering ourselves before him.

C The Demonstration of God's Sovereignty (99:6–7)

99:6. **Moses, Aaron,** and **Samuel** witnessed God's sovereignty. They **called on his name**; and, in spite of the difficulty of their requests, the Lord **answered them.** Divine sovereignty operates in perfect concert with man's prayers, not independent of them. His reign does not bypass people but works in and through their minds, hearts, wills, and actions. God's sovereignty is never contrary to human responsibility. Whenever God desires to do a work, he stirs up a people to pray to that end. God in his sovereignty **answered them.** Providence is God working in this world, causing all things to work together for his glory and for our good.

99:7. In response to the prayers of his people in the wilderness, the Lord answered and provided them divine direction with the **pillar of cloud** (cp. Exod. 13:21–22; Num. 12:5; Deut. 31:15). Further, God directed them through his written Word, his **decrees** and **statutes.** God will do the same in every generation.

D The Delight in God's Sovereignty (99:8–9)

99:8. The psalmist concluded by boasting in God. **You answered them** refers to their cries for deliverance. Yet in spite of God's rescue of his people, they had to live with many of the painful consequences of their sins. In God's dealings with his people, he is **forgiving,** pardoning, and restoring, the God of a second chance. At the same time, he is also a disciplining God, punishing **their misdeeds,** correcting and reproving.

99:9. The psalmist exhorted all to **exalt the LORD our God.** This repeats his familiar refrain declared earlier (v. 5), reinforced again for climactic emphasis. This was a call to come to the **holy mountain,** Mount Zion, to **worship** God. The Lord requires that his people come together publicly to worship him. The reason for this God-exalting adoration is compelling: **For the LORD our God is holy.** Because God is set apart, his people should set themselves apart from the world when they worship him. God is completely set apart from all his creatures, totally separate, unlike his people. Therefore, believers should come together by setting themselves apart in worshipping him.

III. CONCLUSION

God's sovereignty should be the major theme of all believers' lives. It should be the dominant note in every worship service, just as it was in ancient Israel so long ago. "The Lord reigns" should be the central tenet of all that the church preaches, teaches, and sings. God reigns in glory and grace.

Let his people revere him. May all believers glory in this transcendent truth that God rules and reigns in the heavens and does whatever he pleases.

Charles H. Spurgeon once wrote, "Opposition to divine sovereignty is essentially atheism. Men have no objection to a god who is really no God, a god who shall be the subject of caprice, who shall be a servile follower of their will, who shall be under their control. But a God who speaks and it is done, who commands and it stands fast, a God who does as he will among the armies of heaven and among the inhabitants of this lower world, such a God as this they cannot endure. And yet, is it not essential to the very being of God that he should be absolute and supreme? Certainly to the scriptural conception of God, sovereignty is an absolute necessity."

To this, all who love God can declare, "Amen!" Let the church rejoice that God is sovereign and with the psalmist declare this truth far and wide.

IV. TEACHING OUTLINE

- A. The Declaration of God's Sovereignty (1-3)
  - 1. The Rightful Recognition (1-3)
    - a. The Lord is reigning (1a)
    - b. The Lord is enthroned (1b)
    - c. The Lord is great (2a)
    - d. The Lord is over the nations (2b)
    - e. The Lord is awesome (3a)
    - f. The Lord is holy (3b)
  - 2. The Rightful Response (1b, 2b, 3)
    - a. Let the nations tremble (1b)
    - b. Let the earth shake (2b)
    - c. Let the peoples praise (3)
- B. The Description of God's Sovereignty (4-5)
  - 1. The Rightful Recognition (4)
    - a. The King is mighty (4a)
    - b. The King loves justice (4a)
    - c. The King fixes equity (4b)
    - d. The King does right (4b)
  - 2. The Rightful Response (5)
    - a. Exalt the Lord (5a)
    - b. Worship the Lord (5b)
- C. The Demonstration of God's Sovereignty (6-7)
  - 1. The Rightful Recognition (6a-c)
    - a. Moses called upon God (6a)
    - b. Aaron called upon God (6a)
    - c. Samuel called upon God (6b, c)

      2. The Rightful Response (6d-7)
        a. God answered them (6d)
        b. God spoke to them (7a)
        c. They obeyed God (7b)
D. The Delight in God's Sovereignty (8-9)
      1. The Rightful Recognition (8)
        a. God answered them (8a)
        b. God forgave them (8b)
        c. God punished them (8b)
      2. The Rightful Response (9)
        a. Exalt the Lord (9a)
        b. Worship the Lord (9b)

Psalm 100
Into His Courts

"*G*od wants worshippers before workers; indeed, the

only acceptable workers are those who have learned

the art of worship."

A . W . T o z e r

I. INTRODUCTION

Worship can be vividly portrayed as a redeemed subject of God's kingdom, entering the throne room above, coming before God, and ascribing to him the glory due his name. In all true worship, the believer approaches God in humility, entering his courts above with awe. He beholds God's transcendent majesty and, in response, declares his greatness. This involves, first, a vision of God, which leads, second, to expressing thankfulness for his many blessings and offering praise for his glorious name. Herein is the true essence of worship. As a citizen of the heavenly kingdom, the saint enters the courts of the divine throne room in order to have an audience before the King of the universe. Bowing before his supremacy, the believer renders praise and adoration to God. In so doing, he is overwhelmed with gratitude for God's glory and grace. This is the heartbeat of worship.

Psalm 100 graphically captures this heavenly throne scene, one in which worshippers enter God's inner courts, bringing the praises due their King. This psalm is very short, only five verses in length, yet powerfully poignant in what it summons from every heart. Seven imperatives give this psalm a rapid-fire cadence, those verbs being "shout" (v. 1), "worship" (v. 2), "come" (v. 2), "know" (v. 3), "enter" (v. 4), "give thanks" (v. 4), and "praise" (v. 4). These form the skeleton of this much-loved psalm, breaking it into two divisions.

First, there is an initial call to worship God (vv. 1–3), and second, a further invitation to do the same (vv. 4–5). The superscription identifies this as *a psalm for giving thanks,* the only psalm which is so designated as one, specifically, of thanksgiving.

II. COMMENTARY

> **MAIN IDEA:** *The psalmist calls upon all the earth to praise the Lord because he alone is God and is good.*

A Approaching God (100:1–2)

100:1. With a highly charged burst of energy, the psalmist exclaims, **Shout for joy to the LORD**. This is the homage—shout, or fanfare (98:6)—given to a king (66:1; 95:1). This shout is one of loyalty ascribed by a subject to his sovereign (i.e., "Long live the king!") (1 Sam. 10:24). This call to declare allegiance to God goes out to the entire world. Clearly, there is only one God over **the earth** (v. 4), and he alone, not some dumb idol, is to be praised. This summons presupposes that all nations must be brought to the Lord before they can rightly give such praise.

100:2a. Expanding upon the first imperative, the psalmist adds a second command: **Worship the LORD with gladness**. Worship, literally "serve," suggests that we serve God with our worship, or that we minister to him with our praise. This is to be done with gladness, or a rejoicing heart that knows and loves God.

100:2b. The third imperative is **Come before him with joyful songs**. This injunction refers to times of formal worship, later defined in this psalm as coming through the gates of the temple and into its courts. The point is that worshippers are regularly to come before him, in public services, which are designed for God's people to magnify his name (Heb. 10:24–25).

B Apprehending God (100:3)

100:3. The fourth imperative is **Know that the LORD is God** and reveals *why* we must give praise to God. With deepest, personal conviction, worshippers must know that the Lord, Yahweh, is the one, true, living God. This statement of monotheism is the most basic of all theological truths. There is no God but the Lord, who alone reigns over all. This fact of God's sole existence is seen by his exclusive power to create. Thus, the psalmist affirms, **It is he who made us, and we are his**. God alone has made everything out of nothing. Thus, he has made his people for himself. **We are his people, the sheep of his pasture**. Having made us, he now cares for us as a shepherd nurtures his flock. He alone is to be praised.

C Adoring God (100:4–5)

100:4. The second stanza of the psalm is a repeated invitation to worship God, encompassing the call to offer **thanksgiving** to God. This begins with the fifth imperative—**Enter his gates with thanksgiving**, referring to the front **gates** that lead into the temple area. It is through these gates that expectant worshippers must enter to participate in public worship. They must also come into **his courts with praise**. Thus, he repeats his twofold plea, saying, **give thanks to him and praise his name**. The sixth and seventh imperatives are highly charged commands that call for a wholehearted response. Authentic praise should be permeated with much thanksgiving offered to God, recalling the abundant blessings that have come from him. Worshippers should live under the constant theme of gratitude to God.

100:5. This final verse, a repeating of verse 3, explains *why* all people should praise God. All worship has its reasons. Here, it is prompted by God's goodness, love, and faithfulness. **For the LORD is good**, God himself being the source of every blessing that comes to his people (Jas. 1:17). **His love endures forever**, there being no end to the flow of his perfect goodness to his people. **His faithfulness continues through all generations**, again emphasizing the endless goodness of God toward his own. God, who has been **good** in the past, will be so forever. Therefore, praise him always!

III. CONCLUSION

Approaching God is a high privilege for all believers. Such an audience before heaven's King should be carried out with the reverence of one coming before the monarch of the universe. In any monarchy, a citizen who would approach his king must know the proper protocol and respectful behavior upon entering the royal court. Misbehavior would insult his sovereign. So it is in worshipping God. All believers must come properly before God's throne in worship. Such a privileged audience before the sovereign King requires gladness of heart, joyful singing, expressions of thanksgiving, and songs of praise. May all God's people approach him in this prescribed manner. He is the Sovereign, his people are his subjects. So enter his courts with praise.

IV. TEACHING OUTLINE

A. Approaching God (1-2)

1. Acclaim Him with Joy (1)

2. Adore Him with Gladness (2a)

3. Acknowledge Him with Singing (2b)

  B. Apprehending God (3)
     1. He Alone Is Our God (3a)
     2. He Alone Is Our Creator (3b)
     3. He Alone Is Our Shepherd (3c)
  C. Adoring God (4-5)
     1. Enter His Gates with Thanksgiving (4a, c)
     2. Enter His Courts with Praise (4b, 5)
       a. Because he is good (5a)
       b. Because he is loving (5b)
       c. Because he is faithful (5c)

Psalm 101

Personal Integrity

"*The* plainer the diamond, the more it sparkles; the plainer the heart, the more it sparkles in God's eyes."

T h o m a s   W a t s o n

I. INTRODUCTION

In this present hour, personal integrity is fast becoming an endangered species. Everywhere one looks, once highly esteemed values of an upright character are vanishing. Scandals dominate the headlines. Business tycoons sell stock illegally. Government officials accept kickbacks. Corporate executives deceive their own stockholders. Politicians break once-honored codes of ethics. Across the board, integrity is quickly eroding. Our contemporary culture is proficient at producing corrupt people who are skilled at lying, cheating, falsifying, stealing, distorting, and covering up the truth. The crying need of the hour is for God's people to pursue personal holiness and integrity. As they do, Christians will stand out as bright lights in a dark world. Believers must be different if they are to make a difference.

Psalm 101 reflects a passionate commitment to pursue personal integrity in all that one does. As the king of Israel, David, the author, determined to live righteously before God and the people. This psalm records David's desire to see integrity restored to the nation of Israel. Such a pursuit of integrity, he understood, must begin with his own life. Before he could desire to see it in others, David must first live it himself.

II. COMMENTARY

MAIN IDEA: *David determines to live and reign righteously as Israel's king and surround himself with godly people.*

A David's Worship (101:1)

101:1. David begins by praising God with exuberance and enthusiastic worship for his matchless character. Fervent in his love for God, David must **sing** to the Lord. Specifically, David sings over God's steadfast, unfailing **love** by which God pledges himself to care for his people and God's **justice** by which he rewards his servants. In this, his singing was intensely Godward, or vertical, that is, directed to God.

B David's Walk (101:2–5)

101:2. I will be careful (i.e., "be attentive to," "give diligence to") **to lead a blameless life**. David purposed to pursue a life of personal holiness. A blameless life is one that is faithful and obedient, one to which no blatant sin can be charged. He asked God, **When will you come to me?** Here is a desperate prayer that God would strengthen his resolve to pursue the path of personal integrity. His pursuit of holiness should begin in the privacy of his own **house**, where he lived, in his own private world. God's truth must be fully integrated into every area of his life.

101:3a. David understood the close connection between his **eyes** and his heart. Whatever is worthless before one's eyes can produce wickedness within one's heart. The eyes are the gateway to the heart. Through the eyes, temptation enters the heart. If David was to remain blameless in his heart (v. 2), his eyes must remain singular and pure.

101:3b. To the contrary, those who fall into sin are **faithless men** who fail to remain steadfast to God's Word. David pledges to be pure and faithful. He refuses to allow the unfaithfulness of others to pull him down.

101:4. The godly believer shuns evil in every form. **Men of perverse heart** are those who are inwardly crooked, the very opposite of the blameless. David would have **nothing to do with** such evil men lest he be corrupted by their sin. He determined to repudiate everything that was **evil** and, therefore, potentially destructive to his soul. David refused to allow any practice of sin to enter and remain in his life.

101:5. David knew the potential negative influence others could have upon him. Whenever someone comes and **slanders his neighbor** in secret, he would reject that person and refuse this sin. The slander is seen as coming from one with **haughty eyes** and **proud heart**. Neither would David allow prideful people to have close access to the inner circle of his life. If he did, they would influence him for evil.

© David's Workers (101:6–7)

101:6. David purposed to look for **faithful** people with whom to surround himself in his administration. David must work in partnership with people of moral integrity who were faithful to God and his Word. David would look for those who were **blameless** in their personal lives to serve him. The word **minister** is used often in the Old Testament of the priests and Levites who functioned in the tabernacle (Deut. 10:8; Num. 3:6). But it can also be used of court officials who assisted the king in his daily functions (cp. Exod. 24:13; 2 Sam. 13:17–18).

101:7. Conversely, David declared that no one who practiced **deceit** would **dwell in my house**. This refusal involved repudiating evil in many forms, including disloyalty, unfaithfulness, hypocrisy, disguising one's intentions, spreading lies, and gossip. Tolerating any of these sins would create friction in David's court. Such factious people would not serve with him, no matter how gifted, talented, or popular they were. The one who **practices deceit** also **speaks falsely**, eventually, against David. Such an evil person would not **stand** in his **presence**. He would be relieved of his duties and removed from office.

Ⅾ David's Warning (101:8)

101:8. With disciplined resolve, David vowed, **Every morning I will put to silence all the wicked.** This is a pledge to remove from the Lord's kingdom all those who break God's Word. Some sins demand that the offender be **cut off** from the living, a clear reference to the death penalty.

III. CONCLUSION

Personal integrity is a precious commodity that enriches all who possess it. The English dictionary defines the word *integrity* as "steadfast adherence to a strict moral or ethical code, the state of being unimpaired; soundness, the quality or condition of being whole or undivided; completeness." Integrity, in fact, comes from a root word that means a total integration of all the parts of one's life into a consistent whole. When a believer lives with integrity, the Word of God is completely integrated into his life. No area is untouched or unaffected by obedience to the Scripture. Integrity describes someone who is marked by honesty, sincerity, and incorruptibility. He is without hypocrisy or duplicity. Someone with integrity is consistent with his stated convictions.

IV. TEACHING OUTLINE

A. David's Worship (1)
   1. I Will Sing of God's Love (1a)
   2. I Will Sing of God's Justice (1a)
   3. I Will Sing God's Praise (1b)
B. David's Walk (2-5)
   1. I Will Maintain Pure Feet (2)
   2. I Will Maintain Pure Eyes (3a)
   3. I Will Maintain Pure Company (3b-4)
   4. I Will Maintain Pure Ears (5)
C. David's Workers (6-7)
   1. I Will Associate with the Faithful (6a)
   2. I Will Associate with the Blameless (6b)
   3. I Will Associate with the Faultless (7)
D. David's Warning (8)
   1. I Will Silence the Wicked (8a)
   2. I Will Slay the Evildoer (8b)

Psalm 102

Unwavering Hope

"*H*ope can see heaven through the thickest clouds."

T h o m a s   B r o o k s

I. INTRODUCTION

Even in the midst of their darkest hours, believers always have a steadfast hope in God. Theirs is a positive confidence that is unshakable and unassailable. No matter how black the night, no matter how raging the storm, one's hope in the Lord should remain strong. Whenever the outlook is bleak, the uplook remains bright. It is in the darkest night that the stars overhead glow with greatest luster. So it is with one's hope in God. In every dark trial, there is a confident assurance in God—a sure expectation about the future that God will work for his own glory and for the good of his people. Every believer must anchor himself firmly to this immoveable rock. With a strong hope in the Lord, every saint must trust God, especially while in the midst of the difficult circumstances of life. As sure as there is God above, there is hope within.

Psalm 102 was written during a low ebb in the history of God's people. Its setting is the Babylonian captivity of God's chosen people, Israel, a time when God's work had seemingly come to a standstill. It was a time when God's word was not being preached, when God's people were in the minority. It was a time when God's house lay in ruin, when God's holy city was in shambles, and when God's glory was veiled. It is a psalm that begins with despair, but it concludes with a note of triumph. There is always hope in the ongoing sovereignty of God over his people. No matter how impaired God's work may become, the immutability of God guarantees that his work will move forward in God's perfect time. Thus, there is an always unshakable hope in the future.

II. COMMENTARY

> **MAIN IDEA:** *The psalmist depends upon God to intervene and deliver him in the midst of dark, difficult days.*

A The Psalmist's Despair (102:1–11)

102:1. With an abrupt burst of emotion, the psalmist pleaded for a hearing with God. He lifted up his cry to God for his sovereign intervention when his own human strength seemed to be insufficient. It appeared as if God was inattentive to his prayers, given God's present lack of intervention. The silence from heaven made him **cry for help** louder and stronger.

102:2. As if God were avoiding the psalmist, he pled, **Do not hide your face**. There was no answer, no response to his **distress**. It seemed as if God was turning a deaf **ear** to his requests. He pled for God to **answer** him **quickly**.

102:3. This crisis had brought a heavy, physical toll upon his body. He was losing the years of his life under this stress. His physical life was wasting away. His **days** were vanishing **like smoke** before him. His **bones** were burning **like glowing embers**, as if a raging fire was devouring his body.

102:4–5. Acknowledging his own frailty, he confessed that he was losing his strength, passion, and zeal. He was so consumed with this suffering that he forgot to **eat** his **food**. He was so distressed that he could not even think about eating. He lived under a **loud groaning**, or heavy sigh, from his soul. Emotionally and physically drained, he was all **skin and bones**, emaciated and withered.

102:6–7. He felt like a **desert owl**, a **bird alone on a roof**. This is how lonely the psalmist felt.

102:8. The psalmist's **enemies** taunted him, mocking his weakened condition. If he was still in Babylon, these foes were the Babylonians. Most probably, he had returned to Jerusalem from Babylonian captivity, making these opponents men like Tobiah, Sanballat, and Geshen who ridiculed Nehemiah. These were Gentiles who remained in Jerusalem after the Jews had been carried off to Babylon. They did not want God's work to succeed, and they used every possible method to prevent it.

102:9. Depicting great lamentation, the psalmist claimed that he ate **ashes** as his **food**. Ashes on one's head symbolized personal mourning. As God's work languished, weeping was his daily diet.

102:10–11. This situation was so devoid of God's power that the psalmist questioned whether this suffering was the result of his own sin. **My days are like the evening shadow**, he declared. He feared he would not live to see God reverse this spiritual famine in the land. **I wither away like grass**, he sighed. He feared that he would die before he saw God deal with this spiritual barrenness.

B The Psalmist's Devotion (102:12–22)

102:12–13. In spite of the uncertainties of the times, God sits **enthroned forever**, presiding and reigning over all. In due time, God would **arise** to act and show **compassion** to earthly **Zion**, Jerusalem. The psalmist reminded God it was **time to show favor**. The **appointed time** for judgment and deliverance **has come**.

102:14–15. The Lord's **servants** loved even Zion's **stones** and **dust**, in spite of the fact that the temple in Jerusalem had been leveled by the Babylonians. The dust and debris from Jerusalem's broken walls and temple lay everywhere. But the time would soon come when God would restore his work in Jerusalem. When he did, the unbelieving **nations** would see this and **fear the name of the** LORD. Even the **kings of the earth**, men not easily impressed, would fear and reverence God's **glory**.

102:16–17. In the future, God **will rebuild Zion** when he brings his people back from Babylon. When God does, it will be a display of **his glory** for all peoples to see. The divine hand in rebuilding the holy city, Jerusalem, will be in response to the **prayer of the destitute** there. The downtrodden in the service of God will be heard in their prayers and not be despised by him.

102:18–20. Believing that God would work in the future, the psalmist affirmed that a **future generation** would see God's holy city restored. Upon reading this psalm, they would be encouraged to praise God. In answering these prayers, God **looked down** with interest and **viewed the earth** with concern. God heard the **groans of the prisoners**, his people who were imprisoned in Babylonian captivity. He released **those condemned**—his chosen people—from Babylon in order that they might return to Jerusalem and escape death in Babylon.

102:21–22. As a result of this future deliverance from Babylonian captivity, people would declare the name of the Lord **in Zion**. This praise will occur when **the peoples and the kingdoms assemble to worship** God in a rebuilt holy city, Jerusalem.

C The Psalmist's Dependency (102:23–28)

102:23–24. The psalmist believed that it was God himself who **broke** his **strength** as he waited for divine intervention. God, it seemed, had **cut short** his **days** through this extremity. If God was to deliver him before he died, he must act soon. He pled with God not to take him **away** from the earth through death without seeing the deliverance for which he had longed. He asked for an extension of his life so he could live to see God usher in this restoration of earthly Zion.

102:25–26. In his weakness, the psalmist found comfort in God's immutability, which assured his heart that the sovereign **work** of God would move forward. All creation **will change**, but not God, who will **remain** forever the same. God is unwavering in carrying forward his divine work without altering his plans.

102:27–28. God will forever **remain the same**, immutable in his divine person and unchangeable in his eternal purpose. Because the Lord does not change, his future work through his people **will be established**.

III. CONCLUSION

In this present hour, saints find themselves living in a day much like that of the ancient psalmist. As believers survey the state of the local church today, they see much of what the psalmist saw in his day. In so many evangelical places, God's glory is being obscured, his Word is neglected, his house is abandoned, and his work is stalled. In congregations today, exposition is being replaced with entertainment. Theology is giving way to theatrics. The Word is caving in to the world. The sovereignty of God is giving way to the sovereignty of man. Doctrinally rich hymns, once focused upon the cross, are being replaced with crossover, contemporary music devoid of Christ-centered substance. In all this, believers should have a heavy burden for the languishing of God's work in this day. But let us have hope that God will yet prevail.

IV. TEACHING OUTLINE

A. The Psalmist's Despair (1-11)
   1. Hear My Prayer (1-2)
      a. Turn your face to me (2a)
      b. Turn your ear to me (2b)
   2. See My Plight (3-11)
      a. My days are vanishing (3a)
      b. My bones are burning (3b)
      c. My heart is blighted (4)
      d. My groaning is loud (5)
      e. My life is ruined (6)
      f. My sleep is gone (7)
      g. My enemies are railing (8)
      h. My food is sorrow (9-10)
      i. My days are vanishing (11)
B. The Psalmist's Devotion (12-22)
   1. For God's Eternality (12)
      a. He abides forever (12a)
      b. He abides to all generations (12b)

  2. For God's Pity (13-14)
   a. He will have compassion (13a)
   b. He will be gracious (13b)
   c. He will give pleasure (14)
  3. For God's Sovereignty (15)
   a. All nations fear him (15a)
   b. All kings revere him (15b)
  4. For God's Glory (16)
   a. He has built up his people (16a)
   b. He has revealed his glory (16b)
  5. For God's Faithfulness (17)
   a. He will respond to the destitute (17a)
   b. He will receive their plea (17b)
  6. For God's Immutability (18)
   a. His plan is recorded (18a)
   b. His people will rejoice (18b)
  7. For God's Sensitivity (19-20)
   a. He looked down from heaven (19)
   b. He heard their groans (20a)
   c. He released those condemned (20b)
  8. For God's Name (21-22)
   a. It will be declared in Zion (21)
   b. It will be declared by all (22)
 C. The Psalmist's Dependency (23-28)
  1. God Crushed Me (23)
   a. He broke my strength (23a)
   b. He shortened my days (23b)
  2. I Called upon God (24-28)
   a. God controls all (24)
   b. God created all (25)
   c. God changes all (26)
   d. God changes not (27)
   e. God cares for all (28)

Psalm 103
Glorious Occupation

Psalm 103

I. INTRODUCTION

Robert Kennedy, an American missionary to South America, once visited the dense jungle of the Amazon. There he talked with a Brazilian Indian who had recently come to know Christ. Working through a translator, the communication was strained, so the salvation of this newly converted Indian was unknown to Kennedy. He innocently asked the native Brazilian, "What do you most like to do?" He expected to receive a generic answer such as "hunting with bows and arrows" or "canoeing." But to his amazement, the Indian answered, "Being occupied with God." Kennedy was stunned with the response. He said, "Ask him again. Something must be lost in the translation." But the Indian gave the same answer. The constant preoccupation of this new believer was, quite simply, God. He used this occasion to give praise to him who had so greatly blessed him.

This true story provides an excellent definition of authentic worship. It is a redeemed life, being gloriously occupied with the grandeur and greatness of God. It is a believer living every moment of every day adoring God and being enraptured with his majesty. Worship is not about keeping up an outward façade of rituals, rules, or religion. It is about an inward reality of a living relationship with God through his Son, Jesus Christ. Worship is the soul's encounter with the supreme majesty of God and the risen Christ on high. Worship is experiencing God in one's innermost being—all that I *am* responding to all that he *is*. This is every believer's glorious occupation.

This is the heartbeat of Psalm 103. It is a hymn of praise to God that overflows from a heart supremely devoted to the Lord. In this psalm, David surveyed the love and compassion of God toward his people. In every line of this masterful work, he encouraged his soul to join him in praising God. Here David speaks for us all. By speaking to his own soul, he actually speaks to each one of us, inviting us to lift our hearts and voices to God in worship. Some psalms are addressed to God; others are addressed to other people. But this psalm is addressed primarily to the psalmist himself. He calls upon himself to praise God.

II. COMMENTARY

MAIN IDEA: *David calls upon his own heart to praise the Lord for his many blessings and calls upon other people to do the same.*

A The Rejoicing of Praise (103:1–2)

SUPPORTING IDEA: *David exhorts his own soul to praise God, forgetting none of his benefits.*

103:1. The psalmist called upon himself to **praise the LORD**, urging his own **soul** to bless his **holy name**. From the very depth of his **inmost being**, David exhorted his own heart to praise God. Perhaps he was presently discouraged or depressed. Nevertheless, he had every reason to praise God.

103:2. For the sake of emphasis, the psalmist repeated this call to **praise the LORD**. In the midst of his emotional tailspin, he must **forget not all his benefits**. The rest of this psalm will enumerate these many blessings which were his in the Lord.

B The Reasons for Praise (103:3–19)

SUPPORTING IDEA: *David reminds himself of the many reasons he has for praising God.*

103:3–5. Above all, God should be praised because he **forgives all your sins**. As great as the psalmist's sin is against God, God's pardon is even greater. Further, sin is pictured as a life-threatening disease that has spread to his entire soul. But by his grace, God **heals** the deadly plague of sin, giving abundant life. God **redeems** David's **life** out of the **pit** of sin, which he had dug for himself. A pit is dark, confining, and imprisoning, a graphic picture of human sin. By his own efforts David could never escape this grave of his own making. Only by divine grace had he been rescued.

The mercy of God **crowns** the psalmist as though he were a part of the royal family. This is not a literal crown of diamonds but one far more valuable—a crown of divine **love and compassion**. Moreover, God **satisfies your** desires with good things (i.e., pardon). In so doing, David's **youth is renewed like the eagle's.** His heart soars because the burden of sin is removed.

103:6–7. The saints are often under attack in this world by the enemies of God. They are **oppressed,** yet God works on their behalf, bringing **justice** in the midst of their persecutions. On their behalf, God steps in and **works righteousness.** The divine path to follow may often be confusing, especially in many trials. Yet God **made known his ways to Moses** in the confusion of the wilderness. God will do the same for his people today.

103:8–9. God's sovereign rule over the psalmist's life is marked by **compassionate and gracious** dealings. Even in the face of his sin, God is **slow to anger,** withholding swift discipline. The Lord may be justly angry because of David's sin, but he **will not always accuse** him. God will soon forgive and restore him.

103:10–12. God's abounding mercy withholds his judgment. He **does not treat us as our sins deserve.** Nor does God **repay us according to our iniquities.** Christ's atonement has satisfied God's wrath, and, therefore, believers will never be condemned for their sins. **As high as the heavens are above the earth**—an immeasurable distance—is precisely how **great** God's **love is for those who fear him.** Infinite and vast is God's eternal love for his own. **As far as the east is from the west**—another immeasurable distance—is how **far** God **has removed our transgressions from us** (Isa. 1:18; 38:17; 43:25).

103:13–14. As a father has compassion on his children—another figure of extreme measure—is how much **the LORD has compassion** on his people who **fear him.** God **knows** our finite, human limitations and **remembers** that we are as fragile as **dust.**

103:15–16. Man's **days are like grass,** so easily cut off. **He flourishes like a flower** that soon fades away. When **the wind blows,** he is **gone** and forgotten. Man bursts on the scene of human history but then is swept away.

103:17–19. By stark contrast, God's unconditional, loyal **love** toward his elect will never change. His sovereign grace is **from everlasting to everlasting** and will never fade. All believers **obey** the **covenant,** the evidence of true saving faith. As the absolute, unrivaled sovereign Lord of the universe, God **has established his throne** in heaven over all. He is constantly ruling **over all,** causing all things to work together for his glory and the good of his people (Rom. 8:28).

C The Reinforcement of Praise (103:20–22)

SUPPORTING IDEA: *David issues a call to heaven and earth to join him in praising God.*

103:20. This psalm concludes by inviting all things to praise God. **Praise the LORD, you his angels.** The angelic host must join with him in blessing God's name. These ministering spirits exist to **do his bidding** and **obey** God's **word**.

103:21. This invitation is repeated, calling for the angels to magnify God's name. These celestial **servants who do his will** should always **praise the LORD**.

103:22. Finally, the psalmist calls for **all** God's works **everywhere in his dominion** to **praise** him. God's works are his creation, which he made for his own glory and praise. David concludes by addressing his own heart: **Praise the LORD, O my soul.**

MAIN IDEA REVIEW: *David calls upon his own heart to praise the Lord for his many blessings and calls upon other people to do the same.*

III. CONCLUSION

Years ago Thomas K. Beecher was called upon to substitute for his famous brother, the renowned preacher, Henry Ward Beecher. As usual, many curiosity seekers had come expecting to hear the revered Henry Beecher speak. When Thomas Beecher appeared in the pulpit, some of these people got up and started for the doors. Sensing their disappointment because he was substituting for his brother, Thomas Beecher announced, "All those who came here this morning to worship Henry Ward Beecher may withdraw from the church. All who came to worship God may remain."

Worshipping God requires that believers always keep their focus on him, never upon man. God alone is worthy of worship. Let God's people remind their own hearts of this singular gaze in worship. God alone is to be praised.

IV. LIFE APPLICATION

Do you ever have trouble praising God? Do you ever not "feel" like extolling his name? Do you ever get so discouraged that you have lost your joy? And find it hard to praise God? Do you ever get so low that you don't even want to go to church? Do you ever get so downcast that you cannot even sing the hymns and choruses? Maybe that is where you find yourself. Yet the more we know of God, the more we will praise him. To know him is to love him. The key to having a constant devotion to God is to be always growing in the knowledge of God. To see him is to savor him. How can you know him more deeply?

Behold him in the Word. We primarily come to know God more intimately in the Scripture. The Word of God reveals the God of the Word. Study the Bible. See God supremely revealed in the pages of Scripture. There, in the Bible, you will behold his awesome person.

Behold him in worship. Having looked into the Bible, we then should look into his face. Sing the great hymns of the faith, those whose words are solidly built upon Scripture. Sing chorus and spiritual songs that are anchored to sound doctrine. These truth-centered works will lift our spirits upward to God.

Behold him in the world. David said, "The heavens declare the glory of God" (Ps. 19:1). All around us, creation is a testimony to the majesty of God. Behold the skies, stars, and sun above—see God's greatness. Behold the mountains and meadows around—see God's beauty. Behold the rain and harvest—see God's loving provision.

V. PRAYER

God, enable me by your grace to praise you in every situation of life. Rivet my attention upon you. Deepen my heart for you so I may rise up to praise you with all my being. Forgive me for what is, all too often, the shallowness of my worship. In Jesus' name. Amen.

VI. DEEPER DISCOVERIES

A. Love (103:8,17)

The term *love* (*hesed*) means "kindness, mercy, favor, or steadfast love" and is found around 250 times in the Hebrew Bible (cp. Exod. 20:6; 34:6; Num. 14:18; Ps. 136; Mic. 7:18). *Hesed* is derived from *hasad* which means "to bend or bow oneself" or "to incline oneself." It denotes a condescending love of God to his chosen people. Here it is used to express David's confidence in the Lord who would be forever favorable toward him. Sometimes it is called God's covenant love because of its occurrence in Deuteronomy 7:12 and 2 Samuel 7:15.

B. Fear (103:11)

The word *fear* (*yare*) is found approximately 330 times throughout the Old Testament and is most often used to speak of reverential awe produced when a person is before God (Exod. 1:17; 1 Sam. 12:14,18; 2 Sam. 6:9; 2 Kgs. 17:28,35–39; Pss. 33:8; 102:15; Jer. 5:22,24; Jon. 1:16). It is also used of those who honor God and take him seriously (Job 1:1; Pss. 31:19; 33:18–19; 34:9; 128:1; 145:19; Neh. 7:2) or those who fail to do so (Eccl. 8:13). In other instances, as in the present context of Psalm 23:4, *yare* is used as a fear produced by the anticipation of evil (Exod. 14:13; Num. 14:9; Deut. 1:29; 3:2; 7:18; 20:1,3,8; Josh. 10:8,25; Judg. 7:3; 2 Kgs. 1:15; Neh. 4:14; Pss. 27:1,3; 56:3–4,11; Isa. 51:7,12; Ezek. 2:6).

C. Heavens (103:11,19)

The term *heavens* (Heb. *shamayim*) is a plural noun form that literally means "the heights" or that which is raised up or lofty. It refers to the realms of outer space in which the stars, moon, and planets exist (Gen. 1:14–17). The phrase "the skies" (Heb. *raqia*) refers to the atmosphere surrounding the earth. This is the troposphere, or the region of breathable atmosphere that blankets the earth and contains the clouds, weather, birds, winds, and so on. This is where the water cycle occurs (Ps. 147:8).

D. Transgressions (103:12)

This word (Heb. *peshah*) literally means "a going away from, departure, rebellion, or defiance." A transgression is a willful act of rebellion against God's sovereign authority and a refusal to acknowledge his right to rule the lives of his people. A transgression is not merely against other people whom one may hurt by his sin, but it is always, ultimately, a treasonous act against God.

VII. TEACHING OUTLINE

A. The Rejoicing of Praise (1-2)
  1. Bless His Holy Name (1)
    a. From my soul (1a)
    b. From my inmost being (1b)
  2. Remember His Many Benefits (2)
    a. From my soul (2a)
    b. From my mind (2b)
B. The Reasons for Praise (3-19)
  1. God's Pardon Is Great (3-4)
    a. He forgives all sins (3)
    b. He heals all your diseases (3b)
    c. He redeems your life from destruction (4a)
    d. He crowns your soul with love (4b)

      2. God's Pleasure Is Great (5)

C. He Satisfies You with Good Things (5a)

D. He Strengthens Your Life with Great Power (5b)

      1. God's Protection Is Great (6-7)

E. He Works Righteousness for the Oppressed (6)

F. He Revealed His Ways to Moses (7a)

G. He Made Known His Deeds to Israel (7b)

      1. God's Patience Is Great (8-12)

         a. He is compassionate to his own (8)

         b. He is slow to anger (8b)

         c. He is abounding in love (8b)

         d. He is forgiving of sin (9a)

         e. He Is short in anger (9b)

         f. He is merciful toward sinners (10)

         g. He is great in love (11)

         h. He is infinite in forgiveness (12)

      2. God's Pity Is Great (13-14)

         a. He is merciful toward his children (13)

         b. He is mindful of our frailties (14)

      3. God's Perseverance Is Great (15-18)

         a. Man is transitory like grass (15a)

         b. Man is temporal like flowers (15b)

         c. Man is forgotten after death (16)

         d. God is everlasting in love (17-18)

      4. God's Providence Is Great (19)

         a. He established his throne in heaven (19a)

         b. He executes his rule over all (19b)

H. The Reinforcement of Praise (20-22)

      1. All His Angels Praise Him (20-21)

         a. They who do his bidding (20a)

         b. They who obey his word (20b)

         c. They who do his will (21)

      2. All His Works Praise Him (22)

Psalm 104
Almighty God

"The problems of origin and destiny have escaped the philosopher and the scientist, but the humblest follower of Christ knows the answer to both."

A . W . T o z e r

Psalm 104

I. INTRODUCTION

It is hard to imagine anything more absurd than what the secular humanist believes about the origin of all things. His basic statement of faith is this: Nobody times nothing equals everything. Ponder carefully the foolishness of that empty worldview. For the person who rejects the Bible, there is *no* Creator, *no* master plan, *no* higher design, *no* intelligent purpose. For him, everything is the result of a big bang in outer space, pulsating particles, blind chance, and random change. Given enough time, an amoeba became slime, which, in turn, became a tadpole, a fish, a reptile, and then a monkey, which, so they say, finally became a man. Thus, the human race does not know where it has come from, what it is, or where it is going. For the evolutionist, life is random, devoid of God, and, thus, purposeless and meaningless. That is precisely the bankrupt philosophy of secular humanism.

It is against this black backdrop of the world's prevailing darkness that Psalm 104 shines so brightly. It is a praise song that extols God as the true Creator of all, the one who has made the heavens and the earth and all that they contain. This ancient song declares that God himself created the universe with stunning genius, precise detail, and brilliant order. Rather than "aping" the so-called wisdom of this age, this psalm speaks the truth of God. This wisdom from above teaches that God alone has effortlessly spoken everything into being out of nothing. Psalm 104 is a beautiful, poetic restatement of Genesis 1 that portrays the Lord's power, wisdom, and goodness in creation. It teaches that this world has been made by God, for his own glory. As a hymn to the Creator, the psalmist sings the glory of the Maker and Sustainer of all. Let all join their voices and sing to God, the almighty Creator.

II. COMMENTARY

MAIN IDEA: *The psalmist praises God as the sole Creator of the entire universe.*

A First Day: God Created the Light (104:1–2a)

104:1. The psalmist begins by speaking to his own **soul** to burst forth with exuberant **praise** to God (Ps. 103:1–2,22). God is **very great**, the Creator being, infinitely greater than his creation. God is **clothed with splendor and majesty**, wrapped with the dazzling splendor of holiness, the shining forth of his own glory.

104:2a. In poetic fashion, the psalmist portrayed God as wrapping himself in **light**, or as girding himself with blinding, awesome light. Here is a description of the first day of creation, that initial twenty-four-hour period in which God created light (Gen. 1:3–5; 2 Cor. 4:6). This light preceded the sun.

B Second Day: God Created the Heavens (104:2b–4)

104:2b. On day two, God stretched out **the heavens like a tent**. Here the outer universe is described as a mere tent being spread out. Like a camper pitches his tent, so God effortlessly tossed out the vast heavens. The creating and establishing of all the planets in outer space was effortless for almighty God.

104:3. The **waters** are the water vapor in the outer atmosphere (Gen. 1:7–8). They provide the foundational beams for the **upper chambers** where God dwells, much like a royal penthouse placed atop God's created order. Beneath the **waters** in the outer atmosphere are formed **the clouds**, which are made from water vapor. These clouds are pictured as a **chariot**, moving rapidly across the skies. God is driving the clouds as a chariot driver would direct and ride his vessel.

104:4. The **winds** are also directed by God. **Flames of fire** flash from the clouds above. This refers to lightning bolts hurled from the clouds. God sends, governs, controls, and uses the wind for his own purposes.

C Third Day: God Created the Earth (104:5–18)

104:5. On the third day, God created **the earth**. It is **set** on **its foundations**, a poetic way of describing how God established this planet (Gen.

1:9–13; Job 38:4). It can **never be moved** out of orbit or be tilted at a wrong angle. It is firmly established (Pss. 93:1; 96:10), always rotating properly.

104:6–7. God covered the earth with **the deep**, like clothes over the body. This refers to **the waters** that were in the atmosphere that rose **above the mountains**. At God's **rebuke**, they **fled** to their appointed place where they comprised the oceans (Job 38:8–11). God's spoken word was authoritative like **thunder**, and the waters quickly obeyed.

104:8–9. These waters **flowed over the mountains** and then ran **down into the valleys**. In this stage, God put the topography of the earth in its place. All this detail of the earth's surface was **assigned** by God. Further, God set a **boundary** for the waters, which is the coastline with its beaches, so that the land will never be overwhelmed by the sea.

104:10–12. In this process, God also established the **springs**, putting them in their designed place. These springs immediately began to flow into streams and rivers to **give water** to the **beasts of the field**, yet to be created on the fifth day. The trees will grow next to the flowing streams and the **birds** will **nest** in these trees, drinking the water.

104:13–15. God **waters the mountains**, sending the rain down from heaven. The **earth is satisfied** with what God has provided to make things grow. God **makes** the **grass** and **plants** grow, all for a purpose, that is, to provide for the needs of man. **Wine** and **bread** were staples of everyday life in ancient Israel, blessings of God to enrich human life.

104:16–18. God-sent rain causes **the trees** to grow, **the birds** to **make their nests**, and **the stork** to have **its home**. In God's genius, he made the earth suited for all forms of life. He provided a perfect place for all that he created and then good things for them. He gave the birds and the stork a home in the trees, the **wild goats** a dwelling in the **high mountains**, the **coneys** a dwelling place in the rock's **crags**.

🅓 Fourth Day: God Created the Planets (104:19–23)

104:19–20. On day four, God made the planets in outer space which surround the earth. **The moon marks off the seasons**, the **sun** daily sets on the horizon, governing the orderly cycles of the **seasons**. Every planet and star was made by God and put into its perfect place in the universe. With the rotation of the earth, half the earth is always turned away from the light of the sun, resulting in **darkness** for half the day. It is at **night** that the beasts **prowl** and hunt for food.

104:21–23. The **lion** is the king of the animal world and is the ruler of God's creation by night. In the darkness of night these animals **roar for their prey**. But during the light of day, **man** is the ruler of God's creation. Man's work, assigned by God, was good as he was given responsibility to manage what God had created—the earth. This verse looks ahead to man's arrival on the sixth day.

E Fifth Day: God Created the Animals (104:24–26)

104:24. On the fifth day of creation, God made the animal kingdom. With a burst of praise to God, the psalmist worshipped God because his glory is put on display in all creation. The world reveals God's **works** in which his **wisdom** is made known, a divine genius that made all with beauty, diversity, balance, and order.

104:25. On this day, God populated the earth with animals. Specifically, the psalmist mentioned the animals of the open **sea**. These large bodies of water are filled with fish and marine mammals, **beyond number**, too many to count, all revealing the greatness of God.

104:26. The **ships** traverse the seas, anticipating the future time when man will sail the oceans. Then, man will board ships and cross the seas, where the fish and marine mammals live. **The leviathan** is a mighty sea monster that can overwhelm man (Job 3:8; 41:1–34; Ps. 74:14; Isa. 27:1), possibly even a dinosaur. This intimidating animal, fearsome to man, is God's harmless pet, frolicking in the ocean.

F Sixth Day: God Created Man (104:27–30)

104:27–28. On the sixth day of creation, God created man (Gen. 1:24–31). All of God's creation, man included, looks to God to provide food **at the proper time**. This alludes to the various growing seasons, followed by harvest seasons that yield their food. Only God can create food; man simply gathers it. What **good things** God provides, a revelation of his abundant goodness.

104:29–30. If God were to **hide** his **face**, withdraw his presence, and stop providing food, the entire earth would be **terrified**. All creation depends on God for its birth, life, and length of life. The number of days man has to live is set by God (Job 14:5; Ps. 139:16), who then will **take away their breath**. When God sends his **Spirit**, man is made a living soul (Gen. 2:7).

G Every Day: God Should Be Praised (104:31–35)

104:31–32. God's mighty acts in creation should cause him to be constantly praised by man. Let the **glory of the LORD** be put on display through his **works** in creation **forever**. Not only does man enjoy what God has made, but **may the LORD** himself **rejoice** in what he has made. God exercises absolute sovereignty and power over the earth. The earth **trembles** when God looks at it. He merely **touches** the earth, even its strongest parts, **the mountains**, and it melts.

104:33–35a. Here is the rightful response to God's creative power. Man must give him glory and **sing praise** to his name. The psalmist prayed that his **meditation** would be **pleasing** to this awesome God. Those who do not join in this anthem of praise to God will be consumed by God's wrath. **Sinners** refuse to find their gladness in God, but, instead, find it in creation, even themselves.

104:35b–c. The psalmist concluded as he began (v. 1a). He called upon his own **soul** to **praise the LORD.** In hearty response, he answered his own appeal with a passionate declaration of **praise** for the Lord.

III. CONCLUSION

Unique among all God's creation, man is made in God's own image. As the apex of God's created order, the human race is made in the likeness of God in order to know God, worship him, and give glory to his name. Here is the true dignity of man. Here is the real value of human life. Man is created by God with the capacity to enter into a personal relationship with him. Here is the highest purpose of man's existence, his loftiest reason for being. Man was designed with a mind to know God, a heart to love God, and a will to obey God. Man's glory is found in his relationship with God. God has put eternity within his soul. That is, man possesses a transcendent desire to live for what is beyond this physical world. This higher calling upon man to live above a mere temporal existence is planted within his soul by God. This God-shaped vacuum is unlike the rest of God's creation. Thus, let us live to know God through his Son, Jesus Christ.

IV. TEACHING OUTLINE

PRAISE THE LORD (1a)
A. First Day: God Created the Light (1-2a)
   1. God Is Clothed with Splendor (1b)
   2. God Is Clothed with Light (2a)
B. Second Day: God Created the Heavens (2b-4)
   1. God Stretched Out the Heavens (2b, 3a)
     a. Like a tent (2b)
     b. Like an upper chamber (3a)
   2. God Stretched Out the Clouds (3b)
     a. Like a chariot (3b)
     b. Like a flame of fire (4)
C. Third Day: God Created the Earth (5-18)
   1. God Set the Earth on Foundations (5)
   2. God Covered the Earth with Deep Waters (6-9)
     a. Above the mountains (6)

       b. Into its place (7)

       c. Down into valleys (8)

       d. Behind its boundary (9)

    3. God Waters the Earth (10-18)

       a. The springs water the ravines (10)

       b. The springs water the beasts (11)

       c. The springs water the birds (12)

       d. The springs water the mountains (13)

       e. The springs water the grass (14-15)

       f. The springs water the trees (16-17)

       g. The springs water the wild goats (18a)

       h. The springs water the coneys (18b)

D. Fourth Day: God Created the Planets (19-23)

    1. God Orders the Planets (19-20a)

       a. The moon marks the seasons (19a)

       b. The sun ends the day (19b)

    2. God Orders the Night (20a)

    3. God Orders the Day (22-23)

       a. The sun rises (22a)

       b. The animals retire (22)

       c. Man's works (23)

E. Fifth Day: God Created the Animals (24-26)

    1. God Made All Animals (24)

       a. Many of them (24a, c)

       b. In wisdom (24b)

    2. God Made the Sea Creatures (25-26)

       a. Beyond numbering (25a)

       b. Large and small (25b)

       c. The leviathan (26)

F. Sixth Day: God Created Man (27-30)

    1. God Feeds Man (27-28)

       a. At the proper time (27)

       b. With good things (28)

    2. God Terrifies Man (29a)

    3. God Ends Man (29b)

    4. God Creates Man (30)

       a. By his spirit (30a)

       b. To renew the earth (30b)

G. Every Day: God Should Be Praised (31-35)
   1. May the Glory of the Lord Endure (31a)
   2. May God Rejoice in His Works (31-32)
   3. I Will Sing to the Lord (33)
   4. I Will Think upon the Lord (34)
   5. May the Wicked Be No More (35)

Psalm 105

The Invisible Hand

"*What* are all histories but

God manifesting Himself?"

Oliver Cromwell

Psalm 105

I. INTRODUCTION

William S. Plumer once wrote, "Blessed is he who sees God in history and in nature, as well as in revelation." Surely the person who studies the Scripture is enlightened to see the invisible hand of God, presiding over the affairs of human history, directing it toward its appointed end. One's understanding of the flow of world history is dependent upon seeing that God is sovereignly building his kingdom upon the earth to reach the world.

Dr. Martyn Lloyd-Jones said, "The key to the history of the world is the kingdom of God." In other words, world history cannot be understood apart from God's invisible hand upon redemptive history. The course of world events cannot be grasped without observing God at work in and through his people. Here is the hinge upon which all history turns. God is always working through his people to effect the flow of the entire world.

This is the beauty of Psalm 105. It is one of three historical psalms in the Psalter, the other two being Psalms 78 and 106. These historical psalms chronicle in summary fashion the high points of the sacred history of God's people in the Old Testament. In Psalm 105, we see the invisible hand of God upon the many events, circumstances, movements, and causes of history. Here we see God intervening in the affairs of men. We see God closely involved in human lives. We see God not distant and far removed but up close, actively involved in the affairs of men, the events of nations, the rise of rulers, the course of kingdoms, and the direction of history. To be sure, history is his story. There is a divine flow to history. There is a sovereign purpose and strategic plan to world events. History is a seamless garment, tailor-made by God.

Psalm 105 and Psalm 106 form a perfectly matched pair. They stand shoulder to shoulder, closely related, and conclude Book IV of Psalms. Psalm 105 tells how God treated Israel and, conversely, Psalm 106 tells how Israel treated God. Psalm 105 speaks of God's faithfulness to Israel; Psalm 106, Israel's unfaithfulness to God. Psalm 105 speaks of the Lord's grace; Psalm 106, the people's disgrace. In these two psalms, the double theme of the entire Bible is summarized—God's salvation and man's sin, God's divine faithfulness and human unfaithfulness.

The time of these two psalms appears to be after Israel's return to Jerusalem from Babylonian captivity—Psalm 105 being an encouragement, Psalm 106 a warning. Psalm 105 falls into six stanzas of unequal length, covering the history of Israel from God's covenant with Abraham to the settlement in Canaan, a period of approximately five hundred years.

II. COMMENTARY

> **MAIN IDEA:** *The psalmist exhorts God's people to worship the Lord because he rules over history.*

A Israel's Exhortation (105:1–7)

105:1. Ten imperatives launch this psalm, calling God's people to worship him. The first imperative, **give thanks to the LORD**, exhorts all to acknowledge the goodness of God by expressing gratitude to him. Second, **call on his name** summons all believers to lift up their hearts and voices and magnify God's name in praise and adoration. Third, they should **make known** God's mighty deeds to the whole world. Tell of **what he has done** in history among people throughout the earth.

105:2–3. Fourth, God's people are enjoined to **sing** praises to God, who alone is worthy. Fifth, they should **tell of all his wonderful acts**, which are his mighty deeds that have the effect of producing "wonder" in the hearts of all who observe them. Sixth, all saints should **glory** in God's **holy name**, which is the sum total of his divine attributes. Seventh, they should **rejoice** in him who is so awesome.

105:4–5. Eighth, all believers should **look** to the Lord and observe his great **strength**, a power that presides over all. Ninth, they should **seek his face**, that is, pursue the knowledge of God. Tenth, God's people are urged to **remember** the great things that the Lord has done. Call to mind his wonders; never forget his deeds; replay them in one's memory.

105:6–7. All God's people, the **descendants of Abraham** and the **sons of Jacob**, should obey these ten imperatives (vv. 1–5). With solemn declaration, the psalmist announced that the Lord is **God**, whose **judgments** are found in all the earth. These judgments are the decisive, dynamic deeds of God, saving his people and destroying his enemies.

B Israel's Election (105:8–15)

105:8–11. God has remembered **his covenant** with Abraham, keeping and executing its promises (Gen. 12:1–3). He will keep his Word for a **thousand generations**, a generation being basically forty years. Thus, God will preserve his Word for the next forty thousand years, or for the remainder of human history (i.e., forever). This **covenant** God made with **Abraham** (Gen. 12:1–3; 13:14–18; 15:18–21; 17:1–21; 22:15–19) and later confirmed to **Isaac** (Gen. 26:23–25) and **Jacob** (Gen. 35:9–12). God spoke an **everlasting covenant** for all time and eternity, never to be rescinded. In this Abrahamic covenant, God promised to give Israel the **land of Canaan** (Gen. 17:8).

105:12–13. When Abraham and his family were **few**, God promised that he would multiply them to be a large number, as numerous as the stars of heaven and the sand of the seashore (Gen. 13:16; 15:5; 17:2,6; 22:17). Before they entered their land, they migrated from **nation to nation**. Abraham himself sojourned from Ur of the Chaldeans to Haran, Canaan (Gen. 11:31), and Egypt (Gen. 12:10–13).

105:14–15. God allowed no one to **oppress them** but protected and preserved them. He **rebuked kings**. The Lord struck Pharaoh and his house with great plagues when Abraham's wife Sarai was taken into his quarters (Gen. 12:17). God later rebuked Abimelech, king of Gerar (Gen. 20:3–7), to protect Abraham. **Do not touch my anointed ones** is what God spoke to foreign kings on behalf of Abraham, Isaac, and Jacob. They were called **prophets** of God (Gen. 20:7), a title indicating they were anointed with the Spirit's power to speak as God's messengers to men.

C Israel's Exile (105:16–25)

105:16–19. The history of God's dealings with Israel now advances to the days when Joseph was in Egypt (Gen. 37–50). There would be a **famine on the land** as God **destroyed** their food. At this time, **Joseph** was sold by his own brothers into slavery to a caravan that passed through Canaan, bringing him into Egypt. There Joseph was treated as the prisoner of the Egyptians in the land of Egypt. Although he was confined to the prison of Potiphar, Joseph was not forgotten by God. While Joseph was in prison, God kept his **word** spoken earlier to Abraham and acted faithfully toward Joseph.

105:20–22. In due time, the Egyptian king **released** Joseph from prison (Gen. 41:14) and made him **master of his household**. This promotion was in fulfillment of God's earlier promise to make him a ruler over princes (Gen. 37:5–11). Joseph, who was put into chains, was now given authority to **instruct** Pharaoh's **princes** as he pleased. **His elders** refers to Pharaoh's counselors (i.e., older men of wide experience and educated learning).

105:23–25. Thus, with Joseph in Egypt, Israel **entered Egypt** and remained there for the next 430 years. They lived in the **land of Ham**, another name for Egypt, where part of the descendants of Ham, the youngest son of Noah (Gen. 10), had settled. God **made** his people to be **fruitful** in Egypt, to grow in numbers until they were **too numerous** for their foes. Throughout this time, God remained sovereignly in control over Israel's destiny in Egypt (Gen. 15:13). God himself **turned** the **hearts** of the Egyptians **against his servants** (Prov. 21:1), using them to judge and discipline Israel.

🄓 Israel's Exodus (105:26–38)

105:26–28. At the appointed time, God sovereignly raised up **Moses** to lead Israel out of Egyptian bondage. God had already promised that Israel would be delivered out of Egyptian bondage (Gen. 15:14). In this, God's perfect time, he kept his word spoken to Abraham. Moses and **Aaron** did not volunteer for this task. Rather, they were sovereignly **chosen** and providentially sent by God for this assignment. These two men **performed his miraculous signs** among the Egyptians, a reference to the ten plagues of judgment that God unleashed upon Egypt (Exod. 7–12). God so devastated their hearts that the Egyptians caved in and released the Israelites from their oppressions and bondage.

105:29–36. In the first plague (Exod. 7:14–25), God **turned their waters into blood.** In the second plague (Exod. 8:1–15), God sent **frogs to their land.** In the third and fourth plagues (Exod. 8:16–32), God ordered **flies** and **gnats** to judge the Egyptians. In the seventh plague (Exod. 9:13–35) there was the devastation of the **hail** and **lightning,** bringing the loss of crops. In the eighth plague (Exod. 10:1–20), the **locusts** and **grasshoppers . . . ate up every green thing.** In the tenth and final plague, God brought the death of the **firstborn** (Exod. 11:1–12:51). All this was to demonstrate God's sovereignty over Pharaoh and the Egyptian gods.

105:37–38. As God delivered his people out of Egypt, he provided for their financial needs with **silver and gold** as they left (Exod. 12:35–36). So miraculous was Israel's deliverance that Egypt did not even contest it. To the contrary, Egypt was actually **glad** when they left as **dread** had overtaken them.

🄔 Israel's Encircling (105:39–41)

105:39. During the forty years that followed, God **spread out a cloud,** the Shekinah glory, that protected and led Israel in the wilderness. It served as a guide in the wilderness (Ps. 78:14), a shield of protection from the Egyptians (Exod. 14:19–20), and a covering for the fiery manifestations of God's glorious presence (Exod. 16:10; 24:16; 34:5; 40:34–35,38).

105:40–41. God's people asked God for food in the wilderness when they became hungry. So God fed them with **quail**, causing the birds to fly before them. God also fed them manna, the **bread of heaven** (Ps. 78:24–25). In all this, God **satisfied them** with his abundant provision. God also gave them water to drink when Moses **opened the rock** with his rod (Exod. 17:6; Num. 20:11). Throughout Israel's wilderness wanderings, God remained faithful to lead and feed his people.

F Israel's Entrance (105:42–45)

105:42–43. As Israel approached the promised land, God perfectly kept his word. In spite of their many trials, he **remembered his holy promise** to Abraham. In honoring his covenant, God brought out his people **with rejoicing** so that they might enter into the land he had promised. It was a land flowing with milk and honey, beautiful and bountiful. Israel was finally in the place God had prepared for them.

105:44. God gave them the **lands of the nations**, a land previously possessed by Canaanite nations. God gave them this land that they would be an **heir** to what had already been planted by the foreign nations.

105:45. God abundantly blessed his people to motivate their hearts to **keep his precepts**. They who received his good provisions should respond with obedience. Consequently, the psalm concludes as it began, with **praise** being offered to God.

III. CONCLUSION

This psalm records five hundred years of God's unbroken faithfulness toward his people. This unfolding story of redemptive history, drawn from Israel's past, is one seamless garment, one unified whole. This drama is not about individual, unrelated parts but about the sum of its whole, all merged together into one unified plan. Here is one script with many characters, one chronicle of many chapters. This half-millennium span is one epic of God's eternal purposes being worked out in and through the lives of his people. This divinely written story is still being written today. God's eternal purposes are being carried out in the world, heading toward the consummation of the age in Christ's return. What confidence believers should have in God who rules in history. History is his story.

IV. TEACHING OUTLINE

A. Israel's Exhortation (1-7)
   1. Sing to the Lord (1-2)
      a. Give thanks to him (1a)
      b. Call on his name (1)
      c. Tell of his acts (2)
   2. Seek the Lord (3-4)
      a. Glory in his name (3)
      b. Look to the Lord (4)
   3. Savor the Lord (5-7)
      a. Remember his wonders (5)
      b. Reaffirm his judgments (6-7)

B. Israel's Election (8-15)
   1. God Remembered His Covenant (8-11)
      a. He commanded it with Abraham (8-9)
      b. He confirmed it with Jacob (10)
      c. He continues it with Israel (11)
   2. God Regarded His People (11-15)

C. They Wandered to Other Nations (12-13)

D. They Were Protected by God (14-15)

E. Israel's Exile (16-25)
   1. God Called Down a Famine (16)
   2. God Commissioned Joseph (17-22)
   3. God Consecrated Israel (23-25)

F. Israel's Exodus (26-38)
   1. God Commissioned Moses (26)
   2. God Commanded Miracles (27-36)
   3. God Consecrated Israel (37-38)

G. Israel's Encircling (39-41)
   1. God Led Them with a Cloud (39)
   2. God Fed Them with Quail (40a)
   3. God Satisfied Them with Bread (40b)
   4. God Provided Them with Water (41)

H. Israel's Entrance (42-45)
   1. God Remembered His Covenant (42)
   2. God Brought Them Out of Wandering (43)
   3. God Gave Them the Land (44-45)

Psalm 106

Full Disclosure

"*T*he way to cover our sin is to uncover it

by confession."

Richard Sibbes

Psalm 106

I. INTRODUCTION

An old man once suffered inner turmoil as the direct result of unrepented sin in his life. There was no peace for his sin-harboring soul. The more he was convicted of his sin, the more he resisted, until he could bear it no longer. At last, he went to his neighbor who lived on the farm next to his. "Sir, I am sorry," he confided. "I stole a rope from you a while back, and I have come to confess my sin to you and to return the rope."

His neighbor forgave him; and the old man returned home, but still his conscience continued to torment him. So he went back to his neighbor to speak to him again. "Oh, I forgot to tell you," he explained, "that on the other end of the rope was a cow."

The lesson of the story is clear. Only a full confession of sin accompanied by real repentance is a true confession. This is the central theme of Psalm 106, a song containing a full, lengthy acknowledgment of sin. This psalm, in fact, contains one of the longest confessions of sin in the entire Bible. Beginning in verse 6 and extending through verse 46, the written record is one long, continuous confession of sin. An anonymously written historical psalm, Psalm 106 is one of three psalms that provide an overview of much of Israel's history from Egyptian bondage (prior to 1445 B.C.) to its Babylonian bondage (605–536 B.C.). In all, this psalm covers some eight hundred years of Israel's history.

It should be noted that this psalm is a companion psalm to Psalm 105, as the two songs represent two very different ways of telling the same story. Psalm 105 tells Israel's history from the perspective of God's faithfulness, Psalm 106 from Israel's unfaithfulness. An exile psalm, this psalm was written while Israel was in captivity in the foreign land of Babylon. It is the final psalm of Book IV in the Psalms.

II. COMMENTARY

MAIN IDEA: *The psalmist looks to the many long centuries of moral failure by Israel in order to cause God's people to look confidently to the future.*

A. A Prayer for Salvation (106:1–5)

SUPPORTING IDEA: *The psalmist offers thanks to God for his goodness and asks that the Lord deliver his people from great harm.*

106:1–2. This sober psalm begins on a high note with the psalmist declaring, **Praise the LORD**. He then urged all God's people to **give thanks to the LORD**, who is unceasingly **good**, a benevolence that flows out of his unconditional, steadfast **love**. This love **endures forever**, never to be turned away, never to come to an end. God is infinite and so great, **who can proclaim** his **mighty acts**? The answer is none. Worshippers can never adequately speak of his infinitely glorious being.

106:3. **Blessed**, or highly favored, are all who **maintain justice** and **do what is right**. All true worship requires the believer's volitional choices of obedience to practice righteousness. This inner purity, in turn, brings inner joy and happiness.

106:4–5. **Remember me**, the psalmist pleaded, indicating he felt forgotten by God. God, it seemed to him, had set him aside, no longer using him as in previous days. He asked that God **show favor** and deliver his people from their captivity. Desiring to be included in that future rescue, he prayed, **Come to my aid when you save them**. He asked God to deliver him, a reference to Babylonian captivity, and restore him to Jerusalem. The result of God's restoration would be the renewing of his **prosperity** toward his **chosen ones**.

B. A Prayer of Confession (106:6–46)

SUPPORTING IDEA: *The psalmist confesses Israel's long history of rebellion against God.*

106:6. The psalmist shifted to the nation collectively, acknowledging that they had **sinned**, even as their **fathers did**. With this confession, he begins to review the many years of disobedience on the part of Israel. This is why it seemed as if God had forgotten them, as God cannot bless sin.

106:7. In Egyptian bondage, God's people failed to honor the Lord. They gave **no thought** to the ten plagues that God inflicted upon the Egyptians. Instead, they **rebelled by the sea**. These plagues should have drawn the people to God in faith and obedience, but even as early as the **Red Sea**, they blatantly resisted God.

106:8–12. Yet, in spite of their sin, God graciously **saved them**, primarily to make his **mighty power known**. Miraculously, he **rebuked the Red Sea** in order to bring his people across on dry land (Exod. 14:21–22). He **redeemed** them **from the hand of the foe**, Egypt. This divine deliverance was certainly not because they deserved it but solely because of his lovingkindness. As a result of this powerful display at the Red Sea, **they believed** God's **promises** and **sang his praise** (Exod. 15).

106:13–15. But in spite of this dramatic rescue, Israel **soon forgot** this divine parting of the Red Sea. They **did not wait for his counsel** but went their own way, refusing to submit to God. In their impatience, they would not wait for God to provide for them. They grumbled against Moses and Aaron, complaining that they had better food in Egypt, a fate they considered better than starving in the desert (cp. Exod. 16:2–3). Yet God graciously gave them manna. Nevertheless, they soon grew tired of manna and complained that they had no meat (Num. 11:4–6). God graciously answered their complaint. **He gave them what they asked for**, sending quail into their camp. But their discontent was a terrible sin. So he struck them with **a wasting disease**, a necessary discipline.

106:16–18. Subsequently, Korah and 250 of his supporters revolted, rebelling against Moses and Aaron (Num. 16:1–3). They charged that **Moses** and **Aaron** took too much authority to themselves, failing to recognize that they were God-appointed leaders. So God judged these men, as the **earth opened up** and **swallowed** them. **Fire blazed** from the tabernacle and **consumed the wicked**, the accomplices of Korah (Num. 16:32,35).

106:19–23. This next incident involved Israel making a golden **calf** and worshipping **an idol** (Exod. 32:1–14; Deut. 9:7–21). At the base of Mount Sinai, they **exchanged their Glory**, the truth about God revealed to them, for the **image of a bull** (cp. Rom. 1:20,23). **They forgot** God who had delivered them out of **Egypt** through **the Red Sea**. Because of this sin, God said he would **destroy them** and start a new nation with Moses. But Moses **stood in the breach** for the people, and God spared them (Exod. 32:11–14; Deut. 9:25–29).

106:24–27. In Israel's wilderness wanderings, their unbelief was revealed in their refusal to enter the **pleasant land** (i.e., the promised land) when given the opportunity (cp. Num. 13–14). They **did not believe** God's promise but instead **grumbled**, listening to the unbelieving spies, rather than to the sure word of God. Because of their unbelief, God **swore** that this generation would not enter the promised land (Ps. 95:11; Heb. 3:11). He would **make them fall** in the wilderness. Further, God purposed that he would **scatter them throughout the lands**, a prophecy of Israel's Assyrian and Babylonian captivities (Ps. 44:11).

106:28–31. While still wandering in the wilderness, Israel went further into sin, committing apostasy, falling away from the Lord. They joined themselves to **Baal of Peor** as the men of Israel indulged in sexual immorality with Moabite women and made sacrifices to **lifeless gods** (Num. 25:1–3). This **provoked** the Lord, and he sent **a plague** among them. But **Phinehas** intervened by killing two of the most blatant offenders, **and the plague was checked**. As a result, God rewarded Phinehas and his family as **this was credited to him as righteousness for endless generations to come** (Num. 25:4–13).

106:32–33. By the **waters of Meribah**, Israel **angered** the Lord. In yet another sin committed by Israel in the wilderness, they were guilty of insurrection at Kadesh, where the people had no water (Num. 20:1–13). Much **trouble came to Moses** as a result of the sin of the people. **Rash words came from Moses' lips**, and God disqualified him from entering the promised land.

106:34–39. Once they were in the promised land, the unfaithfulness of the people did not stop, but continued in disobedience. They had been told by God to destroy the inhabitants in the land, but **they did not** (Judg. 1:21,27–36). Instead, **they mingled with the nations**, compromising with the pagan, godless inhabitants of the land (Judg. 3:5–6). This coexistence proved to be too great a temptation, and they soon **adopted their customs**, worshipping **their idols** (Judg. 2:12). In reality, **demons** stood behind these idols, receiving their worship, which involved parents killing **their sons and** their **daughters** and sacrificing them to these idols. **They defiled themselves by what they did**, committing prostitution by joining themselves with false gods (Ezek. 23:3,5–8; Hos. 5:3; 6:10).

106:40–43. God became **angry with his people**, and **handed them over** to foreign oppressors, the Assyrians and Babylonians (Judg. 2:14). These foreign powers **ruled over them**, taking them into captivity. The national security of Israel suffered greatly because of their sin. **Their enemies oppressed them and subjected them to their power** (Judg. 4:3; 10:12). Yet in spite of their rebellion, **many times** God **delivered them** from the consequences of their sins (Judg. 2:16–18). Nevertheless, **they were bent on rebellion** and continued to sin.

106:44–46. In foreign exile and captivity, God **took note of their distress when he heard their cry** (Judg. 3:9; 6:7; 10:10). The reason he did so was that **he remembered his covenant** (Ps. 105:8,42). God cannot deny his word.

In the depths of his **great love** toward his people, God **relented** and arose to rescue them once again. In so doing, **he caused them to be pitied by all who held them captive** (Ezek. 9:9–10; Jer. 42:12), leading to their release.

A Prayer for Restoration (106:47–48)

SUPPORTING IDEA: *The psalmist prays for restoration of the Israelites from their dispersion abroad in captivity.*

106:47. Having reviewed Israel's long history of repeated sin, the psalmist held hope for Israel's future amid their Babylonian captivity. God, who had forgiven in the past, would surely do so again. **Save us**, he prayed, the use of "us" indicating that the psalmist himself was in captivity and offered this prayer on behalf of the entire nation. **Gather us from the nations**, he pleaded, requesting that they be regathered from among the nations to replant them once again into their promised land in Judea. **Give thanks to your holy name and glory in your praise.** In Jerusalem, where their temple once was and where it would surely be rebuilt, they would praise God and worship him.

106:48. One final **praise** is offered to God, probably a later addition by the compilers (Pss. 41:13; 72:18; 89:52). This praise forms the concluding verse of Book IV of the Psalter (Pss. 90–106). As such, it also concludes this psalm as it began, with praise offered to God (v. 1). As God's loving-kindness endures forever, so should the praise offered to him by his people. In hope of deliverance and prosperity (vv. 4–5,47), the people of God are urged to respond **Amen! Praise the LORD.**

MAIN IDEA REVIEW: *The psalmist looks to the many long centuries of moral failure by Israel in order to cause God's people to look confidently to the future.*

III. CONCLUSION

One of the most remarkable ministries that God affords to man is the ministry of intercessory prayer. How extraordinary it is that one person can pray and can positively affect so many others. The Bible teaches, "The prayer of a righteous man is powerful and effective" (Jas. 5:16). This is precisely what we discover in Psalm 106. So powerful is intercessory prayer that one man, the psalmist, prayed on behalf of the entire nation and brought about their spiritual good. The intercessory prayer that God hears acknowledges sin. There must be confession of sin with the desire that God will, in turn, bless all believers. A collective confession of sin is necessary before God will restore his own people to her former glory. Only after they repent will God bless them again. May God raise up in this day many intercessors who will pray fervently on behalf of God's people, leading to an outpouring of God's blessing.

IV. LIFE APPLICATION

From this psalm, we learn in confessing sin that we should:

1. *Confess sin as sin.* Sin must always be acknowledged for what it is. There can be no sugarcoating sin when it is confessed to God. All sin is lawless rebellion against the Lord. It is a violation of God's holiness. It is what crucified Christ. Therefore, whenever we name sin to God, whether personal or corporate, we must be careful to own up to the full measure of its offensiveness to God.

2. *Seek forgiveness as undeserved.* The humble soul approaches God as a beggar seeking bread. Forgiveness is not something owed by God for our own goodness. Rather, it is always undeserved, granted only through the perfect merit of the Lord Jesus Christ. All who confess their sin are unworthy of the forgiveness they need. Let us, therefore, come in humility and brokenness, seeking the pardon we do not deserve.

3. *Praise God as Savior.* A forgiven life knows no limits in praising God. Jesus said, "He who has been forgiven little loves little" (Luke 7:47). The person who is most aware of pardon from sin will be the most fervent in praising God for the abundance of divine grace. In response to the forgiveness granted by God, should you not offer much praise to him?

V. PRAYER

God, have mercy upon us in this hour of sin against you. We acknowledge our sin in the church. We confess our sin, the iniquity of your own people! Forgive us for how we have rebelled against your word and have chosen to go our own way. In Jesus' name. Amen.

VI. DEEPER DISCOVERIES

A. Remember (106:4)

David asked for the Lord to remember (*zakar*) him three times in Psalm 25. This Hebrew word is a verb meaning "to contemplate, to recollect, to bring to remembrance when used of past events," yet it does not mean that God has actually forgotten something and is now able to recall it. Rather, it is used to convey the idea that God calls himself into action based upon his past promises to his servant. This word is used throughout the Old Testament to speak of God remembering, or executing, his covenant promises to his people (cp. Gen. 8:1; 9:15; 19:29; Exod. 2:24; 6:5–6; Pss. 98:3; 105:8,42; 106:45; Jer. 31:34).

B. Favor (106:4)

This word (*rason*) means "delight, desire, goodwill, or kindness," often shown from a superior to an inferior (Deut. 33:16; Ps. 5:12; Isa. 49:8; 60:10; 61:2). For example, in the Book of Proverbs, *rason* was used of a king toward his subjects (Prov. 14:35; 16:13,15). However, it is also used from one people in general toward another as meaning "what is acceptable" (Prov. 10:32; 11:27).

C. Depths (106:9)

The term *depths* (*tehom*) is used in various ways to speak of water, whether large bodies of water (Ps. 77:16; Isa. 51:10; 63:13) such as the Mediterranean Sea (Jon. 2:5) or even a subterranean water supply (Deut. 8:7; Ps. 78:15). It is often used as an image of destruction and judgment, as an overwhelming flood of divine wrath. It also speaks of the mounting troubles of life, as when David said that the Lord "reached down from on high and took hold of me; he drew me out of deep waters" (Ps. 18:16). The word is employed for the water that was used by God to judge the evil generation of Noah (Gen. 7:11; 8:2). It also speaks of God bringing the ocean depths over the city of Tyre to destroy it (Ezek. 26:19) and the execution of divine destruction against the nations (Hab. 3:10).

D. Holy (106:47)

The word *holy* (*qodesh*) means, in a primary sense, "that which is consecrated, sacred, set apart, dedicated, hallowed." In Leviticus 10:10 and Ezekiel 22:26, *qodesh* is set over against that which is "common" (*chol*). Like the Holy of Holies (Exod. 26:33–34; 2 Chr. 3:8,10), the temple (Ps. 20:2; Dan. 8:14), and the holy tabernacle (Exod. 28:43; 29:30; 35:19; 39:1), the Holy Hill was holy because of God's intrinsic holiness (cp. Isa. 6:3). The presence of God made the objects near him holy (cp. Exod. 3:5). Because God is holy, his people must be holy (cp. Lev. 11:44; 19:2; 1 Pet. 1:16), which is the very point of this psalm.

VII. TEACHING OUTLINE

A. A Prayer of Salvation (1-5)
PRAISE THE LORD (1a)
    1. Give Thanks to the Lord (1b,c)
      a. For he is good (1b)
      b. For he is loving (1c)
    2. Give Praise to the Lord (2-3)
      a. For he performs mighty acts (2)

        b. For he blesses justice (3)

     3. Bring Petitions to the Lord (4-5)

        a. Remember me when you save (4)

        b. Include me in your prosperity (5)

B. A Prayer of Confession (6-46)

WE HAVE SINNED AS OUR FATHERS (6)

     1. The Sin of Rebellion (7-12)

        a. They disregarded God's power (7a)

        b. They disregarded God's love (7b)

        c. They disobeyed God's word (7c)

        d. Yet God delivered them (8-10)

        e. God drowned their enemies (11-12)

     2. The Sin of Discontentment (13-15)

        a. They forgot God's deliverance (13)

        b. They tested God's patience (14)

        c. They received God's discipline (15)

     3. The Sin of Envy (16-18)

        a. They were jealous of Moses (16)

        b. They were devoured by the earth (17)

        c. They were consumed with fire (18)

     4. The Sin of Idolatry (19-23)

        a. They worshiped metal calf (19)

        b. They exchanged glory for lies (20)

        c. They forgot God who saved them (21-22)

        d. They were spared by Moses' prayer (23)

     5. The Sin of Unbelief (24-27)

        a. They despised the promised land (24a)

        b. They disregarded the Lord's promises (24b)

        c. They disobeyed the Lord's word (25)

        d. They suffered under God's hand (26-27)

     6. The Sin of Apostasy (28-31)

        a. They joined themselves to Baal (28)

        b. They provoked God's anger (29)

        c. They were spared further suffering (30-31)

     7. The Sin of Arrogance (32-33)

        a. They angered the Lord (32)

        b. They rebelled against the Spirit (33a)

        c. Moses Spoke Rash Words (33b)

     8. The Sin of Compromise (34-46)

        a. They did not destroy the Canaanites (34)

        b. They became like the Canaanites (35)

        c. They worshiped like the Canaanites (36-38)

      d. They were defiled like the Canaanites (39)

      e. They were despised by God (40)

      f. They were defeated by God (41-42)

      g. They were delivered by God (43a)

      h. They were disobedient to God (43b)

      i. They were remembered by God (44-46)

C. A Prayer for Restoration (47-48)

    1. A Plea for Deliverance (47)

      a. Save us (47a)

      b. Re-gather us (47b,c)

    2. A Praise for God (48)

      a. Let all Israel praise God (48a)

      b. Let all people praise God (48b)

PRAISE THE LORD (48c)

Psalm 107

Good God!

"*I*f I could write as I would about the goodness of God to me, the ink would boil in my pen!"

F r a n c i s   H a v e r g a l

I. INTRODUCTION

In all his divine perfections and attributes, God is infinitely good. This is a truth of foundational importance to every believer's understanding of God. Everything good in one's life has come down from God above, who is perfectly good. Whether the expression of his goodness be spiritual, physical, or emotional, it is the direct gift of a good God to his people. In the midst of soul-crushing difficulties and when surrounded by life-threatening dangers, believers must remain fixed upon the goodness of God. Let all the saints give thanks to the Lord, who remains immutably good. Even in difficult circumstances and bad times, let us declare that God is good.

Psalm 107 is a stirring exhortation to praise the Lord for his unfailing goodness toward his people. This divine goodness flows out of his eternal loving-kindness and loyal covenant love toward his own. The often repeated chorus "Let them give thanks to the LORD for his unfailing love" is a dominant theme of this psalm (vv. 1,8,15,21,31). The opening line "Give thanks to the LORD" ties this psalm together with the previous two, forming a trilogy (Pss. 105–107), connecting Book IV (Pss. 90–106) with Book V (Pss. 107–150). As Book IV concluded, issuing the call "Give thanks to the LORD," so Book V begins by echoing the same passionate appeal. Let us all give thanks to God who is infinitely good.

II. COMMENTARY

> **MAIN IDEA:** *The psalmist calls all people to praise the Lord for his many providential deliverances.*

A Praise for God's Goodness (107:1–3)

107:1. Here is an initial call to praise. God is to be offered **thanks** because **he is good**. Divine goodness is one of the most fundamental truths about God (Pss. 25:8; 86:5; 106:1; 118:1). His steadfast love **endures forever**, never diminishing toward his people.

107:2–3. The redeemed always should be talking about God's goodness. "Redeemed" is a synonym for being delivered or rescued from danger. **The foe** is probably a reference to Babylon amid their days of Babylonian captivity as Israel's enemies. Throughout the centuries, God had delivered his people from foreign **lands** where they had been held captive and in slavery.

B Portraits of God's Goodness (107:4–32)

107:4–5. In the wilderness, Israel found herself in a forty-year track to nowhere. They **wandered in desert wastelands** for four decades, captive to their own sin. They found **no way to a city where they could settle**, where a supply of food and water could be found to satisfy and sustain them. They were **hungry** and **thirsty**.

107:6–9. They finally became so desperate that they **cried out to the LORD**. He **delivered them**. They did not deserve it, but God by his grace delivered them, an expression of his goodness. God led them by a direct route, **a straight way**, clear of dangerous and difficult obstacles, to provide for their needs. They should **give thanks to the LORD**, a refrain (cp. vv. 15,21,31) for his goodness and love. He has satisfied **the thirsty** and fed the **hungry**, doing good to them.

107:10–12. Some of the people had **sat in darkness**, a vivid imagery for distress, despair, and hopelessness. **Deepest gloom** was theirs, a near-death ordeal. They were **prisoners** in foreign bondage, held **in iron chains**. This imprisonment was disciplinary by the Lord, the result of Israel's rebellion **against the words of God**. Because of their sin, God **subjected them to bitter labor**. Their prison life was brutal, becoming chained slave gangs, subjected to harsh, unending labor (cp. v. 10). As their strength failed them, **they stumbled**, their bodies unable to bear them up.

107:13–14. Finally, **they cried to the LORD**. Having been humbled, they confessed their sin and repented of their evil ways. God heard their cries for help and intervened to save **them from their distress**. God **brought them out**, delivering them. He snapped their **chains** of slavery and imprisonment, releasing them from their hard labor.

107:15–16. In response, the psalmist urged that the people **give thanks to the** LORD **for his unfailing love**. God **breaks down** the city **gates** of Israel's oppressive foe, a reference to the city of Babylon, which had held Israel captive for seventy years.

107:17. Under such severe affliction, some of the Israelites had become **fools**, that is, morally incapable of accepting God's instruction. They pursued **rebellious ways** and **iniquities**. Israel had rebelled against the Lord, amazingly, in spite of the goodness of God in delivering his people out of Egyptian bondage through the Red Sea and feeding them quail and manna.

107:18–19. They **loathed all food**. In their hearts, they did not like God's will or God's timing. They wanted better provision *now*, and when they did not receive it, they grew impatient. **Near the gates of death** means they were dying, at the point of death. Again, **they cried** with a shriek for help, and, again, God **saved them**.

107:20–22. God saved the people by sending forth **his word**. He sent a saving message and **healed them**. God **rescued them from the grave**. "Grave" (a derivative of *shachah*, to fall down in troubles, to sink down in despair, to bow down) means to be plummeted down in trials and pain. Once saved and delivered from their troubles, their hearts should overflow with praise and **thanks** to God for his **wonderful deeds**. They should **sacrifice thank offerings** to God for his **works** of deliverance, accompanied by **songs of joy**.

107:23–27. When God's people launched out to **the sea in ships**, perhaps as merchants in pursuit of trade, they witnessed the works of the Lord **in the deep**. This speaks of terrifying storms in the open sea sent by the Lord. He **stirred up a tempest** and **lifted high the waves**, bringing these storms against Israel because of her sin. In these wave-tossed ships, their **courage melted away** in fear and misery. **At their wits' end**, all their wisdom was swallowed up; they were unable to navigate.

107:28–29. Finally, humbled and convicted of their rebellious ways, they **cried out to the** LORD. Again, he **brought them out of their distresses**. The God who sent the storm is the God who **stilled the storm** and rescued his people.

107:30–32. God's people **were glad** when the angry waves **grew calm**. God then **guided them to their desired haven**, a safe harbor of refuge. God ushered them where they needed to be. As a result, they should give thanks, a refrain in this psalm (cp. vv 1,8–9,15,21–22,31–32). This giving of thanks should be offered publicly before the **assembly** and in the **council of the elders** so that others could hear and be glad.

◖C◗ Principles of God's Goodness (107:33–43)

107:33–34. The Lord sometimes disciplined his people by turning their **rivers** (water supply) **into a desert** (drought) or by turning their

fruitful land into a wasteland. This difficulty was the direct result of their **wickedness**.

107:35–40. Now, God **turned the desert into pools of water**, the reverse effect of verses 33–34. God's discipline is only for a season, and he delights to restore his children who repent of their sin. But what if those blessed by God experience misfortune and are made to experience **oppression, calamity and sorrow** by these arrogant foes? In such cases, God will call their oppressors into account. God will strip their oppressors of their power and influence and cause them to be removed from office, never to harm God's people again.

107:41–42. But unlike God's dealing with these proud princes, he will act as the protector of **the needy** who look to him for help. The **upright see and rejoice** over God's protection and deliverance.

107:43. This psalm ends with an instructive appeal. This song concludes as it began, with a call to **consider**, ponder, and meditate upon the **great love of the** LORD.

III. CONCLUSION

A favorite psalm of the English Puritans who sailed to America, Psalm 107 came to be known as "the Pilgrims' Psalm." Under the leadership of William Bradford, the Pilgrims courageously crossed the Atlantic Ocean in search of religious freedom in the New World and found it as they landed in America. The Pilgrims came ashore at Plymouth Rock on Monday, December 11, 1620, after having spent the previous day worshipping God aboard their ship, the *Mayflower*. Governor William Bradford in his account of the Plymouth Plantation explicitly referred to Psalm 107. His well-known summation of their achievement was based, virtually verbatim, on Psalm 107. This psalm was obviously much on the minds of the Pilgrims as they came to America in search of a new land in which to worship God. This hymn chronicling God's goodness to his people was their guiding light. So should it be for believers today. God guides his people, and where he guides, there he provides. May all who trust him thank him for his providential care and goodness.

IV. TEACHING OUTLINE

A. Praise for God's Goodness (1-3)
   1. Give Thanks to the Lord (1)
      a. For he is good (1a)
      b. For he is loving (1b)
   2. Let the Redeemed Say (2-3)
      a. Those he redeemed from foreign lands (2b)
      b. Those he redeemed from all lands (3)

B. Portraits of God's Goodness (4-32)
   1. He Delivered Those in the Barren Desert (4-9)
      a. They wandered without food, water (4-5)
      b. They called to the Lord (6)
      c. They received God's deliverance (6b-7)
      d. They should give thanks (8-9)
   2. He Delivered Those in Foreign Bondage (10-16)
      a. They were imprisoned in chains (10)
      b. They suffered for disobedience (11-12)
      c. They called to the Lord (13)
      d. They received God's deliverance (13b-14)
      e. They should give thanks (15-16)
   3. He Delivered Those with Deadly Disease (17-22)
      a. They suffered for their sins (17-18)
      b. They called to the Lord (19a)
      c. They received God's deliverance (19b-20)
      d. They should give thanks (21-22)
   4. He Delivered Those on the Perilous Sea (23-32)
      a. They suffered on the open sea (23-27)
      b. They cried to the Lord (28a)
      c. They received God's deliverance (28b-30)
      d. They should give thanks (31-32)
C. Principles of God's Goodness (33-43)
   1. God Disciplines the Disobedient (33-34)
      a. He turns rivers into desert (33)
      b. He turns fruitful land into waste (34)
   2. God Restores the Humble (35-38)
      a. He turns desert into pools (35)
      b. He feeds the hungry (36)
      c. He blesses their labors (37)
      d. He increases their numbers (38)
   3. God Humbles the Proud (39-40)
D. He Decreases Their Numbers (39)
E. He Turns Them to the Desert (40)
   1. God Restores the Upright (41-42)
      a. He delivers the needy (41)
      b. He rejoices the obedient (42a)
      c. He silences the wicked (42b)
   2. God Instructs His People (43)
      a. He teaches them wisely (43a)
      b. He loves them greatly (43b)

Psalm 108
Unsinkable Faith

"*W*here reason cannot wade, there faith may swim."

T h o m a s   W a t s o n

Psalm 108

I. INTRODUCTION

In the face of mounting difficulties and growing dangers, and amid the crucible of fiery trials, a true, God-implanted faith will ultimately remain strong and steadfast. This is the unwavering nature of faith that is anchored in God. Trusting the Lord does not naively explain away one's problems, nor make them less than what they really are. Neither does faith go into denial and pretend that problems do not exist. To the contrary, faith faces problems head-on with a positive, triumphant outlook. Faith believes that God will inevitably work for our good as he pursues his own glory.

In the midst of every difficulty, faith always sees the opportunity for God to work. Faith is always up, not down; always encouraged, not discouraged; always reaching forward, not retreating backward; always overcoming, not being overcome. Faith is always climbing to the top of the pile, not languishing under it. Though it may take on much water in the storms of life, faith is unsinkable.

This is the kind of faith that we see in the life of David in Psalm 108. It is a hymn of trust in God, a song of triumph over God's enemies. This psalm is a repeat of two previous psalms, which are joined together here. In this psalm, David, or possibly a later anonymous collector, combined portions of Psalm 57 and Psalm 60 to form this one psalm. In combining these two psalms, the laments from the previous two works were omitted and only David's exaltation and confidence in God were merged together. Thus, it contains a double portion of triumphant faith in God. This potent psalm provides encouragement for the soul that trusts God.

II. COMMENTARY

MAIN IDEA: *David praises God's great love toward him and petitions divine help against his enemies.*

A David's Faith (108:1–6)

108:1. In the midst of his adversity, David declared to God that his heart was **steadfast**. His soul was fixed and firm, stable and settled, not tossed to and fro. He was **steadfast** because of his sure confidence in God, who is sovereign over all. Such a steady heart is a singing heart. Confidence in God gave David something to **sing** about. Even in the face of battle and deadly foes, David sang to the Lord anthems of praise, not merely with his lips but out of his **soul**, from the very depths of his being.

108:2–4. David called for musical instruments to **awake**, indicating this may be a morning song sung before the day's battle. His songs of praise will be accompanied by the joyful instruments of the **harp and lyre**. Even those who were his enemies **among the peoples** and the **nations** would hear his praises of God. David could sing so confidently because God's unconditional, loyal **love** toward his own people is a love that is fixed forever. Further, God's **faithfulness** is reason to sing. God will keep his word and never forsake his people.

108:5–6. God is exalted **above the heavens**, regardless of David's threatening circumstances. His **glory** is **over all the earth**, no matter how the nations rage against him. In this particular adversity, it will be clear that God is over all. God will show how greatly exalted he is by delivering those whom he loves out of this hour of crisis.

B David's Foundation (108:7–9)

108:7. God has spoken from his sanctuary, David declared. All God's words are holy, transcendent, and true, without any mixture of error. This divine revelation is the very foundation of David's faith. God says he **will parcel out Shechem**, the land east of the Jordan River, to his chosen people to be their possession and inheritance. God promises and pledges to allot **the Valley of Succoth**, the land west of the Jordan River, to his people in spite of his enemies.

108:8. Gilead and **Manasseh** were two portions of the promised land that represent larger areas of the eastern side of the Jordan River, the land occupied by Israel at the time of the conquest under Joshua. **Ephraim** and **Judah** were the two most prominent tribes on the west side of the Jordan River. Judah will be God's **scepter**, a prophecy of the coming of the Messiah who would be born of the tribe of Judah (Gen. 49:10; Mic. 5:2).

108:9. **Moab** will be God's **washbasin**, assigned a position of lowly humiliation before him. **Edom** was another proud nation that would not bow before the Lord. Though it was lifted up in arrogance, God would subjugate it. God would **shout in triumph** over **Philistia** and the Philistines (i.e., Goliath of Gath). These were enemies of Israel whom God had promised to defeat in giving the promised land to his people.

◪ David's Fight (108:10–13)

108:10–11. As David faced this hour of crisis, threatened by surrounding nations, he asked a series of questions. **Who will bring me to the fortified city? Who will lead me to Edom?** This is to say: Who will give him the victory? Where will he look for help? The recent struggles of God's people have given the impression that God has **rejected** them, or has withheld his power on their behalf. The only one who could give David victory over the **armies** was God himself.

108:12–13. Victory ultimately belongs to the Lord. Thus, David offered this petition, that God would **give us aid against the enemy**. David's faith was rightly placed. It was **with God** alone that he would **gain the victory**.

III. CONCLUSION

In an hour of crisis, David drew strength by recalling the promises God had made in his Word. He stood strong by remembering how God gave his people the promised land as their inheritance, just as he had pledged. David was emboldened by clinging to the unshakeable promises in God's Word. Because God had already promised to give his people the promised land, the psalmist believed that victory would be his. A God-given victory would surely be theirs in their fight against surrounding enemies. David was trusting that in this crisis God would keep his promise.

So must all believers stand on God's promises made in his Word. "The grass withers and the flowers fall, but the word of our God stands forever" (Isa. 40:8). God's inerrant, infallible Word must be the firm foundation on which God's people stand.

IV. TEACHING OUTLINE

A. David's Faith (1-6)
   1. My Heart Is Steadfast (1a)
   2. My Heart Is Singing (1b-4)
      a. I will make music (1b)
      b. I will awaken the dawn (2)
      c. I will praise God (3)
      d. For his love and lovingkindness (4)

3. My Heart Is Soaring (5-6)
B. David's Foundation (7-9)
    1. God's Right Hand Is Strong (6)
        a. Able to save us (6a)
        b. Able to deliver us (6b)
    2. God's Spoken Word Is Sure (7-9)
        a. I will parcel out Shechem (7b)
        b. I will measure off Succoth (7c)
        c. Gilead and Manasseh are God's possession (8a)
        d. Ephraim is my helmet (8b)
        e. Judah is my scepter (8c)
        f. Moab is my washbasin (9a)
        g. Edom is under my sandal (9b)
        h. Philistia is under my shout (9c)
C. David's Fight (10-13)
    1. The Searching Question (10)
        a. Who will deliver me? (10a)
        b. Who will lead me? (10b)
    2. The Affirming Answer (11)
D. God Who Has Rejected Us (11a)
E. God Who Has Left Us (11b)
    1. The Affirming Request (13)
        a. Give us aid to fight (12)
        b. Give us victory in war (13)

Psalm 109
Character Assassination

"No greater injury can be inflicted upon men than

to wound their reputation."

J o h n   C a l v i n

Psalm 109

I. INTRODUCTION

Has anyone ever maliciously slandered you because of your faith? Has anyone ever sought to do great harm to your reputation because of your allegiance to Christ? Has anyone ever spread venomous gossip about you because you are a Christian? Jesus said such an attack is to be expected: "Blessed are you when people insult you, persecute you and falsely say all kinds of evil against you because of me" (Matt. 5:11). Maybe it was a coworker in your office. Perhaps a family member. Or it could have been another "so-called" brother or sister in the Lord. Regardless, they have spoken untruths about you and have harmed you. And, unfortunately, you were not there to defend yourself. All you could do was suffer under the injustice.

In one way or another, we can all identify with this. People will reject us and seek to do us harm, especially when they have no answer for what we believe and how we live. Their way of dealing with us is to attack us, and such character assassination is always painful.

This is precisely what David was experiencing when he wrote Psalm 109. He was undergoing a character assassination at the hands of ruthless men. One ruthless man in particular was the ringleader and caused David the greatest trouble. This unknown opponent may have been King Saul, who sought to do him much harm. Or one of Saul's officers may have been the point man in this relentless verbal assault against David. Either way, David was reeling under a painful attack on his character and suffering the devastation of his reputation. His heart was deeply wounded, and he had no way to set the record straight. David responded by taking this matter to the Lord in prayer.

The best way to get rid of an enemy is to leave him or her with the Lord. As we find ourselves in situations similar to David's plight, we should also pray exactly as he did. Ultimately, only God can make it right.

II. COMMENTARY

> **MAIN IDEA:** David appeals for God's protection as he suffers under painful slander.

A David's Lamentation (109:1–5)

109:1–2. David began, **O God, whom I praise**, addressing God as worthy of his praise, even in this painful hour. **Do not remain silent**, he pleaded, petitioning God to answer him in this excruciating ordeal. **Wicked and deceitful men** had risen up to falsely accuse him. Their **mouths** were twisted, wicked, and evil in what they were saying against him. These false accusations against him were spoken with **lying tongues**, assassinating his character, impugning his motives, and slandering his life.

109:3. On every side, David was met with **words of hatred** against him. This verbal assault against him was **without cause**, completely unjustified. He was innocent and blameless yet being wrongly accused as if he were guilty.

109:4–5. David had extended his foes only **friendship** while they, in turn, had shown him **evil** and **hatred**. Throughout this painful ordeal, David committed this matter to God in **prayer**. Literally, "But I am prayer," that is, "I am all prayer." While David's enemies were spewing false words against him, he was speaking to God. David had done them **good**, showing them friendship, but they had shown him evil and hatred.

B David's Imprecation (109:6–20)

109:6. References to David's enemies now change from the plural "they" (vv. 2–5) to the singular "him" and "his" (vv. 6–19). Not until verse 20 do they return to the plural again ("accusers"). These singular pronouns point to the ringleader of this opposition against David. He pleaded with God for this one man, his wicked **accuser**, to find himself on the receiving end of similar slander. May God **appoint an evil man** to be his **accuser** (*satan*), David asked God. **At his right hand**, where a defendant would stand in a law court, let him face an adversary.

109:7–8. David desired that the ringleader of this slanderous attack against him **be found guilty**. Let the truth about his accuser's own evil character be made known. **May the prayers** of his accuser come back to **condemn him**. He prayed, **may his days be few**, so that no more harm may be done to the Lord's work. Let another **take his place of leadership**. This verse was later quoted by Peter regarding Judas forfeiting his position among the twelve disciples (Acts 1:20).

109:9–11. The phrase **may his children be fatherless** expresses this thought: "Cut short his days; cause him to die soon." David did not request that his children be killed but only their father. When this accuser died, his children would be left as **wandering beggars**, leaving them without a father to provide for them. David asked that a **creditor** seize all his possessions, the result of this adversary dying soon. May he die now, unexpectedly, and **strangers plunder** all his property.

109:12–15. Because of the greatness of this accuser's sin, divine judgment must come to him soon. May his surviving children be spared **pity** after his death. **May his descendants be cut off**, not to spread their father's influence of evil. Because children are often like their father, let their names be **blotted out**. David prayed that all influences of this evil man's life be stopped, even through his surviving children. **May the iniquity** of this accuser's **fathers be remembered**. He requested that the guilt of his mother **never be blotted out**. May their sins **always remain before the Lord**. If there is to be no repentance, then let them be put to death by God lest they cause the righteous any more harm.

109:16–20. The evil man should be judged by God because **he never thought of doing a kindness**. He showed much hatred, oppression, and persecution of the godly. He persecuted the righteous man and **hounded** him **to death** like prey. The false accuser **loved to pronounce a curse**. May the cursing that he pronounced on others come back to curse him. The **cursing** of the righteous was such a part of his everyday life that it was **as his garment**, a constant covering and companion. He drank it up like water. His life was saturated with these cursings like **oil**, seeping into his innermost being, down to his **bones**. David pleaded for divine justice and vindication to be exercised toward this evil man, the leader of those who **speak evil of me**.

C David's Desperation (109:21–25)

109:21. In this desperate strait, David turned to the **Sovereign Lord** for deliverance from his false accuser. **Deal well with me**, he appealed to God, asking for divine protection and escape from the relentless attacks of this evil man. David's appeal was **for your name's sake**, that God might be glorified by showing mercy to him. He wanted God to do something so wonderful that it would be clear that this was the hand of God. David desired that God show his great **love** by delivering him from this attack.

109:22–23. David told God that he was **poor and needy** with a **wounded**, broken **heart**. This ordeal was deeply hurtful, caused by his enemies. His life's strength was flowing out of him, like the disappearance of a fleeting evening **shadow**. He was like a dreaded **locust**, the enemy of the farmer. Farmers would shake the locusts off their trees and shrubs to destroy them. This was how David felt, as one who had been shaken off and had fallen to the ground, leaving him cast down and weakened.

109:24–25. David's **knees** were weary from **fasting**, which was associated with prayer. He had been pleading with God for divine strength and help, so much so that he was physically weak and lean from all the prayer and fasting. He was dishonored by their many lies against him, the **object of scorn**. They shook their **heads** at him, a gesture of scorn.

D David's Petition (109:26–29)

109:26–27. David concluded with a passionate plea for God's **hand** to deliver him from the ruthless attacks. Only God could defend him, so he called out to God for protection and deliverance from his enemies. He appealed to God to intervene in such a powerful way that even his enemies must acknowledge that it was God who had acted so decisively in rescuing him.

109:28. Let them continue to **curse** me, David declared. It would only serve to bring God's actions toward him to **bless** him. The more they cursed him, the more it would force the hand of God to favor him. They would realize that they had been opposing God by opposing God's **servant**, causing them to be ashamed of their evil conspiracy. David would **rejoice** as he realized that he was aligned with God.

109:29. When God acts, his accusers will surely be **clothed with disgrace** before men. The **shame** and dishonor his accusers sought to bring upon David are set to recoil and come back upon their own heads.

E David's Adoration (109:30–31)

109:30. David now extolled the greatness of God **with** his **mouth**. He would give thanks for the fact that God would hear him and help him. He will publicly offer his **praise** in the **great throng**.

109:31. Earlier, David asked that an accuser might stand at the right hand of the one doing evil to accuse him of wrong (v. 6). Here, the accuser is replaced by God, who stands at the **right hand** of his own beloved to defend and save them.

III. CONCLUSION

When believers find themselves attacked by those who impugn their character and slander their reputation, they should respond as David did. When persecution comes, God's people should resort to these actions:

Prayer. Commit the injustice to God. Ask God to deal with this vicious person. Seek the Lord to act in vindication. Do not personally seek to make the wrong right.

Patience. Give God time to act. Remember, God is long-suffering with sinners. So should every believer be when wronged. While you wait, turn the other cheek.

Praise. David began and concluded this psalm with praise for God. That should be the pattern for all who trust him. Do not let someone else douse cold water on your flaming love for God. Through it all, give glory to God, who is at your right hand to defend you. The battle belongs to the Lord.

IV. TEACHING OUTLINE

A. David's Lamentation (1-5)
  1. God, Do Not Remain Silent (1)
  2. God, Consider My Suffering (2-5)
      a. Wicked men slander me (2)
      b. Hateful words attack me (3)
B. David's Imprecation (6-20)
  1. Appoint an Evil Man Against Him (6-7)
      a. To accuse him (6)
      b. To indict him (7)
  2. Appoint a Painful Future for Him (8-15)
      a. May his days be few (8a)
      b. May his leadership be gone (8b)
      c. May his children be fatherless (9a)
      d. May his wife be a widow (9b)
      e. May his children be beggars (10a)
      f. May his offspring be homeless (10b)
      g. May his possessions be seized (11)
      h. May his children be neglected (12)
      i. May his descendents be cut off (13)
      j. May his forefathers be dishonored (14a)
      k. May his mother be defamed (14b-15)
      l. May his sin be known (16-18)
      m. May his sin be repaid (19-20)

C. David's Desperation (21-25)
   1. Deliver Me (21)
      a. For your name's sake (21a)
      b. Out of your goodness (21b)
   2. Discern Me (22-25)
      a. My heart is wounded (22)
      b. My life is fading (23)
      c. My knees are collapsing (24a)
      d. My body's thin (24b)
      e. My accusers are scornful (25)
D. David's Petition (26-29)
   1. Save Me (26)
   2. Shame Them (27)
      a. Let them know you did this (27)
      b. Let them hear me rejoice (28)
      c. Let them be put to disgrace (29)
E. David's Adoration (30-31)
   1. The Rejoicing of His Praise (30)
      a. With my mouth (20a)
      b. In the great throng (30b)
   2. The Reasons for His Praise (31)
      a. God stands with the needy (31a)
      b. God saves the condemned (31b)

Psalm 110

Sovereign Savior

"*S*overeignty characterizes the whole being of God.

He is sovereign in all His attributes."

A . W . P i n k

Psalm 110

I. INTRODUCTION

Americans have had a strong sense of the providence and sovereignty of God from the beginnings of the Republic. The preambles to the constitution of all fifty states acknowledge God and his providence as the basis of life and liberty.

In a letter (August 20, 1778) to Brigadier General Thomas Nelson, George Washington wrote: "The Hand of providence has been so conspicuous in all this, that he must be worse than an infidel that lacks faith, and more than wicked, that has not gratitude enough to acknowledge his obligations."

As George W. Bush, the forty-third President of the United States, announced his first candidacy for president, he stated that he believed in a "divine plan that supersedes all human plans." He recognized the invisible hand of God upon the direction of history and nations to carry out his own divinely appointed ends. On February 6, 2004, at the National Prayer Breakfast, President Bush said, "We can be confident in the ways of Providence. . . . Behind all of life and all of history, there is a dedication and purpose set out by the hand of a just and faithful God." By this statement, the President affirmed again his foundational faith in God who, as John Calvin once wrote, "governs the vast machinery of the whole world."

There was another world leader who believed exactly the same way. He also confessed God's sovereign hand over the nations. This king's name was David, the author of Psalm 110. This fact of God's authority over all is precisely the God-centered theology that emerges from the verses of this psalm, a royal psalm. Here is a song that portrays God as King over all the earth and a God who is executing his plans for human history. This psalm is a song that declares the absolute reign of God and his Son, the Lord Jesus Christ, over all the realms of mankind.

II. COMMENTARY

MAIN IDEA: *David represents the sovereign kingship of the coming Messiah as inseparably united with his priesthood.*

A The Providential Reign of Christ (110:1–3)

SUPPORTING IDEA: *David records the Lord's decree in establishing his anointed as king over all in spite of the opposition of man.*

110:1. This psalm begins with a conversation between the first and second members of the Godhead. The LORD, God the Father, **says to my Lord**, God the Son, something remarkable. Jesus Christ, David's Lord, is appointed to **sit** at God's **right hand**, the place of highest authority, privilege, and honor. With stature equal to God's, the Son will share in the universal reign of the Father. Christ is presently seated until the future time when he returns to the earth as a conquering king. Ancient kings often depicted themselves as placing their feet on defeated enemies, signifying their dominance over them (Josh. 10:24). Christ's enemies will become his **footstool**, subjugated and subdued under him.

110:2. Ensuring that this future reign of Christ will come to pass, **The LORD**, God the Father, will **extend** his Son's **scepter** until there is no one left to oppose his rule. This **mighty scepter** given to Christ represents his authorized sovereignty. Once enthroned, the Father commands the Son to **rule** and establish his kingdom over his **enemies**. These enemies are all unbelievers who oppose the gospel and reject his kingdom.

110:3. The Father assures the Son that his **troops**, those true believers who are enlisted in Christ's service, **will be willing** to join and support his kingdom. On a specific **day**, God's power will be unleashed and his chosen ones will volunteer willingly to enter his cause. Christ will be dressed in **holy majesty**, without any sin. The Lord Jesus Christ is pictured here as so strong and mighty that he is perpetually in the bloom of **youth**—strong, vigorous, and aggressive.

B The Priestly Redemption of Christ (110:4)

SUPPORTING IDEA: *David declares that Christ will be appointed as a priest by God.*

110:4a. The LORD, God the Father, **has sworn** to himself that he will send his Son into this world to be a priest. This will be the first time that one person will serve as both priest and king. A priest was one who represented the people before God. Yet the people did not choose their own representative. To the contrary, God the Father ordained his chosen leaders to the priesthood. In like manner, Christ is designated by the Father to this redemptive mission. Regarding this appointment of Christ to this saving work, God **will not change his mind**. His eternal purposes are fixed and unchanging (Acts 2:23; 1 Pet. 1:20; Rev. 13:8; 17:8).

110:4b. In the precreation plan of God, the Father declared to the Son, **You are a priest forever.** Jesus is the final and perfect high priest, never to be succeeded by another. His sovereign appointment is eternally established, based upon the perfection of his divine person and his all-sufficient work on the cross. No need exists for anyone else to make another sacrifice for sins. His work of atonement is finished. He remains a priest forever, seated at the Father's right hand, eternally resting in his once-for-all-time death (Heb. 1:3; 10:12,14). The redemptive merits of his substitutionary sacrifice remain irrevocable (Heb. 10:17–18).

110:4c. In this divine appointment as priest, the Father sent Christ according to **the order of Melchizedek.** Jesus could not be of Aaron's lineage if his priesthood was to be eternal. Melchizedek was a real person, a priest-king of Salem (Gen. 14:17–20). He is a picture of Christ's priesthood in which he is both king and priest (Heb. 5:6; 7:17,21). Thus, his priesthood belongs to a higher order than that of Aaron and his sons, resulting in a perfect work of salvation.

🄲 The Prophetic Return of Christ (110:5–7)

> **SUPPORTING IDEA:** *David foresees a future time when the Messiah will return and defeat his enemies.*

110:5. **The Lord,** God the Father, now stands at the Son's **right hand,** near him in order to assist in the warfare surrounding the time of his second coming (Rev. 19:11–21). Here the Father stands ready to ensure the success of the Son's final mission. This looks ahead to the time of the Great Tribulation at the end of this age. Then the Son will execute all **kings** who oppose him, putting them to death, sentencing them to damnation. That hour will be the **day of his wrath** (Rev. 6:16–17), the final seven-year period of judgment to come to the earth.

110:6. Christ the Son will **judge the nations,** separating the sheep from the goats (Matt. 25:31–46), rendering his judicial verdict for all men. In a day of great carnage, Christ is seen as **heaping up the dead.** This is battlefield imagery, conveying the defeat of all who oppose him. Christ's victory will be global, **crushing the rulers of the whole earth.** None will be left to oppose him.

110:7. In the aftermath of this triumphant return, Christ will drink **from a brook beside the way**. This pictures Christ in his second coming as refreshed and renewed in strength, revived in his mission and reign. **He will lift up his head**, picturing him in holy boldness, courage, and determination.

> **MAIN IDEA REVIEW:** *David represents the sovereign kingship of the coming Messiah as inseparably united with his priesthood.*

III. CONCLUSION

Frederic Farrar, nineteenth-century British theologian, told of a conversation he had with Queen Victoria after she had heard one of her chaplains preach on Christ's second coming. She said, "Oh, Dr. Farrar, how I wish that the Lord would come during my lifetime!" When he asked why she desired this, she replied, "Because I would love to lay my crown at His blessed feet in reverent adoration."

This should be the response of all who hear of the Lord Jesus Christ. He is heaven's enthroned Lord and is the only Savior of sinners. As the High Priest of his people, he offered the perfect sacrifice for sins, a sacrifice so sufficient that it need never be repeated again. In this atonement for sins, Jesus offered himself on the cross, once for everyone who believes. This sovereign Savior is returning soon to judge all who refuse him. The penetrating question is: Do *you* know him? Have *you* repented of your sins and believed on him? If not, do so this moment.

IV. LIFE APPLICATION

This psalm presents Jesus Christ as the sovereign Lord over all and the Savior of all who believe. It is important that every life respond rightly in order to be received by him. We must come to Christ on his terms, not our own. This requires our repentance and faith, these two being inseparably bound together in any true conversion.

We must repent of sin. Repentance was at the heart of the evangelistic preaching of John the Baptist (Matt. 3:2–3,8), Jesus (Matt. 4:17), the disciples (Luke 24:47), Peter (Acts 2:38), and Paul (Acts 20:21). Every sinner who is to be saved must repent. This means there must be a deep, godly sorrow over one's sin and a turning away from sin toward Christ. It involves a change of mind, heart, and will that brings the sinner to a decisive crisis point of brokenness and mourning over his sin (Matt. 5:3–4), a turning from a life of sin and selfish pursuits, and a turning to Christ alone for salvation.

We must believe in Christ. Saving faith is the total commitment of a sin-forsaking soul to Jesus Christ. It is the sinner coming to the end of himself, denying himself (Matt. 16:24), and trusting Christ alone for salvation (Eph.

2:8–9). The faith that saves is the sinner submitting himself to the authority of Christ and surrendering to him (Luke 14:31–33). It is taking up a cross, which is an instrument of death, dying to self, and choosing to follow Christ (Luke 9:23–25). It is transferring one's life to Christ, trusting in his substitutionary death for salvation (1 Cor. 15:3–4). This is the faith that must be exercised toward Christ, the choice of the will to rely exclusively upon him as one's Savior and Lord (Rom. 10:9–10).

V. PRAYER

God, open lost eyes to behold the grace of the Lord Jesus Christ to save from sin. Open unconverted ears to hear the good news of Christ's sacrificial death for undeserving sinners. Open hearts, long closed by sin, to receive Christ as Lord and Savior. Glorify yourself by drawing sinners to Christ to believe on him. Make sinners willing in the day of your power. In Jesus' name. Amen.

VI. DEEPER DISCOVERIES

A. LORD (110:1)

The word LORD uses small capital letters to indicate that it translates the Hebrew word *yehovah,* is the personal proper name of God given to Israel, who knew it to be the "glorious and awesome name" (Deut. 28:58). Derived from the tetragrammaton (YHWH), *yehovah* occurs 5,321 times in the Hebrew Bible, the most frequently employed name of God in Scripture. God was considered to be so absolutely holy that the name *yehovah* was never to be pronounced aloud. Instead, the vowel markings for *adonai* were inserted to direct the reader of Scripture to say *adonai* instead of *yehovah.* The meaning of *yehovah* has been debated, but it is safe to infer that it refers to God's underived self-existence. The ancient Hebrews connected the word with *hava,* which meant "to be," as when God instructed Moses from the burning bush, "I AM WHO I AM" (Exod. 3:14). In this instance, the divine name implies God's eternality, autonomy, independence, and immutability.

This divine name was often used in reference to God's covenants to Israel (Gen. 15:18; Exod. 3:15; 6:2,4–5; Deut. 7:9; 2 Kgs. 17:34–35; Isa. 26:4). The name also signified God's personal relationship and nearness to his people: "I will take you as my own people and I will be your God" (Exod. 6:7; cp. Hos. 1:9). It was to this name that the worship of Israel was to be directed (Deut. 4:32–40; 32:9; Amos 3:2).

B. Melchizedek (110:4)

This name means "king of righteousness." Melchizedek was the king of Salem, probably Jerusalem, and a priest of God Most High. He greeted Abraham on his return from the rout of Kedorlaomer and his allies and received from him a tenth part of his booty (Gen. 14:18–20). In Psalm 110:4, a Davidic king is acclaimed by divine oath as "a priest forever, in the order of Melchizedek." Ultimately, this looked ahead to a greater son of David, the Lord Jesus Christ, who was both priest and king over his people (Heb. 5:6–11; 6:20–7:28).

VII. TEACHING OUTLINE

A. The Providential Reign of Christ (1-3)
   1. He Is Divinely Installed to Reign (1)
      a. At the Lord's right hand (1a)
      b. Over the Lord's enemies (1b)
   2. He Is Divinely Commanded to Reign (2)
      a. Empowered by the Lord (2a)
      b. Charged by the Lord (2b)
   3. He is Divinely Arrayed to Reign (3)
      a. Served by his people (3a)
      b. Strengthened as in youth (3b)
B. The Priestly Redemption of Christ (4)
   1. He Is Divinely Appointed as a Priest (4a)
   2. He Is Divinely Appointed Forever (4b)
C. The Prophetic Return of Christ (5-7)
   1. He Will Shatter Kings (5)
   2. He Will Judge Nations (6a)
   3. He Will Bury Corpses (6b)
   4. He Will Destroy Princes (6c)
   5. He Will Be Empowered (7)

Psalm 111

Awesome Deeds

"*G*ive unlimited credit to our God."

R o b e r t   M u r r a y   M ' C h e y n e

Psalm 111

I. INTRODUCTION

A well-meaning but misinformed person can often be heard saying: "Lord, we praise you, not for what you do, but for who you are." Granted, there is an element of truth in that statement, namely, that God's character is all-glorious. Nevertheless, this statement is not altogether correct. The fact is, the Bible *does* call us to praise God for what he does. *Who God is* cannot be separated from *what God does*. Both the person and work of God are indissolubly one. God's attributes and his actions are inseparably united, the latter being an extension of the former. Therefore, believers *should* praise God for his mighty deeds, which flow directly out of his divine being.

Psalm 111 is a hymn that exhorts everyone to praise the Lord, inspired by the display of his glory in his mighty works. This psalm is an acrostic of twenty-two lines, each line beginning in succession with the twenty-two letters of the Hebrew alphabet. Further, Psalm 111 is joined with Psalm 112. They both are acrostics according to this pattern. Psalm 111 adores the works of God; Psalm 112 affirms the fear of God. These two psalms are twins, probably written by the same author, designed to be studied and sung in tandem. Most likely, they are postexilic. The divine works to be extolled are God's restoration of his people, returning them to their land after years of captivity in Babylon.

II. COMMENTARY

MAIN IDEA: *The psalmist praises God for his mighty deeds.*

A The Declaration of Praise (111:1)

111:1a–b. The psalmist bursts forth with his familiar declaration, **praise the LORD**. It is lifted up with passion, fervency, zeal, and emotion. There is a resolve here, a determination, to praise God. No matter how he feels, or what his circumstances are, in good times and bad times, David will praise the Lord. With deepest gratitude to God, he offers this praise **with all my heart**. If God is known in the heart, he is worthy of our very highest praise.

111:1c. Personal worship must be publicly expressed in the **council of the upright**, referring to the most godly of the saints. The **upright** are the truly godly who gather for corporate worship. Further, the psalmist will praise God **in the assembly** of believers, a reference to the larger congregation in the temple. There are times for private devotions, but they are no substitute for public worship. A life of faith was intended to be a corporate experience, lived in fellowship with other believers, in which worship is an important part.

B The Motivation of Praise (111:2–9)

111:2–3. God is praised, first, for his **works** which he has done for his people. They are **great** (*gadol*) in size and importance. Immense and vast are his **works** (*ma'asim*) in creation, providence, and revelation. These works are **pondered by all who delight in them**, causing them to praise God. They are unfathomable—beyond what man's mind can conceive. God's greatness is also seen in his **deeds**, which are his providential acts by which he governs over all circumstances and events. What God creates he sustains, upholds, directs, and governs. All these divine deeds are **glorious**, revealing God's kingly splendor; **majestic**, manifesting his grandeur; and **righteousness**, displaying his holiness. God's righteousness is displayed through his deeds, which are perfect and right.

111:4. God's works are identified as **wonders** (*pala*), which are usual but which are beyond the ordinary course of events. This refers to the soul-startling effect God's works have on those who observe them, leaving the observers filled with many wonders. It refers to a time of dramatic divine intervention, most often to the saving acts of God when he graciously intervenes and delivers his people out of their trials and distresses. They are **to be remembered**, too awesome to be forgotten, as the result of the **gracious and compassionate** character of God.

111:5. God **provides food** for his people, surely a reference to the manna and quail God gave during the years of Israel's desert wandering. Graciously,

God met their needs (Ps. 78:23–24), remembering **his covenant** that he established on Mount Sinai.

111:6. God **has shown** his **power** in his many **works**. When Israel entered the promised land, he defeated their enemies who lived in Canaan. Further, God stopped the Jordan River, leveled the walls of Jericho, and defeated the Canaanites. In so doing, God gave Israel **the lands** previously occupied by **other nations**.

111:7. God's **works** are faithful, perfectly fulfilling the many promises written in his Word. God's acts are just, meaning always right and equitable. Moreover, **all his precepts are trustworthy**, meaning infallible, dependable, and they will surely come to pass. Not one jot or tittle will fall from the law.

111:8 All the divine works are **steadfast for ever and ever**. They are established for all time, firmly fixed, done forever, never to be undone. God's works are lasting, permanent, irrevocable, everlasting, and eternal. They will not be nullified by man or ever undone.

111:9. Here is God's greatest work, **redemption**. Here is the deliverance Israel experienced from Egyptian bondage and from Babylonian captivity. God is a deliverer who delights in rescuing his people from their trials and afflictions. The work of creation is great (v. 2), but the work of saving his people is even greater (v. 9).

C The Condition for Praise (111:10)

111:10. The reverential **fear of the** LORD is the necessary prerequisite of all wisdom. In this psalm, the wisest thing a person can do is to praise the Lord (vv. 1,10c). The sobering awe of God is **the beginning** (*reshith*) of wisdom; that is, the starting point and first principle of wisdom. Fearing God leads to **wisdom, good understanding**, obedience, and **praise**. This psalm now concludes where it began, with **praise** to God. There should be no end to praising God, which is the primary occupation of the saints.

III. CONCLUSION

Beholding the works of God with the eyes of faith is a cause of great praise for all God's people. They are put on display all around, but, to be sure, they require believing hearts to see them. Unbelieving hearts cannot discern and perceive what God is doing all around them. His providential works are observed only by faith in God. One must fear the Lord and follow his precepts in order to have the spiritual insight needed to behold his doings in the world. Providence has been called "the invisible hand of God inside the glove of human events." By faith we are enabled to perceive the working of the sovereign hand of God in the world. May all believers rejoice in seeing the mighty works of God all about them that are divinely directed for their good and God's glory.

IV. TEACHING OUTLINE

A. The Declaration of Praise (1)
  1. Praise the Lord (1a)
  2. Extol the Lord (1b)
    a. With a whole heart (1b)
    b. In the upright council (1c)
    c. In the public assembly (1c)
B. The Motivation of Praise (2-9)
  1. God's Works Are Great (2)
    a. They are pondered by many (2b)
    b. They are delighted in by many (2b)
  2. God's Works Are Glorious (3)
    a. They are majestic in splendor (3a)
    b. They are righteous in nature (3b)
    c. They are forever in duration (3b)
  3. God's Works Are Memorable (4)
    a. They produce wonder in hearts (4a)
    b. They reveal God's nature (4b)
  4. God's Works Are Benevolent (5)
    a. They provide food for his own (5a)
    b. They fulfill his eternal covenant (5b)
  5. God's Works Are Powerful (6)
    a. They display God's power to believers (6a)
    b. They transfer the promised land from nations (6b)
  6. God's Works Are Faithful (7)
    a. They are just in nature (7a)
    b. They fulfill his precepts (7b)
  7. God's Works Are Steadfast (8)
    a. They are enduring forever (8a)
    b. They reveal divine faithfulness (8b)
    c. They reveal divine uprightness (8b)
  8. God's Works Are Redemptive (9)
    a. They bring salvation to his people (9a)
    b. They execute his eternal covenant (9b)
    c. They reveal his holy name (9c)
C. The Condition for Praise (10)
  1. Fearing God Leads to Wisdom (10a,b)
    a. It produces obedience to his precepts (10b)
    b. It produces understanding in life (10c)
  2. Fearing God Leads to Praise (10c)

Psalm 112

A God-Centered Life

"*The* fear of God is the soul of godliness."

Charles H. Spurgeon

Psalm 112

I. INTRODUCTION

Everyone has someone or something at the very center of their lives. No one is without a driving force and consuming passion at the core of his being. For some people, their lives revolve around good things, like their children, career, parents, or even ministry. For other people, their lives center on shallow things, such as a favorite sports team, their yard, or a hobby. And yet for others, their lives rotate around the shallowest of all things—themselves. But for the Christian, everything in his or her life revolves around one driving passion and one dominant pursuit—God himself. God must be at the center of every life, or it will be off track. Everything and everyone else must be secondary; God must be primary. This is the heart of a God-centered life.

This is the central thrust of Psalm 112. It is a psalm about what it looks like for a believer to live a God-centered life, one in which God is the sum and substance of life. This is a wisdom psalm designed to reveal the path of the godly. The hallmarks of a wisdom psalm, found in this song, are: (1) It begins "Blessed is the man" as do other wisdom psalms (v. 1; cp. Pss. 1:1; 119:1–2; 128:1); (2) it calls for the fear of the Lord (v. 1; cp. Job 28:28; Ps. 111:10; Prov. 1:7; 9:10; Eccl. 12:13); (3) it uses proverbial expressions (v. 3); (4) it sharply contrasts between the roads of life (v. 10; cp. Ps. 1:1–3,4–6); and (5) it uses metaphors ("light," "darkness," v. 4; "horn," v. 9). Also, this is an acrostic psalm, as the twenty-two Hebrew lines begin with the twenty-two letters of the Hebrew alphabet.

II. COMMENTARY

MAIN IDEA: *The psalmist prioritizes the reverence, obedience, and blessings of the person who lives for God.*

A The Character of a God-Centered Life (112:1)

112:1. This psalm begins with a celebration, an announcement of **praise** to God. **Blessed** means happy, satisfied, content, whole, full. It is also in the plural, which intensifies its richness. The heart of the psalmist is full of praise for God because of the immense blessing that comes to the heart of the person who **fears the LORD**. There is no spiritual blessing in our lives apart from fearing the Lord. To **fear the LORD** means to reverence or to revere him. It means to give him first place in our lives and to take him very seriously. It means to stand in awe of who he is, infinitely holy and absolutely sovereign in his glorious being. The person who fears the Lord will **delight in his commands**. You cannot fear God without delighting in his Word. The two are inseparably bound together.

B The Consequences of a God-Centered Life (112:2-9)

112:2. A God-fearing man will leave a spiritual legacy with his own **children** and those with whom he comes in contact. The **generation of the upright** refers to those who live around the God-fearing man—his peers, his contemporaries, his work associates, his neighbors, and such. The powerful influence of a God-fearing man is felt by his generation.

112:3. **Wealth** and **riches** can often attend the life of the righteous. This does not teach a "prosperity gospel" that makes the erroneous claim that godliness always leads to financial prosperity. But it does acknowledge that the person who fears God will often be favored by God's blessing, both materially and spiritually. Thus, both financial riches and spiritual **righteousness** are in view here.

112:4. This **light** is the spiritual light of enlightenment and illumination that comes to the eyes and heart of the God-fearing man. He is able to see in the **darkness** because light is given to him. A God-fearing man is able to see what others cannot see. He sees with spiritual eyes. He sees with a divine perspective and discernment. He is **gracious** or full of grace. His words as well as his actions are gracious—meaning kind, patient, tender, and uplifting. He is also **compassionate**; he feels deeply for others in need, full of sympathy. He is not insensitive or indifferent toward people, but is full of feelings for others. He is also **righteous** or conformed to a standard—that standard being God, who is gracious and compassionate (Ps. 111:4).

112:5-6. The God-fearing man holds what he has with an open hand and **lends freely** what he has to others. He has an anchor for his soul. He is deeply rooted in God and his Word and, thus, **will never be shaken**. Temptation will not sway the god-fearing man. Demons will not move him. Trials will not shake him. He is not given to panic or overreaction in the face of adversity. Rather, he is marked by stability and strength of heart.

112:7–8. The God-fearing man will not fear **bad news**, or threatening reports. He is immovable because his heart is **steadfast**, anchored to the immovable God. He is stable in adversity. The God-fearing man's **heart is secure**, established by God. He knows that God will deal with his **foes**. He need not seek vengeance.

112:9. The God-fearing man recognizes those passed over by the wicked, namely, **the poor**. In spite of what his adversaries (v. 8b) may say or do against him, he will be, nevertheless, honored by God. God will have the last word. Because the God-fearing man humbles himself before the Lord, God will lift him up in due time.

ⓒ The Contrast with a God-Centered Life (112:10)

112:10. The **wicked**, those who do not fear God, will see the blessing of the godly and be **vexed**, bitter, and angry. Becoming full of wrath and envious, he will **gnash his teeth** and **waste away**. The **longings of the wicked will come to nothing**. This means the wicked man will not achieve his purpose, reach his goal, or find his dreams. He will die a disappointed man! While the righteous will endure forever, the ungodly will rot off the face of the earth.

III. CONCLUSION

This psalm begs each reader to ask himself: What is the center of my life? Do I delight in God's Word? Do I desire to study and live the Scripture? Every believer must be growing in a high view of God if he is to have a God-centered life. Consequently, each saint must focus on the character of God— his holiness, sovereignty, righteousness, immutability, omnipresence, omniscience, omnipotence, and wrath.

IV. TEACHING OUTLINE

A. The Character of a God-Centered Life (1)
PRAISE THE LORD (1a)
    1. He Is God-Fearing (1b)
    2. He Is Word-Delighting (1c)
B. The Consequences of a God-Centered Life (2-9)
    1. Its Influence (2)
       a. His children will be mighty (2a)
       b. His generation will be blessed (2b)

2. Its Increase (3-5)
   a. Material riches are his (3a)
   b. Spiritual righteousness is his (3b)
3. Its Insight (4a)
   a. He has light in darkness (4a)
   b. He is enlightened (4a)
4. Its Integrity (4b-5)
   a. He is gracious (4b)
   b. He is compassionate (4b)
   c. He is righteous (4b)
   d. He is not greedy (5)
5. Its Immovability (6-9)
C. He Will Never Be Shaken (6a)
D. He Will Be Remembered (6b)
   1. He Will Not Fear Calamity (7)
   2. He Will Not Fear Foes (8)
   3. He Will Be Lifted High (9)
E. The Contrast with a God-Centered Life (10)
   1. The Wicked Will Be Vexed (10a)
   2. The Wicked Will Waste Away (10b)
   3. The Wicked Will Perish (10c)

Psalm 113

Passionate Praise

"*Man's* chief work is the praise of God."

Augustine

Psalm 113

I. INTRODUCTION

The primary occupation and chief preoccupation of all saints should be rendering to God. This is to be every believer's all-encompassing focus in this life. It will surely be his main vocation throughout the ages to come. God's people have been redeemed to rejoice in him, both now and forever. This is the chief end of man, the magnification of God's matchless name. No matter what surrounds a person's life—whether it be times of prosperity or seasons of adversity, whether it be times of blessing or buffeting, it is always the believer's duty and delight to praise the Lord. This is their highest purpose.

Psalm 113 calls on all believers to praise the Lord. This worship hymn begins with the familiar declaration, "Praise the LORD" (v. 1), and it concludes with the same proclamation, "Praise the LORD" (v. 9). This heartfelt, soul-stirring praise is both the Alpha and Omega of this psalm, the bookends and brackets around this song—Praise the Lord! Psalm 113 begins what is known as the "Egyptian Hallel" (Pss. 113–118), *hallel* meaning "praise" in Hebrew. These six psalms, of which this one is the first, were sung at the great religious festivals in Old Testament times. At the Passover feast, Psalms 113 and 114 were sung before the meal, and Psalms 115–118 were used after the meal. Psalm 113 calls for praise to be given to God for two main reasons: (1) He is exalted on high, but (2) he stoops low to elevate the lowly.

II. COMMENTARY

MAIN IDEA: The psalmist invites God's people to praise the Lord, who is highly exalted and yet reaches down to the lowly.

A The Call to Praise (113:1–3)

113:1. Three times in the opening verse there is the call to praise God, three being the superlative degree. Praise (*hallel*) means "to be bright, to shine, to be splendid, to boast." It carries the idea of an exuberance, radiance, jubilation, or celebration. It means to light up for God, to be radiant for God, to be shining forth for God, to boast in him, to brag on him. **The name of the** LORD is his divine attributes, the sum total of the greatest of his character. God's name represents the entirety of who he is. Thus, praising the name of the Lord centers a person's thoughts and worship on God's matchless, holy character.

113:2. God should **be praised** (*barak*), a different word used here. This word for praise means "to bend the knee, to kneel down, to bless." Praising God involves kneeling before him in order to show submission to him who is infinitely superior. Kneeling conveys the idea of giving homage to this infinitely superior God. The psalmist states **both now and forevermore** this must occur, from this moment forward. Let all believers always praise the Lord.

113:3. All day God is to be praised, **from the rising of the sun to the place where it sets**. It is intended that the entire day is to be given to praising God. From the first moment of consciousness in the morning to the last waking moment before sleep, God should be magnified. When a person sits down to eat, goes forth to work, and comes home to rest, God should be praised.

B The Causes for Praise (113:4–9b)

113:4. **The** LORD **is exalted over all the nations**, unlike the man-made gods of the ancient Middle East, which were limited to a certain tribe or territory. These dumb idols were regional, local gods. But the one, true living God is **exalted over all the nations**. There is no place over which his dominion is not extended. He is above all, the Most High God. His **glory** is the sum total of the supremacy of who God is, the reality and revelation of God's absolutely perfect being. His glory is **above the heavens**, above and beyond the universe, certainly beyond the capacity of human language to describe.

113:5. The psalmist asks, **Who is like the** LORD **our God**? This implies a negative answer: No one is like God. No one compares to him who is unique, one of a kind, and incomparable. Thus, he is the only one worthy of praise. He is **the One who sits enthroned on high** over all the universe. No one is higher than God, as high as God, or even slightly lower than God. He is infinitely higher than his creation, transcendent above, towering in glory.

113:6. Yet this highly elevated God **stoops down to look** at the things on the earth. He surveys this world, reaching down to man to meet him where he is in the trenches of life. This high, holy God **stoops down** and draws near to fallen man.

113:7. In so doing, God **raises the poor** who are also spiritually poor, not an automatic assumption. God bends down and lifts the poor **from the dust** of extreme distress. God reaches down and **lifts the needy from the ash heap**, symbolic of a humble status (Gen. 18:27; 1 Kgs. 16:2). The poor eke out their existence by sifting through the rubbish heaps outside the city walls, sifting through its burned garbage ashes. It is there that God reaches down to them.

113:8. So highly does God elevate the humble that he **seats them with princes**. By his sovereign grace, God raises them from the pit to the pinnacle (1 Sam. 2:8).

113:9a–b. In ancient times, a **barren woman** was considered to be without significance and without joy, confined to a hopeless situation. But God **settles** her, meaning he comforts her and thus brings joy to her heart by bringing her **children**.

ⓒ The Crescendo of Praise (113:9c)

113:9c. This psalm builds to this final crescendo, **Praise the LORD**. All believers everywhere should respond by giving glory to God.

III. CONCLUSION

God's holy transcendence, towering over all peoples, nations, events, and circumstances, should be cause for constant praise from believers. God is high above man's problems, rising above life's circumstances, ordering all according to his eternal plan. No one is elevated above God. He controls and uses all for his own glory. As a result, God's people should never forget to praise the Lord, even in tough times. Believers should never become focused on the storms of life to the exclusion of the sovereignty of God. Too often, the saints lose sight of the Lord in the midst of their trials. In the tough times, when trials are the greatest, let praise be the loudest. Let all who trust God shift their focus off themselves, away from their problems and circumstances, and place their eyes squarely on the Lord. In so doing, their hearts will be filled with praise for God.

IV. TEACHING OUTLINE

A. The Call to Praise (1-3)
PRAISE THE LORD (1a)
   1. Praise the Name of the Lord (1b)
     a. By the psalmist (1a)

   b. By all servants (1b)
  2. Let His Name Be Praised (2-3)
   a. Now and forevermore (2)
   b. From the morning sun (3a)
   c. To the setting sun (3b)
 B. The Causes for Praise (4-9b)
  1. The Lord Is Highly Exalted (4-6)
   a. Over the nations (4a)
   b. Over the heavens (4b)
   c. On his throne (5)
   d. Looking down on all (6)
  2. The Lord Is Reaching Down (7-9b)
   a. He raises the poor (7a)
   b. He lifts the needy (7b)
   c. He elevates the lowly (8)
   d. He blesses the barren (9a,b)
C. The Crescendo of Praise (9c)
PRAISE THE LORD (9c)

Psalm 114

Divine Deliverance

Psalm 114

I. INTRODUCTION

As the deliverer of his people, God delights in intervening in the affairs of this world to rescue believers out of their perils. When it is his will, God comes to their aid, in all his perfect timing. He acts on their behalf and makes a way when, humanly speaking, there is no way for their escape. When God delivers his own, he opens a door that no person can close, ushering them out of their predicament. He then goes before them, leading them into the safety of his will. No obstacle is too great for God to overcome. No enemy is too great for him to defeat. He is the God of new beginnings, the God who releases his people from their captivity. Whether it be from sin or unjust suffering, God longs to set believers free from all that imprisons them.

This message of divine deliverance comes through loud and clear in Psalm 114. It is a hymn that remembers two exodus experiences in which God, first, parted the Red Sea (Exod. 14) and, second, the Jordan River (Josh. 3). This song of celebration commemorates God's mighty deeds in releasing Israel from enslavement to her Egyptian masters and in removing all obstacles before her. The account of the exodus is rehearsed here in highly poetic language as the waters of the Red Sea and Jordan River are personified as fleeing from the presence of God when they parted. Here is encouragement for all believers to be reminded that God delivers his own people from sin and suffering. He makes a way out when there seems to be no way of escape.

II. COMMENTARY

MAIN IDEA: *By looking back at the parting of the Red Sea and the Jordan River, the psalmist assures God's people that the Lord will work for their good in difficult times.*

A The Intervention of God (114:1–2)

114:1. Here is a description of the exodus when God's people, after being in bondage for more than four hundred years in **Egypt**, were led out by God. For four grueling centuries of hard slavery at the oppressive hands of their Egyptian taskmasters, they were, at last, led out by God to begin their journey to the promised land.

114:2. Judah, one tribe of Israel, refers to all of God's people in the Southern Kingdom. **Israel** represents the ten tribes of the Northern Kingdom. Collectively, God's people became God's **sanctuary** and **dominion**. A sanctuary is a place uniquely set apart by God's presence for his own purposes—a holy place. It is a place where the glory of God is manifested, where the greatness of God is put on display. God's people became this special place in the exodus. Wherever God's sanctuary is, there also is his **dominion**—the place over which he exercises his authority. God's people were the place where God's rule and authority were most exercised, working in them, through them, and before them. They themselves were the holy place where God's rule was most demonstrated.

B The Intimidation by God (114:3–4)

114:3. As God led his people through the wilderness, **the sea** (i.e., Red Sea) **looked and fled**. This poetically speaks of God parting the imposing body of water during Israel's journey to the promised land. This occurred at the beginning of the forty-year journey. The second miracle involved separating **the Jordan** at the end of the forty-year journey. Forty years separated these two miraculous events.

114:4. Having crossed the Jordan River, **the mountains** and **hills skipped**, a reference to the elevated topography of the promised land. These high places, once filled with Canaanites, skipped playfully before them, bringing them much pleasure. God gave his people the victory, the land, and their inheritance.

C The Interrogation Before God (114:5–6)

114:5–6. The psalmist raised four teasing questions though he already knew the answer. He asked them only for effect. The **sea**, **Jordan**, **mountains**, and **hills** of the promised land are questioned directly to force them to acknowledge their Creator's power.

D The Invitation to God (114:7–8)

114:7. All the **earth** should **tremble** before God in awesome recognition of his power. Fearing God is the only proper response by nature and man to the omnipotent God. The earth represents all that was mentioned earlier, from Egypt (v. 1) and mighty bodies of water like the Red Sea and the Jordan River (vv. 3,5) to the mountains and hills (vv. 4,6). God himself is the One who brought the Israelites out of Egypt, the One who caused the Red Sea to flee, who turned back the Jordan River, who caused the mountains to skip and the hills to jump. By his omnipotent hand, God intervened. Therefore, people should tremble before God.

114:8. On two different occasions during Israel's wilderness experience, God caused **water** to come gushing out of a rock at the command of Moses (Exod. 17:5–6; Num. 20:8–11). It was God who provided for his people. God refreshed, revived, and sustained his people then and will do so today.

III. CONCLUSION

There is a strange absence today in the evangelical church—a firm belief in the doctrine of providence is missing. Believers fail to see the invisible hand of God in the affairs of men, governing over all things for his own glory. But Scripture is clear that God rules through all events and occurrences as he governs the works of his hands. As R. C. Sproul notes, there are no maverick molecules in the universe. The Westminster Confession of Faith defines the providence of God as follows: "God the great Creator of all things doth uphold, direct, dispose, and govern all creatures, actions, and things, from the greatest even to the least, by his most wise and holy providence, according to his infallible foreknowledge, and the free and immutable counsel of his own will, to the praise of the glory of his wisdom, power, justice, goodness, and mercy."

This timeless theological definition, biblically based, is an accurate statement of the truth that God orders all human events and circumstances according to his own will. The doctrine of providence clearly teaches that God upholds, directs, disposes, and governs all creatures, things, and actions according to his eternal will. All creation is the stage on which God's providence is enacted. Providence is God's gracious outworking of his eternal purpose in the details of human life. The world is not ruled by blind chance or impersonal fate, but by God. It is God orchestrating both big things and small things, carrying out everything according to his divine plan. God does this, even in difficult, dark days.

IV. TEACHING OUTLINE

A. The Intervention of God (1-2)
1. When God Intervened (1)
    a. When Israel came out of Egypt (1a)
    b. When Jacob came out of a foreign land (1b)
2. How God Intervened (2)
    a. Judah became God's sanctuary (2a)
    b. Judah became God's dominion (2b)
B. The Intimidation by God (3-4)
1. The Sea Fled Away (3a)
2. The Jordan Turned Back (3b)
3. The Mountains Skipped (4a)
4. The Hills Skipped (4b)
C. The Interrogation by God (5-6)
1. O Sea, Why Did You Flee? (5a)
2. O Jordan, Why Did You Run? (5b)
3. Mountains, Why Did You Skip? (6a)
4. Hills, Why Did You Skip? (6b)
D. The Invitation to God (7-8)
1. Tremble, O Earth (7)
    a. At the presence of the Lord (7a)
    b. At the presence of God of Jacob (7b)
2. Tremble at God (8)
    a. Who turned the rock into water (8a)
    b. Who turned hard rock into springs (8b)

Psalm 115

Immortal Invisible

Quote

"*It* is visible that God is, it is invisible what He is."

Stephen Charnock

Psalm 115

I. INTRODUCTION

The richest man in the world, Croesus, once asked the wisest man in the world, Thales, "What is God?" The noted philosopher asked for a day's deliberation in which to ponder this profound question. Unable to come to a definite answer, Thales then asked for another day to plumb the depths of this question. Still unable to answer, he requested yet another day, then another, and, finally, another. At last, Thales sadly confessed he did not know.

When the fiery Tertullian, an early church father, later heard about this incident, he eagerly seized on this teaching opportunity. Responding to Thales's inability to answer the question, he declared that it was a clear example of the world's ignorance of God. "There," Tertullian exclaimed, "is the wisest man in the world, and he cannot tell you who God is." Then he surmised, "But the most ignorant, uneducated servant among the Christians knows God and is able to make him known to others."

Psalm 115 is a testimony to the world's ignorance of God. It answers the most basic questions, "*What* is God?" and "*Where* is God?" The truth declared by this psalm is that the Lord alone is God, the One who resides in heaven, who rules over all, who lives forevermore, who protects and prospers his people. *That* is who God is, says the psalmist. This statement of God's true identity is contrasted with the false gods of the pagan nations, who are nothing but dumb idols. There is only one God, the psalmist extols, the God of Israel, the maker of heaven and earth. Rather than mount a philosophical defense for the existence of God, the author simply *declares* the fact of God. By this, he repudiates all false deities. The thought of any allegiance being given to a man-made idol is preposterous and spiritual insanity. There is only one God, the *true* God, the God revealed in creation, history, and the Scripture, Lord over all the nations, Israel's redeemer.

This psalm was placed here in the Psalter to direct the worship of God in the temple, probably on the occasion of the dedication of the second temple (cp. Ezra 6:16). Its central theme presents a contrast between the sovereign God of heaven and the impotent idols of the nations. In this song, the psalmist calls all to trust and worship the true God. It was written at a time when Israel's enemies were taunting and mocking them (v. 2), a time when Israel had suffered devastating defeats, and it appeared that God was nowhere to be found. It was at this time that they were urged to put their trust in the Lord (vv. 9–11). This is the third psalm in the Egyptian Hallel (Pss. 113–118).

II. COMMENTARY

> **MAIN IDEA:** *The psalmist declares the superiority of the one true God over the heathen idols of the nations.*

A A Declaration of God's Glory (115:1)

> **SUPPORTING IDEA:** *The true God, not men, should receive all the glory for his love and faithfulness.*

115:1a. This psalm begins with a bold declaration that all believers are and do is not for their benefit. Rather, it is for God's **name** that everything should bring **glory**. Life does not revolve around man but around God. This theocentric opening directs all praise and honor to its proper focus, the Lord himself.

115:1b. The two divine attributes, **love and faithfulness**, are commonly identified with God's covenant blessings toward his people. Praise should be directed toward God, specifically, who God is. Praise should be given to God because of his eternal, unconditional love toward his people. His loyal love is never rescinding but forever strong.

B A Defense of God's Greatness (115:2–3)

> **SUPPORTING IDEA:** *The true God is in heaven where he does as he pleases.*

115:2. The surrounding, pagan **nations** taunted Israel when it was hit hard by natural disasters or crushed by foreign enemies. Upon observing the defeats and trials of Israel, they mocked God's people, saying, **Where is their God?** The Jews despised this Gentile taunt.

115:3. The psalmist answered this Gentile sneer, saying God is alive in **heaven** and rules over all from his throne. Enthroned above, there is no diminishing of God's sovereignty, even in the presence of many trials. God **does whatever pleases him**, meaning his sovereignty is unequaled, unrivaled, and unopposed (Ps. 103:19). Even if Israel is defeated, it is God's doing, not his failure. When victory comes to Israel, this, too, is God's doing. No so-called god or idol-worshipping nation can oppose him.

C A Denunciation of God's Imposters (115:4–8)

> **SUPPORTING IDEA:** *Impotent idols are made by weak human hands and are powerless.*

115:4. By contrast, the impotent idols of the nations can do nothing. Even if they are made from valuable **silver and gold**, they are still **made by the hands of men**. They are mere figments of fallen human imagination. Thus, they have no power to act. They are utterly worthless.

115:5–6. These idols are dumb with **mouths** that **cannot speak**. They are blind with **eyes** that **cannot see**. Also, **they have ears, but cannot hear** and **noses, but they cannot smell**. They are dead and lifeless (cp. Isa. 44:9–20).

115:7. They also **have hands** that **cannot feel** and **feet** that **cannot walk**. These so-called pagan gods are weak and pitiful. They cannot even **utter a sound with their throats**. They can do nothing except rot and decay.

115:8. The taunting nations who craft these idols and who trust in them **will be like them**—dead. The worship of idols becomes like the idols—spiritually powerless, lifeless, and useless.

D A Dependence on God's Grace (115:9–11)

> **SUPPORTING IDEA:** *All people must trust and fear the Lord.*

115:9–11. The psalmist called on all God's people to **trust in the LORD**. The triple repetition of this urgent plea to **trust in** God underscores how important and necessary it is to do so. Trust should not go to these idols but to God, who provides for his people. "Trust" (*batach*) means "to attach oneself to, to be confident in, to rely upon." The basic idea is associated with firmness and solidity. All believers are called to rely on God and completely rest in the One who does whatever he pleases. **He is their help and shield**—a thrice-repeated refrain proclaiming God's protective care over those who put their trust in him. The **shield** is a symbol of divine protection from one's enemies.

E A Delight in God's Blessing (115:12–13)

> **SUPPORTING IDEA:** *The true God remembers and blesses his people.*

115:12–13. The **LORD remembers** his people and is mindful of their needs. He will not forget them. Four times the psalmist said emphatically that

God **will bless** those who trust him. He will surely multiply his favor toward them. God will bless all who **fear the** LORD with great reverential awe, an indication of saving faith. He is for the **small and great alike**. God is not a respecter of persons but bestows his goodness impartially to all who fear him.

F A Desire for God's Increase (115:14–15)

SUPPORTING IDEA: *The psalmist prays for God's increase to come to his people.*

115:14–15. The psalmist requested that this divine blessing be shown toward all God's people. He asked that God **make you increase** in wealth, numbers, and strength. Again, he asked that they **be blessed by the** LORD. This request is based on the fact that God is **the Maker of heaven and earth**. Only God, who has created all, can bless all.

G A Doxology of God's Supremacy (115:16–18)

SUPPORTING IDEA: *God, who is the exclusive, all-sovereign God, is to be praised.*

115:16–18. The **highest heavens** (i.e., God's dwelling place) **belong** exclusively **to the** LORD. He alone reigns above in glory as the exalted sovereign Lord over all creation. But man's dwelling place, **the earth**, God has **given to man** to cultivate and oversee as its stewards. **The dead** have left this earth and can no longer praise God here. They **go down** into the grave to **silence**. It is only the living who can **extol the** LORD on the earth. This they must do **now** in this life and in heaven **forevermore**. Thus, unable to contain his own heart, he proclaimed, **Praise the** LORD. While he is living and has opportunity, the psalmist will magnify the name of God. So must all believers.

MAIN IDEA REVIEW: *The psalmist declares the superiority of the one true God over the heathen idols of the nations.*

III. CONCLUSION

William Wilberforce, the famed British politician (1759–1833), was one of the great Christian statesmen of history. For years he fought against the evils of slavery and sought to outlaw it in the British Commonwealth. Wilberforce was also a loving and diligent student of the Psalms. Often he meditated on the opening verse of Psalm 115 during the years of his fight against slavery. On March 25, 1807, Parliament passed the bill for the abolition of the slave trade wherever the British flag flew. Wilberforce's response to this victory? By his own testimony, it was first to meditate upon his favorite verse, Psalm 115:1, and give glory to God. "Not to us, O LORD, not to us but to your name be the glory, because of your love and faithfulness." This should be our first and foremost response as well to everything that God chooses to accomplish through us. Our rightful reaction must always be to give glory to God. Will you do this? Will you choose to give praise to God who alone is worthy?

IV. LIFE APPLICATION

Guard against mental idols. Every Christian must guard his own mind from idols. The apostle John warned, "Dear children, keep yourselves from idols" (1 John 5:21). An idol need not be made from wood or stones. It can be any false teaching about the one "true God" (1 John 5:20) that distorts his glory. Twisted doctrines about God are, primarily, the idols from which the readers in the apostle John's day were commanded to protect themselves. Wrong views of God that are contrary to Scripture are blasphemous idols, violating the glory of God. Thus, every believer must be careful to worship God not only in "spirit" but in "truth" (John 4:24). A. W. Tozer warned, "The most important thing about you is what comes into your mind when you think about God." Unscriptural thoughts about God are unworthy of him and must be removed from our minds and smashed as idols.

Guard against heart idols. Further, anything we love, fear, or serve more than God is an idol. Anything that comes between God and us is an idol. Martyn Lloyd-Jones, once pastor of Westminster Chapel, London, wrote, "A man's god is that for which he lives, for which he is prepared to give his time, his energy, his money, that which stimulates him and rouses him, excites, and enthuses him." It is against such idols that we must guard ourselves. For some, these competing gods may be a job, a hobby, a house, or a car. For others, it may be a relationship, a pursuit, or an investment. Whatever it may be, nothing must come between our supreme devotion to God. We must cast down every idol from the heart and worship God exclusively.

V. PRAYER

God, may you alone be glorified in our lives. We choose to live with one holy passion for you. Enlarge our vision of you within our hearts. We desire to treasure your glory above all else. Guard our hearts from any competing loves that would challenge our singular devotion to you. In Jesus' name. Amen.

VI. DEEPER DISCOVERIES

A. Nations (115:2)

This word (Heb. *goy*) refers to a group of people who make up a tribe or nation. The word is often used of the non-Israelite, Gentile nations that surrounded the nation of Israel (Deut. 4:38; Josh. 23:13) and was defined by a political or territorial affiliation or by ethnicity. It was also used of Abraham's descendants, the nation of Israel (Gen. 12:1; 17:20). When used of other nations or groups of people, they were usually pagan and described as wicked (Deut. 9:4–5), without understanding (Deut. 31:21), detestable (Deut. 18:9; 1 Kgs. 14:24; 2 Kgs. 16:3; 2 Chr. 28:3), idolators (2 Kgs. 17:29), ruthless (Isa. 25:3), and uncircumcised (Jer. 9:26). The Lord scoffs at the nations (Ps. 59:8), yet it is the nations whom the promised Messiah would redeem (Isa. 2:2; 11:10; 42:6; 60:10).

B. Idols (115:4)

The term *idols* (*asob*) refers to images or objects that were made for the purpose of worship. To do so was in direct contradiction to the second commandment (Exod. 20:4). The word is found a total of four times in the Psalms.

VII. TEACHING OUTLINE

A. A Declaration of God's Glory (1)
  1. Glory Must Never Be Given to Man (1a)
  2. Glory Must Always Be Given to God (1b,c)
     a. Because of his love (1b)
     b. Because of his faithfulness (1c)
B. A Defense of God's Greatness (2-3)
  1. The Nations Taunt Israel (2)
     a. Where is their God?
     b. Who is their God?
  2. Israel Testifies in Response (3)
     a. God is in heaven (3a)
     b. God reigns in heaven (3b)
C. A Defiance of God's Imposters (4-8)
  1. Idols Are Humanly Made (4)
     a. They are crafted out of silver (4)
     b. They are crafted out of gold (4)
  2. Idols Are Utterly Worthless (5-7)
     a. They cannot speak (5a)
     b. They cannot see (5b)
     c. They cannot hear (6a)
     d. They cannot smell (6b)
     e. They cannot feel (7a)
     f. They cannot walk (7b)
     g. They cannot utter a sound (7c)

  3. Idols Are Eternally Damning (8)
     a. Idol makers will be like them (8a)
     b. Idol worshippers will be like them (8b)
D. A Dependency Upon God's Grace (9-11)
  1. Israel, Trust in the Lord (9-10)
     a. He is your support (9a,10a)
     b. He is your shield (9b, 10b)
  2. God-Fearers, Trust in the Lord (11)
     a. He is their support (11a)
     b. He is their shield (11b)
E. A Delight in God's Blessing (12-13)
  1. The Lord Remembers Us (12a)
  2. The Lord Blesses Us (12-13)
     a. The house of Israel (12b)
     b. The house of Aaron (12c)
     c. Those who fear God (13a)
     d. The small and great (13b)
F. A Desire for God's Increase (14-15)
  1. May the Lord Make You Increase (14)
  2. May the Lord Bless You (15)
G. A Doxology of God's Supremacy (16-18)
  1. God Is Enthroned Above (16)
     a. The heaven is governed by God (16a)
     b. The earth is entrusted to man (16b)
  2. God Is Extolled Below (17-18)
     a. The dead cannot praise God (17)
     b. The living must praise God (18)

Psalm 116

All-Sufficient Grace

Psalm 116

I. INTRODUCTION

An old cliché, often credited with being in the Bible, says: "God helps those who help themselves." But unfortunately, there are two issues at fault with this statement. The first problem is, this statement is not in the Bible. The second problem is, the theology of this supposed truism is also not in the Bible. The fact is, the Bible teaches the very opposite. Actually, God helps those who *cannot* help themselves. If we could help ourselves, then we would not need God's help. To the contrary, we are helpless and weak, in need of grace.

Jesus said, "Apart from me you can do nothing" (John 15:5). *Nothing* means nothing of any eternal, spiritual value. God will certainly help his own people as they humble themselves and call upon his name. This is the all-sufficient grace of God. God strengthens the weak, not those who are self-reliant. There is no one too weak for God to help, only people too strong. The truth is that such self-inflated people are only strong in their own estimation but not in reality. Only when believers confess their weakness are they truly strong.

This is the central theme of Psalm 116—the all-sufficient grace of God to help believers in their weakness. This psalm testifies to the strength of God manifested in the psalmist when he had no power to deliver himself. The psalmist was so ill that he thought he was about to die. There was absolutely nothing he could do to save his own life. In fact, there was nothing anyone could do to help him. If he were to be helped, his help would have to come from God. An old hymn entitled "Abide with Me," written by Henry F. Lyte in 1847, says, "When other helpers fail and comforts flee, Help of the helpless, abide with me." That is what God is: the help of the helpless.

II. COMMENTARY

MAIN IDEA: *The psalmist testifies how God heard him and delivered him from death, vowing always to thank and serve God.*

A The Psalmist's Supplication (116:1–4)

116:1. The psalmist declared with deep excitement and great emotion, **I love the LORD**. He passionately adored God, his entire inner person pulsating with devotion to God. This love is strengthened because **he heard my voice** (Pss. 6:8; 66:19). The Lord is not a deaf idol like the gods of the pagans, incapable of hearing. Rather, God is the living God who hears the prayers of his people.

116:2. Because he turned his ear to me, the psalmist will call on the Lord (Pss. 17:6; 31:2; 40:1). These words indicate that God bends down from on high to hear the voice of his people who cry to him in their distress. Because God presently hears him, the psalmist has every reason to call on God in the future, **as long as I live**.

116:3. The circumstances of the psalmist's distress, which led to his prayer, were his severe sickness, even being on the brink of death. **Cords of death entangled me** like a rope, he declared. They would not release him. His death loomed imminent as the terror of **the grave** overwhelmed him, instilling **trouble and sorrow**.

116:4. In the midst of this ordeal, the psalmist **called on the name of the LORD** for deliverance. He cried, **O LORD, save me** (Pss. 17:13; 22:20–21). God was his only hope.

B The Psalmist's Salvation (116:5–9)

116:5. The psalmist focused on three character qualities of God. He is **gracious** (*channuwn*, "to bend down, to stoop in kindness to an inferior, to favor, to have mercy") and is inclined to be favorable toward his own people (Pss. 86:15; 103:8). The Lord is also **righteous** (*tsadiyq*, "just, lawful, honest, right") and will do what is right with his own people (Pss. 119:137; 145:17). God can be trusted. And the Lord is **full of compassion**, tender in sympathies toward his own.

116:6. The LORD protects (*shamar*, "to hedge about as with thorns, to guard, to protect, such as a shepherd guarding a flock") his people from harm. The Lord also guards **the simplehearted**. That is, God protects the person who is childlike in his dependence on him. When the psalmist **was in great need**, uncertain if he would live, God **saved** him from what appeared to be certain death. God spared his life and extended his years.

116:7–8. The psalmist counseled himself, **Be at rest**, referring to a state of unthreatened security. He had every reason to do so because **the LORD has**

been good to him. He declared, The Lord has **delivered my soul from death** (Pss. 49:15; 56:13; 86:13). God had also kept his **eyes from tears** because of his near-death rescue and his **feet from stumbling**. This is how bountifully God dealt with him.

116:9. His life now spared, the psalmist purposed to **walk before the LORD** in uprightness. Here is a vow of obedience to the Lord. He knew that God had not spared his life in order for him to squander it. He pledged to walk in a way that would honor God.

C The Psalmist's Surrender (116:10–14)

116:10. The psalmist described his faith, which he used to called on the Lord. **I believed** means he fully trusted in God in this predicament. In complete faith in God, he surrendered his life afresh to God while he was **greatly afflicted**. He **believed** that God would work for his good when he prayed to him.

116:11. But people cannot be trusted, since **all men are liars**. This may indicate that the psalmist was subject to false accusations by ungodly men. Further, it is a bold statement regarding how untrue all men were when they predicted the psalmist's death. Certainly, all men offer only a false hope for deliverance (Pss. 60:11; 118:8–9). Only God can save.

116:12–14. The author asked how he could **repay the LORD**. God needs nothing; he owns all. The psalmist recognized what a debtor to grace he was. In response, he pledged, **I will lift up the cup of salvation**—a reference to the drink offering submitted to God in gratitude for his salvation (Lev. 23:10–14). The psalmist will **call on the name of the LORD** in praise. He will **fulfill** his **vows to the LORD**. This dedication refers to the promises he made during the time of his distress (Ps. 116:18). These vows were pledges of obedience (Ps. 116:9). These affirmations were to be made publicly in the midst of God's people.

D The Psalmist's Sacrifice (116:15–19)

116:15. **Precious** are all the **saints** to the Lord. Even when they are near death, it is not as if God no longer cares for them. They are highly valued by God, especially in death. God cares intensely about his saints in their darkest hour. Either in a saint's death or by his deliverance, God would be glorified.

116:16. The psalmist rededicated himself to God, saying, **I am your servant**. The psalmist reaffirmed his devotion to God. He confessed he was the **son of your maidservant**, who follows the example of his godly mother. God had **freed** him from his **chains**, or delivered him from the cords of death, so he would serve the Lord freely.

116:17–19. Reaffirming previous words (vv. 13–14), the psalmist declared, **I will sacrifice a thank offering** to God. This parallels the "cup of salvation" (v. 13). The psalmist will **call on the name of the LORD**, not merely in prayer, but, more importantly, in praise. These **vows** will be performed publicly in the **courts of the house of the LORD** before other believers. He concluded, **Praise the LORD**.

III. CONCLUSION

Are you in need of God's sustaining grace? All believers stand in continual need of such help. God is ready to help his people as they recognize their own weakness and rely on his grace. In what areas of your life do you sense your need of his enabling empowering? When you are weak, then you are strong. In your weakness, his grace is made perfect (2 Cor. 12:9–10). What a blessed place it is when you realize your own inability. It is only then that you will abide in Christ and cling to his grace. As you realize your inability to do what he requires of you, you will learn to look to him and lean upon his grace. Therein will you find the sustaining grace of God that you so desperately need.

IV. TEACHING OUTLINE

A. The Psalmist's Supplication (1-4)
   1. I Love the Lord (1-2a)
      a. Because he heard my voice (1b)
      b. Because he inclined his ear (2a)
   2. I Will Call on the Lord (2b)
   3. I Came Near to Death (3)
      a. Death entangled me (3a)
      b. The grave came upon me (3b)
      c. Trouble overcame me (3c)
   4. I Called on the Lord (4)
O LORD, SAVE ME (4b)
B. The Psalmist's Salvation (5-9)
   1. The Lord Is a Savior (5-6)
      a. He is gracious (5a)
      b. He is righteous (5a)
      c. He is compassionate (5b)
      d. He is protective (6a)
      e. He saved me (6b)
   2. The Lord Is a Deliverer (7-9)
      a. He blessed my life (7)
      b. He delivered my life (8)
      c. He extended my life (9)

C. The Psalmist's Surrender (10-14)
   1. I Trusted in the Lord (10-11)
      a. God can be trusted (10)
      b. Man cannot be trusted (11)
   2. I Thanked the Lord (12-14)
      a. How can I repay God? (12)
      b. I will thank God (13a)
      c. I will call upon God (13b)
      d. I will praise God (14)
D. The Psalmist's Sacrifice (15-19)
   1. All Saints Are Precious to God (15)
      a. In his sight (15a)
      b. In their death (15b)
   2. I Am the Servant of God (16)
   3. I Will Sacrifice to God (17)
   4. I Will Fulfill Vows to God (18-19)
      a. Amid the people of God (18b)
      b. In the house of God (19a)
      c. In the city of God (19b)
PRAISE THE LORD! (19c)

Psalm 117
Ultimate Priority

Psalm 117

I. INTRODUCTION

The loftiest motivation behind the believer's duty in evangelism should be for the promotion of the glory of God. The greatest incentive in missions around the world is that God might have more worshippers of his supreme majesty. This must be the chief force behind the fulfillment of the Great Commission. There must be *more* voices added to the hallelujah choir of those who worship God. Worship is the ultimate goal of global outreach.

Yet sad to say, the main thrust behind evangelism has often devolved downward into baser motivations, often man centered, such as reaching people in order to fill empty pews in overmortgaged church buildings. The drive of witnessing must never be just to add inflated numbers to church growth figures. Rather, the greatest passion fueling evangelism and missions must be the spreading abroad the honor of God's name.

That yet more worshippers must be reached who will magnify the unsurpassed name of our God is the message of Psalm 117. It is the shortest psalm in the Psalter but long in truth. If a psalm could be considered a chapter, this song is also the shortest chapter in the Bible. As such, it has been called a mighty midget of a psalm, the Tom Thumb of the Psalter. Nevertheless, this brief song is played in a major key as it contains towering truth on a grand scale. This brief psalm is one of the most bold in the entire Psalter. This minipsalm is great and its outreach is enormous. More is present in these few lines than what initially meets the eye. The author is anonymous, the setting is unknown, but the message is loud and clear: Let all the nations praise God.

II. COMMENTARY

MAIN IDEA: *The psalmist issues a universal call that all should praise the Lord.*

A The Call to Praise (117:1)

117:1. The psalmist begins, **Praise the LORD, all you nations**. This now-familiar declaration of adoration is actually an invitation to the entire world to declare God's greatness. This summons every living individual to boast in the living God. This means that **all . . . peoples** around the world must turn from their false religions, renounce their false gods, and **extol** the true God in repentance and saving faith. The Lord alone is God, and he only is worthy to be praised. This verse was quoted by Paul (Rom. 15:11) as testimony that the salvation of the Gentiles was not a divine afterthought but a strategic part of the eternal purpose of God.

B The Causes for Praise (117:2a–b)

117:2a. What follows is a word of explanation regarding why God should be praised. Here are the reasons for such exalted worship: **For great is his love toward us**. The word "great" represents something that is large, remarkable, distinguished, or superior. The Hebrew word carries the sense of someone or something prevailing over another because of its vast, superior qualities. This magnificent love is toward us, God's chosen ones. This is the unique, special love that God has for his elect, which is deeper and stronger than his general love for the world. It is the distinction between all "nations" (v. 1) and **us**, "all you peoples" (v. 1).

In a general, nonredemptive way, God loves all people with common grace (Matt. 5:45; Acts 14:17). But he has a selective, special love for his own people that will never cease (Rom. 9:13; Eph. 1:4). This divine loving-kindness is not based on anything intrinsically loveable in the one loved. God loves simply because he chooses to love his own.

117:2b. This love **endures forever**. **Love** and **faithfulness** are two attributes of God that should always stimulate and provoke the hearts of God's people to praise him. These two attributes are often coupled together (Pss. 36:5; 57:3; 61:7; 85:10; 89:14; 96:15; 115:1; 138:2). God's faithful love toward his chosen ones will never come to an end (Rom. 8:38–39).

⬛ The Crescendo of Praise (117:2c)

117:2c. The psalmist ended on a high note, with erupting praise for God. As he considered the love and faithfulness of the Lord, the psalmist could not contain himself. He shouted, **Praise the LORD**. His praise was personal, passionate, and potent.

III. CONCLUSION

John Piper noted, "Worship is the fuel and goal in missions. It is the goal of missions because in missions we simply aim to bring the nations into the white-hot employment of God's glory." This is the thrust of this psalm, a passionate plea that all the nations worship God. The driving force behind missions is to reach the world with the gospel of Jesus Christ, who is the only way of salvation. If lost sinners are to be brought into the vast multitude of adoring worshippers of God, the gospel must be preached to the ends of the earth. May every Christian give his life, prayers, and efforts to this great task of reaching the world for Jesus Christ. But let them do so for the reason set forth in this psalm. Let the church reach the world with the saving gospel of Jesus Christ so that God may receive the eternal praise of the nations. *Soli Deo Gloria*—for the glory of God alone.

IV. TEACHING OUTLINE

A. The Call to Praise (1)
  1. The What of This Praise (1)
    a. Praise the Lord (1a)
    b. Extol the Lord (1b)
  2. The Who of Praise (1)
    a. All the nations (1a)
    b. All the peoples (1b)
B. The Causes for Praise (2a,b)
  1. God's Love Is Great (2a)
  2. God's Faithfulness Is Great (2b)
    a. It is perfect (2b)
    b. It is eternal (2b)
C. The Crescendo of Praise (117:2c)

Psalm 118
Triumphant Thanks

"*T*hanksgiving is good, but thanks-living is better."

M a t t h e w   H e n r y

Psalm 118

I. INTRODUCTION

If the importance of a psalm is measured by the number of times it is quoted in the New Testament, then this psalm, Psalm 118, would be considered the most significant psalm of all. Psalm 118 is the single most referenced psalm in the pages of the New Testament. It is the only psalm quoted by all four Gospel writers—three times by Matthew, three times by Mark, three times by Luke, and one time by John.

When Jesus first wept over Jerusalem and lamented that Israel would not come to him, he quoted this psalm (Luke 13:35). When Jesus later entered Jerusalem on Palm Sunday, the multitude intentionally shouted Psalm 118 (Matt. 21:9). A few days later, when Jesus gave the parable of the landowner to the unbelieving leaders of Israel, he quoted Psalm 118 (Matt. 21:42). A second time Jesus wept over Jerusalem; and when he did, he once again quoted this psalm (Matt. 23:39). When Peter stood before the Jewish Sanhedrin and fearlessly charged them with the murder of Jesus, he quoted this psalm (Acts 4:11). Multiple other times, this psalm was quoted or referenced by the New Testament writers (Eph. 2:20; Heb. 13:6; 1 Pet. 2:7). Clearly, this is a most strategic psalm.

Psalm 118 is classified as a thanksgiving psalm—one in which the author records his thanks to God for his mighty deeds. The author is unknown, but it is probably a Davidic king of Israel, one who was also the military leader of the nation. He writes after a time of great national crisis in Israel, a day when the nation was surrounded by many enemies. The psalmist had earlier called upon God in this hour of distress, and God delivered Israel from this danger. As a result, this psalm was written to call all God's people to worship the

Lord, who dramatically won the war for them. Even more, this psalm is a messianic psalm written with a prophetic anticipation that finds its ultimate fulfillment in Jesus Christ. Specifically, it looks ahead to the Lord's triumphant entry into Jerusalem, his rejection by the nation, his crucifixion on the cross, and his establishment of the church through his death.

II. COMMENTARY

MAIN IDEA: *The psalmist calls upon all God's people to offer thanks to the Lord for his goodness in delivering them.*

A A Call to Thankfulness (118:1–4)

118:1. The psalmist's urgent call is extended: **Give thanks to the LORD.** All believers are summoned to offer their deepest gratitude to God for his many blessings. Two reasons are given why this thanksgiving should be expressed. First, God is **good** and, therefore, all that he bestows upon his people is perfectly suited for them. His will, gifts, and provisions are all good (Rom. 12:2). Second, God's **love endures forever.** There is no end to the boundless mercy he lavishes upon his people.

118:2–4. A threefold invitation is extended to all believers to magnify God's eternal love. **Israel,** all his chosen people who come to God's house to worship, should praise God. Also, **the house of Aaron,** those who lead worship in God's house, should magnify the Lord. Moreover, **those who fear the LORD,** referring to all the rest who worship God (i.e., Gentiles), should worship God. All worshippers and worship leaders should reverence God and say, **His love endures forever.**

B A Call to Trust (118:5–9)

118:5. The psalmist described the specific trial in which God had acted so graciously, prompting this burst of gratitude. The problem resulted in **anguish** (a tight place, a confining place, lack of room), and he could not escape. He was surrounded by impossible circumstances squeezing in all around him (vv. 10–12). God intervened, setting him **free** or, literally, placing him in an enlarged place, which was open, unrestrictive, and no longer threatening.

118:6–7. As a result, the psalmist confidently declared, **The LORD is with me.** The Lord had stood with him, being for him and not for his enemies. Thus, he **will not be afraid.** Perfect peace flooded his heart and soul, displacing all fear. If God was for him, absolutely nothing that man could do would thwart the purposes of God. God is infinitely greater than man. The psalmist would **look in triumph** on his **enemies** because God had soundly defeated them. The author knew that God was with him in all circumstances of life, even in distress and mounting difficulty.

118:8–9. In this soul-crushing crucible, the psalmist had a choice. Either he would trust God or he would look to man. He could rely on **princes**, forging an alliance with foreign leaders who led unbelieving nations to defend him, or he could trust **in the L**ORD. He could place his trust in a human alliance, or in heaven. He testified, quite plainly, that it was **better to take refuge in the L**ORD.

🄲 A Call to Triumph (118:10–14)

118:10–12. Reflecting on this international crisis, the psalmist considered how **all the nations surrounded me**. Four times in these three verses this focus is reinforced, all to underscore the mounting trial he was facing in this excruciating ordeal. **But in the name of the L**ORD, trusting in the sovereign authority and supernatural power of God, **I cut them off**. Literally, he said, "I circumcised them," or utterly defeated and destroyed them. He repeated this three times, emphasizing the victory God gave him. He was responsible to act, but it was only by God's enabling power that he triumphed.

118:13. These surrounding nations with their threatening armies advanced in their violent attacks. This was no empty threat he faced, but an invasion so strong that he was **about to fall** to his own destruction, never to recover. He was in the process of being toppled from his throne and losing his position, leading to the collapse of the entire nation. **But the L**ORD **helped me**, hearing his cry and answering his plea. God alone won the victory for him. Here is the full sufficiency of God's help.

118:14. In the face of this rising opposition, God himself was the psalmist's **strength**, enabling him to overcome his adversaries. God was his **song**, empowering him to overcome his own inner anxieties. God was his **salvation**, delivering him from his adversity.

🄳 A Call to Testify (118:15–18)

118:15–16. The psalmist here reflected on God's mighty works of salvation for his people. Because the Lord had intervened, they were filled with **shouts of joy and victory**. Their song was, **The L**ORD**'s right hand has done mighty things**. God's "right hand" refers to his omnipotence, the divine power to act triumphantly in any seemingly impossible situation. God had freely used his limitless strength to save the people from the surrounding nations. This was their resounding testimony.

118:17–18. The psalmist stated he would **not die** at the hands of his enemies but would **live**. This extended life would be used to fulfill God's greater purposes. He had been spared death in order to proclaim God's greatness to all. Yet he humbly realized that there was another purpose in this conflict. **The L**ORD **has chastened me severely**, he confessed. God was using this trial for his own good to severely discipline, develop, and deepen him. Yet even through this refining process, God set limits as to how far it could go. God withdrew this ordeal at the proper time, just short of his death.

E A Call to Transcendence (118:19–21)

118:19–20. In response, the psalmist must lead all God's people into God's house to declare God's greatness. **Open for me the gates of righteousness**, he proclaimed, referring to either the gates of Jerusalem or the temple gates. The purpose of his entering through these gates was to **give thanks** to God publicly. This **gate of the LORD** is so called because it leads **the righteous** into the house of the Lord.

118:21. Once again, the psalmist gave **thanks** to God for answering his prayers in his day of trouble and delivering him from his enemies. God himself was his **salvation**.

F A Call to Truth (118:22–27)

118:22. This **stone the builders rejected** was, initially, the psalmist himself, Israel's king, who called upon God for the nation. With disdain, he had been looked down upon by the surrounding kings, who had invaded Israel as **builders** of world empires. Although the psalmist was rejected by men, he was, nevertheless, chosen by God, placed as **the capstone** in God's building efforts on the earth. This reveals the central role of Israel and Israel's king in God's purposes in human history. But, prophetically, this **stone** was Jesus Christ, rejected by men, chosen by God, the chief cornerstone of the church (Acts 4:11; Eph. 2:20; 1 Pet. 2:7).

118:23–24. This victory over the surrounding nations had been achieved by God and no one else. **It is marvelous in our eyes** that divine providence has overruled man's plans. They rejoice in God's inscrutable, eternal plan. **This is the day the LORD has made**, meaning the day Israel's king and Israel's people were delivered from the threats of Israel's enemies. Ultimately, this looked ahead prophetically to the death of Christ on the cross, a day which was the eternal plan of God from before time began (Acts 2:23; 1 Pet. 1:20).

118:25. Now rescued, God's people continued to pray, **O LORD, save us** and **grant us success**. This is a request that God would continue to save them from the surrounding nations and send them victory.

118:26. Blessed with divine triumph is Israel's king, who comes **in the name of the LORD**. God is with the earthly ruler, who trusts in his divine power and provision. **We**, the people of Israel, prayed for their king, asking that divine blessing be granted to him. This very verse was proclaimed by Israel when Christ rode into Jerusalem on Palm Sunday (Matt. 21:9; Luke 19:38; John 12:13).

118:27. God's people say from God's house, **The LORD is God**. No foreign idol is God. The Lord of Israel is God alone. This one, true God **has made his**

light shine on his people. Spiritual blessing and favor were theirs (cp. Num. 6:25). With **boughs in hand**, they were to bring a thank offering to God (Lev. 7:11–21).

G A Call to Thankfulness (118:28–29)

118:28–29. The psalm concluded as it began, the author stating, **I will give you thanks**. The psalmist called on all believers to **give thanks to the LORD**. Ultimately, the reason for such praise is that God's **love endures forever**. Thus, praise should also be forever.

III. CONCLUSION

Thanksgiving is to be thanks-living, a daily lifestyle for every believer. In this sense, thanksgiving is to be a way of life, encompassing one's attitude and actions, both words and deeds. Every believer should give thanks to God in all things. Christians have every reason to be filled with gratitude as a result of God's abundant goodness toward them. Most notably, believers should be filled with thankfulness because God delivers them out of their trials. Whether in this life or in the life to come, God *will* surely deliver them from all their adversities. But most of all, God has delivered all believers from his own wrath through the blood of his Son, Jesus Christ. Here is the greatest deliverance of all, a divine rescue of undeserving sinners from the final judgment and eternal damnation. Let them give thanks to the Lord for his great salvation through the cross. Let them give thanks to him who also develops and deepens them for his glory.

IV. TEACHING OUTLINE

A. A Call to Thankfulness (1-4)
  1. Give Thanks to the Lord (1)
    a. For he is good (1a)
    b. For his love endures (1b)
  2. Let All People Praise God (2-4)
    a. The people of Israel (2)
    b. The house of Aaron (3)
    c. Those who fear God (4)
B. A Call to Trust (5-9)
  1. I Cried to the Lord (5a)
    a. He delivered me (5a)
  2. I Was Answered by the Lord (5b-7)
    a. He is with me (6a)
    b. He calms me (6a,b)
    c. He helps me (7a)

        d. He champions me (7b)
      3. I Took Confidence in the Lord (8-9)
        a. Not in man (8b)
        b. Not in princes (9b)
        c. But in the Lord (9a)

C. A Call to Triumph (10-14)
      1. The Nations Surrounded Me (10-11)
        a. They are on every side (10a, 11a)
        b. But I cut them off (10b, 11b)
      2. The Nations Swarmed Me (12)
        a. They are like bees (12a)
        b. They died out like burning thorns (12b)
        c. I cut them off (12c)
      3. The Nations Shoved Me (13-14)
        a. They advance against me (13a)
        b. But the Lord helped me (13b)
        c. The Lord is my strength (14a)
        d. The Lord is my song (14b)
        e. The Lord is my salvation (14b)

D. A Call to Testify (15-18)
      1. Believers Give Shouts of Joy (15-16)
        a. The Lord's arm has done mighty things (15b)
        b. The Lord's arm is lifted high (16)
      2. Believers Give Words of Witness (17-18)
        a. I will not die, but live (17a)
        b. I will proclaim God's acts (17b)

E. A Call to Transcendence (19-21)
      1. I Will Give Thanks to God (19-20)
        a. Open the gates of righteousness (19a)
        b. I will enter through the gates (19b-20)
      2. I Will Give Thanks to God (21)
        a. He answered my supplication (21a)
        b. He became my salvation (21b)

F. A Call to Truth (22-27)
      1. God Has Granted Salvation (22-24)
        a. The rejected stone is the capstone (22)
        b. This is God's doing (23a)
        c. This is our marvel (23b)
        d. This is God's day (24a)
        e. This is our rejoicing (24b)
      2. God, Grant Us Salvation (25-27)
        a. O Lord, save us (25)

    b. O Lord, we bless you (26)

    c. O Lord, shine on us (27a)

    d. O Lord, we thank you (27b)

 G. A Call to Thankfulness (28-29)

   1. I Will Give Thanks to God (28)

   2. You Give Thanks to God (29)

    a. For he is good (29a)

    b. For he is loving (29b)

Psalm 119:1–8
Sola Scriptura (I)

"*I* have made a covenant with God that he sends me neither visions, dreams, nor even angels. I am well satisfied with the gift of the Holy Scriptures, which give me abundant instruction and all that I need to know both for this life and for that which is to come."

M a r t i n   L u t h e r

Psalm 119:1–8

I. INTRODUCTION

In the dramatic days of the Protestant Reformation, the battle cry of the Reformers was *sola Scriptura,* Latin for "Scripture only." By this bold assertion, the Reformers were staunchly committing themselves to the absolute, exclusive authority of Scripture over every church tradition and ecclesiastical council. Regardless of whatever man may say, it is only what God declares in his Word that is binding. This became known as the regulatory principle. Everything in the church and Christian living must be regulated by Scripture, that is, by Scripture *alone.*

Nowhere was this bold statement affirmed more heroically in the sixteenth-century Reformation than when Martin Luther stood trial at Worms, Germany, in 1521. In the wake of posting his *Ninety-five Theses* in Wittenberg and subsequent Scripture-based writings, Luther was summoned to appear before the church authorities at the Diet of Worms. With the Holy Roman Empire Emperor Charles V presiding, Luther's theological works and books were placed on a table before the gathered council. The Reformer was then asked two simple questions: Are these your writings? Do you recant? Luther knew he could not deny his works. They contained the very words of Scripture. To deny his writings would be to deny Scripture.

Thus, on April 18, 1521, Luther delivered his now famous speech, boldly standing on the Word. Luther declared: "Since then your serene majesty and your lordships seek a simple answer, I will give it in this manner, not embellished: Unless I am convinced by the testimony of the Scriptures or by clear reason, for I do not trust either in the pope or in church councils, since it is well known that they have often erred and contradict themselves, I am bound to the Scriptures I have quoted, and my conscience is captive to the Word of God. I cannot and I will not retract anything, since it is neither safe nor right to go against conscience. I cannot do otherwise, here I stand. God help me. Amen."

With these courageous words, the tide of history turned. A torch had been ignited, and Reformation flames spread like wildfire. No church tradition was to take preeminence over the infallible Word of God. Everything must bow to Scripture. The entire life of the church must come *under* the divine authority of Scripture. And further, the Reformers held fast to the sufficiency of Scripture, believing that it was living and powerful, able to perform all that God intends in a person's life in salvation and godliness. Throughout the history of the church, all seasons of reformation and revival have always begun with a restored commitment to God's Word.

Here is the Mount Everest of the Book of Psalms, an expanded treatment of the blessed man of Psalm 1, the person who delights in God's Word. Here are the multifaceted perfections of the Word of God recorded, along with a model of godliness as exemplified by the psalmist. This one psalm, longer than 30 entire books in the Bible, is comprised of 22 stanzas of 8 verses each, making a total of 176 verses. All 8 verses of the first stanza start with the first letter of the Hebrew alphabet. Each line of the second stanza starts with the next letter of the Hebrew alphabet until all 22 letters have been used in successive order, stanza by stanza, making it an acrostic psalm.

II. COMMENTARY

MAIN IDEA: *The psalmist declares the full sufficiency of God's Word in the life of the believer who loves and obeys it.*

A The Internal Delight of God's Word (119:1–2)

SUPPORTING IDEA: *The psalmist announces the blessedness of the person who walks according to God's Word.*

119:1. Blessed are all believers whose daily path is carefully directed by God's Word. "Blessed" (*asher*) pronounces the overflowing delight, deep-seated joy, and supreme satisfaction that is experienced by all who follow the

Word. Abundant grace is theirs to enjoy. These highly favored believers **walk** with a habitual lifestyle of pursuing daily obedience to the authoritative **law** of God.

119:2. The beginning of the second verse repeats the first verse for dramatic emphasis, underscoring how favored are all who **keep** the Scripture. **Blessed** are all who keep the Word, making it their own possession by personal obedience. **Statutes** (*edot*), a title for the Word, emphasizes that God's testimonies are outspoken and speak with frankness and straightforwardness. God's Word openly addresses life as it is, speaking forthrightly. A deep soul-satisfaction is enjoyed by all who **seek** God **with all their heart**, that is, with the entirety of their inner being (i.e., intellect, emotion, and volition).

B The Moral Direction of God's Word (119:3)

SUPPORTING IDEA: *Scripture directs believers into God's ways, restraining them from wrongdoing.*

119:3. God's Word perfectly directs the believer's steps into the very center of God's will. Those who obey the Scripture (vv. 1–2) **do nothing wrong**, being directed away from all evil and wrong. By the precise guidance of the Word, they **walk** in God's **ways**. This is yet another synonym for Scripture, *ways*, indicating the practicality of following Scripture daily. All of life is to be lived on the clearly marked ways of God's Word. The imagery of a **walk** implies a habitual lifestyle or the well-marked path of God's will.

C The Eternal Demands of God's Word (119:4–6)

SUPPORTING IDEA: *God's Word is authoritative and must be fully obeyed.*

119:4. Speaking directly to the Lord, the psalmist said, **You have laid down precepts**, unmistakably affirming the divine authorship of Scripture. God alone has given it, not man. Here is still another synonym for the Word, *precepts* (*piqqudim*), a title which indicates the precise accuracy with which the Scripture speaks. Consequently, it must **be fully obeyed**. Every divine command must be kept, half obedience being no obedience.

119:5. The psalmist yearned, **Oh, that my ways** (i.e., ordered steps) **were steadfast**, that is, marked by long-term endurance **in obeying your decrees**. He desired that he pursue a long obedience in the same direction. Yet another synonym for God's Word, *decrees* (*huggim*), speaks of its immutable character, binding force, and fixed permanence. God's Word endures forever (Isa. 40:8), never to be rescinded. The eternal Word demands man's volitional obedience, never just head knowledge or empty emotional feelings.

119:6. When the psalmist obeyed the Word, he did so even publicly in the face of his enemies: **I would not be put to shame**. He will not suffer humiliation before his enemies, not **when I consider all your commands**. God's Word will never cause him to be ashamed when he obeys it. He is unashamed of what seem to be narrow requirements to an outside world. This synonym for Scripture, commandments (*miswot*), means an authoritative order that is issued by a person superior in position or rank. This is the sovereignty of Scripture over the life of the believer. Not containing mere suggestions or options to consider, God's Word is full of commands to be obeyed.

Ⓓ The Spiritual Dynamics of God's Word (119:7–8)

SUPPORTING IDEA: *God's Word possesses the supernatural power to produce a godly life.*

119:7. God's Word in **an upright heart** stimulates **praise**. The Scripture produces singing and rejoicing to the Lord. The psalmist seeks to **learn** God's **righteous laws**. Still another term for Scripture is *righteous laws* (*mispat*), indicating the perfect equity of its dealings with man, rewarding obedience and punishing disobedience.

119:8. The psalmist concludes this stanza by resolving, **I will obey your decrees**. Here is his firm purpose to keep the Word. He would not be haphazard or lackadaisical about keeping it. Even amid his difficult circumstance, while surrounded by enemies who inflicted their persecution, he pleads to God, **do not utterly forsake me**. In his adversity, he is desperate for God's help to keep the Word. He cannot obey in the sheer willpower of his flesh, weak as it is, but only by divine grace (Phil. 2:12–13; Heb. 12:2). Yet these many personal difficulties would not hinder his obedience to the Word. In spite of his trials, he finds himself singing praises to God with an overflowing joy that far surpasses the pain of his many troubles (Ps. 119:7).

MAIN IDEA REVIEW: *The psalmist declares the full sufficiency of God's Word in the life of the believer who loves and obeys it.*

III. CONCLUSION

John Wycliffe (c. 1329–1384), "the Morning Star of the Reformation," will be long remembered as the first to translate the Bible into the English language. He was a brilliant scholar who taught at Oxford University in England. He also filled various pulpits as a gifted preacher and showed himself to be a prolific writer. In his quest to disseminate God's Word, he sent throughout England teams of preachers called Lollards, who preached the gospel of Jesus Christ. Yet it was his translation of the Bible into the language of the people for which the English-speaking world will long be his debtor. Driving Wycliffe's tireless efforts in this project was his commitment to the truthfulness and sufficiency of Scripture.

Concerning the supernatural power of Scripture, Wycliffe wrote: "God's words will give men new life more than the other words that are for pleasure. O marvelous power of the Divine Seed which overpowers strong men in arms, softens hard hearts, and renews and changes into divine men, those men who had been brutalized by sins and departed infinitely far from God. Obviously such miraculous power could never be worked by the work of a priest if the Spirit of Life and the Eternal Word did not, above all things else, work with it."

This being true, let us devote ourselves to the study and pursuit of this divine Book, the Bible, which alone can so radically transform our lives. The Scripture is, indeed, a supernatural book; and it alone can bring a supernatural change within a person's life. Let us hear and heed its message.

IV. LIFE APPLICATION

Every Christian is greatly dependent on the ministry of God's Word to lead him into the fullness of God's will. How should the Scripture be approached? How should it be read and applied? The following steps should guide every believer's life:

Read the Bible. The Scripture should be read thoroughly, line upon line, precept upon precept. Careful attention should be given to its every nuance and detail. Every Christian should have a systematic plan for reading the Bible.

Study the Bible. As you read, have a pen and paper in hand. Underline key words and truths. Circle important terms and phrases. Indicate, perhaps with arrows, cause and effect. Consider obtaining a study Bible with explanatory notes at the bottom of the page.

Interpret the Bible. Always seek to determine what the passage means by what it says. Avoid superficial interpretations that spiritualize the passage. Instead, always understand the text in its normal, literal, historical, grammatical sense.

Apply the Bible. The Scripture must now be practically applied to your own life. Live the Scripture, and it will transform your life.

V. PRAYER

God, we thank you for the priceless treasure you have entrusted to us in your written Word. We rejoice in the many promises that we find in its pages for our strength and encouragement. We pray that as we get into the Word, it will get into us in a life-changing way. In Jesus' name. Amen.

VI. DEEPER DISCOVERIES

Psalm 119 contains various titles for Scripture, each name emphasizing a different nuance of its comprehensive ability to execute all God's purposes.

A. Law (119:1)

The "law" (*tora*) of the Lord comes from a root meaning "to project" or "to teach" and refers to any direction or instruction flowing from the Word of God that points out or indicates God's will to man. It refers not only to the moral, civil, or ceremonial law but to the entire teaching, instruction, or doctrine of Scripture.

B. Statutes (119:2)

The "statutes" (*edut*) of the Lord is derived from the root "to bear witness" and thus testifies to its divine author. It is a solemn attestation, a declaration of the will of God, the ordinances that became God's standard of conduct. Thus it was used of the two tablets summarizing the law, the Ten Commandments, that were placed in the ark as a witness to the holy character of God.

C. Precepts (119:4)

The "precepts" (*piqqudim*) of the Lord is a poetical word for injunctions found only in the Psalter, used only in the plural. It literally refers to an authoritative charge or order that is binding upon the recipient. In this instance, it is as from the sovereign Lord of the universe, directing and governing all people.

D. Commands (119:6)

The "commands" (*miswa*) of the Lord signifies a definite, authoritative command or anything ordained by the Lord. It designates the general body of imperative commands contained in God's law.

E. Ordinances (119:7)

The "ordinances" (*mishpat*) of the Lord represents a judicial decision that constitutes a precedence, a binding law. It denotes divinely ordered decisions on all kinds of issues in what might be called case-law applications to specific situations of the statutes, precepts, and commands of the law. In the Pentateuch, it referred to the laws after the Ten Commandments. The word can also mean God's judgmental acts on the wicked.

VII. TEACHING OUTLINE

A. The Internal Delight of God's Word (119:1–2)
B. The Moral Direction of God's Word (119:3)
C. The Eternal Demands of God's Word (119:4–6)
D. The Spiritual Dynamics of God's Word (119:7–8)

Psalm 119:9–48
Sola Scriptura (II)

"*In* the divine Scriptures, there are shallows and there are deeps; shallows where the lamb may wade, and deeps where the elephant may swim."

John Owen

Psalm 119:9–48

I. INTRODUCTION

Like no other book ever written, the Bible is divinely authored, truly a supernatural book. The Scripture is the inspired record of the divine voice, the very words of God that speak to every believer's life. Whether the Christian be a spiritual baby or a mature saint, God's Word addresses every life, just as if it were written exclusively for them. Like a multifaceted diamond with many precise cuts, the Scripture is a priceless gem with many sides, each perfectly refracting the pure light of divine truth in profundity that is heart searching and in power that is life changing.

Charles Spurgeon once said, "I hold one single sentence out of God's Word to be of more certainty and of more power than all the discoveries of all the learned men of all the ages." No other book compares with the supernatural power of the sacred Scripture. It alone is a living book that imparts life. The Bible alone reveals the true knowledge of God to hearts that they might grow in godliness.

In this second study of Psalm 119, the second through sixth stanzas (vv. 9–48) will be considered. The message is the same: the all-sufficiency of God's Word in the life of the believer.

II. COMMENTARY

> **MAIN IDEA:** The psalmist extols the many perfections of God's Word, testifying to its all-sufficient power to work wonders in his life.

A God's Word Cleanses the Heart (119:9–16)

119:9–11. The purifying power of God's Word is the theme of this second stanza (vv. 9–16). The psalmist asks a most important question: **How can a young man keep his way pure?** He answers that personal holiness is realized by **living**, or obeying, God's **word**. This outward obedience must arise from one's inward **heart** that seeks the Lord. The Scripture alone has sanctifying power to keep a person from straying into sin. The psalmist confesses that he had **hidden** God's **word** in his **heart**, that is, buried it within his soul like a valuable treasure. Through the Scripture's power he is assured that he might **not sin against** God.

119:12–13. Having acknowledged Scripture's purifying power, he asked that God **teach** him his divine **decrees** so that he might obey it. As the true author of Scripture, God himself must be the primary instructor of the psalmist's heart (cp. vv. 18,26,33,64,66,68,108,124,135). Divine illumination is absolutely necessary to understand God's Word, both in its precise meaning and practical application. Both learning and living the Scripture would come as he would **recount** it over and over in his mind.

119:14–16. The psalmist will enthusiastically **rejoice** in obeying God's Word, as one finding great **riches** (vv. 72,111,162). He will **meditate** on Scripture (i.e., constantly recalling it in his mind), **consider** it often, and **delight** in it with great pleasure. With all his heart, he rejoices in God's Word (vv. 24,35,47,70,77,92,143,174) not with drudgery but delight.

B God's Word Consoles the Soul (119:17–24)

119:17. In this third stanza (vv. 17–24), the psalmist purposes with unwavering resolution, **I will obey your word**. This obedience arises from a grateful heart, motivated by the **good** care and blessing of God. Under great persecution, he is near death. But if God will spare his life, he vows to keep his Word.

119:18. He asks that God **open** his **eyes** so he can **see** by divine illumination (1 Cor. 2:12–13) the deep, profound truths of Scripture. God himself must grant divine understanding of the Word, or it will evade him.

119:19–21. Once the Scripture is grasped, it must be kept through personal obedience. Such a life reality comes at a high price. Persecution for righteousness's sake awaits the person who commits to keeping it (2 Tim. 3:12). Because of this opposition, the psalmist is a **stranger** in this world, never fully accepted here. To the contrary, his familiar abode is in Scripture. God will rebuke the arrogant who violate the Word and who seek his harm.

119:22–23. The persecution he suffers for God's Word is personal **scorn** and **contempt** from unbelievers. This spiritual opposition includes **slander** from **rulers**, who follow worldly wisdom. In spite of this conflict, he will continually **meditate** on God's **decrees**.

119:24. Regardless of this personal attack he suffers, the psalmist finds soul-comforting **delight** in God's **statutes**. Rather than listening to his foes, God's testimonies are his **counselors**. The more he is attacked, the sweeter the Word is to his soul.

C God's Word Comforts the Spirit (119:25–32)

119:25. In this fourth stanza (vv. 25–32), the psalmist pledges that no matter what his circumstances, he will "hold fast" to the Word. He is **laid low in the dust** for holding to God's **word**. He prays that God will **preserve** him by the divine power in the Word.

119:26–27. Teach me your word, he prays yet again (cp. vv. 12,18). Humbly, he acknowledges his limitation in probing the fathomless depths of Scripture. He confesses his need to be taught more of God's **decrees**. In order to be preserved by God's Word (v. 25), he asks that God let him better **understand** the profundity of its eternal message. Only then can he better **meditate** on its astonishing **wonders** that produce within him reverential awe for God.

119:28–29. But he pays a high price for such loyalty to the Word. He is **weary with sorrow** from the direct attacks of those who oppose him for keeping God's **law**. He is not immune from such pain. So he asks God, **strengthen me according to your word.** Only as he would **keep** the Word can he be preserved from **deceitful ways**, paths that initially may seem right, but ultimately lead to destruction (Prov. 14:12).

119:30–32. In spite of the persecution he faces, he does not weaken in his commitment. He pledges, **I have chosen** and **set my heart on** God's **laws.** Further, he adds, **I hold fast** to the Word, implying firm resolution and wholehearted commitment. With great eagerness, **I run** after God's **commands**, pursuing them with eager, personal obedience. No matter what it costs him, he will remain true to Scripture, even in the face of mounting persecution.

D God's Word Counsels the Mind (119:33–40)

119:33–34. In the fifth stanza (vv. 33–40), the psalmist expresses his desire to be more fully instructed by God in the Word. As he reads and studies the Word, he prays, **teach me** in personal obedience (cp. v. 12). Only once receiving divine illumination in what it means and how it applies can he **keep them.** He can only obey what he understands. So he prays, **Give me understanding.** If

God would illumine him, then he could better **follow** and **keep** the divine law. This obedience must come from the **heart**, involving his entire being.

119:35–37. The psalmist requested divine guidance in living God's Word. He asked that God **direct** him in the **path** of obedience. Only in keeping the **commands** would he know **delight**. But to the contrary, disobedience brings much sorrow. Therefore, he requested that God **turn** his **heart** toward his statutes and, conversely, his **eyes away from** the **worthless things** of this world. The Word alone has such sanctifying power.

119:38–39. As he faces heated opposition for God's Word, he asks that God **fulfill** its **promise** to deliver him or preserve him. Such divine intervention would promote the fear of God in his heart. Only by God's protection would he escape **disgrace**.

119:40. In spite of paying such a high price for his allegiance to God's Word, he, nevertheless, does **long** for it. God must **preserve** him in **righteousness** through this anguishing ordeal, not allowing him to weaken in obeying it.

E God's Word Conquers All Fears (119:41–48)

119:41–42. A prayer for deliverance from his persecution is the theme of the sixth stanza (vv. 41–48). The psalmist asks God for divine **salvation**, a rescue out of this fiery trial, which comes because of his loyalty to the Word. This assured deliverance will come, he says, **according to your promise** in the Word, behind which stands God's **unfailing love**. When his enemies mock him, he will **answer** them with God's Word. His **trust** in God's **word** remains steadfast and sure.

119:43. As he waits for God's deliverance, he requests that God **not snatch the word of truth** from his **mouth** through disappointment. He openly confesses his loyalty to God's Word before all. But God's delay would weaken his verbal testimony of **hope** in God's **laws**.

119:44–47. With a fourfold affirmation, he purposes that he will **obey** God's Word always, **walk** in it, **speak** openly of it, **delight** in it, and **love** it. This is how wholeheartedly committed he is to God's Word, even at the expense of suffering for it.

119:48. In the midst of this persecution, he resolves to **lift up** his **hands** to God's **commands**, an act of praise being rendered to God for this truth. Such adoration comes on account of, he says, the divine word **which I love**. In the furnace of affliction, he chooses to **meditate** on the divine **decrees**, reflecting upon their truthfulness.

III. CONCLUSION

In these five stanzas, we read of some of the powerful ministries of Scripture in the lives of the psalmist. These same effects are operative today in the lives of all believers. God's Word is so powerful in the hearts of his people that in spite of the many temptations and afflictions they face, it is able to preserve them with divine purity and peace. The supernatural ability of the Bible is amazing. A saint armed with God's Word is adequately equipped to withstand the greatest assaults brought against his soul. As the believer meditates upon and follows the Scripture, this inspired Book delivers him out of his every temptation and trial, all for the glory of God's name.

IV. TEACHING OUTLINE

A. God's Word Cleanses the Heart (119:9–16)
B. God's Word Consoles the Soul (119:17–24)
C. God's Word Comforts the Spirit (119:25–32)
D. God's Word Counsels the Mind (119:33–40)
E. God's Word Conquers All Fears (119:41–48)

Psalm 119:49–88
Sola Scriptura (III)

"*The* Bible is alive, it speaks to me; it has feet, it runs

after me; it has hands, it lays hold of me."

Martin Luther

Psalm 119:49–88

I. INTRODUCTION

The Bible is a living book, full of the life-giving power of God. Within its sacred pages, the Scripture alone possesses the supernatural ability to produce every God-intended effect in the soul of man. Known as the sufficiency of Scripture, this single truth is immensely encouraging in its implications. When accompanied by the sovereign working of God's Spirit, it is able to accomplish all God's will in the believer's life. Nothing is lacking. This claim does not mean that all truth of every kind is contained in Scripture. Nor does it imply that everything the prophets, Jesus, and the apostles taught is preserved in Scripture. Rather, the sufficiency of Scripture affirms that everything necessary for the salvation of sinners, the sanctification of saints, and the spiritual direction of ministry is provided by God's Word. "The law of the LORD is perfect" (Ps. 19:7), the word *perfect* meaning "whole, complete, lacking nothing, a comprehensive treatment of truth." The Scripture makes the believer "thoroughly equipped for every good work" (2 Tim. 3:17). The Bible claims a supernatural ability for itself, being more than adequate to carry God's work in the Christian. This being so, this study of Psalm 119 continues into the seventh through eleventh stanzas. In verses 49–88, the psalmist continues in his sure confidence in God's Word, an inner certainty that the divine law is more than adequate to carry him through this time of great difficulty in his life.

II. COMMENTARY

MAIN IDEA: *The psalmist testifies that God's Word is the comfort and strength of his life.*

A God's Word Encourages the Heart (119:49–56)

119:49–50. In this seventh stanza (vv. 49–56), the psalmist testifies that the Word is his comfort and guide. Amid his anguish, he asks that God **remember** his **word**. That is, may the Lord fulfill all his promises to help and uphold him, God's **servant**. In the divine Word, God has given him **hope**, even in his seemingly hopeless situation. His **comfort** amid his deep **suffering** is found in the **promise** made by God to preserve him. It is the Scripture that gives him staying power.

119:51–53. Personal pain comes because **the arrogant**, or enemies of God's law, **mock** him. Nevertheless, he will **not turn** from God's **law** but remain devoted to it. As he reflects upon God's **law**, it brings him true **comfort** for his afflicted soul. Nothing heals the broken heart like God's promises. The **wicked** attack him, men who **have forsaken** God's **law**. But holy **indignation** and godly zeal for the Lord's honor consume him.

119:54–55. In this ordeal, his only real comfort is found in God's **decrees**. So strong is the Word that it puts a permanent **song** in his heart, **wherever** he may temporarily **lodge**. This suggests again that he is an alien and stranger here, out of step with the world (v. 19). **In the night**, when sleep eludes him, he is overshadowed by his suffering. But, at those times, he does **remember** God's **name** and **law** and finds true comfort.

119:56. Rather than defeating him, the psalmist's trials actually serve to deepen his daily **practice** to **obey** God's **precepts**.

B God's Word Enriches the Life (119:57–64)

119:57. The theme of the eighth stanza (vv. 57–64) is the fact that God cannot be known apart from his Word. The psalmist declares God is his **portion**, that is, his cherished inheritance and best possession. What better could he have than God himself? Thus, motivated by grace, he has **promised to obey** his **words**.

119:58–60. He seeks God's **face** with his entire being. In so doing, he has promised to keep God's Word. He entreats God that he **be gracious** to him as one pursuing him. The psalmist has carefully **considered** God's Word and **turned** his **steps** to it. He will **not delay** to **obey** God's **commands**. Delayed obedience is no obedience but disobedience.

119:61–62. In spite of persecution from **the wicked**, he will **not forget** God's **law**. They **bind** him **with ropes**, a figurative expression for oppression. **At midnight**, when he awakens because of his suffering, he **thanks** God for his **righteous laws**. He trusts that, one day, God will judge the wicked and reward him.

119:63. Although forsaken by the enemies of God, his heart is especially drawn to all who **fear** God and **follow** his **precepts**. He has become their **friend** through the fires of affliction. Persecution makes fellowship even more precious to him.

119:64. In response to God's vast **love**, he requests, once again, that the Lord **teach** him the divine **decrees** more fully (cp. v. 12).

⦿ God's Word Enlightens the Mind (119:65–72)

119:65. In this ninth stanza (vv. 65–72), the psalmist prays, **do good** to me **according to** the promises of **your word**. Humbly, he identifies himself as God's **servant**, one who is mastered by God's law.

119:66. Teach me the **knowledge** of greater truths in the Word, he prays. **Good judgment** will directly proceed from this knowledge. Adversity has deepened his conviction to follow the divine **commands** all the more. Affliction has taught him obedience to the Word.

119:67–68. Before he suffered this trial, he **went astray** from paths of obedience. **But now**, he chooses to **obey** the Word. Thus, his affliction is good for him. With humble gratitude, he acknowledges all God's ways are **good**. With a teachable spirit, he asks to be instructed.

119:69–70. The arrogant, who refuse to submit to the Word, a law unto themselves, have **smeared** and slandered him. But this vicious attack actually causes him to **keep** God's **precepts** with **all** his **heart**. These enemies of the Word are **callous** toward the **law**. But by stark contrast, he delights in it. Unlike the prideful who are without humility, he gladly submits to divine **law**.

119:71–72. Therefore, he concludes, it was **good** that he suffer for the Word. Such affliction actually drove him to deeper study of the divine **decrees**, leading to greater insight. Having paid an enormous price for his loyalty to God's **law**, he calculates it is **more precious** and valuable to him than **silver and gold**. His pain gave him far more in the Scripture than it cost him in affliction.

⦿ God's Word Emboldens the Spirit (119:73–80)

119:73. In the tenth stanza (vv. 73–80), the psalmist yet again asks for greater **understanding** from God **to learn** the divine **commands**. The Lord who **made** and **formed** him can alone open his spiritual eyes to behold divine truth in Scripture.

119:74. He asks that other believers who **fear** God will **see** this sanctifying work within him and **rejoice**, as they observe his **hope** in God's **word**.

119:75–77. The psalmist affirms his confidence that God's laws are **righteous**, thus bringing the right result in his life, even in disciplining him.

According to divine **faithfulness**, his many trials have **afflicted** him, but they have worked positively to mature him. In his ordeal, God's **unfailing love** and the **promise** of the Word have been his **comfort**. Only by divine **compassion** will he endure this trial. This sustaining grace will be experientially real as he finds **delight** in God's **law**.

119:78–80. The psalmist requests that God deal with the **arrogant**, who have wronged him without cause. In the meantime, he will **meditate** upon the divine **precepts** even more. He asks that others who **fear** God and know the Word **turn** to him in supporting fellowship. In this crisis, he prays that he be found **blameless** in his obedience of the divine **decrees**.

E God's Word Empowers the Soul (119:81–88)

119:81–82. The main theme of the eleventh stanza (vv. 81–88) is that God sustain him through this difficult hour. Sensing his own weakened state, the psalmist **faints with longing** for **salvation** from this present affliction. He endures though because he puts his **hope** in God's **word**. He is anxiously **looking** for God's **promise** to **comfort** him. But **when** will it come?

119:83–87. Though he bears the **smoke** of fiery trials, he will **not forget** the divine **decrees**. How much longer must he **wait** for divine justice to **punish** his **persecutors** who oppose God's Word? **Contrary** to the **law**, these enemies **dig pitfalls** for the psalmist. He cries for God's **help** to preserve and keep him from falling. They **almost wiped** him out, but he did not forsake God's **precepts**. The Word kept him strong and sure.

119:88. In spite of God's preservation by his Word to this point, the psalmist needs to be further kept strong. So he prays, **Preserve my life** from my enemy's attempts to lead me astray. No matter what they do, **I will obey the statutes**, he declares. Obedience to the Word preserves him.

III. CONCLUSION

Verses 81–88 bring to completion the first half of this lengthy but wonderful psalm. What glorious testimony it gives to the divine power of Scripture to work in the lives of God's people. Whatever the believer's spiritual need, the living hope in the Scripture is the answer. This psalm bears marvelous witness to the all-sufficient power of Scripture, attesting to its ability to sanctify the saints in every area of their lives. May all believers immerse themselves in the inspired pages of this divine Book. May minds be enlightened, hearts convicted, souls comforted, spirits revived, feet directed, and wills engaged as they read and heed the message of this holy Book, the Bible. Here is true happiness, holiness, and help for God's people.

IV. TEACHING OUTLINE

A. God's Word Encourages the Heart (119:49–56)
B. God's Word Enriches the Life (119:57–64)
C. God's Word Enlightens the Mind (119:65–72)
D. God's Word Emboldens the Spirit (119:73–80)
E. God's Word Empowers the Soul (119:81–88)

Psalm 119:89–128
Sola Scriptura (IV)

"*There* is no book like the Bible. It is a miracle of literature, a perennial spring of wisdom, a wonderful book of surprises, a revelation of mystery, an infallible guide of conduct, an unspeakable source of comfort."

Samuel Chadwick

Psalm 119:89–128

I. INTRODUCTION

In every generation, those who have most treasured God's Word have been those most mightily used by God. Having a passionate devotion to his Word and being a powerful force for God are inseparably bound together. The former feeds the latter. One is the root, the other the fruit. Loving God's Word is the cause; being used by the Lord is the effect. The fact is, no one can love God without loving his Word. It is in God's Word that the believer learns about the unfathomable glory of God, supremely revealed in the person of his Son, Jesus Christ. The more fully one grows to know the Word, the more deeply he may grow to know the Lord.

It is the Word of God that makes God intimately known to receptive hearts. No one knows more about God than what he learns about him in his Word. For this reason, the saints must cherish this Book, the Bible, for it is the inspired revelation of God to man. A heart fervent toward the Word will soon be glowing toward God.

This exposition of Psalm 119 continues as it leads into stanzas twelve through sixteen. The focus remains the same: the all-sufficiency of God's Word in the life of the believer to mature him in the kingdom of God.

II. COMMENTARY

> **MAIN IDEA:** *The psalmist extols the perfections of God's Word, pursuing and practicing it with all his being.*

A God's Word Stands Forever (119:89–96)

119:89–90. In the twelfth stanza (vv. 89–96), the focus is on the eternal and infinite nature of God's Word. The psalmist testifies, God's **word** is **eternal** and **stands firm in the heavens**, forever immutable, always relevant, and perennially life giving. God's **faithfulness** is a synonym for Scripture, meaning God is forever committed to keeping his promises **through all generations**. As God **established** the **earth** by his spoken word and it stood fast, even so God has spoken by his written Word, and it, too, will come to pass.

119:91. God's ancient **laws endure** to the present **day**, never needing revision or alteration. Even his Word exists to **serve** him.

119:92–93. This unchanging Word of God brings **delight** to the psalmist, even amid his **affliction**. The divine **law** strengthens him, enabling him to endure through much difficulty. He remembers God's **precepts**, which have **preserved** him through deep troubles.

119:94–95. Surrounded by many persecutors, he cries out to God, **Save me**, as he has pursued God's **precepts**. He seeks divine deliverance from this trial. The **wicked** seek to do him harm, but he purposes to **ponder** and meditate on God's **statutes** for his strength.

119:96. As he contemplates God's Word, the psalmist more fully realizes the limitless, **boundless** (literally, "very broad," inexhaustible) perfections of Scripture. All earthly matters are limited, but God's Word is infinite and perfect.

B God's Word Satisfies Fully (119:97–104)

119:97. The central idea of this thirteenth stanza (vv. 97–104) is how meditating upon God's Word makes the psalmist wise. With growing devotion, the psalmist confesses, **I love your law** (vv. 47–48,127,163,165). God's Word becomes more precious and pleasing to him the more he meditates on it throughout the **day**.

119:98–100. As he contemplates God's Word, it makes him **wiser** than his **enemies** who surround him, seeking his harm. The Word gives him **more insight** than his **teachers**. This God-given discernment comes the more he meditates upon God's statutes. Consequently, God's Word grants him **more understanding than the elders** because he obeys its truths.

119:101–102. Applying this God-given wisdom, the psalmist confides that he has kept his **feet** on God's path through obedience. He has **not**

departed from God's **laws** because God himself has **taught** him his Word. Being divinely illumined obligates him to obey God's Word.

119:103–104. He testifies that the **words** of God are **sweeter than honey** to him and give him **understanding**. Thus, he finds distasteful **every wrong path** of worldly counsel that leads to sin.

C God's Word Shines Forth (119:105–112)

119:105–106. Seeking his direction in life from God's **word**, the psalmist declares it is a **lamp** to his **feet**, giving **light** for his **path** in life. Seeing the divinely illumined way, he has taken an **oath** to follow God's **righteous laws**.

119:107. Following God's Word inevitably brings the world's persecution. The psalmist has **suffered much** for righteousness's sake and asks God to **preserve** him by the **word**.

119:108–109. Even in the midst of this painful opposition, he will publicly **praise** God. He will not withdraw from God's Word, even in the face of hostility, but asks that God **teach** him more. This public praise brings threats on his **life**, as if he were taking his own life. Nevertheless, he **will not forget** God's **law**, which sustains him.

119:110. As a result, **the wicked . . . set** a trap to harm him, **but** he will continue to follow God's **precepts**. From this divinely chosen path he has **not strayed**.

119:111–112. In the midst of his persecution, God's Word remains his **heritage forever**, a treasure of **joy** to his **heart**. Regardless of what it will cost him, his **heart** is **set on keeping** the Word **to the very end**.

D God's Word Sustains Firmly (119:113–120)

119:113–114. In this fifteenth stanza (vv. 113–120), the psalmist says that he loves God's Word. He states, **I hate double-minded men**, those who reject God's Word. But to the contrary, he declares, I **love** the divine **law**. Amid such law-rejecters, God is his **refuge**, a hiding place for his soul. He intentionally places his **hope** in the **word**.

119:115. As if speaking to his persecutors, who seek his harm, he commands these evildoers, **Away from me** so that I may devote myself to the divine **commands**.

119:116–117. He asks that God **sustain** him by his Word. Only then will he **live**. God must undergird his **hopes** for deliverance, or his confidence will be **dashed** by despair and defeat. He pleads with God to **uphold** him if he is to **be delivered**. While he waits, he pledges high **regard** for God's **decrees**.

119:118–119. God will **reject** all who reject his **decrees**. Their **deceitfulness** will fail **in vain**. God will **discard** the wicked like **dross**, or scum like slag removed from molten ore or metal. This divine judgment only causes him to **love** God's **statutes** even more.

119:120. As a result, the psalmist's **flesh trembles** in **fear** of God, who judges all who reject his Word. Thus, he stands **in awe** of God's **laws**, quivering out of deep reverence for God's written Word.

E God's Word Strengthens Faithfully (119:121–128)

119:121. The sixteenth stanza (vv. 121–128) highlights the psalmist's prayer for God's deliverance from his **oppressors**. He states that he has **done what is righteous and just**, a synonym for God's law, which is perfectly righteous in its pronouncements and judgments. Thus, he suffers unjustly because he obeys God's Word.

119:122–123. Ensure my safety from **the arrogant**, he pleads. Verse 122 is the only verse in Psalm 119 without a direct or indirect naming of God's Word (see vv. 90,121,132 for indirect references). Bring **salvation** to me from these evil men, he prays, as he looks to God's **righteous promise**, another synonym for the faithfulness of God's Word.

119:124–125. As he is hated by his persecutors, he asks that God **deal** with him in divine **love**. This means that God would personally **teach** him even more of the Word. The more he suffers, the more he wants to be taught by God. In this crucible of crisis, he asks for greater **discernment** and understanding from God in the divine **statutes**.

119:126. It is now **time** for God **to act** and judge those who break the divine **law**. The psalmist cannot bear seeing God's Word **being broken**. He pleads that it is, therefore, **time** for God to **act** in judgment.

119:127–128. Distancing himself from these law breakers, he testifies, **I love your commands more than gold** (vv. 14,72,111,162). God's Word is the greatest treasure of his life. The more he considers God's **precepts**, the more he hates every **wrong path** of worldly counsel, paved with men's lies. He considers God's precepts to be completely right.

III. CONCLUSION

In these stanzas, the psalmist expresses again the all-sufficiency of the Word of God in his life to cause him to live as God intends. He stands in awe of the Scripture, extolling its many perfections. The holy character of God is contained in his Word and is revealed to him as he learns, loves, and lives its truths. His life is immeasurably enriched as he feeds upon and follows its teaching. The Word causes him to be restrained from sin and to pursue righteousness as he progresses in godliness. In the Word, he has a sure lamp and a pure light to direct his feet down the path of spiritual devotion to God in the midst of a dark world that is ignorant of God. The Word is more than adequate to direct him into the fullness of God's will.

IV. TEACHING OUTLINE

A. God's Word Stands Forever (119:89–96)
B. God's Word Satisfies Fully (119:97–104)
C. God's Word Shines Forth (119:105–112)
D. God's Word Sustains Firmly (119:113–120)
E. God's Word Strengthens Faithfully (119:121–128)

Psalm 119:129–176
Sola Scriptura (V)

"*The* Bible is a rock of diamonds, a chain of pearls, the

sword of the Spirit; a chart by which the Christian sails to

eternity; the map by which he daily walks; the sundial by

which he sets his life; the balance in which he

weighs his actions."

Thomas Watson

I. INTRODUCTION

As the church of Jesus Christ enters the twenty-first century, she finds herself standing at a dangerous crossroad. Two roads stand before her, both paths marked "truth." One is paved with the lethal lies of Satan, the other with the life-giving truths of Scripture. Confronted with these two choices, many sectors of the church have abandoned their commitment to the authority of Scripture, and the consequences have been devastating. Choosing to follow worldly wisdom, many have arrived at destinations previously thought to be unthinkable: inclusive universalism, radical feminism, same-sex marriages, annihilationism, and, even worse, atheism.

Yet, in the midst of this rampant apostasy, an amazing phenomenon has occurred. A renewed commitment to biblical inerrancy has emerged in parts of the church. A conservative resurgence has signaled a return to a fundamental commitment to the inspired, infallible Word of God. Such a prospective reformation is, indeed, encouraging.

But having safely negotiated this crossroad, a second intersection now looms on the evangelical horizon, one equally threatening. James Montgomery Boice has observed that while many churches now assert biblical *authority*, they equivocate on biblical *sufficiency*. Boice writes, "Our problem is in deciding whether the Bible is sufficient for the church's life and work. We confess its authority, but we discount its ability to do what is necessary to draw unbelievers to Christ, enable us to grow in godliness, provide direction for our lives, and transform and revitalize society."

Is the Word of God, when rightly taught and carefully followed, capable of performing *all* that is necessary to fulfill God's purposes in the church? *This* is the question of the hour. In the last six stanzas of Psalm 119, stanzas 17 through 22, the psalmist restates the core truth of this masterpiece of the psalms: God's Word is all-sufficient to produce all his good pleasure in the life of the believer.

II. COMMENTARY

> **MAIN IDEA:** The psalmist praises the power of God's Word, which enables him to persevere through his present difficulty.

A God's Word Illumines Minds (119:129–136)

119:129. The psalmist asks God to establish him in the divine Word. He declares that God's **statutes are wonderful**, provoking awe and amazement within him. In light of this, he pledges his obedience to them. He will **obey** them.

119:130–131. As the psalmist looks within God's **words**, the **light** of truth, **understanding**, and discernment is revealed to him. This divine illumination of Scripture increases his desire to **pant** with **longing** for more of God's Word.

119:132–133. As he pursues God's Word, the psalmist requests divine **mercy** toward **those who love** God's **name**. The divine "name" is a reference to God's Word, which reveals his divine glory and attributes. The psalmist requests that God **direct** his **footsteps** to obey his **word**. Only in God's guidance and enabling grace would **no sin rule** over him.

119:134–135. He pleads that God **redeem**, or rescue, him from **the oppression of men**, who oppose him and threaten to weaken his obedience. Even in the face of this personal affliction, he chooses to **obey** God's Word, not man's counsel. He humbly requests that God **make** his **face** to **shine** upon him with divine blessing, favor, and deliverance. In spite of the affliction it has caused, he asks that God **teach** him even more truth in the Word.

119:136. His enemies disregard God's Word, causing **streams of tears** to **flow** from his face. How can he be without sorrow, when God's Word is so hated by others?

B God's Word Incites Zeal (119:137–144)

119:137–138. The psalmist declares that God is righteous, and so is his Word. He begins by affirming God's righteousness, which is perfectly revealed in his **laws**. These laws are perfectly right, meaning just and true. His **statutes** are **righteous**, or equitable and fair, and **fully trustworthy**, that is, absolutely reliable and faithful. God's character is holy and his Word is accurate in every way.

119:139–140. That the Lord's Word is so perfect evokes a response of great devotion. **Zeal** for God's Word **wears** him out when he sees others **ignore** it. But to the contrary, the psalmist **loves** God's **promises**. The Lord's promises have been **tested**, meaning refined by fire and shown to be perfectly pure. They contain nothing worthless, only pure truth.

119:141. Through this ordeal the psalmist has been brought low and feels small compared to his adversaries, even **despised** because of his allegiance to God's Word. Nevertheless, he will **not forget** God's **precepts**.

119:142. Returning to the earlier focus on God's **righteousness** (v. 137), he reaffirms that the divinely written **law** is absolutely **true** (v. 140).

119:143–144. Therefore, even when **trouble** comes upon him through adherence to the Word, he still has **delight** for God's **commands**. No matter what man may say to the contrary, God's **statutes** are **forever right**.

C God's Word Inspires Hope (119:145–152)

119:145–146. In the midst of his affliction, the psalmist pledges to remain completely devoted to keeping God's Word. He vows to **obey** God's **decrees**, no matter what it may cost him. He will **call out** for God's salvation and do so by reaffirming his commitment to **keep** the divine **statutes**.

119:147–149. He is unshakable in his dedication to trust and obey God's inspired record in Scripture. He rises early in the morning and cries for **help**, placing his **hope** in God's **word**. Throughout **the night**, he does the same, meditating upon God's **promises**. As he prays day and night, he appeals to God's **love** and asks that God **preserve** his **life** in proportion to his trust in God's **laws**.

119:150–151. Those who **devise wicked schemes are near** the psalmist, ready to do him harm. But they are **far from** God's **law**. Nevertheless, he knows that God is **near** him. He is sure that God's **commands are true**.

119:152. From **long ago**, he **learned** from God's Word that the Lord **established** his statutes to endure **forever**. They will never be removed or revoked.

D God's Word Increases Faith (119:153–160)

119:153–154. The psalmist again prays for divine deliverance. His entreaties deepen as this prayer continues. He prays that God will see how great his loyalty is to him, having **not forgotten** his **law**. He asks God to **defend** and **redeem** and **preserve** him because he keeps his word. Surely God, in turn, will keep his promise.

119:155–156. To the contrary, the **wicked** will not be saved. They do not **seek out** God's **decrees**. But the psalmist does. God's **compassion** will surely lead him to preserve the psalmist's **life** because he keeps his **laws**.

119:157–158. In spite of many **foes** who persecute him, the psalmist will not abandon God's **statutes**. He loathes **the faithless** who reject the divine Word.

119:159. To the contrary, he loves God's **precepts**, the basis for his deliverance by God. He asks that God **preserve** him from the threat of death by his enemies.

119:160. The psalmist concludes this stanza by extolling the greatness of God's Word. **All your words are true**, he declares, without any mixture of error, **righteous**, executing perfect justice, and **eternal**, never needing to be rescinded.

E God's Word Infuses Peace (119:161–168)

119:161. The psalmist cries out for deliverance because he has kept God's Word. Mighty **rulers** persecute him **without** just **cause**. Nevertheless, the psalmist's **heart trembles** at God's Word.

119:162–164. This properly motivated fear causes him to **rejoice** in God's **promise** as when one **finds** great treasure. He hates the **falsehood** spoken by evil men that contradict Scripture, but he loves the truths of God's **law**. **Seven times a day**, picturing completeness, he praises God for his **righteous laws**.

119:165. Great peace and blessings come to those who love God's **law**. They have stability without stumbling.

119:166–168. Eventually, the psalmist's **salvation** out of this ordeal will come, but in God's perfect time. In the meantime, he is firmly committed to **follow** God's **commands**. In spite of his persecution over the Word, he is determined to **obey** God's **statutes** with greater resolve. This obedience flows from a heart of **love** for the Word, not mere mechanical, legalistic duty. He repeats and reaffirms his commitment to obey God's **statutes**, knowing that God perfectly sees **all** his **ways**. Nothing is hidden from God.

F God's Word Instills Resolve (119:169–176)

119:169–170. In the final stanza, the psalmist declares how the Word affects the entirety of his life. In total dependency upon the Lord, he calls on God to **give** his mind **understanding according to** his **word**. He asks that God **deliver** him from this persecution **according to** his **promise**. God's Word has put this relentless resolve into his prayers.

119:171–172. The psalmist fervently praises God for his Word. His **lips overflow with praise** at the truth he learns. He sings over the Word because God's **commands are righteous**.

119:173. He asks God to **help** him in this predicament based upon the fact that he has **chosen** to delight in and follow God's **precepts**.

119:174–175. With growing desire, the psalmist longs for God's **salvation** from his enemies. In the meantime, God's **law** is his deep **delight**. He asks God to enable him to escape death and **live** so he may yet longer **praise** him on the earth. While he waits, his **laws** strengthen him.

119:176. In this final statement, a humble confession, the psalmist acknowledges, **I have strayed like a lost sheep**, wandering from the Word. The closer he draws to the Word, the more clearly he sees his own imperfections. **Seek your servant**, he implores God, knowing he does truly embrace God's **commands** as fully as he should. They are **not forgotten**, but cherished, by this **servant**.

III. CONCLUSION

For every believer, the *sufficiency* of Scripture must be his confidence as he lives the Christian life. With so many people affirming a renewed belief in the *inerrancy* of the Bible, an equal confidence also must be placed in its *potency* and *power*. This was precisely what occurred in the days of the Reformation as *sola Scriptura* became the battle cry of the Reformers. Armed solely with the Word that cannot fail, Martin Luther explained the phenomenon of the Reformation in his day like this: "I simply taught, preached, wrote God's Word; otherwise I did nothing. And when, while I slept . . . the Word so greatly weakened the papacy that never a Prince or Emperor inflicted such damage upon it. I did nothing. The Word did it all."

Such an unwavering commitment to *sola Scriptura,* the supernatural ability of the Word to execute God's purposes, must be the unshakable confidence of every Christian in this generation. Believers, now more than ever, must live and obey the full counsel of the Word in the power of the Holy Spirit. May God raise up a new generation in our day who will follow the Word with growing confidence in the sufficiency of Scripture to perform all that God intends. May we come to behold in this hour what Luther witnessed so long ago: *The Word did it all.*

IV. TEACHING OUTLINE

A. God's Word Illumines Minds (119:129–136)

B. God's Word Incites Zeal (119:137–144)

C. God's Word Inspires Hope (119:145–152)

D. God's Word Increases Faith (119:153–160)

E. God's Word Infuses Peace (119:161–168)

F. God's Word Instills Resolve (119:169–176)

Psalm 120

Upward Bound

> *"We must take our whole heart to the house of God, and worship like those who listen to the reading of a will."*
>
> J . C . R y l e

Psalm 120

I. INTRODUCTION

An incomparable blessing awaits God's people whenever they come to God's house to hear God's Word. True spiritual growth necessitates that believers regularly attend the gathering of worshippers and sit under the Scripture being taught. Wherever the Word of God is proclaimed, the glory of God is manifested, and the grace of God is magnified in the hearts of the saints. Whatever the distance a person must travel to receive the Word, the effort is always eternally rewarding. Singing praises to God with other like-minded believers makes the journey worth the while. Nothing is more important to one's spiritual life than hearing and living God's Word.

Psalm 120 underscores this basic truth. As the first of fifteen consecutive psalms known as the Ascent Psalms (Pss. 120–134), this hymn was sung by believers as they traveled together to God's house in Jerusalem to worship God. Each of these fifteen psalms is assigned the heading "a song of ascents," or with slight variation. These ascent psalms were originally a self-contained hymnbook unto itself, eventually added to Book IV of the Psalter. This smaller hymnbook, the Ascent Psalms, was used by worshippers as they traveled from all over Judea to make the pilgrimage to Jerusalem three times a year for their annual feasts (Passover, Pentecost, and Tabernacles).

These songs were labeled ascent psalms because those traveling to Jerusalem would ascend upward in topographical elevation. Jerusalem was built on Mount Zion, 2,700 feet high, requiring an upward climb for travelers. These pilgrim worshippers journeyed to the holy city from as far away as Meschech to the north and Kedar to the south. As they did, they sang these psalms until they finally reached the temple (Ps. 134:1–2). These worshippers lived under verbal attack from unbelievers at home. With great anticipation, they traveled with other fellow believers for these regular times in God's house.

II. COMMENTARY

MAIN IDEA: *The psalmist asks God for deliverance from his many enemies.*

A A Cry in Distress (120:1)

120:1. The psalmist calls on **the LORD in** his **distress**, a painful time of personal attack and soul agony. This gut-wrenching trial involved being falsely accused and unjustly slandered by evil men (v. 2). In this ordeal, God hears his plea and **answers** him, either delivering him out of his trouble or giving him the grace to endure. But either way, God answered him.

B A Cry for Deliverance (120:2)

120:2. The psalmist prays, **Save me**, meaning "rescue me out of my difficulty." Though not in life-threatening danger, nevertheless, his reputation and emotional well-being are greatly threatened. Suffering under the attack of **lying lips** and **deceitful tongues**, he is enduring a character assassination from ungodly people who took every opportunity to slander him.

C A Cry of Defiance (120:3–4)

120:3. As if speaking directly to his enemies, he asks, **What will he do to you?** The author is assured that God will act against them. Not taking matters into his own hands, nor seeking his own vengeance, the psalmist leaves room for the wrath of God (Rom. 12:17–19). He desires that God deal with his enemies (Ps. 94:1) if they are not going to repent. The word **more** implies that God has already given some retribution to them. But in stubbornness, these ungodly men have persisted in attacking him.

120:4. He is sure that God **will punish** his accusers with **sharp arrows**. God, who judges rightly, will deal with them as they have dealt with him. The Lord will answer in like manner, dealing severe judgment upon them (Pss. 7:11–13; 45:5). Further, God will punish them with **burning coals** from a **broom tree**, which is a desert bush that grows to fifteen feet high. This means that God will consume the psalmist's enemies with fiery judgment (Ps. 140:10).

D A Cry of Dejection (120:5–7)

120:5. But until the Lord deals with them, the psalmist remains in agonizing pain. He laments in great emotional distress under this verbal attack, **Woe to me**. Their arrows have sunk deep into his soul as if he lived **in Meshech**, in Central Asia (Gen. 10:2), and **Kedar**, in Arabia (Isa. 21:16), both places being far from Jerusalem, inhabited by barbarians and pagans. They slander and belittle him as if he were living among godless bandits.

120:6. For **too long**, the psalmist has endured association with the ungodly who **hate peace** between men. He has been exposed and made vulnerable to the worst of men. He has had this daily dose of reality.

120:7. The psalmist confesses he is a **man of peace**, who chooses not to attack others as he has been assaulted. But when he speaks God's truth from God's Word, **they are for war**, choosing to come against him. His words from God have only provoked hostility against himself, revealing their depravity.

III. CONCLUSION

All believers will suffer persecution from this world (2 Tim. 3:12). This is the sobering reality of the Christian life. While living here, all Christians will find themselves embroiled in the conflict of spiritual warfare between light and darkness, even heaven and hell itself. But the greater the opposition they face in this evil world, the sweeter is their fellowship when they come to worship in God's house. Persecution from the world serves to increase one's love for the brethren. Rejection by unbelievers causes love between Christians to abound even more and more. Under the heat of hatred from a Christ-rejecting world, the truths of Scripture, when proclaimed in God's house, seem all the more precious to the wounded souls of believers. May we be like the psalmist and call out to God in our distress. And, moreover, may we be sure to gather in the Lord's house.

IV. TEACHING OUTLINE

A. A Cry in Distress (120:1)

B. A Cry for Deliverance (120:2)

C. A Cry of Defiance (120:3–4)

D. A Cry of Dejection (120:5–7)

Psalm 121
Finding Strength

Psalm 121

I. INTRODUCTION

David Livingstone, the famous nineteenth-century Scottish missionary, was an explorer of the uncharted interior of Africa. The morning he left Blantyre, Scotland, for the mission field, he gathered with his family and read Psalm 121, seeking the strength he needed for the long, arduous journey that lay ahead. After reading another psalm, Psalm 135, he prayed with his father and sister and set sail for Africa. History records how the endeavors of Livingstone opened up the continent of Africa for the gospel of Jesus Christ. In large measure, it was because of this man's pioneer efforts that the gospel would eventually come to the dark recesses of this land.

Mrs. Moffat, Livingstone's mother-in-law, wrote in a farewell letter that Psalm 121 would be constantly before her as she prayed for him: "Unceasing prayer is made for you. When I think of you, my heart will go upwards— 'Keep him as the apple of Thine eye; Hold him in the hollow of Thine hand,' are the ejaculations of the heart."

Throughout the years that followed, the Lord heard Mrs. Moffat's repeated petitions and granted divine power to enable Livingstone to fulfill the many challenges and hardships he encountered. No matter how great the demands were, the all-sufficient power of God was able to see his servant through this demanding mission.

In like manner, *every* believer desperately needs God's power to live the Christian life, whether it be reaching a continent for Christ abroad or simply being faithful to live for the Lord at home. One of the greatest challenges is to live the Christian life, not in one's own strength but in the power that God provides (John 15:5). This is the lesson of Psalm 121, a marvelous testimony of reliance on God's strength to finish the journey to Jerusalem. The superscription of the psalm is "a song of ascents," meaning it was sung originally by Old Testament worshippers as they made their journey to Jerusalem to worship in the temple. They made such a journey three times a year.

Making the trip to Jerusalem required making an upward ascent in elevation into the holy city to attend the feasts. There were no paved roads but, for the most part, only well-trodden paths across the valleys, along the side of rivers, and over mountain passes. This psalm recounted the arduous journey and the abundant strength they found in the Lord himself to complete their trip. God himself was their strength, sustainer, supporter, and Savior from all harm.

II. COMMENTARY

> **MAIN IDEA:** *The psalmist relies upon the Lord to be his supernatural strength to complete the will of God before him.*

A God Is My Strength (121:1–2)

> **SUPPORTING IDEA:** *The psalmist confesses his trust in God to be his help in traveling to Jerusalem.*

121:1. With singular focus toward God, the psalmist confides, **I lift up my eyes to the hills**. This statement of trust is made as he journeyed upward in elevation to Jerusalem, which is situated atop Mount Zion. Rising up before him, "the hills" are those upon which the holy city rests. Weary from the long, demanding journey, the psalmist is in dire need of divine **help** to complete the trip. In reality, he needs this strength from God in all matters of life.

121:2. He gives the strong testimony, **My help comes from the LORD**. The psalmist affirms all the dimensions of help that he needs—physical, emotional, and spiritual. He is not looking to the mountains for his help or to anything or anyone dwelling on these hills. Rather, he looks to the **Maker** of the mountains—God himself—for this assistance. Only the One who has the infinite power to make **heaven and earth** has the ability to enable him to live triumphantly.

B God Is My Support (121:3–4)

> **SUPPORTING IDEA:** *The psalmist is assured the Lord, ever watchful, will provide the stability he needs.*

121:3. God will not **let your foot slip**, actively keeping believers from falling during their journey. The Hebrew word for **watches over** (*shamar*) is used six times in this psalm, indicating that God himself is the guardian of his people during their trip.

121:4. This sovereign protection is a continual help from God, day and night, who always **watches over Israel**. Though man may close his eyes at night, the Lord **will neither slumber nor sleep**. God is ever awake, ever alert, always focused on the needs of his people. He stands ready to support them if they should slip and fall into difficulty.

ⓒ God Is My Shade (121:5–6)

> **SUPPORTING IDEA:** *The psalmist is confident of God's unfailing comfort during his difficulties.*

121:5. For the psalmist, **shade** provides needed relief from the blazing sun. The danger of sunstrokes in this region is real, as **the sun** drains weary travelers, baking and broiling them. **Shade** provides comfort in the midst of oppressive circumstances, a respite in the midst of fiery times. This is what God provides all believers—comfort and relief.

121:6. The sun and **moon** will not **harm** his people. These two celestial bodies stand for dangers that occur by day and by night. But in spite of these difficulties, God's protection is continuous and constant.

Ⓓ God Is My Savior (121:7–8)

> **SUPPORTING IDEA:** *The psalmist testifies that God is his deliverer in all of life.*

121:7. Travelers on their journey to Jerusalem faced many evils. Thieves and robbers would hide along the way and prey upon them. Spiritual dangers awaited them, discouragement and doubt threatened their **life**. But the Lord himself would protect them **from all harm**, both physically and spiritually.

121:8. The Lord will **watch over** their **coming** to Jerusalem, and their **going** back home. Even as the worshippers conclude their time in Jerusalem and prepare to return home to face the demands of daily life, they do so with the promises of God ringing in their ears. God will protect and preserve them in all their ways.

> **MAIN IDEA REVIEW:** *The psalmist relies upon the Lord to be his supernatural strength to complete the will of God before him.*

III. CONCLUSION

All believers find themselves on a spiritual journey in this life, one in which they are traveling through this world as pilgrims toward their true home in heaven. God's people are aliens and strangers here, merely passing through this world, on the way to their final destination in glory. But while they are here, the demands placed upon them are enormous, requiring extraordinary strength to remain true to God. As the saints traverse this planet, they face many spiritual obstacles and adversaries. To be sure, the Christian life is an uphill climb, an ascent to higher ground. Only by the grace of God does one find the strength to press on faithfully to the upward prize. In God's power, believers can overcome all that confronts them and enables them to live victoriously. Solely in the Lord himself do God's people find strength for the journey of life.

IV. LIFE APPLICATION

How can we find the supernatural strength of God that can empower us for life's journey? Several actions are necessary if we are to advance triumphantly in the will of God.

Look exclusively to the Lord. This is precisely what the psalmist did. When he said, "I lift up my eyes to the hills" (v. 1), he was looking exclusively to God, the Maker of heaven and earth, from whence his help would come. So must all believers. By looking to God, we look away from ourselves and from all others for strength. In so doing, we must rely completely upon God as the source of spiritual power in Christian living. Faith looks to God, not to man.

Listen attentively to the Lord. God's Word is an all-sufficient source of divine grace for pilgrims on life's journey. God's Word is an unlimited reservoir of undeniable spiritual energy for all who will receive his truth. Only by looking into the Scripture can we truly look to the Lord who has spoken to us in the Bible. If we are to know God's strength, we must hear and heed his Word.

Lean wholly upon the Lord. We must rely upon the superabundant grace of God's Spirit in every demand of life. Only as we recognize our own weakness does God's power fill and flood our souls. When we trust in ourselves, we are impotent. But in looking to God, we find great strength. Let us learn to cast our burdens upon him and lean upon him.

V. PRAYER

God, narrow our focus upon you. We confess that we are so easily distracted by the many allures and temptations of the world that would steal our attention away from you. Please forgive us for failing to lift up our eyes to you as we should. In our weakness, cause us to lift up our eyes of faith and look exclusively to you. By your Spirit, work within us so that we might rely solely upon you. In Jesus' name. Amen.

VI. DEEPER DISCOVERIES

A. Help (121:1–2)

The word translated *help* (*ezer*) is a derivative of the root *azar* and means "to help or support." It (*azar*) was used commonly of military support between countries. It is used in the Psalms to refer to God's help from enemy forces (Pss. 46:5; 79:9). *Ezer* is used in the Psalms in reference to God or his divine intervention (Pss. 20:2; 33:20; 70:5; 115:9–11; 124:8; 146:5).

B. Watches Over (121:4)

The phrase "watches over" translates *shamar*, which means "to hedge about" as in guarding or protecting a person or object. It carries the idea of watching over and guarding so as to preserve or save from harm. It was used to describe a gardener tending his garden (Gen. 2:15), a shepherd watching over his flock (Gen. 30:31), and a man watching over a house (Eccl. 12:3).

VII. TEACHING OUTLINE

A. God Is My Strength (121:1–2)
B. God Is My Support (121:3–4)
C. God Is My Shade (121:5–6)
D. God Is My Savior (121:7–8)

Psalm 122
Joyful Arrival

Psalm 122

I. INTRODUCTION

Eager joy should always fill the hearts of God's people as they make their way into God's house. In the company of like-minded worshippers, their hungry souls are satisfied as they sit under the exposition of Scripture. Their spirits are lifted as God is exalted, but never as man is entertained. What a treasured privilege it is to be with God's people as they gather in God's house to hear God's Word. Word-inspired worship is never a drudgery but a delight; never a burden but a blessing. It is in this spirit that believers should gather together with much anticipation, excitement, and enthusiasm for the holy things of God. Such corporate worship serves as a preview of what awaits the redeemed in heaven, a foretaste of glory above. It is with this joy that the saints should always assemble together in God's house.

This is the very joy expressed by the psalmist in Psalm 122 as he arrives in Jerusalem, the holy city, to enter God's house. He is filled with exuberance at this long-awaited prospect of gathering together with fellow believers in the house of the Lord. Psalm 122 is the third of the songs of ascents (Pss. 120–134), a small group of fifteen psalms that captures the progression of worshippers traveling to the city of God for one of their religious festivals. The psalmist, designated in the superscription as David, recalled his delight in going up to Jerusalem to worship God. Compiled later and strategically placed into the Psalter here, it became one of the worship songs sung as believers made their pilgrimage to Jerusalem, the nation's spiritual center.

In Psalm 120, the singers are in a foreign land, beginning their journey toward the city of God. In Psalm 121, they appear to have sighted the city. Here, in Psalm 122, their feet actually stand within the city gates (v. 2), preparing to enter God's house.

II. COMMENTARY

MAIN IDEA: *David expresses exuberance upon arriving in Jerusalem in order to enter God's house and calls upon everyone to pray for its peace.*

A The Procession to Jerusalem (122:1–2)

122:1. With extreme gladness, the psalmist finally arrived in Jerusalem at the house of God to worship there. He **rejoiced**, full of laughter and delight. **Those** who spoke to him, **Let us go to the house of the LORD**, were other pilgrims also making their journey to Jerusalem. The house of the Lord was the tabernacle when David first wrote this, as no temple had yet been built. When this psalm was later compiled and placed here in the Psalter, it had reference to the post-exilic temple.

122:2. Excitement overcame the psalmist and the other worshippers **standing** within the **gates** of **Jerusalem**. To be where God's Word and glory were put on display thrilled them. The psalmist was overwhelmed not merely with the grand buildings of Jerusalem but with what took place inside the worship of God. To stand there was exhilarating as they anticipated the rich blessings to come (Ps. 84:10). To be sure, this journey to God's house was well worth the effort.

B The Praise for Jerusalem (122:3–5)

122:3–4. Jerusalem, the holy city, is built **compacted together**, tight and compressed, bringing the people close together. There, they will **praise** God with grateful hearts, giving thanks. They will also make public declaration of **the name of the LORD**. They are to be thankful for God's saving acts on behalf of his people, both individually and corporately.

122:5. Jerusalem was the center for justice, equity, and the reinforcement of what is right. It was the place where **thrones for judgment** stood, where right was rewarded and wrong was punished. It was the place where the innocent were defended and the guilty were prosecuted. Jerusalem was called **the house of David** because it was the royal city of Israel where David sat enthroned, presiding over the people and dispensing justice. Thus, Jerusalem was not only the central place for worship but also the site where civil judgments and legal decisions were made. It was the seat of government, the place where the king of Israel presided. Not only was the Word of God taught here, but it was reinforced here.

C The Peace of Jerusalem (122:6–9)

122:6. Because of the holy city's strategic importance, David urges, **Pray for the peace of Jerusalem**. This peace involves international peace with surrounding countries, as well as internal peace within Israel. Rather than coming to Jerusalem and finding disharmony, disunity, division, and friction, he urges that there be peace, love, and harmony. If they will seek peace among God's people, then God himself will **secure** them.

122:7–9. Pray for **peace within your walls and security within your citadels**, the psalmist declared. This is a reference to divine protection from hostile nations. They needed an indivisible unity and impregnable safety that can come only from God. Where God finds unity, he commands his blessing there (Ps. 133:1–3). For the common good of all, he is concerned with **peace** within Jerusalem, internally and internationally. To seek peace is to pursue the good of God's people and the blessing of **the house of the LORD**. For the sake of worshippers in God's dwelling place, David vows to pray for its **prosperity**.

III. CONCLUSION

It is of first importance for all Christians regularly to attend God's house for public worship. John Wesley once remarked, "There is nothing more unchristian than a solitary Christian." It is spiritually unhealthy, even disastrous, for any believers to forsake the assembling together with other saints (Heb. 10:25). No believer can lead a spiritually successful life who does not faithfully come to church and be engaged in the spiritual disciplines of the Christian life. How critically important it is to worship with like-minded brothers and sisters of kindred spirit in the gathered congregation of believers. Such must be our regular pattern and joyful experience.

IV. TEACHING OUTLINE

A. The Procession to Jerusalem (122:1–2)

B. The Praise for Jerusalem (122:3–5)

C. The Peace of Jerusalem (122:6–9)

Psalm 123

Gazing Upward

"*F*aith is the sight of the inward eye."

Alexander MacLaren

Psalm 123

I. INTRODUCTION

Faith is always looking up to God. It is seeing beyond the visible to the invisible, peering beyond the temporal to the eternal, squinting beyond the physical to the spiritual. Faith is the upward vision of the believing soul, looking beyond the circumstances of life to the Lord himself, who stands behind those events and presides over them for his glory. Faith sees that God has an eternal purpose in all things, an all-wise plan for all that occurs. The eyes of faith glance away from self and away from this world, focusing upon God who reigns above. Faith is looking beyond this present world to the unseen realm above, beholding God, who rules as the King upon his throne.

Psalm 123 captures the essence of this vision of faith. As the psalmist has journeyed to Jerusalem, he is peering far beyond the holy city to the sovereign Lord, who is enthroned in the heavenly city, Zion. He is gazing beyond the earthly temple in Jerusalem, as important as it is, to the eternal throne above. He has fixed the eyes of his heart on God himself. This song of ascents is the fourth in this collection of fifteen psalms (Pss. 120–134), which chronicle the journey of believers to Jerusalem to worship God. But as they come to celebrate their festivals, they look up to the Lord on high, beyond the earthly temple to the heavenly throne. This should always be the upward vision of worshippers even today as they gather together in church.

II. COMMENTARY

MAIN IDEA: *The psalmist, deeply distraught, looks to God alone for mercy.*

A The Eyes of Faith (123:1)

123:1. With the gaze of faith, the psalmist confesses, **I lift up my eyes to you.** It is to God alone that he looks, riveting the eyes of his heart upon God. Regardless of his distressing and distracting circumstances, he will look exclusively to God. Regardless of his threatening challenges and many disappointments, he will trust in God, not anything else. He will place faith in God to supply his needs, steer his life, and strengthen his soul. God is upon his **throne** in **heaven**, enthroned above, and the psalmist must bow before him as he looks to him.

B The Examples of Faith (123:2)

123:2. Two examples of looking to God in faith are given. First, faith is like **the eyes of slaves** that **look to the hand of their master.** A male servant looks to his master for food, shelter, clothing, and protection. He looks to his master for everything. Second, faith is like **the eyes of a maid** that **look to the hand of her mistress.** A lowly female servant expects her woman master to meet her needs. In the same way, **the eyes** of all believers' hearts must **look to the LORD our God,** continually relying on him with steadfastness, endurance, and perseverance until God supplies the **mercy** they need.

C The Enemies of Faith (123:3–4)

123:3. The psalmist found himself in a difficult situation, desperately needing divine **mercy. For we have endured much contempt,** he declared. He was the object of fierce hatred, fiery persecution, and foul slander.

123:4. The saints have long **endured much ridicule** in the form of verbal taunts and venomous slander **from the proud,** who do not trust God. He suffered **much contempt** as well **from the arrogant,** who look to themselves. In spite of suffering such opposition, the psalmist kept his eyes on the Lord. He chose to look away from his enemies and to focus instead on God.

III. CONCLUSION

Herein is found the encouragement every believer needs. In this psalm is the needed motivation to look beyond all one's present circumstances to the Lord himself. Every Christian needs to be peering beyond an overbearing boss, beyond a dying parent, beyond an unfaithful friend to the Lord himself. He must be looking beyond an unexpected expense, beyond a rebellious child, beyond a stagnant ministry, and beyond a passed-over promotion to the Lord himself. This is the upward vision of faith, a focusing on God for all our needs. The eyes of faith are always looking up to God for life, direction, protection, and provision. Such an upward gaze requires a lowly submission before God, a humble reliance upon him, and a ready obedience to keep his Word.

IV. TEACHING OUTLINE

A. The Eyes of Faith (123:1)
B. The Examples of Faith (123:2)
C. The Enemies of Faith (123:3–4)

Psalm 124
Divine Difference

"*E*veryone who is a man of God has omnipotence as his guardian, and God will sooner empty heaven of angels than leave a saint without defense."

Charles H. Spurgeon

Psalm 124

I. INTRODUCTION

What a difference the Lord makes in a believer's life. With the Lord on his side, victory is always sure, even in the face of mounting opposition. But without the Lord, no matter how hard one may try, all his efforts will fail. If God is for us, who can be against us? If God undertakes our cause, it matters not who is with us or who is not. One plus God always makes a majority. If all the world opposes the weakest saint but the Lord is for him, he will stand victorious. Conversely, if all the world stands with the strongest man but God is not with him, he will surely falter, fall, and fail.

This is the message of Psalm 124, a worship song that testifies to the difference it makes for the Lord to take the believer's side. This hymn is the confident testimony of David regarding this discrepancy when God undertakes one's cause. The historical background is a time when David faced a great enemy, probably the Philistines, who threatened to defeat him. The Philistines had defeated Saul and his armies, killing Saul and his son Jonathan. Now the Philistines set out to capture David. They had spread out in large numbers in the Valley of Rephaim (2 Sam. 5:17–25) to hunt David down like prey. Should they capture him, they would surely destroy him, putting David and his band in great danger. But the Lord was on their side. Thus, it mattered not how large, mighty, or numerous the Philistines were. God was infinitely greater than the Philistines. Therefore, victory belonged to David. This is the fifth song of ascents.

II. COMMENTARY

MAIN IDEA: *The psalmist testifies that God has been his helper and deliverer from all harm.*

A Life Without God (124:1–5)

124:1. The psalmist ponders a hypothetical, provocative statement: **If the LORD had not been on our side**. He considered what it would have been like if God had not been with his people. He contemplated the scenario if God had not been their defense, defender, and deliverer. What if they had been left to themselves to fight their own battles? The outcome would have been vastly different. The psalmist invited the people to join with him in declaring the difference it would have made.

124:2. He repeats verse 1 for emphasis and expands upon it. If they had faced their enemies without God, these **men** who **attacked** God's people would have most assuredly defeated them. The surrounding nations, who threatened Israel's existence, would have triumphed over them.

124:3. Describing the enflamed wrath of their foes, he states, **their anger flared against us**. When these foreign nations were waxing hot in their fuming fury, Israel would have surely been defeated and destroyed. **They would have swallowed us alive**, he declared, borrowing the image of an animal devouring its prey. If God had not intervened, God's people would have been consumed alive by their foes and swallowed whole (Jer. 51:34).

124:4–5. **The flood** of opposition **would have engulfed us**, he acknowledges. Their soul would have suffocated under this rising flood of adversaries. Their hope would have been submerged, their happiness engulfed. These **raging waters** for David were the Philistines.

B Life with God (124:6–8)

124:6. A different tone now suddenly emerges. The mood shifts, becoming upbeat, joyful, and festive. **Praise be to the LORD**, who gives the victory. David now extols God, who has renewed his trust in himself. He knows that the Lord will not **let us be torn** by the teeth of the enemy. Nor will he abandon his people to their enemies, who are like an animal grinding away on a carcass. However, this will not happen to those who trust in the Lord. God will defend and deliver them from their enemies.

124:7. **We have escaped like a bird** is a reference to the psalmist being released from the attack of his enemies who had surrounded him. A bird that has been ensnared, struggling for its life to escape, cannot cut the cords to be freed. But as the doomed bird struggles to escape, suddenly the net loosens, and the bird is free to fly away.

124:8. Loudly they confess, **Our help is in the name of the LORD.** Man is helpless in his own strength. But God is so powerful, especially for the weakest people. He helps even the frailest of believers in their most draining trials. God has intervened and rescued them. Only the Lord, **Maker of heaven and earth**, is an adequate Helper in their weakness.

III. CONCLUSION

Having God in one's life makes all the difference in every circumstance one encounters. Having the Lord on one's side is the decisive factor in one's marriage, schooling, work, and relationships. But the real question is: Are you on the Lord's side? If God be for you, who can be against you? What is necessary for you to be on God's side?

You must be personally converted to faith in Christ. This means that you must deny yourself and come to Christ through repentance and faith (Luke 9:23). To be on the Lord's side requires that you turn from your sin and commit yourself entirely to him.

You must live your life in daily consecration to the lordship of Christ. That is, you must be continually yielded to Christ, living in humble obedience to his Word, willing to go anywhere, do anything, and pay any price (Matt. 19:21).

You must be pursuing a closer personal relationship with Christ. You must have a burning passion to know him and to walk closely with him.

Are *you* truly on the Lord's side?

IV. TEACHING OUTLINE

A. Life Without God (124:1–5)
B. Life with God (124:6–8)

Psalm 125

Rock Solid

Psalm 125

I. INTRODUCTION

When even the weakest saint exercises the simplest faith in God, he becomes anchored to an immovable mountain of stability, the Lord himself. No matter what adversity assails him, his God-trusting soul becomes firmly attached to a sturdy fortress that cannot be swayed—the strong name of the Lord. All who trust the Lord become like a person standing on a firm mountain during earthshaking times. Though the whole earth shake, he will not be moved. He remains immovable as he takes his stand on God and his Word. A sure foundation is fixed beneath his feet. Though the entire earth be in upheaval about him, his soul is undergirded and grounded in God, who cannot be moved. The believer is made to be stable and sure because God is a firm and fixed anchor for his soul.

Psalm 125 declares this great message of hope. It is a song of trust in God who is fixed and firm and who provides stability of every kind for those who rest in him. The psalmist here compares believers with Mount Zion, indicating that they are secure in God, even in treacherous times. This is the sixth ascents song, written for pilgrims traveling up to Jerusalem in the Judean hills, upon which the holy city sits. As the psalmist stands upon Mount Zion in the city of God, looking upward to God, he believes that his faith makes him, spiritually speaking, as strong as the rock-solid mountain on which he has planted his feet. His faith is greatly increased as he trusts in the Lord with a renewed confidence.

II. COMMENTARY

> **MAIN IDEA:** *The psalmist has full assurance in the Lord's strength to provide stability for his life.*

A Stability in the Lord (125:1)

125:1. Those who trust in the LORD are true believers—those who fully entrust their lives to God. Trust (*batoch*, "to attach oneself to, to confide in, to feel safe in, to rely upon") is firmly committing oneself to the Lord without wavering. Those who do so will be like **Mount Zion.** Jerusalem was built on top of a mountain, making the holy city an impregnable fortress on a solid foundation. The holy city **cannot be shaken but endures forever.** Those who attach themselves to God are immovable and secure, regardless of the most earthshaking times.

B Security in the Lord (125:2–3)

125:2. God himself is compared to the **mountains** that **surround Jerusalem.** The holy city is built on one of the seven mountain peaks in the region. The other six surrounding mountains provided protection and security from invading armies, thus making Jerusalem virtually an impenetrable fortress. In the same way, God **surrounds his people** with a strong defense that cannot be moved.

125:3. When the **scepter of the wicked** rises up against God's people, it **will not remain** but will be thwarted by God. The scepter was a rod that a king held in his hand to represent the power of his throne. It was a symbol of a foreign ruler who would rise up against God's people and invade Jerusalem. The rule of wicked rulers will not prevail. The pagan kings who loomed as a serious threat to God's people dwelling in the **land allotted to the righteous,** the promised land, would be defeated.

C Sufficiency in the Lord (125:4–5b)

125:4. The psalmist intercedes for his people, pleading for God's protection to surround them. **Do good, O LORD.** Those **who are good** are those who trust the Lord (v. 1). Similarly, those who are **upright in heart** are these same believers. Their trust is real and genuine, resulting in both a good character inwardly and upright conduct outwardly.

125:5a–b. But those who turn to crooked ways are those who fail to trust God. They do not obey God but turn aside to go their own way. Thus, they walk in sin. God **will banish** them **with the evildoers.** He will withhold his blessing from them and lead them away in the direction they have chosen to go.

D Serenity in the Lord (125:5c)

125:5c. However, those who trust God know his **peace**. The ruling peace of God floods the hearts. The human soul knows true rest only when it rests in the Lord (Heb. 4:3). So the psalmist asks that God's peace be poured out on the one who is firmly attached to the Lord (v. 1). The cause and effect between the first and last lines of this psalm are now completed (vv. 1a,5c).

III. CONCLUSION

What difficulties are you facing? What disturbing circumstances are threatening your peace? For what demanding challenge, threatening problem, or imminent crisis do you need God's help? Be assured that God is infinitely greater than whatever threatens you. This is the time to anchor yourself firmly to the Lord. God is a sure foundation and solid rock for all who trust him. No matter what earthshaking experiences you may be facing, trust in the Lord will strengthen you to stand secure (Isa. 40:31). May this be a time to rest in God and to rely on his unchanging grace. Then—and *only* then— you will be a rock-solid believer.

IV. TEACHING OUTLINE

A. Stability in the Lord (125:1)
B. Security in the Lord (125:2–3)
C. Sufficiency in the Lord (125:4–5b)
D. Serenity in the Lord (125:5c)

Psalm 126

Pivotal Times

"*A* revival means days of heaven on earth."

Martyn Lloyd-Jones

I. INTRODUCTION

Martyn Lloyd-Jones, famed preacher of Westminster Chapel, London, once preached a series of sermons on the subject of revival. In those messages, Lloyd-Jones stated, "The history of religion is the history of revivals." By that he meant that redemptive history is marked by peak seasons of the Spirit's power which raises God's work among his people to a higher level. But, eventually, the Spirit withdraws his power, and the people of God descend to a lower level. Revival times are high times in God's kingdom, divinely appointed seasons when God intervenes in the affairs of history, reviving and restoring his work. It is after the darkest times in history that God has made the pure light of his truth to shine the brightest. These seasons of revival among his people, though relatively few in number and brief in duration, are, nevertheless, pivotal times of "heaven and earth" when God dramatically advances his kingdom.

Regarding those seasons of revival, Martyn Lloyd-Jones has said, "God does more in five minutes than man did in the previous ten years." In those pivotal times, God acts powerfully, and his languishing work is restored. The Reformation of the sixteenth century was such a time. After a thousand years of spiritual darkness that shrouded Europe during the Medieval Age, a time when the Scriptures became a closed book, the pure light of the gospel once again shined from pulpits. *Sola Scriptura,* Latin for "Scripture only," became the watchword of the day. Men like Martin Luther and John Calvin were preachers of light who extinguished the darkness and brought to light the gospel of God's grace. The full counsel of God was declared, and the church once again became the blazing torch of truth that she had been in the first century. In the darkest hour, the light of Scripture suddenly shined the brightest.

Psalm 126 records a similar time in the Old Testament, a dramatic day of reformation and revival among God's people. The historical background of this hymn points to the time when Israel returned from captivity, most likely the Babylonian captivity. This return occurred in three stages: the first under Zerubbabel (Ezra 1–6, 538 B.C.), the second under Ezra (Ezra 7–10, ca. 458 B.C.), and the third under Nehemiah (Neh. 1–2, ca. 445 B.C.). The occasion for the celebration of this song was either the laying of the foundation of the second temple (Ezra 3:8–10) or, more probably, the reinstating of the Feast of Tabernacles during the revival under Ezra's ministry (Neh. 8:13–14).

What is described in this psalm is one of the greatest revivals in the annals of God's kingdom—the revival at the Watergate when the people cried out to Ezra to "bring out the Book" (Neh. 8:1), referring to God's Word. Here is the seventh of the fifteen songs of ascents.

II. COMMENTARY

MAIN IDEA: *The psalmist rejoices in the Lord's restoration of his people to their land, causing even the unbelieving nations to be astonished.*

A A Release from Captivity (126:1)

SUPPORTING IDEA: *The psalmist describes the restoration of God's people like a dream, too good to be true.*

126:1a. The psalmist speaks of the time **when the LORD brought back the captives to Zion**. This represents the past hour of divine intervention, when God restored his people to their land. The nation Israel had been removed from their land in the Babylonian captivity for over 70 years. It had been seven long decades of slavery, exile, defeat, humiliation, and devastation. Then, in a moment, the hand of God **brought** them **back** to Jerusalem. The psalmist himself was probably a part of this dramatic return.

126:1b. This release from Babylonian captivity was so marvelous that it seemed like a startling dream. The wonder of their return was so amazing that the people hardly dared to believe it. Some of them could barely remember living in the promised land as a child. So dramatic was their restoration that heading back was like fantasy, a dream come true.

B A Rejoicing in Hope (126:2–3)

SUPPORTING IDEA: *The psalmist describes how the laments of the people were turned into laughter by their return.*

126:2. In their release from Babylon and return to Jerusalem, the psalmist notes, **Our mouths were filled with laughter**. No longer in exile, they were delirious with joy. Their deep sorrows were turned to **songs of joy**. This restoration was so extraordinary that even the unbelieving, pagan **nations** took notice and were forced to admit that **the LORD has done great things** for Israel. God was greatly honored before a watching world as he regathered his people to their land.

126:3. God's people said the same: **The LORD has done great things**. This was their cry as they acknowledged the hand of God upon them. The believers are now saying the same as the unbelievers. The psalmist includes himself with God's people who made this return. He asks for God's favor, blessing, and a fully restored prosperity to be upon them in the land.

C A Restoration of Fortunes (126:4)

SUPPORTING IDEA: *The psalmist asks God to restore their fortunes to the fullest.*

126:4a. The psalmist earnestly prayed, **Restore our fortunes**. This was a request that God would replenish the nation's blessings. The people, who had returned to Jerusalem, needed God's prosperity in their new home. Only God could truly replenish what had been lost in years past because of their sin.

126:4b. The psalmist compared the returning exiles to **streams in the Negev**, a reference to the arid region south of Beersheba. In the dry summer season, these riverbeds had no water. But in the springtime, the rainy season, the dry riverbanks overflowed with gushing floodwaters in the desert. Even so, the psalmist prayed that Israel's fortunes would pour into their lives, changing swiftly from adversity to prosperity.

D A Return to Blessings (126:5–6)

SUPPORTING IDEA: *The psalmist acknowledges that sorrow sown in difficulty will reap joy in prosperity when God works mightily in their midst.*

126:5. The psalmist stated, **Those who sow in tears will reap with songs of joy**. Seventy years ago, God's people had been carried to Babylon in tears. Yet their sorrow, leading to repentance, reaped tremendous rewards, bringing this new joy (Jer. 31:12–13). Possibly, this could refer to the promised land, which had been neglected during the days of their Babylonian captivity, leaving the land virtually impossible to recultivate. It had gone so long without plowing. The planting would be difficult, the sowing strenuous. But if they **sow** with **tears** of repentance, they will **reap with songs of joy.**

126:6. The returning believer, **who goes out** to work the field, replants **seed** in the promised land, **weeping** over sin. He will surely reap a great harvest. The repentant worker will be a rejoicing worker, knowing God's blessing upon his labor. By God's grace, he will be **carrying sheaves with him.**

MAIN IDEA REVIEW: *The psalmist rejoices in the Lord's restoration of his people to their land, causing even the unbelieving nations to be astonished.*

III. CONCLUSION

As this psalm reveals, a true revival ushers in dramatic days when God's people are restored to God's work. Long languished, God's kingdom work is suddenly advanced. Such times of restoration always follow long periods of spiritual drought, times in which God's work has wasted away. Revivals come when the Spirit's power has seemed to be nonexistent. The Word appears to be a closed Book. Pulpits become barren of truth. A famine in the land exists, a famine for hearing the Word of the Lord. The church becomes captive to worldliness. But then the wind of the Spirit blows. Suddenly, hearts are revived. God's truth is restored. God's work is renewed. And God's church is returned to her former power and glory. This is the work of a heaven-sent revival in divinely appointed days.

IV. LIFE APPLICATION

How can we see a mighty revival in our day? We must understand that any awakening is a sovereign movement of God's Spirit, who cannot be manipulated or controlled. A revival will come only when, where, with whom, and how it pleases God. Nevertheless, there are certain forerunners of revival that have always preceded the dramatic days when God's people are restored to their former power. The Spirit visits a people marked by three primary qualifications:

Prayer. Revival always starts with believers on their knees. Prayer is the primary forerunner of any season of revival. It is in humble intercession that the church acknowledges it is totally dependent upon the grace of God. This may involve an extraordinary season of intercessory prayer. Or it may involve a group of people asking for God to invade their lives, ministries, and church. But prayer is the forerunner of all revival.

Preaching. Any movement of God's Spirit in history has been ushered in by a time of renewed emphasis on the preaching and teaching of God's Word. There has never been a Word-less revival. Any awakening has always been accompanied by a return to strong, biblical preaching that exalts Christ and exposes sin. When a fire is built in the pulpit, it will soon spread to the pews.

Purity. Revival always requires a time of sin-confessing, sin-rejecting repentance. The Holy Spirit will never work through unholy people. It can be argued that a concentrated time of repentance is produced by the revival itself. Or it may be that the repentance precedes the revival. Either way, repentance is an indispensable part of any awakening. A season of self-humiliation on the part of God's people must come. Only in lowering themselves before God can there be an exaltation of the saints by God.

V. PRAYER

God, how we need a mighty restoration of your work in these days. Release us from the entangled captivity of our sins. Cause our hearts to rejoice in hope again. Return the full blessing of your hand upon us. Bring the harvest. Replenish the celebration of our souls in the glory of your name. Work as you have in days of old. In Jesus' name. Amen.

VI. DEEPER DISCOVERIES

Restore (85:4)

The word *restore* (*shub*) means to return, to turn around, to come back, to be brought back. *Shub* is the twelfth most used verb in the Old Testament, appearing 1,060 times, and is used 71 times in the Psalms. *Shub* is best understood to mean repentance, a turning away from evil to God. According to the context the meaning of *shub* may be properly delineated, for it is used in both the figurative and physical senses. Here it refers to a spiritual restoration.

VII. TEACHING OUTLINE

A. A Release from Captivity (126:1)
B. A Rejoicing in Hope (126:2–3)
C. A Restoration of Fortunes (126:4)
D. A Return to Blessings (126:5–6)

Psalm 127

A Faith-Forged Family

"*W*here we have a tent, God must have an altar."

Matthew Henry

Psalm 127

I. INTRODUCTION

A team of New York state sociologists once attempted to calculate the lasting influence of a father's life upon his children and those who followed in subsequent generations. In this study, two men were researched who lived at the same time in the eighteenth century. The lasting legacies that each man left upon his descendants stand as different as night and day.

The first man was Max Jukes, an unbeliever, a man of no principles. His wife also lived and died in unbelief. What kind of lasting influence did he leave his family? Among the 1,200 known descendants of Max Jukes were: 440 lives of outright debauchery, 310 paupers and vagrants, 190 public prostitutes, 130 convicted criminals, 100 alcoholics, 60 habitual thieves, 55 victims of impurity, and 7 murderers. Not exactly a distinguished legacy.

The other man studied was Jonathan Edwards, the noted Colonial pastor and astute theologian, arguably the greatest preacher and intellect America has ever produced. This renowned scholar was the primary instrument that God used to bring about the Great Awakening in colonial America. Jonathan Edwards came from a godly heritage and married Sarah Pierrepont, a woman of great faith. Together, they sought to leave an entirely different kind of legacy. Among his male descendants were: 300 clergymen, missionaries, or theological professors, 120 college professors, 110 lawyers, over 60 physicians, over 60 authors of good books, 30 judges, 14 presidents of universities, numerous giants in American industry, 3 United States congressmen, and 1 vice-president of the United States. There is scarcely any great American industry that has not had one of Jonathan Edwards's descendants among its chief promoters. This was a legacy that lasts, one that honors and glorifies God.

Psalm 127 brings a strong message on the house that God builds. It is a wisdom psalm about the priorities and practices of the family that is forged by faith. Instruction is given on how to establish a godly family with children who are used by God to further his kingdom. As the eighth song of ascents (Pss. 120–134), this hymn reminded pilgrims in the temple in Jerusalem that all life's blessings, especially in the home, are gifts from God. Normally, families would travel together in caravans when they made their pilgrimages to the holy city. It was a family time as they came to worship. Here we find needed instruction that dependence upon the Lord is absolutely necessary if a person is to have a God-blessed home. This is one of only two psalms attributed to Solomon, Psalm 72 being the other.

II. COMMENTARY

> **MAIN IDEA:** *Solomon teaches that a godly home and successful work cannot occur apart from the Lord's blessing.*

A The Builder of the Home (127:1a)

> **SUPPORTING IDEA:** *Solomon instructs that God must build and bless the house and city.*

127:1a. Any activity attempted without the Lord is launched **in vain**. This is especially true in raising a family. Vain ("empty, useless, meaningless, or futile") is all home-building and family-raising without God. The words "in vain" appear first in each Hebrew clause, the emphatic position, doubly emphasizing the sheer folly and failure of building a home without God. Raising a family is futile **unless the LORD builds the house**. The idea is not that the Lord literally uses a hammer and nails, but metaphorically. God must be the architect, builder, and foundation of every successful home.

B The Protector of the Home (127:1b)

> **SUPPORTING IDEA:** *Solomon declares that God is the true protector of the home.*

127:1b. Unless the LORD watches over the city, it, too, is built **in vain**. Builders put up houses, but **watchmen** guard them. A city is made up of many homes, living in close proximity to one another. Thus, God himself must also be the protector of our families. Again, the idea is not that the Lord takes up a literal sword and shield to defend the houses. Rather, his invisible hand guards the very homes that he builds from the evil influences that would harm those who live within.

The Provider of the Home (127:2)

SUPPORTING IDEA: *Solomon counsels that one's time and energy must be kept in proper balance.*

127:2a–b. All who live in houses with families must labor hard to provide for their families. Again, it is **vain** to **rise early and stay up late**, striving hard, without God in the center of one's life. This does not de-emphasize hard work, a virtue valued throughout Scripture (Prov. 6:6–11; 10:26; 13:4; 15:19; 19:24; 22:13; 24:30; 26:13–16). Rather, he warns against being a person who burns the candle at both ends, neglecting one's family, and failing to trust God. **Toiling** speaks of feverish activity, rising before sunrise to begin working, coming home late, long after the sun has gone down, working long hours to put bread on the table. Without time for God, their **food** only maintains people in their miserable existence.

127:2c. God **grants sleep to those he loves**, symbolizing the rest and peace one receives when he commits himself to the Lord. The person who trusts God, while working hard yet within certain boundaries, lies down at night and sleeps well, believing God will give the increase. God gives inner tranquility and contentment to the person who works in humble obedience to him.

 The Rewarder of the Home (127:3–5)

SUPPORTING IDEA: *Solomon affirms that children are God's gifts and a sign of his blessing.*

127:3. **Sons are a heritage from the LORD**, gifts graciously bestowed by God on parents. Fathers and mothers must acknowledge that each child is a divine gift. Further, their sons and daughters are a **reward**, an expression of divine favor. Children are a highly valued prize, not a burden. They are the expression of God's goodness upon one's life, bringing great pleasure to a home, a demonstration of his love and mercy.

127:4. Moreover, children are **like arrows in the hands of a warrior**. A father is pictured like a warrior in battle, and their children are like arrows. Arrows are indispensable for a warrior to succeed in defeating the enemy. So are children invaluable to parents in warring against the enemy of God's kingdom, Satan. Children are invincible weapons to be shot into the world for the kingdom of God.

127:5. **Blessed** (*asher,* "happy, favored") **is the man whose quiver is full of them.** Fathers with many sons and daughters **will not be put to shame** when they come under the attack of evil men, who oppose the cause of righteousness. Such a godly father shall not be slandered without the defense of his sons. His sons, now spiritual stalwarts, will rise up publicly to join their father's cause, defend his integrity, and undergird his work. His children will do so **in the gate**, the public entrance into the city, where community business was transacted.

> **MAIN IDEA REVIEW:** *Solomon teaches that a godly home and successful work cannot occur apart from the Lord's blessing.*

III. CONCLUSION

As long as one's sons and daughters are living under one's roof, parents must shape and direct their children with a godly influence. Tragically, many fathers and mothers wait until it is too late. Or, worse, some choose to be absent throughout the process, burning the candle at both ends. Other parents pass their God-assigned responsibility to others. But childrearing is every parent's duty before God. This God-given ministry cannot be assigned to a school, a teacher, or a minister. Such a stewardship is granted to every parent by God. And it is to God to whom they will one day give an account.

When Woodrow Wilson was president of Princeton University, he spoke these words to a parents' group: "I get many letters from parents about your children. You want to know why we people up here in Princeton cannot make more of them and do more for them. Let me tell you the reason we cannot. It may shock you just a little, but I am not trying to be rude. The reason is that they are your sons, reared in your home, blood of your blood, bone of your bone. They have absorbed the ideals of your homes. You have formed and fashioned them. They are your sons. In these malleable, moldable years of their lives, you have forever left your imprint upon them."

IV. LIFE APPLICATION

As sons and daughters are like arrows, the following truths must be implemented early in Christian childrearing:

Arrows must be shaped. No arrow begins straight, ready for battle. The soldier who would shoot a straight arrow must spend time whittling and shaping the branch into a well-fashioned arrow. So it is in raising children. Sons and daughters must be trained at an early age to pursue righteousness. Solomon wrote, "Train a child in the way he should go, and when he is old he will not turn from it" (Prov. 22:6). This involves biblical instruction, moral correction, firm discipline, and loving affirmation.

Arrows must be directed. A well-shaped arrow must also be carefully aimed at the target. An old adage says, "Aim at nothing and you will hit it every time." This is most true in childrearing. One's sons and daughters must be directed at the right target while they are in the parents' hands. They must be directly pointed at God's enemies, armed with the gospel of Christ, if they are to score a direct hit. This involves teaching and instructing them with God's Word, as well as modeling it before them.

Arrows must be released. The time eventually comes for the warrior in the day of battle to release his arrows. Only then will they be successful and victorious. They cannot defeat the enemy as long as they are in the warrior's hands. Arrows must be shot from the bow. Even so, parents must release their grown children at the appointed time. Every parent must send his or her children into the world with a sense of eternal mission, not merely to make a living but to make a difference for the kingdom of God. This, in the end, requires much prayer, daily modeling, and ongoing encouragement.

V. PRAYER

God, we look to you and you only to build our homes. In this world of evil influences and seductive temptations, we ask that you guard and preserve the purity of our families. Protect us from becoming a part of the world system and losing our sense of mission with our children. While they are in our hands, grant us grace to shape them into godliness and direct them for your glory. In Jesus' name. Amen.

VI. DEEPER DISCOVERIES

Vain (127:1–2)

The Hebrew word (*rig*) translated "vain" means "emptiness, senseless, or futility." In this case, it refers to the utterly foolish plan of man to attempt to do something outside of God's sovereignty. Such anarchy against God is utterly insane and foolish.

VII. TEACHING OUTLINE

A. The Builder of the Home (127:1a)
B. The Protector of the Home (127:1b)
C. The Provider of the Home (127:2)
D. The Rewarder of the Home (127:3–5)

Psalm 128
Successful Living

"*I*f I had to die like a dog, and there were no hereafter, I would still choose to be a Christian, for of all lives that can be lived, there is none that can compare with this."

Charles H. Spurgeon

Psalm 128

I. INTRODUCTION

A basic desire of all people everywhere, whether they be saved or lost, is to be happy. No one wants to be miserable. Everyone wants to be content and satisfied. The Christian is no different. The believer talks about his primary drive to pursue holiness and heaven. But in so doing, he may give the impression that his desire for happiness is an illegitimate desire. It is not. The first recorded sermon that Jesus preached, the Sermon on the Mount (Matt. 5–7), begins by promising happiness and fulfillment to all who would follow him (Matt. 5:3–12).

The first psalm begins the same way—with God promising joy and peace to those who meditate on his Word (Ps. 1:1–3). So it is not wrong to desire to be happy. The only question is: How will one find happiness? The world promises happiness in many things such as possessions, popularity, position, prestige, and promotions. But true contentment will be found in enjoying God himself. In Philippians 4:4, Paul declared, "Rejoice in the Lord." God wants us to rejoice, and it is found in the passionate pursuit of loving him.

Psalm 128 is written that believers may know the soul-elevating joy that only God can give. Happiness is not determined by one's physical or financial condition but by one's spiritual condition—not by where one works but by where and how one worships. Not by external circumstances but by internal contentment. Not by finances or fame, but by faith in God. Christ is the source of eternal joy and everlasting happiness.

II. COMMENTARY

MAIN IDEA: *The psalmist declares God's blessedness to the person who reverences and obeys the Lord.*

A The Requirement for God's Blessing (128:1)

128:1. This psalm states the indispensable requirements of a truly fulfilled life. To be **blessed** with divine favor, it can be argued, is the primary message of the entire Psalter (Pss. 1:1; 94:12; 112:1; 119:1–2; 128:1), certainly the central theme of this psalm. God's blessing belongs, first, to the person who will **fear the LORD** (Job 28:28; Ps. 111:10; Prov. 1:7; 9:10; Eccl. 12:13). This person takes God seriously, reverences him deeply, and honors him greatly. Second, one must **walk in his ways**, which is to live in daily obedience to the Word and will of God. No one will be truly happy while living in disobedience to God. Only in walking in God's ways will he be truly satisfied and content.

B The Realms of God's Blessing (128:2–4)

128:2. This God-blessed man will **eat the fruit** of his **labor**, referring to the divine blessing upon all he does (Ps. 58:11). Heaven's favor will be upon his work, his labor graced by God. If one fears and obeys God, his endeavors will be fruitful and rewarded, but only to the extent that God chooses to bless, which will be either in this life or in the world to come.

128:3. Further, God's blessing will also abide upon one's home life. **Your wife will be like a fruitful vine.** The God-fearing man will have a childbearing wife, a clear indication of God's favor (Ps. 127:3). He will also have **sons . . . like olive shoots** (Ps. 128:3). Olive trees, common in the Middle East, take time to mature and become profitable. When patiently cultivated, they produce crops for many years. When one's children are rightly nurtured over time, they will become productive and prolific for God. They also will know God's blessing, a grace that will further come back to bless their father.

128:4. The psalmist summarizes, **Thus is the man blessed who fears the LORD.** The person who reverences God, repeated here for emphasis, is divinely favored. He knows grace upon grace, the goodness of God upon his life in double measure.

C The Request for God's Blessing (128:5–6)

128:5. The psalmist petitions, **The LORD bless you from Zion,** whether this be from God's heavenly throne room in glory or his earthly temple at

Jerusalem. Heavenly Zion is the place where the divine glory most resides, the center from which all our blessings flow (Ps. 20:2). Earthly Zion was a local extension of Zion above. The blessings already described include seeing **Jerusalem** prosper, spiritually so as well as militarily, economically, and culturally. May this **prosperity** be a lasting blessing, the psalmist prays, one that will endure **all the days of your life**.

128:6. He concludes, **May you live to see your children's children**, a request for a long, blessed life. It is a request for physical health in the face of sickness, a petition for military victory in the face of Israel's enemies, and an asking for abundant crops in the face of famines. It is a request for all that will keep them alive and prosperous into the future. **Peace** (*shalom*, "prosperity") **be upon Israel** was his closing petition.

III. CONCLUSION

Wherever people live, they are seeking to experience the inner happiness that this psalm offers. There is a universal cry from every human heart, longing to be fulfilled, satisfied, and content. But the people of the world never find this happiness. Such bliss evades all unbelievers. They look for it in all the wrong places. True happiness is found not in things but in God. Genuine satisfaction is found in knowing God. Deep-seated contentment is discovered only in fearing and obeying God. The key to a fulfilled life is having a right relationship with the Lord, trusting and walking with him. Only in fearing and following God does a person experience successful living.

IV. TEACHING OUTLINE

A. The Requirement for God's Blessing (128:1)
B. The Realms of God's Blessing (128:2–4)
C. The Request for God's Blessing (128:5–6)

Psalm 129
Irrepressible Resilience

Psalm 129

I. INTRODUCTION

Resilience marks the determined drive of God's people to be faithful to God's calling. An overcoming perseverance causes them to bounce back from defeat. The person who trusts God may be knocked down but never knocked out. "We are hard pressed on every side, but not crushed; perplexed, but not in despair; persecuted, but not abandoned; struck down, but not destroyed" (2 Cor. 4:8–9). God never promised that the Christian journey would be easy. In fact, becoming a believer brings new challenges. Serving God will never lead to a trouble-free life. But God has promised that he will see his saints through their problems victoriously. Christianity is not the subtraction of all problems but the addition of God's grace to overcome those problems. God promises to give us the victory, no matter what we face, even in the face of many difficulties. The battle belongs to the Lord.

This is the soul-strengthening message of Psalm 129. In this prayer, the psalmist encourages Israel to say that the Lord delivered her from the attacks of the wicked. Time and time again, God's people were opposed and oppressed. And repeatedly God intervened and fought for them. In the face of defeat, God gave them the victory. In fact, such God-given victory marked the entire history of his people, Israel. God's people sinned, and God saved them; Israel disobeyed, and God delivered them; Israel rebelled, and God rescued them. This is the undeserved grace of God poured out upon his people. Failure is never final as long as there is the grace of God. The divine rescue celebrated here is probably from Babylonian captivity (v. 4). This is the tenth of the ascent songs (Pss. 120–134) sung during their annual pilgrimages to Jerusalem.

II. COMMENTARY

MAIN IDEA: *The psalmist reminds God's people how God has delivered them in the past to give them hope for the future.*

A The Persecution of God's People (129:1–3)

129:1. Speaking on behalf of the nation, the psalmist invites **Israel** to say, **They have greatly oppressed me from my youth.** From the time God's chosen people were first enslaved in Egypt, they have suffered much from godless nations. They have been **greatly oppressed** (Exod. 1:12–13) from their nation's **youth.** Adversity and hostility is all Israel has known since its conception as a people. **From my youth** indicates that this persecution began in the early days of the nation and has continued until the time this psalm was written.

129:2. The psalmist repeats verse 1 for dramatic effect. This is surely all that Israel has known, an unbroken history of persecution. But these hostile nations **have not gained the victory.** They have not eliminated Israel as a people. Rather, Israel has withstood the relentless onslaught of foreign oppressors and has endured as a people.

129:3. Israel here is pictured as a scourged man with deep welts on his **back** from many inflicted lashes, like **furrows** in a **plowed** field. Over the years, Israel's enemies have plowed long rows down her back in deep persecution.

B The Preserver of God's People (129:4)

129:4. Israel has survived only because the LORD **is righteous.** He is faithful to execute all the promises he has made, specifically those promises to preserve Israel as a nation forever (Gen. 12:1–3; 15:4–5; 22:17–18). God has **cut me free from the cords of the wicked,** the psalmist declared, setting Israel free from the harness of foreign nations.

C The Petition of God's People (129:5–8)

129:5. The psalmist offers an imprecatory prayer, calling for the destruction of God's enemies. He pleads that they be **turned back in shame.** He requests that these oppressive foreign powers be repelled through an ignominious defeat at their hands. May their armies be routed and sent back to their homeland. This is not just a desire for embarrassment but for their complete devastation and utter humiliation.

129:6–7. Further, he asks that God's enemies be like **grass on the roof,** which **withers**. Their wicked enemies may initially sprout like grass, but only with shallow roots. Soon they will wither and die. The writer prays that they wither to the point that the **reaper cannot fill his hands**. May they be short-lived so they can no longer harm God's people.

129:8. In greeting a person, it was normal to wish God's blessing on him (cp. Ruth 2:4). But the psalmist asked that God's people not do this toward the wicked. **May those who pass by** (i.e., God's people like harvesters in a field) **not say, "The blessing of the LORD be upon you."** He asks that the hands of their oppressors be empty. May Zion's enemies not hear the customary greetings of friends.

III. CONCLUSION

How do God-fearing believers survive the many persecutions they face in a Christ-rejecting world? The God who stood with his people, Israel, through many wars and conflicts, is the same God who will stand today beside his saints through the spiritual opposition they face. In the face of such turbulence, Christ has promised that he will never fail us or forsake us. In such trials, the Lord grants grace to his people, enabling them to persevere, even in the face of defeat. "But thanks be to God, who always leads us in triumphal procession in Christ" (2 Cor. 2:14). No matter how fierce spiritual warfare is, Christians are always led victoriously by God.

IV. TEACHING OUTLINE

A. The Persecution of God's People (129:1–3)
B. The Preserver of God's People (129:4)
C. The Petition of God's People (129:5–8)

Psalm 130

Full Forgiveness

"*T*he way to cover our sin is

to uncover it by confession."

R i c h a r d   S i b b e s

I. INTRODUCTION

John Wesley, eighteenth-century Methodist evangelist, was ordained into the ministry in 1728. But by his own admission, he was not personally converted to Christ until ten years later in 1738. For a full decade, Wesley labored as an evangelist and missionary, preaching on both sides of the Atlantic while lost. Yet, throughout this time, this famed preacher was not a true believer in Christ. However, on May 24, 1738, Wesley attended St. Paul's Cathedral in London and heard Psalm 130 sung as an anthem. "If you, O LORD, kept a record of sins, O Lord, who could stand?" (v. 3). Deep conviction came over his heart. How could he find acceptance with God, who kept perfect records of his many sins? Later that night, Wesley visited a small group of believers where he heard read the introduction to Martin Luther's commentary on Romans. His regenerated soul was "strangely warmed," and John Wesley was converted to Christ.

Psalm 130 is a hymn which records the psalmist's confession of sin and the forgiveness he found in God's pardoning grace. This penitential psalm is primarily directed to worshippers who are already justified by faith and have received the cancellation of the penalty of their sins. As they come to worship God, they have unconfessed sin that must be acknowledged to God if they are to find pardon from God. In this psalm, God also calls unbelievers to seek his grace, a forgiveness that John Wesley found and is offered today. This is the eleventh song of ascents. The author is unknown.

II. COMMENTARY

MAIN IDEA: *The psalmist confesses his sins, seeking forgiveness from God, and he encourages others to do the same.*

A A Cry of Repentance (130:1–2)

130:1. **Out of the depths** of severe distress, the psalmist cried to God. Figuratively, he was drowning in the deep waters of despair, overwhelmed by the rising waves of anguish. This despondency was coming not from his many foes around him but from within himself. His greatest enemy was within—his own sin. The sharp awareness of his own personal sin was overwhelming him. In the very depths of his soul, he was submerged in an ocean of guilt.

130:2. He pleads with God, **Hear my voice**. Desperation fills his heart, causing him to cry out with urgency. When confession of sin and repentance are real, they will not be mumbled in a casual, halfhearted manner. True repentance always has an element of brokenness, a feeling of guilt that must be cleansed. His **cry for mercy** is a confession of sin, seeking forgiveness from God.

B A Cry of Forgiveness (130:3–4)

130:3. If God **kept a record of sins**, never to forgive them, no one could **stand** with acceptance before him. Even the best of men, apart from divine pardon, could not access God. All have sinned (Rom. 3:23), and the wages of sin is death (Rom. 6:23).

130:4. But with God there is **forgiveness**, a full, free cancellation of one's sin debt. God is the only one who can forgive our sin. The good news of grace is that he is willing to do so. It is his very nature to forgive man of all his sin. The result of true forgiveness is never a lackadaisical attitude but holy fear toward God. Divine pardon, rightly understood and humbly received, will always lead to deep reverence for God.

C A Cry of Patience (130:5–6)

130:5. The psalmist says, **I wait for the LORD**. For what specifically was he waiting? Forgiveness had already been granted and received (v. 4). He was waiting for a full restoration by God of his divine power and peace. As he waits, he trusts **in his word**. This refers to God's Word, which promises the full blessing of the Lord.

130:6. The writer pledges, **My soul waits for the Lord** to restore him to the fullness of his blessing. He waits as the **watchmen** on the wall, guarding the city, waiting for the morning. This metaphor refers to those who have the night watch, which ends with the sun's rising early in the **morning**. The psalmist waits for God's grace as eagerly as the watchmen look intently for the dawn, when other guards would relieve them.

D A Cry of Confidence (130:7–8)

130:7. The psalmist now speaks to all others, encouraging them to do the same. **Put your hope in the LORD** is a call to have a strong confidence in God to forgive sin and restore hope. **For with the LORD is unfailing love.** God's people should rest in his **love** (*hesed,* "unconditional, permanent loyalty"), which is God's unbreakable covenant love for his own. Israel should have hope based upon the eternal, immutable electing love of God. Moreover, there is abundant, plentiful **redemption** with God from their many sins.

130:8. The psalmist ends on a high note. He declares that God **himself will redeem Israel**. This is a word of absolute certainty! God will save his people from all the effects of **all their sins**. Glory to his name!

III. CONCLUSION

This psalm asks a penetrating question, one that every person must ask God. The question is: "If You, O LORD, kept a record of sins, O Lord, who could stand?" (v. 3). If God should uncover and calculate our sins, who could escape his judgment? If God should charge them to our account and hold them against us, who among us could stand before God? The answer is: No one could stand before God in their sin and find his acceptance. Not a single person could gain approval with a holy God if his sins were marked and held against him. Every sin is, ultimately, against God, who is holy and just. Even when one person sins against another individual, that sin is, eventually, against God.

In light of this verdict, every person desperately needs forgiveness from the Lord. Divine pardon has been secured through his Son, the Lord Jesus Christ, and is offered freely to all who will confess their sin, repent, and believe upon Christ. Call upon the name of the Lord for forgiveness. Acknowledge your sin. Turn from your wicked ways. Do so today and you will receive his pardon.

IV. TEACHING OUTLINE

A. A Cry of Repentance (130:1–2)
B. A Cry of Forgiveness (130:3–4)
C. A Cry of Patience (130:5–6)
D. A Cry of Confidence (130:7–8)

Psalm 131
Simple Trust

"*H*ope is never ill when faith is well."

John Bunyan

Psalm 131

I. INTRODUCTION

The more a believer matures spiritually, the more childlike his faith will become. Growing to trust God involves assuming many of the qualities of a young child who looks to his parents with an unquestioning acceptance and unwavering reliance. This is not to say that believers should be childish, which is immaturity. Instability, selfishness, and complaining are undesired marks of carnality, not maturity. Rather, the Scripture calls us to be childlike in our faith (Matt. 18:3), a much desired virtue characterized by a simple, unquestioning, accepting dependence on God. As a child looks to his father to provide for his needs, so the child of God should look to his heavenly Father. Those believers who rely upon God like trusting children are those who exemplify that faith for which this psalm calls.

Psalm 131 is another song of ascents (Pss. 120–134), the twelfth in this series. It is a hymn in which the psalmist confesses a simple trust in God. David is the author, but the specific circumstances are not apparent. He expresses his trusting faith in the Lord, strategically placed after Psalm 130. The person who knows the forgiveness for which the previous psalm calls is one who exercises childlike faith, as this psalm encourages. Here is a psalm of humble trust that invites everyone to do the same.

II. COMMENTARY

MAIN IDEA: *David confesses his childlike trust in the Lord, urging others to do the same.*

A Humility Before God (131:1)

131:1. David begins by making three great denials. He is **not proud . . . not haughty** and does **not concern** himself **with great matters**. These three denials suggest that this has not always been the case. Pride, haughtiness, and selfish ambition have previously shaped his life. **Things too wonderful for me** refer to heroic exploits and personal achievements in competition with God's works. But now he chooses a new path of self-humiliation. He desires no longer to be self-elevated, self-exalting, and self-centered. No longer will he pursue things **for me** but for God.

B A Hush Before God (131:2)

131:2. David purposes to be **stilled** and **quieted** before God. He is not giving God the solution to his problems but is waiting for him to speak. David describes what this humble faith within him looks like. It is like a **weaned child**, possibly about four or five years old, who walks beside his mother, old enough to be weaned off his mother's breast but not yet old enough to care for himself, trusting his parent for everything. This is to be the position of the believer, quietly submissive and trusting in God.

C A Hope in God (131:3)

131:3. Childlike trust always has an element of **hope**. As a person trusts God, a positive confidence in God regarding the future floods his soul. Hope believes that God is always working toward a positive outcome. God who causes all things to work together for the believer's good is the basis of this assurance for the future. This assurance is his from this time forth. Regardless of one's circumstances, or the personal storm that has blown in, he should have a firm hope in God.

III. CONCLUSION

This psalm should be the confession of all believers. Every saint should have a childlike faith in God. But such a trust is never automatic. If it were easy, there would be no need for the instruction of this psalm. Childlike trust must be nurtured. Although it sounds paradoxical, the more one matures in the Lord, the more childlike his faith in the Lord becomes. We never outgrow a childlike trust in God, one that is unpretentious and unassuming.

J. Oswald Sanders said, "There is no conceivable situation in which it is not safe to trust God." God is always worthy of our full trust. Corrie ten Boom said, "Never be afraid to trust an unknown future to a known God." It is always right to trust God. How do you need to develop childlike faith?

IV. TEACHING OUTLINE

A. A Humility Before God (131:1)
B. A Hush Before God (131:2)
C. A Hope in God (131:3)

Psalm 132

A Place of Grace

"*W*herever we see the Word of God purely preached

and heard, there a church of God exists,

even if it swarms with many faults."

John Calvin

Psalm 132

I. INTRODUCTION

Throughout the centuries, God's house has always been a special gathering place for believers. For Old Testament saints, the tabernacle and temple were the places where God's glory was put on display. It was there that God's Word to his people was kept in the ark of the covenant. For New Testament believers, wherever God's people meet to hear God's Word and to worship God's greatness, whether it be an ornate cathedral or a dusty warehouse, that place becomes a sanctuary of God in which his transcendent truth is housed.

What makes God's house so special is not the building or the architectural style or the materials. What truly counts is the spiritual reality of what happens inside that place—the purity of the pulpit, the fidelity of the ministries, and the sincerity of the hearts. This is what makes God's house a true place of worship. Better to be in a crude, little facility where the Word of God is elevated and the glory of God is exalted than to be in an extravagant, large edifice where the Scripture is minimized and the glory of God is trivialized. God's house should be that place wherever his truth is openly declared, his glory is clearly revealed, and his Son is publically magnified.

This is the focus of Psalm 132, a royal psalm that describes the special blessing that accompanied God's house, presumably when the ark of the covenant was brought there by David. This psalm was written to describe the momentous occasion when the ark was brought to Jerusalem and placed into the tabernacle. As long as it was located there, Israel prospered and knew God's success. This psalm is a prayer of the congregation, requesting that the Lord remember David's vow concerning the dwelling place for the ark. This is the thirteenth song of ascents, placed here in this cluster of psalms (Pss. 120–134) to encourage worshippers who had traveled to worship in the rebuilt temple—God's new house.

II. COMMENTARY

> **MAIN IDEA:** *The psalmist prays for God's blessing to rest upon his people in fulfillment of his promises to David.*

A A Passion for God's Glory (132:1–5)

132:1. This song begins with the appeal, **O LORD, remember David**. It is a prayer that God would remember the promises he had made earlier to David regarding the establishment of his house and throne (2 Sam. 7:10–14,16; Pss. 89; 132:10–11). The psalmist petitions God to remember **the hardships** they have suffered in relationship to these promises made to David. In considering God's faithfulness to David, the psalmist sought to draw strength in the face of his many **hardships**.

132:2–5. David **swore an oath to the LORD** not to rest until he found **a place for the LORD**. David vows he will **not enter** his house to **sleep** until he secures a dwelling place on earth for God. This refers to David's consuming passion to build the temple, a request denied by God. David, instead, provided the materials for God's house of worship built by his son Solomon (1 Kgs. 6). The psalm calls upon God to keep his promises to David at a time when they seemed forgotten.

B A Pursuit of God's Glory (132:6–9)

132:6. The people recalled how David's passion for God's glory propelled him into action. He and his men **heard** of the whereabouts of the ark of the covenant **in Ephrathah** and soon found it. It had been **in the fields of Jaar**, a reference to Kiriath Jearim (1 Sam. 7:1–2), for twenty years until David moved it to Zion (2 Sam. 6).

132:7–8. The congregation purposed to **worship** where David had earlier rallied the people in bringing the ark to Jerusalem, **his dwelling place**. In actuality, it was God's dwelling place in that it was his earthly throne. Here is the prayer of the people that God would visit them again: **Arise, O LORD, and come to your resting place**. It was called the **ark of your might** because it symbolized God's power to deliver them from their enemies.

132:9. The people's prayer requested that the **priests** would **be clothed with righteousness**, or personal holiness. These spiritual leaders must be right with God if this work was to know God's support and to succeed.

C A Petition for God's Glory (132:10–12)

132:10. A prayer is offered on behalf of each successive Davidic king **for the sake of David**, or on the basis of God's covenant with him. The people requested that the Lord **not reject** his promises to their **anointed** kings. Ultimately, this prayer looked beyond David to a greater King who would come—Jesus Christ (Isa. 61:1; Luke 4:18–19).

132:11–12. God's promise to David is condensed and reiterated (2 Sam. 7:11–16; 1 Kgs. 9:1–9). God **swore an oath to David**, promising that David's future **descendants** would sit upon his throne and rule successfully. But there was a conditional aspect to the **covenant**, requiring that they keep **the statutes** of God's Word. Obedience would usher in God's blessing.

D A Prophecy of God's Glory (132:13–18)

132:13–14. This final stanza looks ahead prophetically to the coming, future day when Jesus Christ, the greater Son of David, will be divinely installed on the throne of David in Jerusalem to rule the earth (Pss. 2; 89; 110). Earthly **Zion** will be God's **resting place for ever and ever**, a reign that will never end in the ages to come, even in the new Jerusalem.

132:15–16. In this future day, the Lord promises to **bless** his people with **abundant provisions**. God will **clothe** their spiritual leaders with the eternal blessings of **salvation**. Further, all the **saints** will forever know great joy.

132:17–18. Still looking ahead prophetically to the coming of the Messiah, God promises to **make a horn**, a symbol of strength, **grow for David**. This is a reference to Jesus Christ, the true **anointed one**, who will come in power to rule forever. In that day, Messiah's **enemies** will be utterly shamed in defeat. Christ's **crown** will be **resplendent**, shining in preeminence and power.

III. CONCLUSION

God's house is to be a place where Christ is magnified. If God's Word is expounded there, the glory of God fills that house of worship. If God's Son is magnified there, the grace of God is manifested in that place. No matter how stunning or simple God's house is, if the Word of God and the Son of God are honored, that place becomes a glorious house of praise. What ultimately makes any church a special place is not its architecture but its adoration; not its size but its substance; not its entertainment of man but its exaltation of God. May every believer find and support that church where the truth of the

Word of God is proclaimed and the glory of God is guarded. Such is a place for grace.

IV. TEACHING OUTLINE

A. A Passion for God's Glory (132:1–5)
B. A Pursuit of God's Glory (132:6–9)
C. A Petition for God's Glory (132:10–12)
D. A Prophecy of God's Glory (132:13–18)

Psalm 133

Indissolvably One

"*U*nity must be ordered according to God's holy

Word, or else it were better war than peace."

Hugh Latimer

Psalm 133

I. INTRODUCTION

In his book *The Pursuit of God*, A. W. Tozer gave the following illustration: Suppose you were to have one hundred concert pianos, all needing to be in tune with one another. If you tune the second piano to the first, and the third piano to the second, and the fourth piano to the third, and so on, until you have tuned all one hundred pianos accordingly, you will still have discord and disharmony. But if you tuned each piano to the same tuning fork, there would be a different result. Then you would have perfect unity and harmony among all the pianos. So it is in the body of Christ, Tozer argues. When believers try to tune themselves to one another, it results in disharmony. But when each saint brings himself into one accord with Jesus Christ, glorious unity results in the body of Christ.

Psalm 133 is a song about unity among God's people, who are in tune with the holiness and supremacy of God. Nowhere is the true unity that binds believers together more vividly described or beautifully illustrated than in this short psalm. Genuine harmony is a precious thing, like sacred oil flowing down the head and beard of the priest, emitting a sweet aroma. It is like the sweet morning dew, which comes down from the mountains to cool and satisfy the dry arid places. David is identified as the author, but the exact background is not known. It may refer to David's coronation at Hebron or the precious sight of the multitudes, who came from all parts of Palestine to be present in Jerusalem for one of the great national feasts.

Many commentators believe this psalm refers to the time of the return of Israel from Babylonian captivity, a time when there was no longer any division within the kingdom. The jealousy of the tribes had ceased, and all who returned were incorporated into one united nation. If so, then this song was dedicated to the past leadership of David. Regardless of its historical background, it is this vision of unity and the divine blessings that attend it that prompted the psalm to be written. As such, it is the fourteenth song of ascents (Pss. 120–134), written to encourage unity among God's people as they journeyed to Jerusalem to celebrate together.

II. COMMENTARY

MAIN IDEA: *The psalmist extols the blessings of unity among God's people.*

A The Praise of Unity (133:1)

SUPPORTING IDEA: *The psalmist declares how good and pleasant unity is.*

133:1. The psalmist begins with a burst of excitement, **How good and pleasant it is when brothers live together in unity.** "Good" (*towb*) means "excellent, choice, agreeable to the senses." Further, it is "pleasant" (*naiym*), meaning that which is "sweet." To **live together** is to function in close and intimate association with others. They were to so live **in unity.** This does not mean uniformity, where they are all alike, but harmony in the midst of their differences. They are to live together with oneness of mutual support, fellowship, direction, and affection.

B The Pictures of Unity (133:2–3a)

SUPPORTING IDEA: *The psalmist pictures unity among God's people as anointing oil and falling dew.*

133:2. The psalmist shows what unity looks like, beginning with Aaron, who was a high priest. He could not minister until he was anointed with **oil.** Thus, the oil was **poured on the head**, in a sacred anointing (Exod. 29:7; 30:30), picturing a rich spiritual blessing. But the anointing oil did not remain confined to the top of Aaron's head where it was applied. It was soon **running down on** Aaron's **beard** and then **down upon the collar of his robes.** In the same way, Christian love and harmony spreads blessing to the entire body.

133:3a. Unity is like **the dew of Hermon** coming down from the mountains of **Zion.** God creates the cool, refreshing dew that revitalizes everything. So God creates true unity and the blessings that come from it. Unity comes down from above, just like the water vapor comes down to form the dew. Mount Hermon is the tallest mountain peak in the Middle East. At 9,232 feet tall, it is a source of perpetual freshness and coolness. In times of dryness, it gives nourishment. So does unity among God's people.

🄲 The Power of Unity (133:3b)

SUPPORTING IDEA: *The psalmist testifies that God commands his blessing where he finds unity.*

133:3b. The psalmist maintains that **there**, where brethren dwell in close unity, **the LORD bestows his blessing**. By sovereign decree, God orders his grace to be bestowed where his people live together in harmony. It is where true unity is found that God sends the fullness of the Holy Spirit. This **blessing** is the eternal favor that God pours out upon his people. Further, this is also where God commands **life forevermore**, which is fullness of life, or abundant life (John 10:10). Among united brethren is where God issues the full experience of his grace.

MAIN IDEA REVIEW: *The psalmist extols the blessings of unity among God's people.*

III. CONCLUSION

A father once had a family of quarrelsome sons who had trouble getting along with one another. So he called them together and handed a stick to the strongest of his sons. "Snap it," he said. The son did so with a gesture of contempt. The father then handed him two sticks. "Snap them," he said again. The son did so. The old man handed him increasing numbers of sticks—four, five, six sticks. "Snap them," he said each time. Soon the son was having to strain to snap the sticks, until finally he had to admit defeat. The old man then gave his sons a valuable life lesson. "Unity is strength," he reasoned. "A house divided cannot stand. Be assured, anyone can overthrow you one by one. But stand together in unity, and your combined strength will give your enemies second thoughts."

What is true in one's physical family at home is true in the family of God. There is great strength in our unity. Together, as we stand as one, we have a combined strength, able to resist and overcome our greatest enemy, Satan. Unity is what God desires for his people to promote. Unity is what Satan dreads and works to undo. Unity is what Jesus prayed for and what the Holy Spirit came to achieve. Unity is what will convince the world of the gospel. Unity is a precious commodity for which we must all strive.

IV. LIFE APPLICATION

In the Book of Acts, we read of the extraordinary unity of the first church in Jerusalem. The marks of their unity must be recovered today. Is it any wonder that they were so Spirit empowered? God's power is poured out upon brothers and sisters who meet together in unity. This unity includes the following:

One central purpose. The early church in Jerusalem was united in one common mission—reaching the world for Christ. They never lost sight of their singular purpose. As a result, they were all pulling together in the same direction—the fulfillment of the Great Commission (Acts 1:8). God supernaturally empowers a people who are mutually committed to serve as witnesses for Christ in all the world. Do you share this one purpose with your Christian brothers and sisters?

One common place. The first congregation birthed on the day of Pentecost came together regularly in one and the same place. Originally, that was the upper room in Jerusalem (Acts 1:13); then "they were all together in one place" (2:1); then they were together "in the temple courts" (2:46) and "in their homes" (2:46). The point is, they were not isolated from one another. They met regularly together in one place. Do you regularly meet together with the church?

One corporate prayer. When these first disciples came together, they prayed together. What is more, they prayed together for the same things. Scripture records, "They all joined together constantly in prayer" (Acts 1:14). They met together for appointed prayer times (Acts 3:1). Do you gather together when your church prays?

One chief pursuit. These early believers all pursued together the same spiritual disciplines—the apostles' teaching, fellowship, the breaking of bread, and prayer (Acts 2:42). They studied God's truth together, held God's Son together, worshipped God's glory together, and prayed for God's grace together. They were joined together—one mind, heart, and soul. Are you involved in one chief pursuit like this with your church?

V. PRAYER

God, we desire to maintain Christianity with our brothers and sisters in Christ. We ask that you enable us, by your Spirit, to be patient and longsuffering with them as we fellowship with them. May we forgive others as you have forgiven us. May the world know we are Christians by our love. In Jesus' name. Amen.

VI. DEEPER DISCOVERIES

Unity (133:1)

The Hebrew word translated "unity" (*yahad*) refers to a unit of people who are together. It and its derivatives are found numerous times throughout the Psalms (Pss. 2:2; 4:8; 14:3; 19:9; 31:13,15; 35:4,26; 37:38; 40:14; 41:7; 48:4; 49:2,10; 53:3; 55:14; 62:9; 71:10; 74:6,8; 83:5; 88:17; 98:8; 102:22; 122:3; 141:10).

VII. TEACHING OUTLINE

A. The Praise of Unity (133:1)
B. The Pictures of Unity (133:2–3a)
C. The Power of Unity (133:3b)

Psalm 134

Transcendent Worship

"Man's chief work is the praise of God."

Augustine

Psalm 134

I. INTRODUCTION

John MacArthur, noted author and pastor of Grace Community Church in Los Angeles, California, has remarked, "I can tell the depth of any church spiritually after being in their worship service for only five minutes." When asked to explain, he replied, "If the words of the music are unusually experience-oriented, man-centered, me-focused, and so fast-paced that the service more resembles a pep rally than a worship service, that church is, more than likely, shallow and superficial." Then MacArthur expounded, "You must first take a church down deep in the Word if you would lead them up high in worship. The depth determines the height. The depth in the Word determines the height in worship. Shallowness in the Word leads to shallowness in worship. Too many churches try to fake it simply by turning up the volume."

This is a correct analysis, an accurate diagnosis that the contemporary church needs to hear and heed today. Worship is not to be a performance before men but a proclamation to God. It is not the entertainment of men but the exaltation of God. All this is built upon the deep exposition of the Word.

This is why Psalm 134 is such a needed message today. What is immediately striking about this psalm is its simplicity. One certainly cannot conclude from these few verses that worship is a show. Rather, we learn that it is a song of praise to God. This psalm is the fifteenth and final song of the songs of ascents (Pss. 120–134). It focuses upon God's house and those who serve in it. Addressing the priests and Levites who serve in the temple, the hymn of praise encourages worship leaders to remain faithful in their ministry duties.

It pictures spiritual leaders in the temple as encouraging the people to continue in their faithfulness to God.

II. COMMENTARY

> **MAIN IDEA:** *The psalmist summons worshippers to praise the Lord and receive God's blessing.*

A The Call to Worship (134:1–2)

134:1a. All God's **servants** are summoned: **Praise the LORD**. This call to worship is to be singularly Godward in its focus, not man centered. Believers should boast in the Lord for who he is and what he has done. They should give glory to God as their first call of duty. These servants are those who served daily in the temple, a reference to the priests and Levites who lived and ministered in the temple.

1134:1b. These worship leaders are exhorted to worship God also **by night**. Worship should be a lifestyle—morning, noon, and night. They should worship God not only publicly during the corporate gatherings but also privately at night, after the people have left and the **house of the LORD** is empty. They were to worship God all day and all night, even where they lived.

134:2. In the Old Testament, it was a common practice for worshippers to **lift up** their **hands** to God in worship. This act signified a looking to God, a reaching up to the Lord for help. It represented the upward focus of their praise and prayer, a symbolic gesture of a teachable spirit and submissive will.

B The Consequences of Worship (134:3)

134:3. This is a benediction offered by the priests and Levites upon the people as they prepared to leave God's house in Jerusalem and return to their homes throughout the region. **May the LORD, the Maker of heaven and earth, bless you from Zion**. Here is a request that the Lord favor and benefit them. The worship leaders ask the Lord to lift up the hearts of the people, renew their faith, and ignite their passion for God.

III. CONCLUSION

The church today is in dire need of a new reformation, one that will restore its purity in worship. On Sunday mornings, performances are crowding out praise, entertainment is replacing exposition, and drama is supplanting doxology. Worship is, as A. W. Tozer wrote years ago, "the missing crown of the evangelical church."

Kent Hughes, pastor of College Church, Wheaton, speaks an insightful word for us as he addresses the need of the hour:

The unspoken but increasingly common assumption of today's Christendom is that worship is primarily for us—to meet our needs. Such worship services are entertainment focused, and the worshippers are uncommitted spectators who are silently grading the performance. From this perspective, preaching becomes a homiletics of consensus—preaching to felt needs—man's conscious agenda instead of God's. Such preaching is always topical and never textual. Biblical information is minimized, and the sermons are short and full of stories. Anything and everything that is suspected of making the marginal attender uncomfortable is removed from the service. . . . Taken to the nth degree, this philosophy instills a tragic self-centeredness. That is, everything is judged by how it affects man. This terribly corrupts one's theology.

IV. TEACHING OUTLINE

A. The Call to Worship (134:1–2)
B. The Consequences of Worship (134:3)

Psalm 135
Bold Praise for a Big God

"*I* feel like that good old saint, who said if she got to

heaven, Jesus Christ should never hear the last of it."

Charles H. Spurgeon

I. INTRODUCTION

Burning within the heart of David Livingstone was the passion to reach people around the world for Christ. Having received a medical degree from the University of Glasgow, Livingstone soon joined the London Missionary Society and went to southern Africa, where he labored to open up Africa for the gospel of Jesus Christ. One of the key passages of Scripture that reverberated in his soul was Psalm 135. It was with this psalm that David Livingstone bade farewell to his family and home at Blantyre, Scotland, to go to Africa.

Of his dramatic departure, Livingstone's sister wrote:

> I remember my father and him talking over the prospects of Christian missions. They agreed that the time would come when rich men and great men would think it an honor to support entire stations of missionaries instead of spending their money on hounds and horses. On the morning of the seventeenth of November 1841, we got up at five o'clock. My mother made coffee. David read Psalm 121 and Psalm 135 and prayed. My father and he walked to Glasgow to catch the Liverpool steamer [for Africa]. David never saw his father again.

With Psalm 135 ringing in his ears, David Livingstone headed to Africa to spend over three decades serving Christ under the most adverse conditions. What was it about this psalm that so captivated the heart of this pioneer missionary? Why did he read this psalm as he left home for Africa? What made this sacred hymn so special to him? What about it inspired him to go to Africa for thirty-two years and serve until he died? The answers to these questions lie in the fact that this is a "big God" psalm. It is a psalm that lifts high the name of our great God and calls for towering praise to be given to him.

Psalm 135 is a call to praise the Lord, the one true God over all the earth. Here is a passionate plea to come and worship God, who is Lord over all creation and over all nations. The author and occasion of this psalm are unknown, the background most likely postexilic. But the message is abundantly clear: Praise God, who is Lord over creation, the nations, and redemption. The psalm begins and concludes with the same powerful line: Praise the Lord! Further, its opening and closing stanzas are also calls to praise God.

II. COMMENTARY

MAIN IDEA: *The psalmist invites God's people to praise the Lord, who is mighty over all creation and history.*

A The Call to Praise (135:1–2)

SUPPORTING IDEA: *The psalmist invites everyone to praise the Lord, especially those who are worship leaders.*

135:1. Three times in the opening verse believers are called upon to **praise the LORD**. Repeating something three times raises what is said to the superlative degree. Thus, praising God is to be one's highest goal, greatest passion, and noblest activity. The word translated "praise" (*hallel*) is the intensive form of the Hebrew *halal,* which means "to boast." Praising God means boasting in the Lord or bragging upon him.

135:2. Especially is this praise to come from **you who minister in the house** and **courts of the house of our God**. These are the ones who serve God in the temple complex area (cp. 134:1–2). The primary expression of this praise is in the public gathering of God's people, who come together in the **house of the LORD**.

B The Causes for Praise (135:3–18)

SUPPORTING IDEA: *The psalmist encourages praise because of who God is and what he does.*

135:3. What follows are several reasons for God's people to **praise the LORD**. The first reason is because **the LORD is good** (*tob,* meaning "beneficial, positive, giving what is needed, dealing bountifully with"). God's beneficial acts toward his people call for praise. God's **name** represents his holy attributes and perfect character. They should **sing praise to his name** because God is **pleasant**. Both the act and object of worship are lovely.

135:4. Second, God should be praised because he **has chosen Jacob** for himself. Here is the pride-crushing truth of God's sovereign grace and electing love, which is sweet and satisfying to the spiritual man. For reasons known only to himself, God chose his own people for himself unto eternal life. From the depths of such soul-lowering humility arises the height of God-honoring praise to God.

135:5–7. Third, praise belongs to God because he **is great** in his authority to rule and reign over all. God alone is **greater than all gods**. This is demonstrated by the fact that he **does whatever pleases him**, a clear declaration of his sovereign authority and power. One example of God's absolute sovereignty is his control over the weather. He **makes clouds rise**, **sends lightning**, and **brings out the wind**.

135:8–12. Fourth, praise should be rendered to God who **struck down the firstborn of Egypt** in the days of the exodus. This is a reference to the ten plagues with which God struck the Egyptians when Pharaoh refused to let God's people go. **Signs** are clear evidences of God's character. **Wonders** leave a sense of awe and terror in their hearts. In the display of his wrath, God **struck down many nations**, not just Egypt. He **killed mighty kings** in addition to Pharaoh. Many peoples felt the fury of God and were sent staggering to the grave, all because they turned away from the true God to serve false gods. Under this divine anger, Moses and Israel defeated **Sihon king of the Amorites** (Num. 21:21,32) and **Og king of Bashan** (Num. 21:33–35). Further, **all the kings of Canaan** were devastated during Joshua's conquests of the land (Josh. 6–12). God took the land from the Canaanites and gave it to **his people Israel**, as he had promised Abraham (Gen. 15:18–21).

135:13–14. Fifth, God should be praised because his **name**, his character, **endures forever**. He is forever the same, never diminishing, never changing. His divine person is renowned **through all generations**, immutable and fixed. Even when God's people are faithless, needing to be disciplined, he remains unchanging in his **compassion**. Even so, God is unchanging in his relationship with his people.

135:15–18. Sixth, God is to be adored because he is the living Lord. How infinitely superior God is when compared to the dumb **idols** of the pagan nations. They are **silver and gold**, and tarnished, corrupted, and needing polish. These false gods **cannot** hear. They are lifeless, and **those who make them will be like them**, that is, dead.

C The Crescendo of Praise (135:19–21)

> **SUPPORTING IDEA:** *The psalmist consummates his call to worship with a final crescendo of praise.*

135:19–21. This psalm concludes by calling all believers to **praise the** LORD. Addressed to all who are assembled at the temple, this call to worship is extended to all who **fear** God, or to all who know him.

> **MAIN IDEA REVIEW:** *The psalmist invites God's people to praise the Lord, who is mighty over all creation and history.*

III. CONCLUSION

Anthony Collins, a famous agnostic of years past, wrote a book titled *Discourse on Freethinking.* Filled with humanistic philosophy and disseminating high thoughts of man and notoriously low thoughts of God, Collins's treatise greatly impacted his day. One Sunday, Collins encountered a poor English laborer who was walking to church. Collins thought he would belittle him, so he asked, "Where are you going?" "To church, sir," answered the common laborer. "I am going to worship God." Attempting to confuse the simple fellow, Collins asked him sarcastically, "Is your God a *great* God, or a *little* God?"

The humble churchgoer never missed a beat. He immediately replied with an answer far more profound than what the philosopher was prepared to hear. "My God is so great, sir," the man said, "that the heaven of heavens cannot contain Him, and so little that He can dwell within my lowly heart." Collins was disarmed at such a grand thought and had no rebuttal for this reply. Years later the lettered philosopher admitted that this uneducated man had had a far more powerful effect on his sophisticated mind than all the volumes he had read that argued in favor of Christianity.

IV. LIFE APPLICATION

All believers should be filled with praise for God at all times. God never changes. Neither should the worship of believers change. God is always worthy of our praise. Let us praise him in this fashion:

Praise God fervently. We should be wholehearted in our worship of God. Lukewarmness is a tragic sin. Our praise should be intense and passionate. We should always be fired up for God in our worship of him.

Praise God continually. There is never a time not to praise God. Whether we are in good times or bad times, on the mountaintop or in the valley, we should always praise him. He never changes. Neither should our praise.

Praise God publicly. We should always be gathering together with other believers in public places of worship in order to praise him. In the midst of the congregation, we should observe his greatness. Others should be able to hear our praise and be encouraged to join with us. Let us go to God's house and worship the Lord with God's people.

Praise God privately. We should have regular times in our personal schedule when we are alone with God. It is in these quiet moments, secluded and isolated, cloistered with God, that we should also praise him.

Praise God intelligently. All worship is a response to who God is and what he has done. The more truth we learn, the more we should worship God. Jesus said, "His worshipers must worship in spirit and in truth" (John 4:24).

V. PRAYER

God, we delight to worship you. We know that our hearts were made for you and they find their greatest joy when focused on you. Increase our passion for you. Ignite our souls for you. Fan the flame of our hearts for you. Make our greatest pleasures to be found in you. We do praise your glorious name. In Jesus' name. Amen.

VI. DEEPER DISCOVERIES

Name (135:1)

This word translates the Hebrew *shem*, which means "to mark" as in designating a person or place. In biblical history, a person's name often described personal characteristics such as one's destiny or position. The various names of God reveal important aspects of his nature (i.e., God Most High, Almighty God, I AM). "The name of the LORD" encompasses the whole of who God is, incorporating all the divine names into one. The name of the Lord should be praised and used with honor and respect (Exod. 20:7).

VII. TEACHING OUTLINE

A. The Call to Praise (135:1–2)
B. The Causes for Praise (135:3–18)
C. The Crescendo of Praise (135:19–21)

Psalm 136

Everlasting Love

"*G*od never repents of His electing love."

Thomas Watson

Psalm 136

I. INTRODUCTION

The love of God toward his saints is higher, deeper, wider, and longer than anyone can comprehend. Throughout all the ages to come, God's covenant love for his people, like a mighty river, will be flowing as strong in eternity future as when it first began in eternity past. This is the awe-inspiring wonder of being the special object of his everlasting love. God's love endures forever. But this is not true toward unbelievers. When they die lost, God's common grace and gospel invitation will no longer be extended to them. In hell, there will be no eternal love demonstrated as God's mercy is absent and only his wrath is present. But for believers, his divine love will endure forever. What a cause for praise this is for God's people. His love endures forever.

This is the comforting message of Psalm 136. This reoccurring refrain—"His love endures forever"—is the repeated chorus of this psalm, one that echoes at the end of each of the twenty-six verses in this song. Twenty-six times the psalmist declares this truth, "His love endures forever." There is no other psalm like this in the entire Psalter. Most likely this psalm was originally sung in the tabernacle or temple. The Levitical song leader sang or spoke the first line of each verse, and in response the Levitical choir, or perhaps the entire congregation, or even both, responded with this refrain: "His love endures forever." With dramatic epiphanal effect, this psalm was sung with a volley of praise, from worship leader, to choir and people, and back. May it ring in our hearts today.

II. COMMENTARY

> **MAIN IDEA:** *The psalmist elicits praise for God for his mighty power and endless love.*

A Thanks for God's Creation (136:1–9)

136:1. **Give thanks to the LORD** is a call to express gratitude to God publicly. The reason is clear: **for he is good** (Ps. 135:3), the source of all blessings for his people. The often-repeated refrain, **His love endures forever**, is spoken. This is the first of twenty-six times this chorus will be sung in this psalm, a declaration and celebration that God's loyal love will never fail or falter toward his people.

136:2–3. **Thanks** should be offered to the Lord who is **God of gods**. This is a Hebrew superlative meaning he is the supreme deity, the sovereign ruler over all. Further, **thanks** should be given to him who is **the LORD of lords**, that is, the Ruler of rulers. God is to be praised who uses his supreme authority for our good. He is a loving Sovereign to be adored forever.

136:4–6. God has especially displayed his generous rule in his works of creation. He **alone does great wonders**, having performed awe-inspiring feats that produce "wonders" in the hearts of his people. He created **the heavens** above **by his understanding**, divine genius, stunning wisdom, and perfect insight. The planets and starry hosts decorate the sky above, manifesting God's love. Further, God **spread out the earth upon the waters**, referring to the skillful way God made this planet. God did all this as an expression of his loving-kindness toward his own people.

136:7–9. Praise should also be given to God because he **made the great lights**, which are the celestial bodies overhead. He made **the sun to govern the day**, and **the moon and stars** to rule **the night**. Again, all this is according to God's loving-kindness revealed in his creation. Let them respond, **His love endures forever.**

B Thanks for God's Conquests (136:10–22)

136:10–12. God is to be praised for his many great acts of deliverance, first, in bringing his people out of Egypt in the exodus (Exod. 12). In a series of ten devastating judgments (Exod. 7–12), God, climactically, **struck down the firstborn of Egypt.** This final destruction was an act of love toward God's people. In so doing, God **brought Israel out from among** the Egyptians **with a mighty hand** of salvation and **outstretched arm** of triumph over his enemies.

136:13–15. Further, God's conquests continued at the Red Sea. There the Lord **divided the Red Sea asunder**, bringing **Israel through the midst of it** and drowning **Pharaoh and his army** in its waters. This violent act was, in reality, an evidence of God's everlasting love for his own people.

136:16–20. Moreover, God's victories were demonstrated in the wilderness. He **led his people through the desert**, never abandoning them but faithfully going before them as he **struck down great kings**. God soundly defeated **Sihon king of Amorites** and **Og king of Bashan**, slaying them (Num. 21). It was God's special, electing love for his people that moved him to devastate these pagan kings. Let all God's people declare, **His love endures forever**.

136:21–22. Finally, God is to be praised for the victories he granted his people as they entered the promised land. The Lord **gave** them **their land as an inheritance**. He took the land, previously belonging to the Amorites, and transferred it to become the possession of **his servant Israel**. Why would God do this? He did so because of the greatness of his love for his chosen ones.

C Thanks for God's Care (136:23–26)

136:23. Having sovereignly given his people these mighty victories, God tenderly cared for them in the land. God **remembered** them in their **low estate**. He could never forget those upon whom he had set his eternal love. No matter how little regarded they were by this wicked world, they were highly esteemed by God (cp. Deut. 7:7–10).

136:24–25. All whom God remembers, he rescues. God **freed** them from all their **enemies** because his eternal love was so strong toward them. He **gives food to every creature** among his people. Those for whom he fights, he feeds. This is God's love in action.

136:26. In conclusion, the psalmist invites everyone to sing, **Give thanks to the God of heaven**. This last verse echoes the opening line of this psalm. Here is one final call to worship God, whose **love endures forever**. His unconditional, loyal love is everlasting, never to be extinguished, ever to be expanding.

III. CONCLUSION

Commenting on the subject of God's perfect love, Charles Haddon Spurgeon wrote these words: "God is good beyond all others; indeed, He alone is good in the highest sense; He is the source of good, the good of all good, the sustainer of good, the perfecter of good, the rewarder of good. For this, He deserves the constant gratitude of His people. It is this divine goodness that has been showered upon us."

Spurgeon is right. God is good. His love never ceases or diminishes toward his beloved. As a result, so must our praise toward God be without end. May we forever give him praise as his love is forever toward us. Let us give thanks to this God publicly and passionately, acknowledging his supremacy over all things. May we always express our gratitude, knowing he uses his sovereignty for his glory and our good.

IV. TEACHING OUTLINE

A. Thanks for God's Creation (136:1–9)
B. Thanks for God's Conquests (136:10–22)
C. Thanks for God's Care (136:23–26)

Psalm 137

Evasive Praise

"You that are called born of God, and Christians,

if you be not criers, there is no spiritual life in you."

John Bunyan

Psalm 137

I. INTRODUCTION

There can be times in the life of the believer when he feels so overcome with grief that he is too sad to sing praises to God. Granted, the saints should always praise the Lord. But the sober reality is, there are seasons of life that are marked by great disappointments and defeat. When praise evades God's child in such low valleys, his heart may become so filled with despair that it becomes virtually impossible to lift his voice upward to God. Sometimes it is because God's kingdom has suffered a devastating loss. A visible Christian leader has fallen into sin. A denomination chooses to stray further away from God's Word. A church loses its zeal and closes its doors. A false religion or cult makes considerable inroads in a region, overshadowing the Christian witness in that place. The result of all these losses is a deep sense of sadness that sweeps over the soul of a follower of Christ. His heart can become too sad to sing.

This is precisely the kind of trauma the psalmist felt when he wrote Psalm 137. God's people had been taken captive by the Babylonians, their beloved temple was destroyed, and they found themselves exiles in a foreign land. They were suffering under God's disciplining hand, and the pain they felt cut deep into their souls. In pagan Babylon, they heard the stinging taunts of their captors, mocking their God, chiding them to sing their songs of Zion. No doubt, their heads hung low, their shoulders sagged, and tears streamed down their cheeks. They were too full of despair to lift up their voices to God.

They had suffered an ignominious defeat and were aware they were reaping the bitter harvest from seeds of disobedience they had sown for many years.

Written in pathetic, plaintive, sorrowful language, this psalm mourns the sad plight of God's people when they wept in a foreign land and could not sing their songs of Zion. Possibly, this psalm was written toward the end of the Babylonian captivity, reflecting back on that troubling time. More probably, it was written upon their returning from Babylon to the promised land. In either case, the author's reflections upon the exile brought bitter memories. Nevertheless, his love for Zion remained strong, a devotion that would be rekindled in the land and in a rebuilt temple.

II. COMMENTARY

> **MAIN IDEA:** *The psalmist remembers the sad days of Babylonian exile, praying that God will judge their captors.*

A The Psalmist's Lament (137:1–4)

> **SUPPORTING IDEA:** *The psalmist laments those past days when God's people wept beside the rivers of Babylon, too sad to sing.*

137:1. This psalm begins in a different land. Babylon was one of the great empires in the ancient world, occupying the large land mass of modern-day Iraq. It was there that God's people had been taken into exile and captivity. The **rivers of Babylon** refer to the Tigris and Euphrates rivers and the many canals associated with them that helped make Babylon a great kingdom. There in captivity, they **remembered Zion**, Jerusalem, the place where the temple was destroyed by the Babylonians. They bitterly **wept**, mourning the loss of the city of God.

137:2. In deep despair, they **hung** their **harps** on the trees beside the rivers, having no use for these instruments of joy. There could be no joyful singing in Babylon, not in this depressed state of ignominious defeat. In this low condition, they refused to make any joyful music.

137:3. Their **captors**, the Babylonians, tormented and taunted them, demanding that they entertain them with **songs of joy**. This mocked God's people as if to say, "Sing us the worship songs of your once beautiful but now destroyed Zion."

137:4. God's people could not **sing** any of **the songs of the LORD while in a foreign land**, not on unclean soil. Hopelessness filled their hearts. They could not sing, not while Zion lay in ruins and they were in foreign captivity.

B The Psalmist's Loyalty (137:5–6)

SUPPORTING IDEA: *The psalmist declares the exiles will never forget the glories of Jerusalem.*

137:5. The psalmist talks directly to **Jerusalem**. His body is in Babylon, but his heart is in Jerusalem. This shows the deep love he has for Jerusalem. His love for God and for God's holy city cannot be separated. **May my right hand forget its skill.** For a right-handed person, this expression refers to his greatest ability and strength, most probably the hand used to play the harp (v. 2). If he should **forget** Jerusalem, then he has no real reason to play his harp. He must play for the glory of God or not play at all.

137:6. The psalmist refuses to betray his loyalty to God and to the holy city, Jerusalem. He vows not to sing while Jerusalem lies in ruins. He pledges not to sing and entertain these God taunters, not while being made sport of by Jerusalem's enemies. Jerusalem is his **highest joy** in all that it represents to God's kingdom. Jerusalem was where the temple once stood, where the glory of God had dwelt, where the Word had been preached, where the songs of Zion had been sung, where God's name had been magnified. Exalting Jerusalem was exalting all these things.

C The Psalmist's Longing (137:7–9)

SUPPORTING IDEA: *The psalmist prays that God will punish the Edomites and Babylonians.*

137:7. The psalmist called for God to **remember** their oppressors to judge them. **The Edomites** were hoping for the destruction of Jerusalem's **foundations.** The word *foundations* implies not only the actual base of the buildings of Jerusalem but also the God-established order of the city (Ps. 11:3) and the rule of Yahweh upon the earth. The details of Edom's horrific crimes against God's people are found in Obadiah 11–14.

137:8. The psalmist turns to Babylon and speaks directly to their captors. Babylon is personified as the **Daughter of Babylon**, meaning the people and all that she represents. The pagan empire is **doomed to destruction**, an acknowledgment that Babylon would be devastated (Isa. 13; 21; 47; Jer. 50–51; Hab. 2). **Happy** is the one who **repays you** the destruction you have brought upon us.

137:9. This psalm comes to a shocking end. Happy will be the one who **seizes your infants** for destruction and **dashes them against the rocks.** This is precisely what the Babylonians themselves had done to their Hebrew babies when they entered the land, invaded Zion, and defeated God's people. They had killed their babies. He prays the cruelty of war will come back to them in a stroke of divine justice.

MAIN IDEA REVIEW: *The psalmist remembers the sad days of Babylonian exile, praying that God will judge their captors.*

III. CONCLUSION

It is easy to relate to the psalmist's lamentation here. The joy of God's people is inseparably bound to the state of God's work. When churches are strong, believers' hearts soar to great heights. But when the glory of God and the name of Christ are defamed in the church, it is cause for deep sadness among all followers of Christ. It is heart-wrenching to consider the low state of spirituality in so many congregations today.

When one considers that 85 percent of all churches in America today are either plateaued or declining in membership, it is cause for weeping. When we consider what nonsense comes out of many pulpits, a complete lack of "Thus says the Lord," it is cause for weeping. When we see the man-centered entertainment that passes as worship in so many churches today, it is a cause for weeping. In these days of spiritual decline, may we pray that God will once again restore his work through the years. And may God bring the church back to her glory days seen in the Reformation.

IV. LIFE APPLICATION

As we consider some of the imprecations expressed by the psalmist, admittedly shocking, let us hear the words of Charles H. Spurgeon, the great Baptist pastor of London, before we try to soften these curses. Spurgeon wrote:

> Let those find fault with these curses, that were not causeless, who have never seen their temple burned, their city ruined, their wives ravished, and their children slain; they might not, perhaps, be quite so velvet-mouthed if they had suffered after this fashion. It is one thing to talk of the bitter feeling which moved captive Israelites in Babylon, and quite another thing to be captives ourselves under a savage and remorseless power, which knew not how to show mercy, but delighted in barbarities to the defenseless. The song is such as might fitly be sung in the Jews' wailing place. It is a fruit of the captivity in Babylon, and often has it furnished expression for sorrows which else had been unutterable. It is a gemlike Psalm within whose mild radiance there glows a fire which strikes the beholder with wonder.

V. PRAYER

God, we can relate to the lament of the psalmist. We, too, are grieved and saddened by the low state of your work in these days. We find it difficult sometimes to laugh and be giddy when your church is so weak and worldly. Our hearts break with the heart of the psalmist. But more than that, we know that your heart breaks over the low state of the church. Encourage us, Father, by allowing us to see in these days a revival among your people. Show yourself to be God over all. Revive your church. In Jesus' name. Amen.

VI. DEEPER DISCOVERIES

Destruction (137:8)

The word *destruction* (*shadad*) means "to ruin, to wreak havoc, to spoil." In its verb form, as it is found here, it is used to speak of the destructive nation of Babylon. This destructive nation destroyed Jerusalem (Jer. 6:26; 12:12) and would, thus, incur God's destruction (Jer. 51:48,53,55–56).

VII. TEACHING OUTLINE

A. The Psalmist's Lament (137:1–4)
B. The Psalmist's Loyalty (137:5–6)
C. The Psalmist's Longing (137:7–9)

Psalm 138

Audacious Faith

Psalm 138

I. INTRODUCTION

Every believer should live with a bold confidence in the sovereignty of God over his life. While he remains responsible for all his choices and must take reasonable steps to protect and extend his life, his times, nevertheless, are in God's hands. God has appointed the number of days he has to live upon the earth. Further, the Lord has preordained good works that he is to perform. Every follower of Christ follows a divinely written script that God purposes to accomplish through his life. Therefore, as the Christian faces daily challenges, many of which are momentous, he should move forward with an unwavering, audacious faith that God's eternal purposes will be brought to pass. Even in the midst of mounting trials, he should trust God to fulfill his plan for his life.

This is the focus of Psalm 138, a psalm of praise for God, who has exalted himself above all. The Lord has delivered David from threatening foes, sustaining his life. Therefore, David magnifies God for this dramatic rescue. With mounting confidence, he is certain that God will fulfill his purposes for his life. He expresses absolute trust in the overruling will of God for him. No wonder David pledges such praise to God who answered his prayers and saved him out of his dangers. Although the specific occasion of the psalm is unknown, it represents a lifetime of trust that the psalmist had in God.

II. COMMENTARY

MAIN IDEA: *David expresses praise to God for the certainty of divine promises made to him in the Davidic Covenant.*

A The Expression of Praise (138:1–3)

138:1. In spite of the difficult circumstances of his life, David states, **I will praise you**. This adoration is a volitional choice of his will. His volatile emotions may not feel like it, but he purposes to do so regardless. He will worship God **with all my heart**, not halfheartedly but from the depth of his soul. **I will sing your praise**, not mumbled but upbeat, triumphant, and overflowing. Other **gods** indicates that other deities were recognized in David's time. Canaanite gods were everywhere, but David gave thanks to the one true, living God.

138:2. I will bow down toward your holy temple, offered humbly in a posture of lowly humility. God has **exalted** his name **above all things**. The divine **name** refers to the essence of his holy character and sovereignty. He is without rival. Further, his **word** is "above all things." All that he commands will come to pass, especially his promises. God's word here refers to the written revelation of holy Scripture, which reveals God's loving-kindness and faithfulness to believers, two attributes associated with his divine promises (Pss. 108:4; 115:1).

138:3. When David **called** to the Lord, God answered. The fact that God heard and heeded his prayers caused David's soul to be **bold and stouthearted**. He has confidence to move forward.

B The Extension of Praise (138:4–5)

138:4. Other pagan **kings** were not giving praise to the Lord. David was probably the only monarch on the earth doing so. He prayed that all **the kings of the earth** will render praise to God. They must hear the **words of your mouth** (i.e., God's saving truth); and when they respond in faith, they will praise God.

138:5. David prayed that all the kings, yet to be converted, will **sing of the ways of the LORD**. They will see clearly that their earthly glory is nothing. God's eternal **glory** is everything.

C The Explanation for Praise (138:6–8)

138:6. God is **on high** and lifted up in heaven. Yet at the same time, he **looks upon the lowly** to lift up and honor those who bow before him. **But the proud he knows from afar**. A great chasm separates holy God from the haughty proud.

138:7. This was not an easy time for David, who walked **in the midst of trouble**. Yet he knew God would **preserve** his **life**. God would **stretch out** his **hand against** his **foes**. David felt invincible within God's will.

138:8. With extraordinary confidence in God, David declared, **the LORD will fulfill his purpose for me**. Here is unwavering faith in the overriding, overruling sovereignty of God. No matter what others may do to David, God's eternal purposes will be carried out in his life. God's **love** toward him **endures forever**. God's eternal purposes for him are unchanging, even in the face of threatening foes.

III. CONCLUSION

No matter what circumstances a believer faces, he always has good reason to praise God. He must realize that God's sovereign will for his life will be executed, regardless of whatever circumstances threaten him. No matter what trials a believer faces, he must hold fast to the confidence that God will over-rule all until his divinely appointed purposes are completed. He should see his life as resting in God's hands, not his enemies' clutches. As a result, all followers of Christ are able to move forward confidently and serve God triumphantly. This audacious faith should be found in all who have committed their lives to him. May we live with a bold confidence in our sovereign God, who presides over all.

IV. TEACHING OUTLINE

A. The Expression of Praise (138:1–3)
B. The Extension of Praise (138:4–5)
C. The Explanation for Praise (138:6–8)

Psalm 139
Infinite, Yet Intimate

"How shall finite comprehend infinite? We shall apprehend Him, but not comprehend Him."

R i c h a r d   S i b b e s

Psalm 139

I. INTRODUCTION

The greatness of God is infinitely vast. His majesty far exceeds man's ability to comprehend him. Consider, for example, the size of the universe he has created, the sheer dimensions of which are staggering. Scientists tell us it would take 500 billion years to journey around its perimeter, traveling at the speed of light—186,000 miles per second. The sun has a diameter of 864,000 miles and can hold over one million planets the size of the earth. The star Betelgeuse has a diameter of 100 million miles, larger than the earth's orbit around the sun. It takes sunlight traveling at the speed of light about 8.5 minutes to reach earth. Yet that same light would take more than four years to reach the nearest star, Alpha Centauri, some 24 trillion miles from earth.

The galaxy to which our sun belongs, the Milky Way, contains hundreds of billions of stars. And astronomers estimate that there are even billions of galaxies, perhaps the number of all the grains of sand on all the beaches of the world. How immense must God be who, as Creator, far exceeds the size of his creation.

Yet this infinite God is intimately aware of every individual on the planet. In the midst of over six billion persons on the earth, God knows each and every one perfectly. The very hairs of their heads are numbered. He knows what each person will say before he says it. He is present everywhere, personally involved at even the most minute level. Having created every life, God presides over every aspect of each of these lives. Every thought, attitude, word, and deed is an open book before him. How can a God so immense be so immanent? Such is the mind-boggling yet soul-comforting reality about our infinite yet intimate God.

Psalm 139 is a wisdom psalm, intensely personal, written by David. It reveals the awe and astonishment he felt toward God, who created the heavens and the earth yet who actually knew him and was intimately involved in the minute details of his life. This beautifully poetic song describes some of the most incomparable attributes of God—his omniscience, omnipresence, omnipotence, and vengeance. David sees them not as mere theological abstractions but as dynamic realities that deeply impacted his life. Here is a personal testimony by this beloved man of God that surveys four great divine attributes which should influence every believer's life. The occasion of this psalm is unknown, but its message is unmistakable.

II. COMMENTARY

> **MAIN IDEA:** *David meditates upon the momentous truths that God is all-knowing, all-present, all-powerful, and all-holy.*

A God Is All-Knowing (139:1–6)

> **SUPPORTING IDEA:** *David is overwhelmed that God knows all about him.*

139:1. Nothing in his life, David realized, was hidden from God's all-seeing gaze. He declared, **O LORD, you have searched me**, using a word meaning "to explore, spy out, to dig deeply into, to explore a country." God knew the very depths of his being, what no one else saw. **You know** (*yadah*, "to know intimately, experientially") **me** thoroughly (i.e., his character, being, his very heart).

139:2. You know when I sit and when I rise. These two activities are intended to represent when David rests and rises to work during his day's activities and everything in between. He pondered how God knew his **thoughts from afar.** Others saw his actions, but God saw into his heart.

139:3–4. God does **discern**—that is, "to sift through something, to winnow as grain, to sort out the good from the bad"—his life. He sees through his **going out** to labor and his **lying down** to sleep. God saw David's morning departure to work, his evening retiring at home, and, implied, all the other events of the day. God was deeply **familiar** with all his **ways.** He even knew what he was going to say before he said it. David could only conclude, **You know it completely.**

139:5. God surrounded David like a city being besieged with no way of escape. There was no way for him to escape his all-knowing thoughts. God had **laid** his **hand upon** him so that he was always near. Under this kind of close scrutiny, God saw the entirety of his life up close, inside out.

139:6. David's response to all this is, **Such knowledge is too wonderful** and too high. God's omniscience is both convicting and comforting. For David, it was humbling, beyond his human capacity to grasp.

𝔹 God Is All-Present (139:7–12)

> **SUPPORTING IDEA:** *David is overcome that God is always with him.*

139:7. Further, David understood that God is all-present, and he could never escape the divine presence. **Where can I go from your Spirit?** or **Where can I flee from your presence?** These two rhetorical questions imply a negative answer. There is nowhere God is not present. God's "Spirit," a reference to the Holy Spirit, is omnipresent.

139:8–10. **If I go up to the heavens**, David declared, God is **there**. Heaven above is God's eternal dwelling place. Or **if I make my bed in the depths** of hell, the other extreme, God is there. David would never be more face-to-face with God than after he died. **If I rise on the wings of the dawn** and fly to the east, or **if I settle on the far side of the sea** (i.e., the Mediterranean Sea), God is there. North, south, east, and west are represented here. No matter where he goes in life or after death, **your hand will guide me** into the divine will and **your right hand will hold me fast**. God is always in touch with his life, which is never beyond the divine reach.

139:11–12. If David says, **The darkness will hide me**, even then, God sees in the dark and is present there. This **darkness** refers to the dark nights of the soul (i.e., dark trials). **Even the darkness will not be dark to you**. Dark times are light to God. He is present in them, knowing perfectly all that is transpiring and what his eternal purposes are.

ℂ God Is All-Powerful (139:13–18)

> **SUPPORTING IDEA:** *David is astounded that God precisely created him and ordained the number of his days.*

139:13. Moreover, David knows that God is all-powerful. This is proven in that the Lord has made him skillfully in his mother's womb. God created his **inmost being** (i.e., his kidneys, symbolic of his vital organs, his heart, liver, lungs, even his innermost emotions and moral sensitivities). God **knit** him like a skilled artisan would weave a beautiful tapestry. This work of creation was done in his **mother's womb**, beginning nine months before he was born.

139:14. David could only **praise** God for this display of wonderful omnipotence. He understood he was **fearfully and wonderfully made**, producing awe and astonishment within him toward God who created him so perfectly.

139:15. My frame (i.e., bones and skeleton) **was not hidden from** God but in full view to divine eyes. God **made** David **in the secret place**, a euphemism for the womb, that unseen place concealed from human eyes. There he was **woven together** like a multicolored piece of cloth or fine needlepoint. All these threads picture his veins, arteries, muscles, and tendons.

139:16. God **saw** his **unformed** body before he was made. **All** his **days** were sovereignly **ordained** for David before he came into the world. The span of his life was **written** by God in his divine **book** containing his eternal decree. The precise length of his life was determined by God before he was born. There could be no changing the number of his days (Job 14:5).

139:17–18. These divine truths were **precious** to David, **vast** and beyond his human comprehension. If he tried to list these truths about God, **they would outnumber the grains of sand** on the beaches of the world, far past his ability to understand. When he awakens, his thoughts are still dominated with God. He cannot remove such towering thoughts about God from his mind.

D God Is All-Holy (139:19–24)

SUPPORTING IDEA: *David appeals to God to destroy his wicked adversaries and search him for any hurtful way.*

139:19–20. With holy zeal, David pledged his loyalty to this awesome God. He desired that God would **slay the wicked** because **they speak** against him and oppose the Lord. God's enemies were his enemies. They blasphemed God and abused the divine **name**. David could not bear this. Nor could he be accepting of those who so despise God.

139:21–22. David said that he did **hate those who hate** God. This means he rejects and refuses those who would rise up against God (cp. Ps. 1:1). He cannot be neutral toward those who attack God: **Count them my enemies**. Strictly speaking, he had not made them his enemies, but they had made themselves his enemies. To oppose God was to oppose David. David was so burdened for God's kingdom work to move forward that he asked for all obstacles to be removed, even these adversaries.

139:23. In dealing with sin, David was equally hard on himself. He invited God to **search** and explore his own heart, a fact he had already acknowledged (v. 1). He wanted God to **know** his heart so God could make it known to him. He could not fully know his own heart because of the self-deceptiveness of sin (Jer. 17:9). **Test me**, he asked God, as a refiner would test and purify metal. **Know** intimately **my anxious thoughts**, he prayed.

139:24. David asked that God would **see** and reveal to him any **offensive way** in which his sin grieves the Lord. Only then, once his own sin is confessed and removed, could God lead him **in the way everlasting**, the way of holiness.

> **MAIN IDEA REVIEW:** *David meditates upon the momentous truths that God is all-knowing, all-present, all-powerful, and all-holy.*

III. CONCLUSION

How can God, who is infinite, be at the same time so intimate with us? How can God be so transcendent and immanent? So highly perfect and highly personal? To be sure, God who knows all and controls all is directly involved with each one of us at the deepest level. Not only does God operate on the macro-level, but on the micro-level as well. God is all and in all. No creature is hidden from his sight. No individual is away from his presence. This great God has skillfully made us and ordained all our days. This psalm invites every one of us to live humbly before our God. Do you want to walk with God intimately? Then respond appropriately to God at each level of this psalm. Yield your life to him, knowing that this God who knows you the best also loves you the most. This God is with you wherever you go. This God reveals your own heart to yourself. May you grow to know *this* God more deeply each day.

IV. LIFE APPLICATION

In this psalm, David's response to God must be our response to him. As this man after God's own heart pursued the Lord, so must each one of us. How should we live out the message of this psalm? The personal application and direct appropriation of this inspired psalm begin with an overwhelming sense of the infinite greatness of God. Such an awareness should sweep over our souls, leaving us amazed and astonished. As we ponder the immensity of his greatness, yet intimately involved in a personal relationship with us, our hearts should be awestruck, even dumbfounded, that he should be so mindful of and involved with us.

Can we respond in any way other than by worshipping him? The greater our vision of God's attributes, the greater will be the wonder-filled love that will flood our hearts for him. We could never adore a God we could completely understand. The fact that he exceeds the limits of our human comprehension causes our hearts to be filled with even greater amazement toward him. That this infinite God would make himself known to us is truly amazing. That he would make himself known to us in such an intimate relationship should confound us all our days.

V. PRAYER

God, great Creator of heaven and earth, how we praise you that you would choose to dwell within finite, fallible lives such as ours. We are stunned that you would take such notice of us and be involved at such a deep level with us. We invite you to search us and make known to us what you find that is hurtful to you. We will repent and deal with it. In Jesus' name. Amen.

VI. DEEPER DISCOVERIES

A. Depths (139:8)

This word (*sheol*) occurs sixty-six times in the Old Testament and is a reference to the realm of the dead, the grave, and the underworld. Both the righteous (Gen. 37:35) and the unrighteous (Num. 16:30) will go to *sheol*. People enter the sheol because it is God himself who brings them there (1 Sam. 2:6). It is a place of man's conscious existence (Ps. 16:10) from which no one will return (Job 16:22; 17:14–16). The New Testament equivalent is not the Greek word *gehena* but rather *hades* (cp. Matt. 11:23, where Jesus quotes Isa. 14:13–15). The body of every person will go to *sheol,* although all souls will not enter into the same final destiny.

B. Guide (139:10)

The term *guide* (Heb. *naha*) means "to lead or to direct someone down the right path" (Exod. 13:21; 32:34; Num. 23:7; Neh. 9:12; Job 38:32; Isa. 58:11). It occurs thirty-nine times in the Old Testament. Nowhere is this verb more vividly demonstrated than in the Book of Exodus, where God guided Israel with a cloud by day and fire by night (Exod. 13:21; Ps. 78:14). In the Psalms, this guidance describes God guiding his servant (Pss. 27:11; 31:3; 61:2; 77:20; 139:24; 143:10). This guidance leads a person down the path of righteousness (Pss. 5:8; 23:3; 67:4).

C. Eyes (139:16)

The word *eyes* is an anthropomorphism, a literary device that portrays God in human terms. The term itself is derived from two Greek words—*anthropos* ("man") and *morphe* ("form"). Anthropomorphisms are descriptions of God using words that indicate a human physical form and must be taken figuratively. It is the transcendent God repeatedly portrayed in earthly and human terms with such descriptions that are figurative rather than literal. These figurative terms (e.g., eyes, ears, face) are used so that the eternal, incomprehensible God can be made intelligible to finite, fallen man.

Anthropomorphisms are intended to depict the infinite God to the limited minds of human beings. Most occur in Old Testament poetry and prophecy (for examples of anthropomorphisms, cp. Gen. 3:8; 6:8; 49:24; Exod. 15:3; 24:11; Josh. 4:24; Num. 12:8; Deut. 11:12; 13:18; 32:10; 2 Chr. 16:9; Pss. 10:17; 17:6; 18:6; Isa. 59:1–2; Jer. 7:13; Hos. 11:8). These human-like terms assigned to God are not to be taken literally because the Scriptures are clear that "God is spirit" (John 4:24) and is without bodily form (cp. Deut. 4:12). This is why the Israelites were forbidden from making any image to portray the invisible God (Deut. 4:15–19). No graven image can rightly portray God who has no physical form. It should be noted, of course, that the second member of the Godhead became incarnate in the person of Jesus Christ.

VII. TEACHING OUTLINE

A. God Is All-Knowing (139:1–6)
B. God Is All-Present (139:7–12)
C. God Is All-Powerful (139:13–18)
D. God Is All-Holy (139:19–24)

Psalm 140

Desperate Cry

"Let us never despair while we have Christ

as our leader!"

George Whitefield

Psalm 140

I. INTRODUCTION

The storms of life either make us or break us. They either mold us into the persons God wants us to be, or they cause us to lose heart and crumble. Fiery trials either drive the believer closer to God, or they drive him farther away. But no one ever remains the same after experiencing a severe distress. Affliction either softens the believer or sours him. It either makes him better or make him bitter. This is the powerful effect of trials upon our spiritual lives. All believers go through storms, but none pass through them unchanged.

David seemed to live most of his days submerged in the fiery trials of life. Psalm 140 is a prayer for deliverance from the plots and profanities of impious men. This is no small trial David faces. Yet, in the midst of all his trouble, this affliction actually drives him closer to God. In this painful ordeal David calls upon God with a sense of great urgency, and God hears him.

II. COMMENTARY

> **MAIN IDEA:** *David petitions God's deliverance from evil men who seek to do him great harm.*

A David's Cry (140:1–8)

140:1. David exclaimed, **rescue me**, an urgent appeal for God's help amid great difficulty. His danger was **evil men**, those who continually harm the innocent and prey upon the godly. In the meantime, David prayed, **protect me** until you rescue me. These **men of violence** are harsh and ruthless, not caring who they hurt. They will stop at nothing, destroying the reputation, livelihood, family, and peace of the godly.

140:2. The **evil plans** they **devise** are harming David and his supporters. They attack the innocent, creating strife and conflict. Their violence is never accidental but planned, purposeful, and premeditated. They hatch evil plans **in their hearts**. They **stir up war**, sowing discord among the brethren and pitting people against the godly.

140:3. Their most destructive weapons are **their tongues**. They run their mouths, slandering and tearing down. Their tongues are **as sharp as a serpent's** fangs that puncture and penetrate. Once they bite, they inject their **poison** into their victims.

140:4. David pleads, **Keep me, O LORD, from the hands of the wicked**. This shows the desperation of David's situation as if they literally want to lay their hands on him and do him bodily harm. These **men of violence** are intent on destroying him, seeking to **trip** his **feet**, causing him to fall.

140:5. All these hunting words—**snare, cords, net, traps**—represent the fact that these evil men seek to entrap and ensnare David like an animal. He senses correctly that he is their prey as they try to trap him in their ambush of words, a character assassination.

140:6. The ground for David's appeal to God is his relationship to the Lord. **You are my God**. In the midst of this difficulty, his faith was active and dynamic. **Hear, O LORD, my cry for mercy**. He pleads for divine favor, protection, and deliverance.

140:7. David acknowledges the **Sovereign LORD** as his **strong deliverer**. God is infinitely more powerful than his enemies and is able to deliver him from his foes. God has figuratively been David's helmet in battle, his protection from harm. God is the divine warrior who will deliver his people.

140:8. David pleads with God to act lest evil **succeed** and wickedness triumph. Their **desires**, unholy and unlawful, were to destroy David and take over God's work without his restraint. Do not let their evil plans succeed, he pleads.

𝕭 David's Condemnation (140:9–11)

140:9. David prays that their evil plots will come back on their own heads: **Let the heads of those who surround me be covered with the trouble their lips have caused**. This is not a personal vendetta, but it is spoken with godly zeal for God's glory on the earth. Further, it was said in self-defense, not personal offense. The psalmist prays that what they have spoken with their **lips** will recoil on their own **heads**.

140:10. David asks for **burning coals**, **fire**, **miry pits** to destroy his enemies, all metaphors for divine judgment. They picture the fire of God's retribution reserved for his enemies. The **burning coals** may be a reference to the story of the destruction of Sodom and Gomorrah, a destruction which the inhabitants of these cities brought upon themselves. The fire and miry pits are traps and pitfalls that they have dug for others.

140:11. The term **slanderers** refers to the evil, violent men who seek to harm David. These are men who stir up wars through their razor-sharp tongues. It is these tongues that slander him. May the evil committed **hunt down men of violence** and overtake them.

C David's Confidence (140:12–13)

140:12. David's deep confidence in God remains firm. He is unwavering that God will preserve **justice for the poor**, David himself being one of them. In the face of such slander by his enemies, he believes that God will maintain his cause. He is persuaded that God will vindicate him. Although evil may temporarily succeed and harm God's people, God will act justly and make right every wrong.

140:13. David himself is one of these **righteous** who will **praise** God's **name**. Because God maintains the cause of the poor and afflicted, **the upright will live** for God's glory.

III. CONCLUSION

This psalm describes the persecution that all believers today still face for being followers of Jesus Christ. Christians live in a fallen world of evil people who plot against the godly and seek their harm. Slanderous gossipers would impugn their reputations. Gospel opponents would do them much harm. The apostle Paul left no doubt, "Everyone who wants to live a godly life in Christ Jesus will be persecuted" (2 Tim. 3:12). When we find ourselves under spiritual attack in these difficult situations, we must call upon God to deliver us. To whom else would we turn? If you find yourself under attack for your faith, cry out to God who alone can comfort, strengthen, and deliver you. He will *never* forsake you.

IV. TEACHING OUTLINE

A. David's Cry (140:1–8)
B. David's Condemnation (140:9–11)
C. David's Confidence (140:12–13)

Psalm 141

Prevailing Prayer

"*P*rayer is the great engine to overthrow and rout my spiritual enemies, the great means to procure the graces of which I stand in hourly need."

Charles H. Spurgeon

I. INTRODUCTION

Anyone who has ever been mightily used by God has been strong in prayer. The ministry of intercession is a powerful weapon available to all believers. Granted, few will ever step into the pulpit to preach. Few will ever go overseas to the mission field. But all Christians are called to the ministry of prayer. All *can* pray, and all *must* pray. Prayer, it has been said, moves the invisible hand that moves the world. Prayer can do whatever God can do. Prayer is mighty because it summons the divine power to accomplish his sovereign will. Prayer unleashes the power of God to do the will of God. No Christian's ministry or life will advance any further than his prayers. There is no greater need than to pray.

This is one of the benefits of Psalm 141. It records a prayer of David seeking deliverance from wicked men and their evil ways. But more than the prayer itself, it is a psalm that teaches us how to pray. Here is not only what David prayed, but how he prayed. It is an individual lament psalm of David in which he pours out his heart to God in passionate petition. The occasion is unknown. But the lessons to be learned here are clear. Here is a powerful example of how to pray.

II. COMMENTARY

MAIN IDEA: *David petitions God for deliverance from the wicked and asks for divine guidance in holy living.*

A David's Desperation (141:1–2)

141:1. David cries, **O LORD, I call** (*qara,* "to cry out, to call aloud, to roar, to proclaim, to preach") **to you**. David calls upon God with a loud **voice**. He cries out loud, **Come quickly**, that is, "God, do not delay. There is not a moment to lose." An urgency and emergency fill David's plea. **Hear my voice when I call**. "God, pay attention to my cry."

141:2. David compares his prayer to a pleasing offering to the Lord. **Incense** was presented to the Lord every day (Exod. 30:7–8), usually together with the burnt offering (Lev. 2:1–2) and often in connection with the **evening sacrifice** (Exod. 29:38–42). This pictures his prayers to God, pleasing to the Lord. The **lifting up** of his **hands** is symbolic of his dependence on the Lord (Pss. 28:2; 63:4).

B David's Dedication (141:3–4)

141:3. Pursuing his own personal holiness, David dedicates his **mouth** and **lips** to God. His mouth must be pure in prayer and every conversation. He asks that God direct his words rightly and restrain his speech carefully. David petitions God to be like a watchman on the wall and to **keep watch** over what comes out of his **mouth**.

141:4. Let not my heart be drawn to what is evil, he prays. There exists an inseparable cause and effect between the heart and mouth. He humbly requests that God prevent his heart from taking part in **wicked deeds**. This will best guard his speech.

C David's Determination (141:5a–c)

141:5a–c. David calls upon God to use a **righteous man** to **rebuke** and discipline him. He asks that wise people help restrain his lips, heart, and actions. Words of rebuke from others would be like **oil** on his **head**, a courtesy shown a weary guest by a gracious host. Even so, David will **not refuse** their critique, which is God's discipline leading to divine favor.

D David's Discernment (141:5d–7)

141:5d. David's prayer is **against the deeds of evildoers**. He intercedes against these wicked men who are performing many wicked deeds against him. In this, he seeks God's protection, even retaliation, in defending him.

141:6. David prays that **their rulers**, the leaders of the wicked, will be **thrown down from the cliffs** in divine judgment. He asks that the wicked will learn that his **words are well spoken**. His words spoken in prayer are power-ful, bringing the wicked under divine wrath.

141:7. As when a farmer **plows and breaks up the earth**, so **our bones** have been attacked and assaulted by evil men. Their bodies are devastated, left at the doorstep of the grave, ready to be buried.

E Davids Devotion (141:8–10)

141:8. David's **eyes** are riveted on God while he is praying. This is true faith, which is a looking away from what threatens David and a gazing upon God who is triumphant. **In you**, he pledges himself, **I take refuge**. David anchors, attaches, and aligns himself to God. **Do not give me over to death**, he pleads. God must not abandon him or leave him vulnerable to his enemies.

141:9. David asks for divine protection from **the snares they have laid for me**, a reference to the evil plots of wicked men to bring him down. He feels like a hunted animal with **traps set** for him and pleads with God to pro-tect him from **evildoers**.

141:10. David concludes, **Let the wicked** harm themselves. Let what they have laid for David **fall** upon them. Let them fall into **their own nets**. Let them be caught in their own evil devices while he, David, passes **by in safety**.

III. CONCLUSION

Like David models in this psalm, every believer needs desperation in his prayers. We are often too passive in our intercessions and, thus, too stoic. More urgency and expediency are needed. As long as we are convinced that we can make things happen in our own strength, our prayers will be flat. But Jesus said, "Apart from me you can do nothing" (John 15:5). This truth alone ought to infuse a healthy desperation in our prayers. A high view of God's supremacy reveals that only God can cause good to happen in our lives.

Consider, for example, our prayers for lost sinners to come to Christ. Only God can open the sinner's blind eyes to see spiritual truth, open the sin-ner's closed heart to receive truth, and open the sinner's deaf ears to hear the gospel presented. Only God can convict the lost sinner of sin, righteousness, and judgment. Only God can draw the unconverted to Christ. Only God can enable the dead sinner to repent and believe. Therefore, it is God to whom we must pray for the salvation of unregenerate sinners. And when we do pray for their conversion, we must intercede with great desperation. When we mean business with God, he will mean business with us.

IV. TEACHING OUTLINE

A. David's Desperation (141:1–2)
B. David's Dedication (141:3–4)
C. David's Determination (141:5a–c)
D. David's Discernment (141:5d–7)
E. David's Devotion (141:8–10)

Psalm 142

Never Alone

"*My* God and I are good company."

Richard Sibbes

Psalm 142

I. INTRODUCTION

Even when the believer is alone, the truth is that he is never alone. Although he may live by himself, he is never unaccompanied. Though isolated, the Lord is always with him. He may be in a lonely place, removed from family and friends, but he is never isolated from God. The Lord is *always* with the believer. This truth has been a source of immeasurable comfort down through the centuries for all the saints who have found themselves in lonely places. No matter what the predicament is in which believers find themselves, God is always with them to strengthen them. A saint may be separated from friends, forsaken by a spouse, released from a job, cut from a team, or living by himself, but in spite of all this, he is never alone. The Lord is always with him.

This is precisely where David found himself as he wrote Psalm 142—alone but not alone. According to the superscription, the circumstances pointed back to his desperate days of hiding in the cave of Adullam (1 Sam. 22:1) while Saul attempted to take his life (1 Sam. 18–21). At the time, David's predicament appeared to be hopeless apart from divine intervention. Although David was by himself in a cave, surrounded by Saul and his supporters, he was, nevertheless, in the presence and fellowship of God. Even when he was alone, he was not alone because the Lord was always with him. This psalm is a plaintive prayer for deliverance at the time when David's plight seemed hopeless.

II. COMMENTARY

MAIN IDEA: *Alone and powerless, David expresses his firm trust that God hears his prayers and will act.*

A David's Cry (142:1–2)

142:1. The psalmist says, **I cry aloud**, as his crushed soul is calling out to God for help. This is not a muted cry, not a halfhearted appeal to God but one that is loud and fervent. David is voicing this plea to God, who alone can help. **I lift up my voice** pictures an inferior stooping before a superior, looking up to him, beseeching, requesting, and seeking help. He cries to the LORD (Yahweh, Jehovah), the active, self-existent, self-sufficient One who alone can help.

142:2. I pour out (*shaphak,* "to spill forth") **my complaint** as a drink offering or libation would be spilt out on the altar. The words **I tell my trouble** boldly declares his needs to God.

B David's Collapse (142:3–4)

142:3. David's **spirit** is devastated. He is emotionally imploding; everything is crashing in on top of him. He grows **faint** under the pile of these heavy trials. God knows (*yadah,* "to know intimately") David's path, a knowledge far deeper than a mere intellectual cognizance. Rather, God is with David on the path, intimately involved. When David is ready to give up, he looks up to God and anchors himself to God. David's adversaries, Saul and his men, **have hidden a snare** to capture David like an animal.

142:4. The **right** is where one's help would normally be found, the side of one's strength and security. David cries that there is **no one** on his right side to protect him. He has no one to defend him against his adversaries. He has no defender, no advocate, no one to rescue him out of this difficulty. There is no **refuge** for him. What is worse, no one **cares for** his **life**. David is totally abandoned, alone.

C David's Confidence (142:5–7)

142:5. Here is the second summit of faith as the psalmist lays hold of God afresh. David prays firmly and pointedly, **I cry to you, O LORD**. Although he feels shut up in this cave, God is his **refuge** (*machseh*), a place of shelter, a stronghold. God is **my portion**, meaning God is his allotment, or all he has. But God is all he needs, the sustainer and strength of his life in **the land of the living**, that is, as long as he is alive.

142:6. Repeating his earlier plea (vv. 1–2,5), David pleads that God heed him. David laments that the adverse circumstances in which he finds himself have humbled him and brought him low. Specifically, he has been brought low by **those who pursue** him, meaning Saul and his henchmen. They are **too strong** for David, far beyond what he can handle.

142:7. The cave in which David finds himself, hiding from Saul, has become a **prison** for him, a place of solitary confinement. He cannot escape it as he finds himself between a rock and a hard place. But more than that, he is in an emotional prison, a psychological black hole. Only God himself can deliver him, something he believes God will perform.

III. CONCLUSION

Desperate times produce desperate prayers. Troubles cause us to throw ourselves on God in new, desperate ways. When there is none to help but God, we learn to pray aggressively, casting ourselves upon him completely. What do we need to commit to God in prayer? First Peter 5:7 encourages us to cast "all your anxiety on him because he cares for you." That is, we are invited to transfer the weight and pressure of our trials into God's mighty arms (Phil. 4:6). It is in committing our trials to God in prayer that we find his peace. "You will keep in perfect peace him whose mind is steadfast, because he trusts in you" (Isa. 26:3). Like the prophet urged so long ago, will you cast your burdens on the Lord?

IV. TEACHING OUTLINE

A. David's Cry (142:1–2)
B. David's Collapse (142:3–4)
C. David's Confidence (142:5–7)

Psalm 143
Real Repentance

┤ Quote ├

"*To* do so no more is the truest repentance."

M a r t i n   L u t h e r

Psalm 143

I. INTRODUCTION

After Martin Luther wrote his Ninety-five Theses, he nailed them to the front door of the Castle Church at Wittenberg, Germany, beginning one of the momentous events of human history—the Protestant Reformation. History has never been the same since. The very first thesis read, "When our Lord and Master, Jesus Christ, said 'repent,' He meant that the entire life of believers should be one of repentance." Luther declared that Scripture taught that repentance is an absolute necessity for all people and that it involves a radical change of the entire person—mind, emotion, and will.

First, real repentance is a change of mind in which one is confronted with his sin by the Word of God, and that sin is acknowledged for what it is—a grievous offense against God. Second, repentance involves a change of emotions as one becomes broken over his sin with a godly sorrow. Third, the believer experiences a change of will in which he turns away from his sin in order to obey God and pursue holiness. This is the true repentance for which Luther called amid the religious hypocrisy in the church of his day.

This soul-wrestling repentance is precisely what David expressed in Psalm 143. This psalm is known as a penitential psalm, one containing a confession of sin and a turning from that sin. It is a psalm acknowledging personal sin, the seventh and last such psalm in the Psalter. The other repentance psalms are Psalms 6; 32; 38; 51; 102; 130. In each of these psalms, there is the acknowledgment of personal sin against God and the expression of heartfelt remorse over that sin's offense toward God. At first glance, it may not be immediately apparent to see why Psalm 143 is so classified. Only verse

2 acknowledges wrongdoing, while the rest of the psalm is about David's enemies (vv. 3–4) from whom David asked to be delivered (vv. 7–12). Nevertheless, it does contain this somewhat brief, veiled confession of sin; thus, it is rightly classified as a penitential psalm. Here is the last psalm in which David acknowledged his sin to God.

II. COMMENTARY

> **MAIN IDEA:** *David acknowledges his sin, seeking deliverance from his enemies.*

A David's Repentance (143:1–2)

143:1. David throws himself upon the Lord's mercy, seeking his mercy and help. **Hear my prayer**, he pleads. **Listen to my cry for mercy.** That is, turn your ear toward my supplications. All true forgiveness of sin is based on God's **faithfulness and righteousness.** Fervently, David appeals to God's holy character as the basis for the answer to his petitions—not David's sinful character.

143:2. He explains why he needs God's mercy. He sins constantly and thus suffers divine **judgment**, or God's chastisement. Yet the psalmist is aware that he can make no claims upon God based on his own merit. **No one living is righteous before you**, not even David. David's words imply his own unrighteousness. He realizes that if he is to be delivered, it will be because of God's righteousness, not his own.

B David's Reproach (143:3–4)

143:3. Under painful persecution, **the enemy**, a group of people, seek to do David harm. They have already attacked him and registered a direct hit on his soul. David is constantly being attacked by enemies, proving the higher one rises in leadership, the more visible he is and, thus, a target. The more David stands for God, the more he is attacked by the enemy. Here they are instruments of divine discipline upon David. His adversary crushes him **to the ground** a devastated man. He feels as if he lives in **darkness, like those long dead** in the grave, robbed of the pleasures and enjoyments of life.

143:4. David's persecution is not without its emotional effect. **So my spirit** (i.e., his inner emotions, thoughts, and attitudes) **grows faint.** He is devastated psychologically, emotionally, and spiritually. He is a crushed man, buckling under this onslaught. He is reeling under this personal attack, **dismayed** to the point of suffering despair from this oppression.

C David's Remembrance (143:5–6)

143:5. David musters confidence as he remembers **the days of long ago** when God's favor and divine blessing were clearly upon his life. Throughout the day, David meditates on God's gracious past deeds in his life. He considers how God has been with him in the past through many providences, good-nesses, and blessings.

143:6. David desperately spreads out his hands to God. Reflecting upon past days of God's blessing causes him to pour out his soul to God in prayer. David compares his own **soul** to that of a dry, **parched land** in the wilderness, desperately longing for water. As the dry ground opens itself for rain, so he longs for the outpouring of God's care.

D David's Restoration (143:7–12)

143:7. David prays, **answer me quickly,** showing an urgency to have this matter resolved. He cannot continue to live this way. Living in spiritual luke-warmness and disobedience is destroying him. Emotionally drained, his **spirit fails** within him. His zest for living is gone. **Do not hide your face from me,** he prays. God seems so far away and distant. **I will be like those who go down to the pit,** devoid of passion for living any more, he declares.

143:8. This time of spiritual decline in David's life is as dark as the night. He longs for a new **morning** to dawn in his spiritual life. He longs for the warm sunrise of God's **unfailing love** to rise upon his soul and to radiate God's presence in his life. Turning to God with a repentant heart, he puts his **trust** in the Lord. David asks that God **show** him the steps that lead back to walking in close fellowship with him. He requests that God teach him how to get his life back on spiritual track. Sin has led David astray. Only God can **show** him **the way** to come back.

143:9–10. David realizes that only God can **rescue** him out of this time of divine discipline at the hands of his **enemies.** He calls on God to rescue him and provide relief. David pleads with God to **teach** him the way to return to the right path of obedience. He reminds God of their relationship as if to bind God to teach him again. Once God has taught him the way to take, the Lord must yet **lead** him on to this divine path.

143:11–12. David appeals to God's **name's sake,** that is, to divine honor and glory. **Preserve my life** is to admit his weaknesses, asking God to renew a steadfast spirit within him. Not only must God show him the way to go and strengthen him along this path; the Lord must silence his **enemies** who are seeking to do him harm. David's confidence lies not in his own strength but in the fact that he is the Lord's **servant.** To attack God's servant is to attack God. This will surely bring God to the defense of his servant.

III. CONCLUSION

If greater spiritual sensitivity were ours, we would realize that, like David, many of our troubles are the direct result of sin in our own lives. This is precisely what David acknowledged in this psalm. The psalmist did not pass blame to others for his painful trial. Rather, he assumed personal responsibility for his own sin, which had brought it. This is what we should acknowledge in our own lives as well. It is our own sin that so often invites God's discipline in our lives. God often raises up troublesome, even ungodly, people in our lives to be used as the rod of his anger to discipline us. We must be careful in such cases to confess our sin to God. True repentance must fill our hearts. When we forsake our sin, we are positioned to get back on track with God.

IV. TEACHING OUTLINE

A. David's Repentance (143:1–2)
B. David's Reproach (143:3–4)
C. David's Remembrance (143:5–6)
D. David's Restoration (143:7–12)

Psalm 144

God-Given Victory

I. INTRODUCTION

In the spiritual conflict of any believer's life, his greatest defender and ally is the Lord himself. Victory belongs to God, who is *with* him and *for* him. God stands with his people in every circumstance of life, in the valleys and on the mountaintops, in his battles and in his peace, in the storms and in the sunshine. What is more, God works *for* the believer, always working for his good. God is *for* him in whatever situation he finds himself. In fact, he stands with and fights for the believer when the enemies of God are against him.

Psalm 144 is a royal psalm in which David petitioned God for victory over threatening enemies. He called out to God who was for him and with him. This psalm bears a close similarity to Psalm 18 (esp., vv. 1–15), and if the historical background is the same, the enemies to which David referred here were Saul and his men (2 Sam. 22:1–18). It is also possible that this psalm was used in the training of Israel's army, much like Psalm 149. It should be remembered that warfare in ancient Israel was closely tied to the worship of God. Victory in battle was always a matter of worshipping God before the conflict, praising the Lord who alone gives victory.

II. COMMENTARY

A David's Praise (144:1–2)

144:1a. The psalmist declares, **Praise be to the LORD my Rock**, the strong refuge of his people. David's foundation in life is God himself, who is like a large mountain, solid and unshakeable. God is an immovable place to stand when attacked, an unshakeable stronghold in whom to find protection from his enemies. This is what David has in God, a firm place to stand in the midst of earth-shaking circumstances.

144:1b. David acknowledges that God is his personal trainer who prepares him for **battle**. If David's arrows land in the enemy's side, it is because the Lord has trained him and enabled him to strike a direct blow. He finds in the Lord not only his protection in battle but also his preparation for battle. God is the One who maximizes his skills and enlarges his strength in battle. God is the One on whom David can depend. God is unconditionally committed to his servant, forever loyal to his promises.

144:2. My fortress (*mesudah*) compares God to a high place of refuge and defense to which David must flee for protection. **My stronghold** (*misgab*) is protection in a high, safe place of retreat. Further, God is his **deliverer** from the attacks of the enemy. David trusts God to be the One who repels the fiery arrows of the enemy. A **shield** was held up by a soldier in the day of battle to deflect the incoming arrows of the enemy. God is a shield to David, turning away the deadly advances of the enemy. Whatever came against him had to come through God first.

B David's Powerlessness (144:3–4)

144:3. What is man is intended in an autobiographical sense, as if to say, "God, who am I but a mere man, a mere creature, weak and weary? Who am I that you would look down and take notice of me?" Omnipotent God (vv. 1–2) is contrasted with weak David. How can you even **think** of me, he wonders, when I am so weak?

144:4. Man is like a breath, a vapor, that appears for a moment and then disappears (Jas. 4:14). His **days are** flickering, without stability, empty, and hollow **like a fleeting shadow.**

C David's Petition (144:5–8)

144:5. David prays, **Part your heavens**, inviting God to **come down** and invade this war. David appeals to God to make his presence known and to rescue him from all the evil forces. **Mountains** represent the strongest and tallest of this world. **Touch** them, and they will be torched by your presence. This highly figurative language portrays God as the heavenly warrior who comes to fight on behalf of David against his enemies. He longs for God's presence to come as fire, bringing his smoldering judgment.

144:6. David calls for **lightning**, a symbol of God's blazing judgment that will strike David's enemies. He prays that God would burst on the scene like a lightning bolt, stretching across the skies, reaching downward to smite David's foes. He prays that God will **scatter** his adversaries. These lightning bolts are fiery, flaming **arrows** shot from God's bow, designed to score a direct hit, not only to scatter but to confuse his enemies.

144:7. Reach down your hand, David prays. That is, lay bare your mighty right arm and fight for us, O God. David prays that God will **rescue** and **deliver** him out of this stormy trial and day of battle. The great **waters** is a symbolic allusion to these **foreigners** or aliens who are as powerful as a flood.

144:8. The **mouths** of these evil foes speak great deceit, meaning slanderous **lies** against David. Their tongues are set on fire by hell itself. Their destructive lying and slanderous mouths are their most vicious weapons against David. What they say, they carry out with all the strength of their **right hands**. They back up their monstrous lies with destructive deeds.

D David's Proclamation (144:9–10)

144:9. While surrounded by his evil foes, David purposes, **I will sing a new song to you**. David will lift up his voice to God to offer a new song, or a fresh word of praise, expressing his renewed confidence in God's ultimate victory.

144:10. David sings this new praise to God **who gives victory to kings**. God, he believes, **delivers** those divinely anointed kings who put their trust in him. This is precisely what David is doing.

E David's Plea (144:11)

144:11. David prays that God will **rescue** him out of this threatening war against foreign powers. Clearly, David's trust is not in himself or in his own resources but in God alone. God is opposed to such people who are **full of lies** and carry out their **deceitful** schemes and conspiracies.

F David's Prospects (144:12–15)

144:12. David declares, **Our sons** will be like **well-nurtured plants**, indicating maturity, productivity, fruitfulness. **Our daughters** will be like **pillars carved to adorn a palace**, picturing strength of character, health, beauty, and dignity. Here is pictured a prosperous, peaceful future, one with no military threat.

144:13–14. Our barns will be filled with a full harvest of crops, overflowing with abundant **provision. Our sheep will increase by thousands, by tens of thousands in our fields**, a provision that comes from God. There will be **no cry of distress** in our streets but the blessing of peace.

144:15. Blessed are the people who are favored by God. They are abundantly provided with families, fields, and flocks. They are prosperous and so situated in the midst of God's blessing. **Blessed** is repeated twice for emphasis, indicating the double overflowing favor of God upon the psalmist. How favored by God are those who trust in him.

III. CONCLUSION

The believer's strength and security are found in God. One title is not sufficient to describe his greatness. All six titles for God found in this psalm are needed by believers. God's names reveal him to be our Rock, Trainer, Fortress, Stronghold, Deliverer, and Shield. God is *all* this to us—and more! In other words, God is our *everything!*

Regarding these many names for God, John Calvin wrote in his monumental commentary on the Psalms these God-honoring words:

> It is not superfluous, but designed to strengthen and confirm; for men's minds are easily shaken, especially when some storm of trial beats upon them. Hence, if God should promise us His succour in one word, it would not be enough; in fact, in spite of all the props and aids He gives us, we constantly totter and are ready to fall, and such a forgetfulness of His lovingkindness steals upon us, that we come near to losing heart altogether.

So let us take these words to heart. God is all this and more to us.

IV. TEACHING OUTLINE

A. David's Praise (144:1–2)
B. David's Powerlessness (144:3–4)
C. David's Petition (144:5–8)
D. David's Proclamation (144:9–10)
E. David's Plea (144:11)
F. David's Prospects (144:12–15)

Psalm 145

Perpetual Praise

"*P*raise is the rehearsal of our eternal song."

Charles Haddon Spurgeon

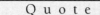

I. INTRODUCTION

The chief purpose of the believers, both now and throughout the ages, is the pursuit of the glory of God. Praising and practicing the greatness of God should be the primary passion of God's people all day, every day. Adoring the Lord should be the constant delight of their souls, the endless theme of their hearts. In every circumstance of life, believers should magnify his glorious name. Perpetual praise offered to God should be the grand pursuit of all that the saints do, their ultimate priority in this life, their chief business in the world to come.

Psalm 145 is a summons to every believer to practice this pursuit—the unending praise of God. Here is the last of David's psalms. In many ways, the Psalter is David's book. Certainly, he is the author of more psalms than anyone else—a total of 75 of the 150 psalms. David was certainly the obvious choice to write the most psalms, being "the sweet singer of Israel." A talented musician who often played his harp for Saul in earlier days, he was a man after God's own heart. Possessing a high view of God and commanding communication skills, David became, in reality, the worship leader of the entire Bible. In this, the last of David's psalms, we are not surprised to find that it is a powerful song of praise to God. The heading above the psalm reads "a psalm of praise," the only psalm so designated. While the entire Book of Psalms is a praise, this psalm, most especially, is the clearest praise of all. David saved his best for last.

II. COMMENTARY

MAIN IDEA: *David praises God for every good reason, especially extolling his divine greatness over all.*

A Praise for God's Greatness (145:1–6)

145:1. **I will exalt you, my God** reveals a deliberate, determined vow to praise the Lord. This praise is a purposeful choice of David's will. *Exalt* means "to elevate to a high place, to lift up, to elevate." David chooses to raise high the name of God above all other names. This lofty adoration flows out of a personal relationship with "my God." David was king over Israel, but God was **King** over David. **I will praise** (*barak*, "to bend the knee, to give a blessing") God's **name**, representing all his holy character. This offering of praise is not a momentary whim, quickly offered and soon forgotten, but a fixed resolution that will be carried out forever. Praising God presently is only an abbreviated prelude to praising God **for ever and ever** daily in heaven.

145:2. Worship is to be a daily lifestyle for the believer. **Every day**, whether in good or bad times, **I will praise** God, expressing love and devotion for him. This is one earthly occupation that will continue **for ever and ever**.

145:3. **Great is the LORD** in his person and works. Thus, God is **most worthy** to be praised. **His greatness** is unsearchable, beyond our human comprehension, never fully realized by finite man.

145:4. Each **generation** of believers will add to the telling of what God has done. This is their unique contribution in praising God. Their worship includes a magnifying of God's great acts in human history, an exuberant telling again and again of God's mighty acts.

145:5–6. The psalmist will **meditate** on God's **glorious splendor**, referring to the sum total of his divine attributes and actions. He is glorious in holiness, sovereignty, and grace. Splendor is the radiance and revelation of these attributes of God. Each generation **will tell** of God's **power** to alter nations and overturn kingdoms on behalf of his people. These **awesome works** provoke fear and reverence in the hearts of all who observe them.

B Praise for God's Goodness (145:7–10)

145:7. God's people will **celebrate** his **abundant goodness**. There is no scarcity of good things over which to celebrate. Because God shares his good provisions generously, they will **joyfully sing of your righteousness**. God's greatness is always used in a righteous, or right, way. His righteousness is consistent with all his other divine attributes. He never misuses his sovereignty.

145:8–9. **The LORD is gracious** (i.e., kind and merciful), having pity and **compassion** on those who are in need. He is **slow to anger**—patient, longsuffering, extending time to repent—and **rich in love**, being unconditionally committed to seeking the highest good of those whom he loves. God is **good to all**, even to his enemies, showing them common grace. He is not merely good to the good, but he shows favor to the undeserving, delaying his judgment, extending further opportunities to repent.

145:10. All you have made will praise you. All God's works will show his perfections, revealing who he is. This divine disclosure causes his saints to praise him.

C Praise for God's Government (145:11–13a)

145:11–12. All generations will **speak** of the greatness and **glory** of God's **kingdom** over all. As men see and understand the perfections of this divine kingdom, they will be compelled to **speak** about it. Their enthusiastic talking about God's government will make his glory known to others. This kingdom involves **mighty acts** of divine sovereignty and **glorious splendor** of radiant beauty.

145:13a. God's **kingdom** is **everlasting**, never to be usurped or overturned. His reign endures forever, never to pass away as earthly empires do. It will never be overthrown as human dynasties are or crumble from within. Rather, his government **endures through all generations**.

D Praise for God's Generosity (145:13b–16)

145:13b–14. The LORD **is faithful to all his promises**, never failing to keep his word. He is **loving** to all people **he has made**, faithfully executing his promise. God **upholds** the life of **all**, providing for their needs. God **lifts up** all who are **bowed down** under the heavy trials of life, strengthening them so they can bear up under burdens.

145:15–16. God restores **all** who are dependent on him. While he does not always do so immediately, he does in the **proper time**. God does **open** his **hand** to provide for the needs of his own children. In doing so, God satisfies their **desires**. Their bodies are fed and strengthened; their hearts are gratified and gladdened.

E Praise for God's Grace (145:17–21)

145:17–18. God is **righteous** toward his people, always just **in all his ways**. He never deals with his creation wrongly, nor does he ever mismanage them with inequity. God is infinitely **loving**, never needlessly harsh. God is **near** to those in need, ready to extend favor. He does not abandon his people who confess his name. Rather, he comes to the aid of **all who call on him** with grace and love.

145:19–20. God **fulfills the desires of those who fear him**, granting them true soul satisfaction. No person can be happy if he does not fear God.

The fear of the Lord is the beginning of everything good in one's life. The Lord **watches over** his own, protecting and preserving them. They keep God in their love, and he keeps them by his love. But to the contrary, **all the wicked**, or those who do not fear and love God, **he will destroy.**

145:21. No matter what others may say, David declares, **my mouth will speak in praise of the LORD.** This is a straightforward resolution to praise God (cp. vv. 1–2). **Let every creature** join this chorus of praise to God **for ever and ever.**

III. CONCLUSION

What David has declared in this psalm must be our daily, personal experience. Rising up from within our souls must be an anthem of perpetual praise to God. We must be always lifting our voices in magnifying the name of the Lord. God is so worthy of our praise that we should never cease extolling his name. He is great and, therefore, greatly to be praised. His sovereignty is unsearchable, far beyond our human comprehension. His incomparable glory produces wonder and astonishment that overwhelm us. His mighty deeds induce within us awe-filled worship that must be offered up to God, forever.

IV. TEACHING OUTLINE

A. Praise for God's Greatness (145:1–6)
B. Praise for God's Goodness (145:7–10)
C. Praise for God's Government (145:11–13a)
D. Praise for God's Generosity (145:13b–16)
E. Praise for God's Grace (145:17–21)

Psalm 146

Purposeful Praise

"*T*he most holy service that we can render to God is

to be employed in praising His name."

J o h n   C a l v i n

Psalm 146

I. INTRODUCTION

One of the most accurate measures of where any believer is spiritually is the intensity of his praise to God. A growing Christian is one who is growing in the fervency of his praise of God. Wherever there is advancement in the grace of the Lord Jesus Christ, there will be an ever-increasing sacrifice of praise ascending from his heart to the Lord. Jesus said, "For out of the overflow of the heart the mouth speaks" (Matt. 12:34). That is, what fills the heart overflows the mouth. When Jesus Christ is genuinely loved , there will be a growing surge of adoring praise. A soul enraptured with God will be evidenced by a mouth exalting him.

Psalm 146 is a declaration of praise to God who reigns forever. It is the first of five Hallelujah psalms that close the Psalter (Pss. 146–150). The chief focus of these last five psalms is the rendering of praise to God. They form the capstone of this house of worship known as the Psalter. These last five psalms have been called "the double Hallelujah psalms" because they each begin and end with "Praise the LORD." In the earlier psalms, the psalmist laid bare before us his griefs and shames, his doubts and fears, even his sins and confessions. But in these five final psalms, all this is behind us and virtually every word is directed toward praising the Lord. Charles Spurgeon, in his classic commentary on the Psalms, *Treasury of David,* said, "We are now among the Hallelujahs. . . . All is praise to the close of the book. The key is high-pitched.

The music is high-sounding cymbals. O for a heart full of joyful gratitude that we may run and leap and glorify God, even as these Psalms do."

II. COMMENTARY

MAIN IDEA: *The psalmist encourages all God's people to praise and trust the Lord.*

A The Proclamation of Praise (146:1–2)

146:1–2. The psalmist begins, **Praise the LORD**, which is an exuberant, boisterous shout to God. He follows by summoning his own heart, **O my soul**, to do the same. More than merely commanding others to praise God, the psalmist does so himself. This he will do **as long** as he lives. This shows his resolute determination to praise God that goes far beyond the mood of the moment.

B The Preservation of Praise (146:3–4)

146:3. **Do not put your trust** in even the best of people who may render aid, the psalmist advises. **Princes** who appear to have authority to bail one out of predicaments are but **mortal men** not to be trusted. These mighty men need God just like all the saints. They cannot even help themselves, much less others.

146:4. At death, princes **return to the ground**, or the grave. **On that very day** when they die, **their plans** for personal greatness **come to nothing**. They expire and their ambitions come to an end.

C The Pleasure of Praise (146:5–10b)

146:5–6. On the other hand, **Blessed is he whose help is the God of Jacob**. Here is the last of several beatitudes in the Psalter (cp. 1:1). The person who praises the Lord (vv. 1–2) will also trust him in all of life. The divine name **God of Jacob** emphasizes that God has always been faithful to his people, extending back to the patriarchs. The Lord has never veered from his promises. As **the Maker of heaven and earth**, God is unlike mortal man, who is frail, who dies, and who passes off the scene (vv. 3–4). God, the Creator, is worthy of the believer's trust. He is deserving of the saint's confidence as **the LORD, who remains faithful forever**.

146:7–8. God continually **upholds the cause** of those who are **oppressed** by princes who abuse their power. He overrules these finite rulers whom man is tempted to trust. The Lord **gives food** to those who have been oppressed by ungodly princes. God reverses their decisions and feeds his people. These **prisoners** are denied justice by evil princes, falsely accused and thrown into confinement where they are denied food. But God, in due time, sets them free. **The blind** are given **sight** to see their needs met. Those **bowed down** are the oppressed, hungry prisoners. The **righteous** are believers who have suffered for the sake of righteousness.

146:9. The Lord protects **the alien**, or the foreign Gentile, who suffers injustice because he is an outsider. God also **watches over** him. The Lord **sustains the fatherless** and husbandless in the face of abuses to justice. God **frustrates the ways of the wicked** who carry out the malicious deeds against these helpless victims. He will deal with these wicked men.

146:10a–b. In the midst of these social injustices by ungodly rulers, God's perfect justice will prevail. **The LORD reigns forever** throughout **all generations**. His just reign will never end.

D The Preeminence of Praise (146:10c)

146:10c. **Praise the LORD** is the proper response to all that has been revealed here about God. This divine revelation demands a wholehearted response. Thus, this strong shout of praise climaxes this song.

III. CONCLUSION

Praising God is a choice. It is an intentional choice of the will to magnify God in every circumstance and situation of life. Sometimes our trials momentarily obscure our view of God and threaten to steal away the praise that belongs exclusively to God. Whenever the tribulations of life mount, we must maintain our God-centered focus and choose God-enthralled praise of the Lord. We must never allow our praise to be controlled by our circumstance. Instead, we must allow our praise to control how we respond to our circumstances. Let us always choose praise. We have every reason to magnify the Lord's holy name.

IV. TEACHING OUTLINE

A. The Proclamation of Praise (146:1–2)
B. The Preservation of Praise (146:3–4)
C. The Pleasure of Praise (146:5–10b)
D. The Preeminence of Praise (146:10c)

Psalm 147

Proper Praise

Psalm 147

I. INTRODUCTION

Coming to public worship of God's people is one of the most important aspects of any Christian's life. It is doubtful that any believer who is capable of attending church but who remains irregular in coming can be growing in the grace and knowledge of Christ. The Christian life was never intended to be lived in isolation from the body of Christ. The divine design is that all saints should live in close fellowship with one another. A key part of this community experience is assembling together in worship. All believers need the psalmist's urging to come to God's house and give praise to God with other like-minded saints.

This is the focus of Psalm 147, a praise song that reminds believers how good God is and how good it is to worship God. This psalm is considered to be postexilic, written after the time of Israel's return to Jerusalem from the Babylonian captivity. It was probably written to celebrate the completion of the rebuilt wall around Jerusalem under Nehemiah's leadership (Neh. 12:27,43). That was a joyous occasion, one that called for fervent praise to God for all that he had done in restoring them to the holy city, Jerusalem. The psalm is comprised of three stanzas, each with its own call to worship followed by the causes for worship.

II. COMMENTARY

MAIN IDEA: *The psalmist invites all God's people to praise the Lord for his abundant goodness.*

A Praise for God's Restoration (147:1–6)

147:1. This psalm begins with a call to **praise the LORD**. It is **good** and **pleasant** to **sing praises** to God. How pleasurable and appropriate it is to sing the Lord's greatness.

147:2–3. God should be praised because he **builds up Jerusalem**. This psalm was probably written on the occasion of the dedication of the reconstructed walls of Jerusalem (Neh. 12) under Nehemiah. Returned to their promised land, these **exiles of Israel** had strong reason to praise God. They were **brokenhearted** because they had been in Babylonian captivity and had suffered much. But God healed their despair and bound up the **wounds** of their devastated souls.

147:4–5. The billions of **stars** are all named by God and kept up with by him. Everything is in its rightful place in the universe. He counts and names the vast starry host above and **calls them each by name**. To name something is to assume the care of that thing, as a parent does in naming a baby. God is **mighty** in strength to order the starry hosts and planets above. **His understanding** of each of the stars **has no limit**. He knows their exact location and size.

147:6. Even more so, God watches over **the humble** on this earth. The Lord **sustains** and undergirds them as they start this new phase in the promised land. The Lord's great strength and infinite understanding is applied to caring for his people. He knows they are afflicted, so he comforts them. Further, the Lord's great strength is able to bring down and defeat **the wicked** in and around Jerusalem who threatened to overturn their work.

B Praise for God's Provision (147:7–11)

147:7. This second stanza begins as did the first stanza with a call to praise God. All believers are summoned to **sing to the LORD**, accompanied by musical instruments such as the lyre, a multiple-stringed instrument much like a **harp**.

147:8–9. God should be praised because he provides for the needs of his people after having placed them in the promised land. God sends the **clouds**, which cause **grass**, which grows **food**, which feeds **the cattle** and **young ravens**. Even more so, God provides for his people.

147:10–11. God's real **pleasure is not in the strength of the horse**, the result of feeding them. **Nor is his delight in the legs of a man**, developing their physical strength. Rather, the Lord **delights in those who fear him**.

God's greatest delight is when his people revere him, serve him, and **hope** in him.

🅲 Praise for God's Protection (147:12–20)

147:12–13. The third stanza of this psalm begins with a third invitation to **extol the LORD**. The psalmist stands in Jerusalem, on Mount Zion, and calls on all the people to praise their God. The Lord **strengthens the bars** of the city **gates** in order to protect them. In so doing, he guards them against the surrounding nations who have threatened them. It is this protective wall around Jerusalem—fortified by God—that secures the city and **blesses** his **people**.

147:14. God **grants peace** within the **borders**, the city walls of Jerusalem. The people are at peace with one another, and this harmony is from God. This is God's grace within their midst. The Lord **satisfies . . . with the finest of wheat**, bringing prosperity to those who farm the surrounding land. God causes their crops to grow and their fields to be fertile.

147:15–18. All the world is at God's **command**. He directs and ordains everything in his created order. **His** spoken **word** orders the affairs of providence. In the wintertime, God **spreads the snow**, and it covers the ground like a white **wool** blanket. God orders the **frost**, and it is so. **Hail**, or ice particles, litter the ground **like pebbles**, all by divine decree. **Who can withstand his icy blast?** The winter God sends is so cold that people must retreat inside. In springtime, **He sends his word and melts them**, reversing the weather. All nature is at God's command, ready to do his bidding. The snow and ice melt, causing the **waters** to **flow** into creeks and streams.

147:19–20. God's written Word is equally powerful. **He has revealed his word to Jacob.** The written **laws** and **decrees** are mighty to work in his people. God has done this **for no other nation**. God chose Israel alone to be recipients of the Scripture. Other nations **do not know his laws**. But this privilege of receiving divine truth brings great obligation and responsibility to obey this Word. Knowing God's Word is the greatest blessing to come to a nation or a people, but obeying it is the greatest duty. Thus, this psalm concludes with the call to **Praise the LORD**.

III. CONCLUSION

This psalm is a call to worship as well as a reminder of why the Lord should be praised. Believers have every reason to come to God's house to praise him. It is good to be reminded of those most basic truths for which we should magnify the name of the Lord. Strong doxology is always built upon sound theology. All worship is centered in God—who he is and what he has done. Proper worship is to be "in spirit and in truth" (John 4:24), this truth being from God, but most of all, about God. A knowledge of the truth about God is the foundation and fountain for all dynamic praise. Thus, a substantive psalm like this one is necessary because it stimulates passionate praise for God.

IV. TEACHING OUTLINE

A. Praise for God's Restoration (147:1–6)
B. Praise for God's Provision (147:7–11)
C. Praise for God's Protection (147:12–20)

Psalm 148

Powerful Praise

"*W*hen God is praised, we have come to the ultimatum.

This is the thing for which all other things are designed."

C h a r l e s   H a d d o n   S p u r g e o n

Psalm 148

I. INTRODUCTION

The highest purpose of all creation is to glorify God. Whether they be in the heights of heaven or in the depths of the earth, this is the crowning reason for all that God has made. All creatures find their ultimate purpose in rendering praise to the Lord. As those created in the image of God, all the saints must be constantly reminded to magnify their Creator and Redeemer. In the midst of the many duties and responsibilities of life, the believers need to heed this admonition to praise God.

This is the main message of Psalm 148, a worship psalm designed to call all to praise the Lord. The author and background are unknown, but its message is clear in its summons to all to worship God. Its placement here in the five Hallelujah psalms that climax the Psalter is to further broaden the scope of the repeated calls for praise. Let all creation praise their Creator. There are three stanzas in this praise psalm, each containing an invitation to a different group to offer its worship to God. Praise is to come from the heavenly choir (vv. 1–6), the earthly choir (vv. 7–12), and the redeemed choir (vv. 13–14).

II. COMMENTARY

MAIN IDEA: *The psalmist calls upon the entire universe to praise God.*

A Praise from the Heavenly Choir (148:1–6)

148:1. Thirteen times in this psalm creation is called upon to **Praise the LORD**. Beginning with the **heights** of heaven, the psalmist invites all who dwell in **the heavens** to lift up their voices and magnify the name of the Lord. Heaven is to be alive with praise to God.

148:2–4. All the **angels** and **heavenly hosts** are summoned to praise the Lord. Myriads of angels are invited to lift their praise to God. So should the **sun**, **moon**, and **stars** praise God. The psalmist does not imagine that heavenly bodies are literally to speak words of praise to God. Rather, they reflect the glory of God (Ps. 19:1). They are silent, visible testifiers of the greatness of God. The psalmist also speaks of the **waters** that are in the upper atmosphere (cp. Gen. 1:7), which also testify to the glory of God.

148:5–6. The entire heavenly order is to **praise the name of the LORD**. God **commanded** the word and they were **created**. He spoke them all into being out of nothing (cp. Ps. 33:6). God **set them** in place **for ever and ever**. The placement and regularity of the heavenly bodies has been established by God alone. Nothing happens by chance.

B Praise from the Earthly Choir (148:7–12)

148:7–8. The focus of the psalmist now shifts to the **earth** below, calling upon the earthly realm to praise God. He begins with the **sea creatures** in the **ocean depths** and all that is found in them (Gen. 1:7,10,21). **Lightning and hail**, **snow and clouds** and **wind do his bidding**, meaning that God's sovereignty creates them and directs their activity. Everything in the atmosphere above the earth reflects God's glory, testifying to his immutable greatness. The weather elements testify to the unstoppable power, benevolent goodness, and absolute faithfulness of God.

148:9. The towering **mountains** reveal God's transcendence. The grass-covered **hills** testify to God's beauty. **Fruit trees** reveal the sweetness of God's provision. The **cedars** are majestic, proclaiming God's greatness. All created things on the earth are invited to praise God. They declare God's grandeur, causing us to praise God.

148:10–12. Even **wild animals** (i.e., lions, tigers, bears) and **all cattle** (i.e., cows, horses) are called to praise God. So also are the **small creatures** that creep on the ground (i.e., caterpillars) and **flying birds** (i.e., eagles, hawks) summoned to praise God. Likewise, **kings** and **princes** (i.e., crowned heads of state) and **all nations** (i.e., their subjects) should praise God. So should **all rulers on earth** praise God. **Young men** and **maidens, old men,** and **children** are to praise God. Both great and small are to behold God's greatness and give him praise.

⬛ Praise from the Redeemed Choir (148:13–14)

148:13. Here the third choir is invited to praise God. All the redeemed should **praise the name of the LORD.** The divine name represents all that God is, the entirety of his character, the sum of his attributes, the glory of his being (i.e., God's holiness, sovereignty, power, righteousness, wisdom, unchangeableness, love, and grace). The **splendor** of the Creator is far **above the earth and the heavens.** The glory and the name of God are one and the same. Both are highly **exalted** and above heaven and earth.

148:14a. This highly exalted God has **raised up** a **horn,** a reference to the exercise of his strength. The psalmist was probably thinking about the restoration of strength to his ancient people, Israel. They have endured difficult days in Babylonian exile. In their weakness, God has lifted up a horn for his people, replenishing their strength and renewing their hope as they are regathered to the promised land. This is a cause for **the praise of all his saints.** God has raised them up so they can praise him.

148:14b. This psalm concludes as it began with this ringing declaration, **Praise the LORD.** The psalmist boasts in the Lord whose divine sovereignty (v. 13) and strength (v. 14) have been clearly displayed.

III. CONCLUSION

It is apparent from this psalm that every person is summoned to praise the Lord. This is the highest purpose for which each soul is created. Who needs to hear this psalm?

The person who is busy serving God. It is possible to become so busy in our ministries for God that we forget to cultivate our hearts for God. Let us never become so active in serving God that we forget to bring our praise to God. Our ministries are to be the overflow of our relationship with God.

The person who is suffering the deepest hurt. The despondent heart often takes its eyes off the Lord and wallows in self-pity. Our trials cause us to become so focused upon self-preservation that we lose sight of the Lord. If you find yourself down and discouraged, be careful to keep your eyes on the Lord. Lift up your voice and praise him.

The person whose heart is lukewarm. If you find your spiritual heart is at room temperature, then you need to look to the Lord and praise him. Consider the Lord's greatness and grace toward you. Consider his sovereignty and strength that have been demonstrated in your life. You will soon find yourself giving him the glory due his name.

IV. TEACHING OUTLINE

A. Praise from the Heavenly Choir (148:1–6)
B. Praise from the Earthly Choir (148:7–12)
C. Praise from the Redeemed Choir (148:13–14)

Psalm 149

Preeminent Praise

"Be not afraid of saying too much in the praises of

God; all the danger is of saying too little."

M a t t h e w   H e n r y

Psalm 149

I. INTRODUCTION

Praising God is the highest privilege afforded to the saints. Whether it be offered by glorified beleivers in heaven or by those living on earth, they are truly blessed to enter God's presence and exalt his name. That the holy God would allow mortal man to come before his throne, beholding the beauty of his holiness and bringing their praises to him, is a privilege never to be taken for granted. Worshipping God is the glory of all the saints, an indescribable grace afforded to redeemed believers. To obtain this privileged access before heaven's throne and ascribe to God the greatness that belongs to him alone is a prize above all the treasures of this world. Worshipping God is never to be viewed as a rote ritual or as empty drudgery. Rather, it is joyful delight, the highest honor of the Lord's people.

This is the central theme of Psalm 149. It is a call to participate in the greatest privilege afforded to the saints—giving glory to the name of God. The author and specific circumstances of this psalm are unknown though it is considered to be postexilic. The occasion was a time when Israel was being threatened by encroaching enemy powers. Even in the face of this life-threatening peril, God's people were invited to come worship God (vv. 1–3,5) for his grace in their lives (v. 4). As they must prepare to go forth into battle to defeat their adversaries (vv. 6–9), they were implored to bring their praises to God. This next-to-last psalm is another summons to God's people to praise him in the midst of turbulent times. Praising God puts earthly extremities into perspective.

II. COMMENTARY

MAIN IDEA: *The psalmist calls all God's people to worship the Lord for his grace, even in the presence of threatening enemies.*

A The Call to Worship (149:1–3)

149:1. Like so many psalms, this song begins with a call to worship God, summoning his people to praise the Lord. They are to **sing to the LORD a new song**, which can be even an old song sung in a new day with a new awareness of its truthfulness and importance. This **praise** is a boasting in the Lord to be sung in the public **assembly of the saints**. God's people are to join their hearts and voices together in declaring God's glory.

149:2. The saints should **rejoice** in the Lord, their **Maker** and **King**. He is Creator and controller of all things. Believers should **be glad** in him, even in the face of great dangers (vv. 7–9). God's people should worship with much joy because the Lord rules over all.

149:3. The people are invited to **praise his name**, all his divine attributes, **with dancing**. In ancient Israel, great military victories were often celebrated with joyful dancing (Exod. 15:20), a spontaneous response to a supernatural triumph. Accordingly, the people should **make music . . . with tambourine**, which is a timbrel, **and harp**, which is a stringed lyre. This praise should be offered to God publicly and passionately in anticipation of the victory he will give over their enemies.

B The Causes of Worship (149:4)

149:4a. The psalmist provides clear, compelling reasons God should be so joyfully worshiped. First, **the LORD takes delight in his people**. Although they are hated and despised by the pagan nations who threaten them, they are deeply loved by God. This delight reveals the abiding pleasure the saints bring to God's own heart because they are his chosen inheritance (Pss. 35:27; 147:11). That they are the object of God's love and the source of his enjoyment should be the cause of much praise by the saints.

149:4b. Second, God **crowns the humble with salvation**. That is, he will grace the afflicted with his saving, sustaining mercy. Those afflicted with sin and suffering will be delivered by God as they place their trust in him. Those who confess their inadequacies will be given divine aid to overcome their enemies. Therefore, fervent praise should be given to the Lord.

C The Confidence in Worship (149:5–10)

149:5. In response to God's grace and goodness (v. 4), all **the saints** should **rejoice in this honor** of worshipping God. This **honor** is the undeserved privilege of being made the object of God's delight and deliverance. Their joy is so real that even when they lie down at night **on their beds**, they do so without worry. Because their confidence is in the Lord, they do so without panic. Adoration, not anxiety, floods their souls.

149:6. A mounting God-centered confidence continues to build in the heart of the psalmist. As the threat of war surrounds Jerusalem, the author calls upon God's people to have **praise** in **their mouths and a double-edged sword in their hands**. Worship and warfare are to be their dual commitment. These worshippers are to be aggressive warriors, fully engaged in fighting God's enemies.

149:7. As these worshippers go forth into battle, they will surely **inflict vengeance on the nations**, these foreign powers who threaten Israel's national security. In reality, this is God's vengeance, his just retribution, carried out by the saints upon those who have attacked his kingdom. The saints will execute divine **punishment on the peoples** who war against them.

149:8. In battling these enemies, they will subdue **their kings** and imprison them **with fetters**, or chains. Also, **their nobles** will be confined with **shackles of iron**. This is their confident expectation as they prepare to go into battle.

149:9–10. In this divine retribution, God's people will **carry out the sentence written against them**. This scripted record is a reference to the written prophecies of Scripture in which God had promised to defeat the nations that had occupied the promised land (Deut. 7:1–2; Josh. 1:3–9). Scripture had already recorded their defeat. It will surely come to pass. God's Word is infallible. Thus, these worshippers were confident of victory in battle. All **this** (i.e., their worship and warfare) **is the glory**, or highest honor, **of all his saints**. It is a grand privilege to praise God, as well as to fight for him. The only proper response to all this is, **Praise the LORD**.

III. CONCLUSION

Praising God is the highest honor afforded believers. It should never be allowed to become a dreary duty. As long as the saints focus on the divine glory of God's unrivaled supremacy, their worship is breathtaking. Hearts soar with enraptured joy as they behold the transcendent majesty of their exalted King. Upon seeing the beauty of God's holiness, magnifying the Lord becomes treasured as a prized possession. Thus, a low view of God produces lukewarm, insipid worship. But a high view of God produces fervent, zealous adoration. The key is to maintain a transcendent view of God's glory. May every Christian answer the call to worship extended in this psalm. Come, give glory to your God. Lift high your praises to his name. Sing to the Lord a new song. This is your priceless privilege.

IV. TEACHING OUTLINE

A. The Call to Worship (149:1–3)
B. The Causes of Worship (149:4)
C. The Confidence in Worship (149:5–10)

Psalm 150
Climatic Crescendo

┌─── Q u o t e ───┐

"Give praise to God who reigns above

For perfect knowledge, wisdom, love.

His judgments are divine, devout,

His paths beyond all tracing out.

Come, lift your voice to heaven's throne,

And glory give to God alone!"

J a m e s   M o n t g o m e r y   B o i c e

Psalm 150

I. INTRODUCTION

True worship is awesome. This is true because God is awesome. Authentic worship is the most soul-thrilling, heart-stirring experience any redeemed being can enjoy. There is nothing boring about worship. There is nothing boring about God, the object of worship. Worship may be defined as the proper response of the entire person—mind, heart, and will—to all that God is—Creator, Ruler, and Redeemer. It involves all that one is acknowledging the greatness and grandeur of God. Flat worship is an oxymoron, a contradiction in terms, an inconsistency of highest order. Empty, tired praise is an insult to God, insinuating that his matchless glory is anything but glorious. God is infinitely magnificent and exponentially supreme. All worship should reflect this. Because God is the sovereign Lord, absolutely holy and incomprehensibly august, worship is awe-inspiring for all who know him. May all believers humbly approach him to give him praise.

Psalm 150 is the last psalm, and it contains the final great hallelujah. Here is praise to God that is full of life, passion, and dynamic energy. This psalm is exhilarating in its adoration of God. Although its composer and occasion are unknown, its message is loud and clear: All that has life and breath should praise the Lord. Every person in every place should give praise to God, who alone is worthy. Such is the proper ending and powerful crescendo to the book of praise.

II. COMMENTARY

MAIN IDEA: *The psalmist calls upon all God's people to praise the Lord for his unsurpassed greatness.*

A Where to Praise God (150:1)

150:1a–b. This final psalm begins with a loud crescendo, proclaiming **Praise the LORD**. The psalmist cannot be silent about such a supreme, sovereign God. He should be praised **in his sanctuary** (literally "holy place"), a reference to the earthly temple in Jerusalem. The list of musical instruments (vv. 3–5) argues for this earthly designation of the sanctuary. God's house is to be filled with praise and worship.

150:1c. Further, God is to be praised in **his mighty heavens** above. This is a reference to his heavenly sanctuary in glory. Redeemed saints and elect angels are to worship God in the heights of heaven. God is to be praised everywhere, whether on earth below or heaven above. There is no place where praise is out of place.

B Why to Praise God (150:2)

150:2a. Having called for praise in every place, reason is now given for this worship. God is to be praised **for his acts of power**, referring to the major areas of divine works (i.e., creation, providence, salvation, and judgment). All his acts work together perfectly with precise unity of purpose and should be the cause for great praise.

150:2b. In addition, praise is to be rendered to God **for his surpassing greatness**. This greatness refers to God's person—the essence of his divine attributes. The Lord should be worshipped for his holiness, sovereignty, righteousness, omniscience, omnipotence, and omnipresence. Everything about God is to be praised, for both his acts and his attributes.

How to Praise God (150:3–6)

150:3. The psalmist gives instruction regarding the manner in which God is to be praised. Both musical instruments (vv. 3–5) and human voices (v. 6) are to be employed. **The trumpet**, a shofar, or ram's horn is to be sounded. The **harp and lyre**, a smaller harplike, portable instrument, were also to be used. Both wind and string instruments are listed here in praising God.

150:4. Also, God is to be praised with **tambourine** and **dancing**. These two often went together, the former used by women when they danced after God-given victories (Exod. 15:20). Moreover, God is to be worshipped with **strings**, a general term for all kinds of stringed instruments, **and flute**, a pipe-like percussion instrument.

150:5. Finally, God is to be praised with **the clash of cymbals**, instruments usually made of either brass or silver. These were the smaller and higher pitched kind, like our castanets. **Resounding cymbals** were also to be used, larger and louder, making a more crashing sound. These verses (vv. 3–5) are not intended to cover every instrument that is acceptable to God but to be a sampling of every kind of musical instrument to be played in God's house.

150:6a. Those who should **praise the LORD** encompasses **everything that has breath**. This includes all the redeemed who gather at God's house. The human voice is the greatest instrument of all. As God's people sing, they are to be accompanied by the trumpet (v. 3a) blown by priests; harps and lyres (v. 3b) played by the Levites; tambourines (v. 4a) played by women; and strings, flutes, and cymbals (vv. 4b–5) played by men. Everyone in God's house is to sing praise to God, supported by the playing of instruments by the priests and people, men and women.

150:6b. This psalm, as well as the entire psalter, now concludes with this dramatic declaration, **Praise the LORD**. This final, great Hallelujah is proclaimed by a mighty choir not only by the psalmist but by all people in heaven and earth. Here is the ultimate purpose for all that lives and breathes. All should praise the Lord.

III. CONCLUSION

Will you answer the psalmist's call to worship? Will you bring your wholehearted praise to God? This requires the total response of your entire life. Worship is a lifestyle, not an isolated act, never to be segmented from the whole of your life. Worship must be a passionate life pursuit of rendering praise to God, a deepening reality that should permeate your entire existence. If God is real in your life, then you should be praising him with all of your being. This, of course, includes times involving the corporate gathering of God's people when they come together to sing his praises. May you give to God the praise he so rightfully deserves in the midst of the great congregation.

IV. TEACHING OUTLINE

A. Where to Praise God (150:1)
B. Why to Praise God (150:2)
C. How to Praise God (150:3–6)

Glossary

confession—Admission of personal sin and seeking forgiveness from others

conversion—God's act of changing a person's life in response to the person's turning to Christ in repentance and faith from some other belief or from no belief

covenant—A contract or agreement expressing God's gracious promises to his people and their consequent relationship to him

creation—God's bringing the world and everything in it into existence from nothing

cross—Two wooden beams shaped as a letter *t* or *x* used as an instrument to kill criminals by the Roman government; the wooden beams on which Jesus was killed and thus a symbol of Christian faith and responsibility

discipline—Instruction or training used by God to train his children in righteous living

evangelism—The central element of the church's mission involving telling others the gospel of salvation with the goal of leading them to repentance and faith in Christ

evil—Anyone or anything that opposes the plan of God

exile—Israel's life in the Assyrian kingdom after 722 B.C. and Judah's life in Babylon after 587 B.C.

exodus, the—The most important act of national deliverance in the Old Testament when God enabled the Israelites to escape Egypt

faith—Belief in and personal commitment to Jesus Christ for eternal salvation

fall, the—The result of the first human sin, which marred the image of God in humans and created an environment for and a tendency toward sin for all people

firstborn—The oldest son born into a Jewish family or the first offspring of livestock; the firstborn were dedicated to God in a special sense

forgiveness—Pardon and release from penalty for wrongdoing; God's delivery from sin's wages for those who repent and express faith in Christ; the Christian act of freeing from guilt and blame those by whom one has suffered wrong

glorification—God's action in the lives of believers, making them able to share the glory and reward of heaven

Godhead—The unity of the triune God: Father, Son, Holy Spirit

grace—Undeserved acceptance and love received from another, especially the characteristic attitude of God in providing salvation for sinners

hell—The place of everlasting punishment for the lost

holy—God's distinguishing characteristic that separates him from all creation; the moral ideal for Christians as they seek to reflect the character of God as known in Christ Jesus

holy of holies—The innermost and most sacred area of the tabernacle and temple, where God was present and where sacrifices were made by the high priest on the Day of Atonement

idolatry—The worship of that which is not God

intercession—A prayer presenting one person's needs to another as Christians presenting the needs of others to God or as Christ or the Holy Spirit representing believers before God

Jerusalem—Capital city of Israel in the Old Testament; religious center of Judaism in the New Testament; also name of the heavenly city John describes in Revelation (New Jerusalem)

joy—The inner attitude of rejoicing in one's salvation regardless of outward circumstances

judgment—God's work at the end time involving condemnation for unbelievers and assignment of rewards for believers

law—God's instruction to his people about how to love him and others; when used with the definite article *the, law* may refer to the Old Testament as a whole but usually to the Pentateuch (Genesis through Deuteronomy), indicated in the HOTC by capitalizing (Law)

mercy—A personal characteristic of care for the needs of others; the biblical concept of mercy always involves help to those who are in need or distress

Messiah—the coming king promised by the prophets; Jesus Christ, who fulfilled the prophetic promises; Christ represents the Greek translation of the Hebrew word *messiah*

millennium—A thousand-year period when the righteous will reign on earth

Passover—The Jewish feast celebrating the exodus from Egypt (Exod. 12); celebrated by Jesus and his disciples at the Last Supper

perseverance—The response of enduring even in the face of difficulty; Christians develop this trait by facing and overcoming hardship and adversity

repentance—A change of heart and mind resulting in a turning from sin to God that allows conversion and is expressed through faith

righteousness—The quality or condition of being in right relationship with God; living out the relationship with God in right relationships with other persons

sacrifice—According to Mosaic law, an offering to God in repentance for sin or as an expression of thanksgiving; Christ as the ultimate sacrifice for sin

saints—Those holy or set apart to God; any person in Christ

salvation—Deliverance from trouble or evil; the process by which God redeems his creation, completed through the life, death, and resurrection of his Son Jesus Christ

sin—Actions by which humans rebel against God, miss his purpose for their life, and surrender to the power of evil rather than to God

sovereignty—God's freedom from outward restraint; his unlimited rule of and control over his creation

total depravity—The condition of humanity after the fall, including involvement of each member of the human race in sin

trials—Afflictions and hardships permitted in our lives by God to develop stamina and endurance in us (Jas. 1:2–4)

Trinity—God's revelation of himself as Father, Son, and Holy Spirit unified as one in the Godhead and yet distinct in person and function

truth—That which is real and reliable; opposite of falsehood and error; descriptive of the divine Father, Son, and Spirit as the full revelation of the one true God

worship—Reverence, honor, praise, and service shown to God

wrath of God—God's consistent response opposing and punishing sin

Yahweh—The Hebrew personal name of God revealed to Moses; this name came to be thought of as too holy to pronounce by Jews; often translated LORD or Jehovah

Zion—Another name for Jerusalem

Bibliography

Popular Expositions
Beisner, Calvin. *Psalms of Promise.*
Boice, James Montgomery. *Psalms.* 3 vols.
Maclaren, Alexander. *Expositions of Holy Scripture.* Vol. 4.
Phillips, John. *Exploring the Psalms.* 2 vols.
Stedman, Ray. *Psalms of Faith.*
Swindoll, Charles. *Daily Grind.* 2 vols.
Wiersbe, Warren. *Meet Yourself in the Psalms.*

Devotional Commentaries
Alexander, J. A. *The Psalms Translated and Explained.*
Henry, Matthew. *Matthew Henry Commentary.*
Lockyer, Herbert, Sr. *Psalms: A Devotional Commentary.*
Scroggie, W. Graham. *A Guide to the Psalms.*
Spurgeon, Charles H. *Treasury of David.* 7 vols.

Exegetical Commentaries
Davidson, Robert. *The Vitality of Worship.*
Dickson, David. *Psalms.* Geneva Series of Commentaries.
Harman, Allan. *Psalms.*
Kidner, Derek. *Psalms.* 2 vols.
Leupold, H. C. *Exposition on the Psalms.*
Perowne, J. J. Stewart. *The Book of Psalms.*
Ross, Allan P. *Psalms.* Bible Knowledge Commentary.
Unger, Merrill. *Psalms.* Unger's Commentary on the Old Testament.
Wilcock, Michael. *The Message of Psalms 1–72.*
Wilcock, Michael. *The Message of Psalms 73–150.*

Technical Commentaries
Calvin, John. *Calvin's Commentaries.* Vols. 4–6.
Craige, Peter C., Marvin E. Tate, and Leslie C. Allen. Word Biblical Commentary. Vols. 19–21.
Delitzsch, Franz. *Keil-Delitzsch Commentary on the Old Testament.* Vol. 5.
Gameren, Willem Van. *Psalms.* The Bible Expositor's Commentary. Vol. 5.

Hebrew Tools

Armstrong, Terry A., Douglas L. Busby, and Cyril F. Carr. *A Reader's Hebrew and English Lexicon of the Old Testament.*

Brown, Francis, Samuel R. Driver, and Charles A. Briggs. *A Hebrew and English Lexicon of the Old Testament.*

Even-Shoshan, Abraham. *A New Concordance of the Old Testament.*

Gameren, Willem Van, ed. *New International Dictionary of Old Testament Theology and Exegesis.* 5 vols.

Harris, R. Laird, Gleason L. Archer Jr., and Bruce K. Waltke. *Theological Wordbook of the Old Testament.* 2 vols.

Owens, John Joseph. *Analytical Key to the Old Testament.* 4 vols.

Ringgaren, Butterweck, ed. *Theological Dictionary of the Old Testament.* 10 vols.

The Englishmen's Hebrew and Chaldee Concordance of the Old Testament.

Torrey, R. A. *Treasury of Scripture Knowledge.*

Weingreen, Jacob. *Practical Grammar for Classical Hebrew.*